A FULL LIFE

A Full Life

HELEN GAHAGAN DOUGLAS

1982
Doubleday & Company, Inc.
Garden City, New York

Library of Congress Cataloging in Publication Data
Douglas, Helen Gahagan, 1900–1980
A full life.
Includes index.
1. Douglas, Helen Gahagan, 1900–1980. 2. United
States—Politics and government—1933–1945. 3. United
States—Politics and government—1945–1953. 4. Legisla-
tors—United States—Biography. 5. United States.
Congress. House—Biography. 6. Actors—United States—
Biography. I. Title.
E748.D677A33   973.9'092'4 [B]
AACR2
ISBN 0-385-11045-6
Library of Congress Catalog Card Number 81–43289

ACKNOWLEDGMENTS

The family of Helen Gahagan Douglas wishes to pay tribute to the selfless contributions of many people who helped Helen work on this book and who, after her death, assisted in the completion of the manuscript as they knew she wanted it.

Foremost are Evelyn Chavoor and Nan Stevens. Each spent a good part of her life at Helen's side and each lovingly saw this book to the finish.

Amelia R. (Chita) Fry of the Regional Oral History Office, Bancroft Library, University of California at Berkeley, conducted the interviews that resulted in the Helen Gahagan Douglas oral history which is stored there. That process inspired and facilitated Helen's efforts to put her autobiography on paper. Thanks are due also to Willa Baum and Malca Chall in the Regional Oral History Office of the Bancroft Library, who cheerfully and with dispatch made transcripts available.

We appreciate the warm cooperation of the University of Oklahoma's Western History Collections, where the Helen Gahagan Douglas archives are stored, and, especially, of Jack D. Haley, who catalogued them.

Ingrid Winther Scobie, a writer who spent many years researching a biography of Helen, freely shared her extensive knowledge of her subject. And special thanks are due to Elizabeth Evans, who helped Helen a great deal in the early years of the project, and to Patrick Hardy, who was Helen's assistant and put the pieces together.

The final draft was done by June Callwood.

Contents

Introduction

Not long after her seventieth birthday, Helen finally yielded to friends who had been urging her for years to write a book about her remarkable life. She tried to make it a priority but generally failed; she was too busy addressing students on campuses, protesting the arms race, supporting the women's movement, campaigning for presidential candidates, making study tours all over the world, enjoying her family—and fighting cancer.

In her twenties she was a brilliant star on Broadway, hailed as another Ethel Barrymore and once described as "ten of the twelve most beautiful women in the world." She abandoned that career at its height in order to study voice. In her thirties she dazzled critics in the music capitals of Europe. She is best known for her third career, as a U.S. congresswoman, and for her defeat by a fledgling politician, Richard Nixon, in a 1950 senatorial race in California which some describe as the dirtiest campaign in American political history.

Helen refused for twenty years even to discuss what happened in that bitter autumn. Only at the time of Watergate, when reporters searched her out, did she express some courteously worded criticism of Richard Nixon. She had to be persuaded not to omit all mention of that campaign in this autobiography. Her reasoning was that she had been fortunate to walk away from that defeat without a burden of hatred and resentment that might have crushed her. She was delighted to find herself on the morning after the election a whole woman, even a happy one, eager to go on with her life.

She plunged into research and lectures to warn Americans that the arms race was folly of unimaginable magnitude. She remained passionately concerned about conservation and about the miserable conditions of farm workers, the two issues that had attracted her to politics in the first place.

In 1978 Helen's cancer returned and this time it was inoperable. She continued to work on the manuscript of her book, and she never stopped speaking out on the issues. In June 1980 she died in a hospital room piled with reports, clippings, revisions, inserts and notes—still striving to finish the book before the deadline her disease imposed on her. June Callwood has assembled this material with much help—from two women who were Helen's secretaries, from Nan Stevens and Evie Chavoor, from Helen's brother Walter Gahagan, from the interviews Helen did with Chita Fry and Ingrid Scobie, and with some input from me.

Helen and I were married almost fifty years. In all that time she was radiant, confident, loyal and loving. She paid a high price for sticking to her principles but she never complained. There was never a moment when she didn't know who she was and what she was about.

She was entranced always by light. In every house we ever occupied, she wanted the windows to be wider. She thought no room could have too many windows. She would exclaim about the light on a mountain in Vermont or on a wall in New York. She was always saying, "Look at the light! Isn't it beautiful?"

She was the light. And she was beautiful.

Melvyn Douglas

A FULL LIFE

The First
Two Careers

The windows of our big house in Brooklyn stood open to the warm night. In the parlor, two floors below my bedroom, I could hear the angry voice of my father shouting that I was going back to college the next day. His daughter, by god, was not going to be an *actress*. In his mind, *actress* and *whore* were interchangeable.

Harry Wagstaff Gribble, a playwright-producer of great charm, had been confident that he could change Father's mind. Harry had accompanied me home from the final dress rehearsal of *Dreams for Sale*, assuring me all the way that my father's opposition would melt once he understood that I was beginning what would be a great career on the stage.

I knew better about my father once his mind was made up, but I accepted Harry's naïve offer gratefully. From the age of five I had been consumed by dreams of going on the stage, and from the age of five had been told by my father that he wouldn't allow it. We had come to this night with neither giving an inch.

Their voices drifted up to me, Father furiously declaring I was going back to Barnard College in two days, Harry smoothly, patiently explaining what a great opportunity it was for me that Brady insisted on signing me to a five-year contract. Father's bellow, "NO!" could be heard down the block.

I was twenty-two years old and had never defied Father in my life. Few did. He was an impressive man who seemed to use up all the breathable space in a room. A successful civil engineer, fiercely principled and paternalistic in the Victorian style, he was physically big, full of impatient energy, and possessed of a flaming Irish temper. In many respects we were alike and we had been clashing about my acting aspirations all my life.

Mother used to caution me gently, "Don't make such a fuss, Helen. If it is right for you to be an actress, you'll do it."

Meanwhile I never stopped preparing myself for my career on stage. Night after night, after prayers were said and the lights turned out, I would stand on my bed and perform for the delight of my younger sister Lilli. My daytime stage was the top of the pool table on the third floor, where I assembled an audience of children who had come to play in our side garden.

In my teens I acted in school productions or, almost as good, debates and spent my allowance on tickets for Saturday matinees in Brooklyn playhouses. I couldn't understand why my desire to flesh out characters should be considered so different from Father's wanting to build a bridge or a railroad.

One day when he judged I was old enough he explained his aversion to the theater. Some of his friends had mistresses who were on the stage, from which evidence he was convinced that all actresses were tarnished. I was revolted by his assumption and fled the room, my usual reaction to my father's edicts. I was called back. Still, he was unable to convince me why a talented actress should be less honorable than a talented engineer.

Father was reflecting the upper-class sentiment of his era and Midwestern background. In February of 1922, only months before our confrontation over *Dreams for Sale*, my producer-director William A. Brady was involved in a much-publicized debate in the Calvary Baptist Church in New York with the pastor, the Reverend John Roach Straton, on the burning issue of the morals of "theatrical folk." According to the New York *Evening World*, the flamboyant Brady won the crowd when he accused the clergyman of slandering "poor little Mary Pickford," then America's stainless sweetheart.

Father took his responsibilities as head of a family very seriously. He came from pioneer Irish stock who had helped found Dayton, Ohio, and made his fortune building railways across the West. He picked my mother as his bride only after his mother checked her out. His plan was to raise sons to join him in his Gahagan Company and she obliged handsomely with her firstborn, twin boys, William and Frederick.

Her next child, however, was me and he hadn't planned on a

daughter. I was born on November 25, 1900, in Boonton, New Jersey, where Father was supervising the building of a dam. I worried him. I was gregarious, outgoing, demonstrative. He never let me out of the house without a chaperon.

Unlike many of his generation, he had no contempt for women's intelligence. He would have approved heartily if I had wanted to be a doctor, lawyer, teacher or scientist. He believed that education was essential for a woman because it provided her with a defense against life's challenges. His example was his unusual mother, the formidable Hannah Gahagan, who was sent to Antioch College by her father despite family outrage and intense opposition.

The education proved invaluable when Grandmother Hannah was widowed at the age of thirty-eight. Her husband died of an illness contracted during the Civil War, leaving her with a large Ohio farm to run and three children to raise. She accomplished that and became a leading feminist as well. It was Grandmother Hannah who integrated libraries in Ohio which previously had been closed to women on the grounds that women didn't really want to read books, they only wanted to flirt. Grandmother didn't argue the point. She simply marched in and insisted on borrowing some books.

When the Ohio Assembly, to the dismay of many, passed a law allowing women to vote for and serve on school boards, Grandmother Hannah helped organize the first political meeting of women in Troy. Two women were selected to run against the male candidates. Grandmother was one of them and she won.

She and another woman started the Women's Christian Association in Troy. This was an activist group that succeeded in forcing the county to stop putting orphans in infirmaries with criminals and the insane. Like my father, Grandmother Hannah was a hard person to stop once her mind was made up.

Everything his mother did Father found praiseworthy and proper, but he did not extend that endorsement of one independent woman, Hannah Gahagan, to the ambitions of another, me. Of all his children, I was the one with whom he most often clashed. The twins, two years older than I, avidly looked forward to joining the family business as he wished. Lillian, two years

younger, was like Mother, gentle and sweet. Walter, born eight
years after Lillian, was still in short pants.

Father loved the outdoors and never would allow the draperies
to be drawn when he was in a room, so lights from the parlor
where he and Harry Wagstaff Gribble were arguing over my future streamed across the lawn. I leaned out of my window to listen better. Harry was not moving Father one inch.

Four years earlier, when I was eighteen, I had spent an entire
day fighting with Father on the subject of my stage career. The
setting was our summer home in Vermont, where Father had
confronted me with my high school report. I had failed every subject.

"Have you stopped studying?" he asked coldly.

I said truthfully, "Yes."

Father taught us at an early age not to lie or equivocate. When
asked if we had done something wrong, we were expected to answer yes or no. He conducted his business on his reputation for
honesty. His word was his bond and everyone knew it.

He asked for an explanation and I said I had been working
with Elizabeth Grimball to prepare myself for the theater, leaving
me no time for academic activities. Elizabeth Grimball was a
young woman who had come from Charleston to the Berkeley Institute, a private school for girls a block from our home where
Lilli and I were enrolled. She ran the drama department at the
school and her arrival dazzled the stagestruck person I was. My
dreams had a focus, her department. She became my adviser,
coach and ally.

Her job at Berkeley was a stopgap until she went on to become
a Broadway producer, which she soon did. Meanwhile her school
productions attracted professional critics. The Brooklyn *Eagle*
gave me my first rave review. In those days I took approval for
granted. If the critic had written that I couldn't act, I would have
been in shock.

Father tolerated my obsession with Elizabeth Grimball's department, at least until the fateful report card, but he was furious
when he discovered that I was branching out. I had cut classes
one afternoon in order to help Broadway stars, among them Al
Jolson, sell war bonds from the steps of the New York Public Li-

brary. At eighteen, I gave a speech about the brave French army at Verdun and ended with a famous war poem, *They Shall Not Pass*, which caused large numbers of the audience to rush forward to buy bonds. As a result I was invited to repeat my address at the final bond drive performance in New York City. I refused. It was to be held at night and it wasn't possible that Father would permit me to go.

As Father listened impassively, my awful report in his hand, I poured out my hopes for a theatrical career and rashly told him of my successes to date. He descended upon me in wrath. Compliments had addled my brain, he told me. Young, attractive girls always were flattered. If I didn't understand that, I lived in a dream world. I would get no compliments later on unless I was educated. I must buckle down at once. Education alone was the safeguard against a life without purpose or interests.

Did I want to be just a breeding machine? he thundered. An uneducated woman was just that, a breeder. The tirade continued all day and into the night. The rest of the family fled from us. His car was waiting to return him to the railway station at Fairlee. He ignored it.

"Forget about acting," Father ordered. "*Think!*"

He outlined my future. He would take me out of Berkeley, away from the distraction of Elizabeth Grimball's classes, and send me in the fall to a boarding school. I would stay there until I had learned enough to be ready for college. Then I would go to college and graduate. "*Think!*" he repeated.

Thinking was a theme of Father's frequent lengthy lectures to his children. To think was to be in control of oneself, to be less likely to be manipulated, to avoid being a slave to emotion. Thinking, he told us, doesn't come naturally. It requires training. One must gather facts with which to ponder a subject.

When I began to read avidly, as he did, he cautioned me to be skeptical. Printing something did not make it true. The written page should be tested. Once, during one of our family summer tours of Europe, he pointed to a book-lined corner of the Bibliothèque Nationale in Paris. If I spent the rest of my life reading I could not cover more than the books in that one corner, he told me.

"Obviously," he concluded, glaring at me to drive the point home, "you must do more than read. You must learn to *think* about what you read."

Finally Father could delay his departure no longer and left me on the porch in the Vermont darkness to contemplate my bleak prospects. I stood a long time, feeling intensely sorry for myself. The house was so silent behind me that it seemed empty. It was only ten o'clock, a normal retiring time for Mother but not for Lilli and the boys.

I went up to Mother's room and stood by her bed. Her soft hand reached for mine. Mother always understood, I thought gratefully. As I leaned over to kiss her good night, she asked, still holding my hand, "Helen, do you enjoy upsetting the family?"

I blurted, "No, Mother," and fled the room in tears. Did no one care about *my* life? If Mother, my last defense, didn't or wouldn't support me, how could I hope to change Father's mind?

Undressing in the dark, I pulled the covers up to my chin. I felt cold. Lilli whispered from the next bed:

"Helen, was it ghastly?"

"Yes," I answered tersely, unwilling to discuss my hurt.

"Now what?" she asked.

"Boarding school!"

"What!" A pause. "Are you going?"

"No. *I am not.*"

"But, Helen—"

"Good night," I said rudely.

I slept poorly. At four in the morning, watching the glow in the sky that precedes sunrise, I had a compulsion to walk in the woods. Dressing hurriedly in a blouse and long, pleated skirt, I moved quietly through the house so as not to wake the family, my pumps in my hand. I strode along the road leading through the forest that rings Sawyer Mountain and up a path leading to a plateau, a favorite picnic spot.

Sitting on a familiar flat rock, I brooded over my dilemma. I suddenly recalled a story Mother had told us about a Welsh great-uncle, crippled with rheumatism, who made a deal with the Creator. This man, racked with pain, shut himself into his room and informed God that he couldn't go on. God would have to tell him what to do. He emerged from the room to announce that God wanted him to live on bread and water for the rest of his life. He did so and lived to an old age, free of pain.

I resolved to try my old uncle's method of relieving misery. A dialogue with God, I decided, should take place on a mountain-top. I searched until I found a path leading upward and began to climb. Hours later, panting and sore, I realized I was lost. The mountain seemed to have no summit where I could ask God to tell me what to do. I sank down and sobbed, feeling bound on every side—by the mountain, by the trees, by my father.

My mother, I knew, would not approve of my quest for an easy solution to my problem. When I was five years old, and possessed of such a quick memory that I could bluff an ability to read after she had read aloud only once from one of my books, she caught me out and gave me a scolding. "There's no easy way to learning, Helen," she told me. "In life, there are no shortcuts."

I started for home, through brush that scratched my arms and tore my skirt, in a direction that seemed vaguely downward. Suddenly I began to slide in my slick-soled pumps—slowly at first, then faster and faster until I was out of control. I managed to grab a sturdy outcropping just before I would have plunged over the edge.

I looked down. Five feet straight below was a narrow ledge that was clearly a traveled path. As I considered the mess I was in, my head began to clear. I saw myself as bullheaded, unreasonable. My father was concerned for my well-being. I recalled my mother's patient advice, "Stop arguing with your father, Helen. If it is right for you to be on the stage, you'll do it."

My rebellion was self-obstructive and foolish. If I defied my father I would defeat everything I wanted to accomplish later on. I resolved that I would prove to him and to myself that I could concentrate on studies when I wanted to, and that I could sail through college. Father wasn't blocking me. *I* was. After I paid my dues, I could become an actress.

The mountain had provided the answer after all, but the problem of getting down safely remained. Unfastening my long skirt, I threw it and my pumps to the ledge below and examined the face of the sheer cliff for handgrips. Summoning my courage, I slowly eased myself down until I stood safely on the ledge.

I reached home almost at dusk as the family was finishing dinner. No one spoke of my absence. I went straight to bed after eating. Lilli followed soon after.

"How was it on the mountain?" she asked.

"How did you know where I was?"

"Mother sent the boys to look for you," she explained. "When they saw you slide down the cliff in your underpants, they knew you'd make it."

I was scalded with resentment. After muttering about people minding their own business, I told Lilli I was going to college after all.

"Are you going to boarding school too?" she asked in amazement. I nodded.

I was up early the next morning. If I had to go to college, there was no time to lose. Lilli wanted to know where I was going this time. Hanover, I told her. I was going to enroll in the Dartmouth summer tutoring school. "They manage to get know-nothing football players ready for Dartmouth, so they can just go to work on me," I said.

"But Helen," she protested. "It's only for *boys!*"

"What of it?" I threw back over my shoulder as I departed. "Now they'll take their first girl."

That morning I persuaded the summer school to take me and found a boardinghouse in Hanover where I could stay the rest of the summer. Mother approved it and together we pored over a list of girls' boarding schools. We decided on the Capen School in Northampton, Massachusetts, a starkly scholastic no-frills institution.

That fall Father enrolled Lilli and me in Capen and I plunged into saturation study. The twins were not far away, at Williams College. By spring I was admissible to a college. I picked Barnard because it was in New York, close to Elizabeth Grimball who was now running Inter-Theatre Arts, a school and production company, near Broadway. Father agreed to it, possibly because he didn't expect I could pass the required sight examination in Greek or Latin.

That summer I went back to Dartmouth and persuaded the head of the department of classical languages to tutor me in Latin. When the time came, I passed all my Board exams and the sight reading as well.

Barnard suited my thirst for drama perfectly. I played leads in Barnard's famous Greek Games, debated passionately the cause of Irish independence, took all the drama courses offered under Professor Minor Latham, and belonged to the college drama society, Wigs and Cues.

In my sophomore year my complaints that Wigs and Cues should stop rehashing stale Broadway shows bore fruit. I was allowed to choose and direct a rarely performed Hauptmann play, *And Pippa Dances*. In my zeal I instructed the cast that they should come to first rehearsal with their lines already learned. I was informed icily that this was an amateur production, not Broadway.

A professor noted that I talked a good deal about Irish independence and my Irish heritage, while another student was in love with Yeats's poetry. He thought we would get along well and introduced us. Alis de Sola, later a distinguished playwright and screenwriter, became a lifelong friend.

That spring we collaborated on a one-act play we called *Shadow of the Moon* for a term paper. It was based on a folk legend—Irish, of course. Elizabeth Grimball read it and was impressed enough to offer to mount a studio production of it in the Lenox Little Theatre, starring me. An associate of Elizabeth's, Harry Wagstaff Gribble, came to see it out of curiosity.

Gribble had written a satiric comedy, *Shoot*, which had a part he thought just right for me. He invited me to play it, the lead, in an off-Broadway tryout so that he could see how the play looked on the boards and what changes he should make in it. Somehow I managed to keep up my studies, go through ten days of rehearsals and play two weeks of night performances.

My parents watchfully insisted that a chauffeur and car deliver me and return me home promptly every time I left the house at night. They assumed that my absences had to do with another student production and I didn't dare tell them otherwise. Because of the secrecy I couldn't enlist Mother's help in finding a suitable dress for my role, which required something flossy and glamorous. Somehow Elizabeth and I concocted an overly trimmed creation that would do.

A Broadway director, John Cromwell, came to see the production and telephoned me the next day to ask if I was interested in playing a small part in *Manhattan*, a play he was producing in the summer. Cromwell was an associate of the famous Broadway producer William A. Brady, who owned the Playhouse. I was dazzled by the offer. To look more grown-up, I wore the flouncy *Shoot* outfit, complete with feathered garden hat, for my interview with Cromwell.

If Cromwell was taken aback by my garish costume he gave no sign. I agreed to do the part and went home to break the news to my father and mother. There was no possibility of concealing it from them, since I would be unable to accompany them to our summer home in Vermont in June.

To my surprise, my parents didn't seem to mind, providing I was chaperoned everywhere by my father's sister, my Aunt Mary, our next-door neighbor. As I learned later, both expected that the experience would cleanse me of theatrical ambitions and I would return to Barnard happily in the fall.

Manhattan opened out of town and Aunt Mary Clyde went with me to protect my honor. I was disappointed when none of the family came to see it in New York, though Father was in the city attending to the family business. It seemed they reasoned that their attendance would only encourage me in my folly.

Unknown to me, the Broadway actress Gladys George came to a performance of *Manhattan*, bringing with her a friend who was married to the playwright Owen Davis. Davis had just completed a new play, *Dreams for Sale*, whose leading role required an ingenue. Bill Brady, Gladys George's husband, was producing it but hadn't yet cast the part of the debutante. Both women decided I was perfect for it.

The next morning I received a call from William Brady himself. He ordered me to stop whatever I was doing (cleaning Mother's closets) and come at once to the Playhouse. I found his office on the second floor and took a seat in an anteroom crowded with actors waiting to audition. After an hour the door of his inner office was thrown open and Brady stuck out his head and roared, "Where the hell is that girl?"

I divined that he meant me. When I introduced myself he glowered. "What the hell are you doing out here? Come inside."

I followed him into his office and recognized John Cromwell among the men lounging about the room. Cromwell was the one who rose politely to greet me. Brady handed me the script of *Dreams for Sale* and ushered me into an adjoining room. He said I should read it and tell him if I wanted the lead.

I found the play trivial and the part silly but decided it didn't matter. I had a chance to open on Broadway in a starring role! When I emerged Brady said, "Well?"

I smiled and answered, "Mr. Brady, I can play it on my eyebrows." I don't know why I put it so oddly, but that's what I said.

He instructed me to take the play home and study the first act. He would hear me read the part the next day.

When I returned to the Playhouse, Brady and Cromwell and some others were waiting in the dark and empty theater. A young actor, script in hand, was ready to run through the scene with me. Brady asked me in irritation, "Where's your script?"

I told him I didn't need it. I knew my lines in the first act. In truth I knew all the lines in the entire play.

When we finished the reading, Brady invited me to join him in the auditorium. There he introduced his wife, Gladys George, a cool, poised, aloof woman of exquisite grooming and manners, and Owen Davis and his wife. I was startled at the contrast between Brady and Gladys George, whom he clearly adored. Since he was a blustering, rough-tongued Irishman who had been a fight manager, they made an unlikely couple.

Father objected strenuously when I broke the news about *Dreams for Sale*. Mother calmed him with assurances that Aunt Mary would never leave my side. I suspect she also advised him that it was best to give me my fill of Broadway in one massive dose. In any event he reluctantly agreed to it.

The day before Aunt Mary and I were to leave with the com-

pany for the out-of-town tryout of *Dreams for Sale*, we had a
dress rehearsal in the Playhouse. Brady exploded when he saw
what I was wearing for my first act entrance.

"Jesus Christ!" he yelled. "Take that thing off! Wear your own
clothes! It's awful." He turned to his wife and groaned, "What is
that fancy designer trying to do to the girl? Ruin her?" Gladys
George agreed with him, and so did I. The offending garment
was in the flapper style, with a tight flat bodice, a short pleated
skirt, and purple velvet flowers appliquéd all over it.

Brady stopped the rehearsal while Gladys George gave me some
helpful tips on a stage wardrobe. She advised me never to be a
slave to fashion. If the style was unbecoming, I shouldn't wear it.

Mother returned from Vermont to learn that the plan to give
me my fill of acting hadn't worked. I bravely told my parents that
I would not be going to Barnard after all. Brady wanted me to
sign a five-year contract even before the opening of *Dreams for
Sale*. In fact he was so anxious to secure me as his property that
he said he wouldn't open the play unless I signed. Father told me
flatly that I wasn't signing: I was going back to Barnard for my
junior year.

And there the impasse stood. Harry Wagstaff Gribble had been
a sympathetic spectator during an exhausting day of dress rehearsal and setting the lights. Brady, tense with nerves, behaved
outrageously to the straining crews. He stood in the middle of the
middle aisle, a cigar in his mouth, bellowing curses at Louis Hartmann, head electrician of the Playhouse, and Hartmann passed
along the crackling bad temper in booming instructions to his
lighting assistants.

Brady treated me with elaborate consideration, in contrast to
his usual obscene approach to producer-cast relations. Sometimes
he even removed his hat, which was so much a part of him that
when he doffed it half his head seemed missing.

I fell asleep exhausted that night while Harry was still trying
futilely to get Father's approval. When I awakened, Father had
already left the house. I went to the Playhouse to prepare for the
opening and was putting on my makeup—ineptly, as usual—
when a bang on the door announced that Brady wanted a word
with me. He came in, his hat pulled low on his face, drunk. Since

I had never seen anyone drunk before, I didn't realize why his behavior was so strange.

He threw the five-year contract on my dressing table, knocking over pots of rouge and cold cream, and slurred a command at me. "Sign that, young lady, or the curtain doesn't go up and we don't open." He wheeled, staggered out of the room, and slammed the door.

I was sitting as he left me, numb with misery, when there was another knock. John Cromwell came in and drew up a chair. He said Brady was serious about canceling the opening. He urged me to sign the contract. Father would be reconciled to my decision after he saw me perform.

When Cromwell left, I did what my father always recommended, "Think it all out." I reasoned that he would never know whether or not my talent was worth the sacrifice of my education unless he saw me act. The play would have to open in order to show him that I had a talent worthy of his respect. *If* he attended —another unknown.

Still I hesitated. After demanding my independence for so long, was I afraid to grasp it? Couldn't I pick up the pen and sign? I groaned. Then I was struck by another thought. If I didn't assert myself now, I would never be independent of my father.

I signed.

Brady was in a high state of excitement when I gave him the contract. He hung around backstage, pouring solicitude and advice on me. I felt like one of his prizefighters—James J. Corbett or James J. Jeffries—about to climb into the ring. If I hadn't been such a secure and confident person, I would have been rattled by his "go get 'em" style.

The audience cheered when the final curtain came down. My dressing room was packed with my brothers and Lilli, other relatives, friends from Barnard, teachers, and people I didn't know, all praising me to the skies. From Lilli I learned that Father and Mother had attended after all. They were waiting outside.

When the room finally cleared and I had changed, I went out the stage door and apprehensively approached my parents, who were standing beside our car. Mother embraced and kissed me warmly. I kept my eye on Father but couldn't read his mood. He didn't seem angry, but he wasn't pleased either. His expression was sad and withdrawn. He nodded, which I took to mean approval.

Brady burst from the theater and rushed up. "Aren't you proud of your daughter?" he demanded. Mother surprised me. She said she would be proud of me when I *sang* in the theater. Brady was taken aback. He turned to my father, who looked him over silently for a long time and then said:

"Keep her decent. Good night, sir."

The ride home was funereal. The telephone began to ring at an unconscionably early hour the next morning, as the twins were preparing to leave for engineering school at Columbia University and young Walter was setting out for the Polytech Preparatory Country Day School. They gave me affectionate hugs, unusual at that early hour, said something about wonderful reviews in the newspapers, and left. Lilli, still in her dressing gown, announced she wouldn't be going to Barnard that morning. She refused to miss the excitement.

"What's going on?" I asked, dazed.

"Your notices," she told me gleefully. "Everyone we know has been phoning. Walter ran down to the corner and brought back the papers. You're *famous!*"

None of us had thought of buying the papers the night before. I collapsed in a chair and read the headline in the Brooklyn *Eagle* that Lilli handed me: HELEN GAHAGAN BECOMES STAGE STAR OVERNIGHT. Below, in smaller type: *Parents Opposed Career.* The reviewer wrote:

> The first-nighters had gone to the Playhouse wondering who this newcomer might be who was entrusted with the leading role in the new Owen Davis play. They left wondering how she could have gained her poise and evident stage experience without Broadway ever having heard of her. . . .

Lilli asked, "Do you know who Heywood Broun is, Helen?"

"Of course."

"Well, see what he says about you."

I took the paper she handed me and read:

> The event of the evening was the performance of a young leading woman called Helen Gahagan. . . . Unless we are mistaken, here

is a light comedienne capable of challenging comparison with the best whom our theatre has to offer. . . . Miss Helen Gahagan is ten of the twelve most beautiful women in America.

"That's irrelevant," I complained.
"What are you talking about?"
I said, "Looks have nothing to do with acting."
Father and Mother came into the breakfast room. Father's mood of gloom subdued even Lilli. We ate in dense silence, broken by telephone calls from Father's business friends who asked, "Walter, is that your daughter they're talking about this morning?" Father looked more depressed with every call. The world knew it. His daughter was an *actress*.

I crossed the front porch to say good morning to my grandmother, Hannah Gahagan, who lived with Aunt Mary in a twin house attached to ours. She asked some thoughtful questions about the theater and my plans and considered for a moment. At last she found a way to accept the bad news. "Well, Helen, theater is a kind of teaching." She was a former schoolteacher. I grinned and kissed her gratefully.

Back home I ran up the stairs two at a time to the top floor and threw myself on my bed. I found I was depressed. My performance in *Dreams for Sale* on opening night hadn't been my best, but I was certain I could improve it with work. And *Dreams for Sale* wasn't worth doing, but I promised myself I would never accept a second-rate script again. And I was exhausted, but a twenty-two-year-old woman can recover quickly from that. My despair stemmed from something else—the reviews.

I felt self-conscious and alarmed. All my good reviews in the past had been general statements and had meant little to me. But the New York critics had not only heaped praise on me, they had analyzed gestures and movements and voice quality. I knew instinctively that a performer could be led astray by such examination. It was possible that I might shape my performance, perhaps unconsciously, to the perception of the critics and lose my own thread.

After *Dreams for Sale* I never again read the reviews the morning after an opening, preferring to wait a week or two until I was certain of what I was doing in a part.

Brady, sober and delighted, greeted me warmly at the Playhouse that night. The critics had been unkind about the play but their acclaim for me was a confirmation of his judgment. He turned up in my dressing room with some advice.

"An actor's greatest contribution is originality," he told me. "You're unique and you want to stay that way. I'm telling you that you should stay away from the theater crowd. When actors spend a lot of time together they tend to pick up one another's mannerisms. If you want to keep your freshness, stay away from other actors."

The advice seemed somewhat lame, since his wife Gladys George was a leader of the theater crowd. I suspected that Brady was trying to comply with Father's admonition to keep me "decent." Whatever prompted his heart-to-heart talk with me, I considered his advice and decided it was sound.

Father may have been heartbroken that I disobeyed him, but there was no question of my leaving home. Family ties were too strong for either of us to have considered it for a moment. He required only that the family car take me to the theater every night and pick me up immediately after the final curtain. And life went on.

We were raised in acute awareness of our family lines. My maternal grandfather was James Mussen who pioneered in Lodi, Wisconsin. His future wife, Tamer Griffith, immigrated from Wales. His people were known for their strength and hers for their pure singing voices.

With Grandfather away serving in the militia, Tamer was taken with labor pains. She crawled two miles on her hands and knees to the nearest farm. Women there brought her back home in a buckboard and helped deliver her eighth child, my mother. Tamer called her Lillian Rose.

When Mother was five years old, she and Tamer were stricken with pneumonia. Racked with high fevers, they begged for water. A medical superstition held that it was hazardous to give water to pneumonia patients. Tamer was denied anything to drink but some water was given Mother, just to keep her quiet.

Tamer lay in a coma until Easter morning, when she sat up in bed, sang a few lines of "Nearer, My God, to Thee" in a clear, sweet voice, and fell back dead. James was left with nine children to raise. Two years later he married a widow with daughters the same age as his oldest children.

Mother, lonely and mourning for Tamer, found comfort in her brother Frank, the youngest child. Their chore was to watch the cows to see that they didn't stray. In the afternoons they listened to the distant, mournful whistle of a train and Mother was swept with longing to be on it, traveling far away.

When she was ten she rebelled. Blamed for something she hadn't done at school, she announced that she wasn't going back. After that her stepmother required her to rise at four in the morning to help the kitchen girl prepare breakfast, and then she washed dishes, cleaned, cooked, and looked after farm animals until dark.

She was a quick, intelligent child. That year at harvest time she drove a four-horse hitch when Grandfather couldn't find anyone else to bring in his crop. She had learned to do it by watching. As a reward, he bought her a sealskin hat she had been longing to own. The feel of the luxurious fur, she once told me, stirred her to the soul. Her stepmother sent it back to the store, saying it was too fine for Lillian Rose.

Loss of that hat put steel in Mother. She determined she would get away. A visit to a sister who taught school in a distant town provided her with a method. She would become a schoolteacher. After that she took her school books off the shelf where she'd flung them and studied every night by candlelight when the family was in bed.

When she judged herself ready, she asked an older brother in the nearby town of Lodi to find a place for her to stay while she attended high school. A kindly minister and his wife took her in and made her feel wanted for the first time since Tamer's death. Lillian Rose sailed through high school with top grades, to the surprise of her stepmother who had predicted she would fail, and took a train to Rice Lake to begin teaching.

Another brother met her there, concerned for her safety in that school. The last teacher, a man, had been thrown bodily into a snowbank by his oversized students. Mother saw the problem her first day in the classroom. It was full of huge teenagers, burly

Irishmen, sensitive because farm chores had played such havoc
with school attendance that they could not read or write though
they were in their teens.

She put away the textbooks and taught them orally. Since she
was a natural-born storyteller, her accounts of the early settlers, of
the Revolution, of pioneers in the West, fascinated them. From
that beginning she introduced them to memorizing, first the
names of Presidents, then the National Anthem, and by degrees
into poetry.

Four months after her arrival, her pupils gave a concert for the
parents. The adults were amazed and thrilled to be entertained
with recitations, songs and a one-act play Mother wrote for the
occasion. A special meeting of the school board was called at
which it was decided to extend the school year by a month, a big
sacrifice for farmers who needed their children's help. The next
year the progress of the students was so encouraging that the
board voted to have school last for eleven months.

Mother was promoted to a less isolated school in Rice Lake,
where she lived with her sister Myra. Myra's husband was a lum-
berman, absent for months at a time. Mother thought Myra
should have something to occupy her time.

Mother adored hats. On Mother's ninetieth birthday Lilli flew
to Vermont with the perfect gift, four boxes of hats. Mother was
ecstatic.

Since Rice Lake lacked a good millinery shop, Mother determined that Myra should make hats. That summer she dragged
Myra to Chicago and they offered to work without pay in a
wholesale house, beginning in a back room where shapes were
blocked and advancing rapidly through trimmings to display.

Laden with a collection of year-old Paris hats and boxes of silk,
satin, lace and wire, they returned to Rice Lake in the late summer. Mother found a vacant shop and the two women set themselves up in business as milliners. Mother continued to teach
school, but her project prospered so well that in a few years she
had expanded. She was running the biggest department store in
Rice Lake, with Myra's husband in the front office.

Meanwhile her father had a new wife, Ida Waterbury, a
woman Mother knew and liked. Ida wrote that there was a milli-

nery business in Lodi for sale. She begged Mother to come home. Her father had moved from the farm into a hotel in Lodi, a three-story wooden building he'd acquired as payment for a bad debt. He was having trouble running it and needed Mother's help.

Mother returned, moved into the hotel, bought the vacant shop and opened for business with a tea party that had the town agog.

At six one morning, the occupants of Grandfather's hotel were roused from their beds by a fire in the chimney. That's how Mother met Father. He was a civil engineer, Walter Homer Gahagan, from Ohio, living in the hotel while he supervised the laying of double track for a railway from Chicago to Baraboo.

The year was 1896. Father had been traveling too much to settle down to marriage. Fresh from M.I.T., he helped build the first bridge across the Mississippi River, the Eads Bridge at St. Louis. His latest job had been in Arkansas where he supervised the building of seven bridges over the Snake and the Red rivers. His Gahagan Company would take on anything.

He was attracted to Mother's beauty and her competence— Hannah Gahagan's son was bound to respect ability in a woman —but what won him was Mother's voice. That Friday night he attended a meeting in the Methodist Church, heard her sing, and fell in love on the spot.

For months he courted her, but he didn't propose until Grandmother Hannah arrived in Rice Lake, met Mother, looked her over sharply, and approved. Mother was so insulted that she decided to make him wait. When he did ask her to marry him, she said she would let him know. He was certainly a catch, as Rice Lake would say—prosperous, dignified, handsome, and possessed of courtly, formal manners.

Mother accepted him even though she had a taste of his possessiveness. She was the proud owner of a bicycle, the rage of the early nineties, and loved to ride off on picnics with her friends. Father couldn't bear to see her so free and mobile. He insisted she sell it. She did, and they were married.

An Episcopal minister came to perform the ceremony. Father was an Episcopalian.

Father took Mother to Ohio to stay with Grandmother Hannah while he went East to supervise the construction of the Manhattan pier of the Williamsburg bridge. Mother joined him a few weeks later and found herself, for the first time in her life, with time on her hands.

One day, walking through Union Square, she heard singing. She traced the source to a music school and went inside. She had always been curious to have a professional opinion of her voice. An operatic coach at the school heard her and begged her to bring her husband.

Father reluctantly went and the coach told him, "There hasn't been a voice like this since Melba. Only once in a generation is there a voice as beautiful and as naturally placed as your wife's. If she begins studies with me, in three years she'll sing in opera. I'll give her lessons free if she'll sign a contract with me. She will have a brilliant career."

Father looked at Mother, then at the coach waiting for his answer, then at Mother again. He said, "Come."

They walked a few blocks before he spoke. "Lillian," he said, "you must give up this notion of having a singing career or I'll take you back to Wisconsin and leave you there. I love your voice but I didn't marry you to have you become a professional singer. I want you to be my wife and the mother of my children. If you want to live with me, you can't sing opera."

Mother cried all night. When Father left the house the next morning he was as unhappy as she, but he was adamant. "It was a bitter pill to swallow," Mother wrote in a memoir almost sixty years later. She knew he meant it. She put aside her hopes for voice training.

Nine months later the twins were born. After that, she said, "My heart and hands were full."

The division of labor in their marriage obliged Mother to take complete responsibility for the house. She learned early that Father wanted no part of it. "I don't want to hear about it!" he exploded one day when she described a servant problem. "My work is outside the home. Yours is in the home. Manage as best you can."

The arrangement suited Mother, who after all was an experi-

enced and astute businesswoman. She ran the big house so effortlessly that Father came to believe it ran itself. I'm afraid we all
thought so. I didn't appreciate that Mother was a miracle-worker
until I married and ran a household of my own.

Two years after the twins, in 1900, I was born. A year or so
later Father decided to establish the Gahagan Company headquarters in Brooklyn. He instructed Mother to find a suitable
house. She picked an enormous double house in the elegant Park
Slope area of Brooklyn, at 231 Lincoln Place, choosing it for its
large garden and because there was a good private school for girls,
Berkeley, just down the street and a good private school for boys
around the corner.

The house looked like the set of *Life with Father*, with large,
airy, high-ceilinged rooms, marble fireplaces in almost every room,
tall windows looking out on the garden, and fine paneling everywhere. Father agreed the house was ideal in every respect save
one, the steep stairs that ran from the first to the second floor and
from the second to the third without a landing. He was concerned that Mother would trip in her long skirts.

Father obtained a corroborating opinion from another engineer, who agreed that the stairs would be the death of Mother.
Mother laughed. We moved into one of the houses in 1902 soon
after Lilli was born.

Father bought both houses. His business was thriving and he
needed more help in the office so he brought his sister Mary and
her husband George Clyde from Troy, Ohio, and settled them
next door. Their only child, Walter, was twelve and I was five. I
fell in love with him on sight. At first the families were amused.
As we grew older and I proved tenacious in my adoration of my
handsome, dashing cousin, tolerance gave way to alarm. As soon
as Walter finished school, Uncle George and Aunt Mary shipped
him off to the Klondike.

The Park Slope was a tranquil neighborhood at the turn of the
century. The streets were lit by gas lanterns and echoed to the
clop-clop of horse-drawn carriages and the cries of vendors. A lone
policeman patrolled, a friend to us all. Our spacious house, aglow
with gaslight, was utterly peaceful except for the uproar of five
hearty children.

On Sundays the family usually went to the nearby Montague Club for supper. It was the only day of the week when women were permitted. Father used to tell us of the events we missed. One story concerned Senator Chauncey Depew, railway baron and famed orator, who spoke there one night. He delivered his address without notes and it was a triumph. Afterward a member congratulated him for delivering such an impressive impromptu speech. Depew was indignant.

"*Impromptu!*" he retorted. "Young man, I've been preparing that speech all my life!"

Years later when I found myself delivering speeches without notes, I remembered Chauncey Depew. No one speaks in a vacuum. A talk is a summation of the speaker's experience and hard-earned perspective; it is an intensely self-revealing process. A seemingly offhand address takes a lifetime of preparation.

We were a noisy, gregarious, affectionate family. When Mother could tolerate no more of our games of tag through the house, shouting and taunting one another at the top of our lungs, she would say sternly, "Stop it now. Stop it! And you, Helen, stop at once or you'll be crying by nightfall." For a long time I tired more quickly than the others because I was growing quickly and because a severe hemorrhage following a tonsillectomy had left me weakened. Mother called me her "white potato sprout."

We loved sliding down the banisters of the stairs Father disliked. They were our normal transit. Just before dinner one evening, Billy, Fritz and I were descending with speed when Father arrived home unexpectedly. He yelled for Mother, who came to the head of the stairs and answered sweetly, "Yes, Walter?"

"Lillian, do you see what the children are doing?" Father bellowed. "*They're sliding down the banisters.*"

Mother said, "Yes, I know. I taught them how."

Father was dumbfounded. "Do you want them to fall and break their necks?"

"No," she said, "that's why I showed them how. I've been sliding down myself to set an example."

Mother, a chameleon of adjustment to circumstances, fitted herself to Father's uncertain schedule with ease. Time meant nothing to him, a failing I share. When he was engrossed in something he stopped only when it was finished. Because he returned home so late, we children often had two dinners, one at the usual hour and the other when he sat down for his. We would jump out of bed, slide down the banister, and join him in the dining room while he ate.

On bank mornings Father was up at eight, but on other days he stayed in bed until he was rested. He liked to have Mother sit by him while he read the morning paper. She had no tolerance for idleness but would sit still for as long as she could bear it before rushing off. One of her activities was the study of medicine. She took courses to equip herself for giving emergency treatment to her large, active brood.

Her other major activity consisted of finding after-school training for us. She was always optimistic that the new project would work out, but fortunately she gracefully accepted the frequent collapse of her ambitions for us. One such disaster was her plan to have me dance like Anna Pavlova. Eventually the ballet lessons stopped but music did not. Her passion for music filled the house. She had season tickets to the Metropolitan Opera and took me to every performance from an early age.

Mother actively supported the Episcopal church two and a half blocks from our home. Father refused to attend, but all five Gahagan children were required to pass through the sequence of Sunday school, confirmation and regular attendance at the Sunday services in the family pew. Father saw to it that we left on time. He explained that he had had enough of sermons in Troy to last his lifetime.

In the afternoon we went to the Brooklyn Museum. Mother thought the museum would stretch our minds. It certainly did. It made world travelers of us all.

Sunday morning after breakfast was reserved for the family council. When we were little it consisted of exhortations to behave better, but as we grew older the discussions concerned more serious matters—ethics. Father was famous for his honesty. His business was built on handshake agreements. He would tell us, "Your word is your bond. You must keep your word always."

Our household didn't resemble the formal, dignified establishments of some of our friends, where families ate in subdued

surroundings attended by unobtrusive servants. At the Gahagans'
no two of us ate breakfast or lunch at the same time. We usually
snatched something from the table and ate on the run, late for
school. We did sit down for dinner but it was a noisy meal. Like
Father, we were all talkers and we expressed our ideas, more often
than not, simultaneously.

Our maids were inexperienced, since trained help wasn't drawn
to such a hubbub. Mother patiently trained a succession of
Swedes and Germans, some of them supplied by the same large
family, one at a time.

The activities of the twins appealed much more to me than
playing with dolls, as Lilli did. When my brothers were given
boxing lessons, a form of athletics popularized by President
Teddy Roosevelt, I insisted on learning to box too. After much
pleading, Frederick agreed to spar with me. "I'm not going to
treat you any differently than I do William," he warned. I told
him to go ahead. He knocked me out.

When I came to, Frederick asked if I still wanted to box. Father answered for me, *"No!"*

The whole family skiied but somehow I managed to avoid it. I
got the impression from watching them that there was nothing to
it. Why do they make such a fuss about it? I wondered. One winter day I went to the highest place I could find. I rented some
skis from an instructor, who was worried about me. "You haven't
skied before, have you," he reminded me. "Don't you want to—"

"No, no," I told him impatiently. "I can see what you do. You
just lean over, like this, and go down the hill."

I leaned over and plunged down the hill, faster and faster, until
I hit a bump and flipped into the snow headfirst. I suppose I was
lucky my neck wasn't broken. That was the beginning and the
end of my skiing.

My golf career was similar. My brothers loved golf so I refused
to play, not wanting to compete with them. One day, out of curiosity, I put a ball on a tee, picked up a golf club, took a hefty
backswing, and knocked myself unconscious. That finished golf
for me.

The boys were like Father—smart, quick-moving, big, indepen-
dent-minded. Lilli was like Mother, easygoing and sweet-tem-

pered. I resembled my father in several ways, sharing his love for books for instance; also, I had his explosive temper.

His refusal to allow me out of the house without a chaperon used to infuriate me. Once when he wouldn't allow me to take a Sunday stroll with a girl friend I was so enraged I threw over a table, just missing some guests.

Hours later Mother came into my bedroom where I had retreated shamefacedly. "It's good to have a temper, Helen," she told me kindly, "but you'd better get it under control or you'll go through life apologizing."

I struggled to heed her wise counsel but it was some years before I achieved a measure of restraint. One of my better-known furies occurred at school when I found an older girl abusing a crippled student in the locker room of the gymnasium. I grabbed the bully's arm, threw her to the floor and sat on her, shouting "You don't do that, *you don't do that!* Do you hear!"

Of course she heard. The entire school, including the principal, heard me.

I was aware on some level that my existence was protected. When newsboys came down the street at night calling, "Extra! Read all about it . . . ," I was filled with alarm. What was going on? What awful things were happening beyond the safety of Park Slope? I shivered with dread. My only knowledge of poverty, child labor, debtors' prison and Christmas without a turkey came from reading Charles Dickens.

At the age of ten I came to the realization that Mother and Father kept important information from us. It happened on the day that Aunt Mary took me and Lilli out of Berkeley without explanation. A servant kept us occupied all day, bringing us home at six o'clock. We both felt that something was very wrong.

When Aunt Mary opened our front door to us, my heart sank. "Where's Mother?" I asked.

"Upstairs, Helen. Do be quiet."

I ignored her and raced up the stairs screaming, "Mother!" With Lilli close behind, we burst into her bedroom and found her with a tiny baby beside her.

"You have a little brother," Mother told us. "Isn't he beautiful?"

I was stunned and speechless. Lilli, enraptured, leaned over the baby making ridiculous noises, the kind she made to her dolls, but I was repelled. Mother patted my hand reassuringly but I felt betrayed. My parents had explained that babies sat on lily pads waiting for a stork to gather them up and deliver them. I was certain my brother hadn't arrived that way.

I ran from the room. How, then, had he come? Why hadn't Mother and Father told us the truth? What was being kept from us?

Two years later the family went to Europe *en masse*—Father, Mother, the twins, me, Lilli, two-year-old Walter with his nurse, Uncle George and Aunt Mary. We stayed at Baden-Baden, a spa in Germany's Black Forest, where I improved my German while the twins went cycling down the Rhine with a tutor in charge.

That summer in Europe in 1912 was all beauty, the glorious period of *La Belle Époque* that provided me with a yardstick against which to measure the destruction of the two world wars that were to follow.

Soon after our return Uncle George left Father's company to form his own, the Clyde Literage Company, and my cousin Walter returned from the Klondike to join him. I was overjoyed. I was infinitely resourceful at finding reasons to go next door to "visit Aunt Mary."

Walter had become dangerously handsome. He was six-foot-six, lean, exuding vitality and charm. I found him irresistible; most women did. My parents were so concerned about my infatuation that they sent me that summer to visit Grandmother Hannah in Ohio.

Though I pined for my dashing cousin, the visit proved rewarding. Grandmother Hannah was an extraordinary woman. Two years earlier, she and Uncle George's mother, Sarah Clyde, both in their seventies, had traveled alone to the Holy Land and Europe and even climbed one of the Alps.

Hannah Gahagan was tall and straight as an arrow, with a grave, solemn manner. Her grooming was immaculate. Until the last year of her life not even her daughters were permitted to see her when she wasn't fully, impeccably dressed.

She lived on Plum Street in Troy. After raising her three

children—Father, Mary and Bess—she sold the farm and moved
into the town where she appeared to run the local Presbyterian
church. She was consumed with interest in her family genealogy
that summer, poring every day over charts and old Bibles and correspondence with distant relatives. She wasn't communicative but
Martha Schnibel, my cousin, gave me some information gleaned
from her mother, Aunt Bess.

My paternal great-great-grandfather, William, was a feisty
young Irish immigrant who enlisted in General "mad Anthony"
Wayne's army of Indian fighters in Ohio. He and fourteen others
traveled down the Ohio River to its mouth and in 1796 established a new settlement they called Dayton. Later he took his
wife and son, William Hammer Gahagan, to homestead in the
fertile riverland up the Miami River north of Troy township.
President James Madison signed the deed for the farm that was
called the Gahagan Prairie.

William Hammer Gahagan appears to have been a natural
leader. He organized county fairs and citizen committees to promote the growth of Troy, and made a gift of a piece of his land
for the First Presbyterian Church and adjoining graveyard. His
son, my grandfather, was named after William Henry Harrison.
He was a captivating, handsome man who loved fine horses, silk
vests and acting. *Acting!* I was thrilled to learn that after the
Civil War Grandfather performed in Shakespearean plays produced by his own Thespian Company.

Grandmother Hannah hired a horse and buggy and drove
Martha and me to New Carlyle where her family farm was located. Her brother told us that the farm had been one of the stations on the underground railway along which runaway slaves fled
to freedom in the North.

Discovering my Gahagan-Smith roots gave me an important
sense of family continuity which was a source of strength and stability during my political life. The three William Gahagans were
a solid link with the country's pioneer past, tracing a pattern from
sod-busting through community-building to appreciation of the
arts. Like them, Father was a builder and a cultivated man. The
twins and my brother Walter extended both developments. I
note the same growth, generation by generation, all over the

world. Seeing it in my own family I can identify with it everywhere.

I found my roots in Ohio.

One morning, shortly before I was to return home to Brooklyn,
I woke with a shock and ran downstairs in bare feet and nightgown. I found my grandmother in the kitchen preparing breakfast. "What's the matter with me?" I cried. "I'm *bleeding!*"

She told me to go back to bed. She would bring up breakfast
and explain what had happened. There was nothing to worry
about; it was quite normal.

Soon she put the tray on my lap and sat down beside my bed. I
was apprehensive about what she would tell me. I rattled on
about the delicious hot rolls and plum jam. I wasn't sure I wanted
to know what she was waiting to say. While she talked, I concentrated on eating and managed to shut out her voice about half
the time. We finished together, I with breakfast and Grandmother
with a clinical explanation of menstruation and puberty.

She put the tray on a hall table, brought me the necessary
supplies, and sat by the bed again. She fixed me with a gaze I
couldn't fathom, very tender and loving and sad. She put her
hand on my forehead with such sweet intimacy that I squirmed.
It was so unlike her normal distant reserve that I was confused.

After a long moment I was grateful that she broke the spell.
She stood up briskly and told me to get dressed. We were going
to Aunt Bess's where I would spend the day with Martha. I was
relieved. Within the hour I had forgotten the strange moment.
Years later I understood its significance. Grandmother was ex-
pressing her deepest feelings about becoming a woman; she was
giving me her blessing.

By our early teens, the twins, Lilli and I had moved to the
third floor of our Brooklyn house and Mother was resigned to the
fact that we were a family of night owls. She went to bed early,
shutting her door and ignoring us all. We Gahagans resisted sleep
as long as possible. Father used to read late into the night, always
falling asleep over a book with the light still on.

At the stroke of midnight we would stop reading or studying
and run down to Father's room. "Don't you think we ought to

have a snack, Father?" we would ask. Invariably, he agreed. In the kitchen the twins would construct enormous sandwiches. Lilli and I made only slightly smaller versions of their concoctions. Father was content with bread and milk. He wasn't really interested in eating. He was there to visit with us.

His daytime communication with us consisted almost entirely of long, severe lectures. At midnight we really talked. He asked what we were doing and thinking, and he told us about his current engineering projects as though we were expert adults. We visited him on the site regularly. Father not only took the twins, who from the age of ten couldn't wait to be engineers and work in the family business, but Lilli and me as well. We all knew exactly what was happening on every job and during our midnight snacks we would question him avidly.

After that 1912 summer in Europe, Father announced that he didn't want his children to spend another summer in resort hotels. It wasn't healthy, he said. He didn't really care for cities. He instructed Mother to find us a summer home in the country. She chose Vermont and one morning we boarded a train for the Upper Connecticut Valley. Late that afternoon we were in Fairlee, where the stationmaster, Joe Alger, greeted us warmly. Mr. Munn drove us to our rented cottage.

The road ran through a dense forest, giving us occasional glimpses of Lake Morey. The lake has a special history. It was named for a renowned Vermont inventor, Captain Samuel E. Morey, who may have invented the steamship before Robert Fulton did. He had a steam-driven sidewheeler on the Connecticut River in 1790, sixteen years ahead of Fulton. Vermonters say that Fulton stole Morey's design. Morey, in disgust, sank his steamship, the *Aunt Sally*, in the lake named for him.

A little paddleboat called the *Miss-It-Walk-It* took passengers around the lake. Mother had a ride on it and spotted a large wooden house perched high above the shore. Festive with Victorian gingerbread with a broad veranda running all around, it resembled a wedding cake. She decided she wanted it but was informed that it wasn't for sale.

"Well, when it is, let me know," she said.

The following winter word came that the house could be bought. Sight unseen, except for that glimpse from the deck of the paddleboat, Cliff Mull became ours.

The next summer was 1914. In June a newsboy came down our street hawking papers with headlines about the assassination of Archduke Ferdinand, heir to the Austrian throne, the event that led to the First World War. A few weeks later we drove to our new home in Vermont. Father decided we should leave at four in the morning in order to arrive before dark. It didn't work out that way. The car had one blowout after another, a common occurrence on the unpaved roads of the day. After each disaster, the chauffeur would pull into a garage for repairs. The fourth delay was too much for Mother. Thoroughly exasperated, she announced, "We'll not stop again for any reason!"

Thirteen hours after we waved Father good-bye in Brooklyn we clattered into the town of Fairlee—on four rims.

Life at Cliff Mull was intoxicating. After obligatory piano lessons and physical exercises every morning, we were free to live in or on the water, roam the woods, or hike seven miles to Chapman's Drug Store to gorge on his incomparable homemade ice cream topped with solid marshmallow—to be found nowhere else in the world, then or now.

We all played tennis on the court below the house. When Father came for weekend visits it would madden us that he could beat us without appearing to move, his long arms reaching out to return the ball. The twins also played golf and fished. By the second year at Cliff Mull they were possessors of a Model T, Father's reward for their high grades in their freshman year at Williams College. Locals called them the GO-hagan twins. Neither Fritz nor Billy would teach me to drive their precious Tin Lizzie, which made me determined to learn.

I watched closely to see how they operated it. Cranking to get the engine going seemed to be the hardest part. At five one morning, while the family was still asleep, I stole down the hill to the garage and started to crank. A half hour later I was almost ready to concede defeat. I decided to try one more time. To my great joy, the engine sputtered and then caught.

I backed the car out safely and set off down the driveway to the road around the lake and then up and over the mountain to Bradford. I didn't dare stop for fear the engine would stall and I wouldn't be able to start it again.

Four hours later, elated, I turned into the gates of Cliff Mull. Unfortunately, the twins, Lilli, Walter and Mother were all down at the tennis court and I was in plain view. The twins came running toward me, shouting at the top of their lungs. In a panic to escape, I reversed the engine without looking where I was going. I went off the road and came to rest, unharmed, against a poplar tree on the edge of the drive.

Lilli and Walter were proud of me but the twins were furious. The car wasn't much damaged but it was a long time before they forgave me.

Lilli didn't think much of hiking or swimming, or of Vermont either; she preferred the sea. She also loved horses and was always ready to join me on buggy rides. We would rent a horse and buggy at Munn's and set off after the preliminary argument about who would drive first. Lilli usually won. She would cry "Giddee-up" and away we would go.

We'd cross into New Hampshire over a covered bridge that spanned the Connecticut and explore the country roads for a perfect picnic spot. When we found one, we'd climb out, tie the horse, and eat our famous Gahagan three-decker sandwiches.

We all adored overnight picnics, except Mother. She had no taste for sleeping in the woods with a rock for a pillow or, worse, in the middle of her back. As a result we were on our own. Half the pleasure of the outing was the organization and planning. We selected the menu, bought the food, packed it on our backs to the selected campsite, collected wood for the fire, and cooked dinner. The bigger the group the better; we invited people from miles around. At dawn we hurried back to Cliff Mull in time for a swim and a delicious kitchen-cooked breakfast.

None of this distracted me from my main ambition, to prepare myself for a career on the stage. I practiced eye exercises daily in front of a mirror, trying out changes of emotion. I was practicing flirting one day at lunch, using the twins and two of their friends as subjects. By the middle of the meal, they'd had enough. To laughing protests from Mother and Lilli, they picked me up bodily, carried me out of the house and down three flights of stairs, and threw me fully dressed into Lake Morey.

I was laughing so hard when I hit the water I almost drowned. I *had* overplayed the flirting, I decided. Too Carmen-like.

With or without clothes, I'm happy in water. I enjoy walking in rain or snow bareheaded. I love storms, especially Vermont storms. I would take a front seat on the porch of Cliff Mull and watch the storm advance across the lake and catch me up in its wildness.

I dream about Vermont when I travel. Touring in plays, as I did later, singing in Europe, traveling the world, when I'm tired I imagine that I'm in a Vermont woods listening to the silence. It brings me peace. I expand and feel the sweetness and the sadness of this transitory life. Every time I leave Vermont I think of Deirdre's line in John Millington Synge's play *Deirdre of the Sorrows*: "It's a heartbreak to the wise that we have the same things for a short space only."

The twins were too young to consider enlisting in the army in the First World War, but my beloved cousin Walter Clyde tried to join when the fighting started in Europe. He was turned down because the Clyde Literage Company was ferrying arms and munitions to cargo ships standing outside New York Harbor, an essential service for the Allied cause.

The Clyde house next door was filled with young women who also were smitten with my dashing cousin. For a short time he was engaged to someone in Ohio, but nothing came of it. In 1917 he met Kitty Lovett and after a brief, ardent courtship of only a few weeks they were married. They returned from a short honeymoon to take up residence in a brownstone only three blocks away.

Undeterred by his new status, I continued to adore him. I managed to be on the porch to exchange a few words with him every day when he drove his father home from the office.

On a Monday six weeks after the wedding, Walter delivered his father as usual but came in, threw himself on the sofa, and said he didn't feel well. The next day he stayed home with a severe cold. On Wednesday, Kitty told us he had chills and a slight fever. Aunt Mary and I went at once to see him. Walter looked dreadfully ill and was racked by painful coughing spells.

The following day his temperature rose to 104 degrees. Aunt Mary called the doctor. Walter had pleurisy in his right lung, the doctor said. We weren't concerned at the news. One of the twins, William, had recovered from three bouts of pneumonia.

Kitty called us early on the morning of the fourth day of Walter's illness. The doctor had just left. Walter now was critically ill with double pneumonia. By the time I arrived with Uncle George and Aunt Mary, he was delirious. We stayed with Kitty that day but nothing we did seemed to help. The wonder drugs that were to cure pneumonia readily were unknown. Walter was burning with fever, talking wildly and laboring to breathe.

We stood around his bed, helpless. The next few hours were unbearable. We watched his dying struggles. I don't remember if anyone cried. I didn't. I was intensely involved in his fight to live. As he neared the unmistakable crisis, I gripped the back of my neck with my hands. I had a strong sensation that my head would topple off if I didn't hold it.

The crisis passed and Walter, long, lank and warm, lay still. I couldn't believe he was dead. The sound of his fevered cries was still in the room. Then a chilling silence descended and I was filled with a sense of irretrievable loss.

The doctor moved first and broke the dreadful stillness with a comment. Sometime in the early morning Uncle George insisted that we return home, taking Kitty with us. I felt it was barbarous to abandon Walter to the care of strangers from the undertaker. I still think so. We shouldn't flee from the corpse of someone we love. Death is not contagious.

After a time Uncle George adjusted to the death of his splendid son. Mary Clyde never did. Kitty was dazed; she had known him a cruelly brief time. For myself, I was shattered.

Grieving over Walter Clyde in some ways protected me against the infatuations to which my friends were prone. I was free to devote my energies exclusively to the theater. I was relieved that Father had accepted my decision about *Dreams for Sale* so mildly. I assumed he would no longer try to direct my life but I should have known better. Father didn't give up so easily.

Soon after I began to receive my regular salary checks he came to me with an offer. If I would put my money in a savings account he would match it, dollar for dollar. I could continue to draw my allowance. I saw through his strategy at once. He really was uncomfortable with the idea of a woman having independence and mobility, as he had been when Mother rode a bicycle.

His offer was generous, since Brady was paying me $250 a week, but I turned Father down flat. Nothing on earth could have persuaded me to give up my new financial self-sufficiency. I had hated receiving an allowance from him from the age of seven when I used to avoid collecting my twenty-five cents a week whenever I could.

The weekend reviews of my performance in *Dreams for Sale* were dazzling. Gilbert Seldes wrote in "Talk of the Town":

> Not since Helen Hayes made her first tumultuous appearance . . . has any unknown scored so superlatively. . . .

On the same day Colgate Baker wrote in the New York *Review:*

> HELEN GAHAGAN: A NEW ACTING SENSATION
> The day of miracles is not past for William A. Brady. . . . He has discovered a real acting genius in the person of the young woman who was never heard of before in all theatredom. She is Helen Gahagan. . . . She could not help outshining everything that opening night at the Playhouse any more than the sun can help shining over the landscape at dawn and dwarfing everything else into petty littleness. . . . In a word, Miss Gahagan showed that she is a real inspirational actress by birthright.

The day after the opening of *Dreams for Sale* Brady handed me a script to read. I returned it, saying, "I'm sorry but I can't play in this one."

Over the next few weeks Brady gave me many more scripts and I rejected them all. Brady was offended that I refused to accept his judgment about my next play. For my part I suspected that he had a closet full of dusty old scripts and was running them by me, one at a time. I was determined not to appear in any more trashy, poorly written productions.

In an honest play, speech expresses thinking and feeling that can touch an audience. Elizabeth Grimball had taught me to consider the inner thoughts of a character I intended to portray, to work on the emotions below the lines. That is the essence of the creative process in acting. Even a familiar role achieves a different shape from the substrata that a new actor finds in it. I was determined not to play any cardboard characters where it would be impossible for me to express any depth of feeling.

Brady was becoming irritated with me. At the point where our relationship was deteriorating, he surprised me by giving me a new play by the Hungarian genius Ferenc Molnar whose best-known work, *Liliom,* much later was the basis for the hit musical *Carousel.* The Molnar play Brady offered me was *Passions for Men.* The characters leaped off the pages and I couldn't wait to begin rehearsals. Brady confessed it wasn't his property. He was so anxious to keep me before the public that he was allowing me to work with another producer.

The Molnar play, renamed *Fashions for Men,* opened in Philadelphia in 1922 for a three-week tryout. At the end of the first-night performance there was a stir backstage. Leopold Stokowski was coming to see me. He was escorted to my dressing room by the producer, the director, and the stage manager, followed by everyone else who could crowd into the corridor behind him.

The glamorous conductor complimented me lavishly. Embarrassed, I changed the subject and told him that I was sorry I was unable to get matinee tickets to his concert, which was sold out. He promised to send me tickets if I would go backstage afterward to see him.

In those years Philharmonic Hall was always packed to watch the dramatic Stokowski, who was at the height of his career. Music lovers used to scream and swoon at his entrance, much as they did over Frank Sinatra a generation later, and the Beatles in a subsequent generation. Stokowski was handsome, tall, slender, sensual, straight as an arrow, with a mane of yellow hair springing from his forehead. As he turned to the orchestra and lifted his baton, the houselights dimmed and a powerful spotlight centered on him, turning his head to flaming gold.

After the concert the audience exploded with adoration and

brought him back for curtain call after curtain call. It was some
time before I summoned courage to go backstage. I knocked on
his dressing-room door and was informed that he was busy. He
was having a massage. As I turned away his voice called out, "Is
that you, Miss Gahagan? Please wait. I won't be long."

A few minutes later he appeared in a heavy dressing gown and
invited me in. He explained that he perspired so profusely during
a performance that he was concerned about colds or, worse, arthritis. To avoid risk it was his habit to strip down for an alcohol
rub and massage.

I thanked him for the ticket, expressed my admiration for his
performance, and turned to leave. He invited me to have lunch
with him the following Monday. I accepted, flattered. The lunch
proved to be boring. Stokowski spent the entire two and a half
hours lecturing me about proper diet. He was a very early proponent of health food.

The morning after my visit to Stokowski's home, a Philadelphia matron whom I scarcely knew telephoned me. She
wanted to have lunch with me and wouldn't be put off by my
evasions. We were barely seated when she opened the conversation by asking me about lunching at Stokowski's country estate.
I was astonished that she knew. She went on, leaning forward
conspiratorially:

"Leopold Stokowski is a great musician, a great musician." Em-
phasizing every word, she went on, "He . . . admires . . . beautiful . . . women. He *collects* them. You are young and beautiful. I
think it is best you don't see him again. Ever."

I was so flustered that I gave her a detailed account of the innocent conversation that had passed between us at the luncheon.
She brushed my protests aside.

"I think it better for your reputation," she told me, giving me a
meaningful look and stressing *reputation,* "if you never see him
again—*alone.*"

I sighed. Father's long arm had reached me in Philadelphia.

Fashions for Men had a successful run in New York and then
went to Chicago where we opened in the Playhouse. This time
Mother went with me, to my great joy. She and I took a small
apartment with another actress in the company, Frances Good-

rich, who later married Albert Hackett and with him became a successful writing team best known for their dramatization of *The Diary of Anne Frank.*

I was very social the first few weeks in Chicago, attending lunches and after-theater parties almost every day. I accepted one invitation to the racetrack and was so smitten with racing that I persuaded Mother to go with me regularly. Angel that she was, she agreed. I lost most of my salary every week but I couldn't keep away.

All that activity came to an end abruptly when I became ill with a low-grade fever that persisted. A doctor prescribed a diet not unlike the one Leopold Stokowski had recommended: Two meals a day, no snacks, no fried foods, no desserts, no starch.

The fever vanished and I lost pounds.

The Playhouse Theater in Chicago was splendid in many ways but had one curious failing. The architect had omitted dressing rooms. The building was almost completed before the oversight was noticed. The only space still available was in the basement, so we dressed in cubicles with corrugated metal partitions, the women on one side of a narrow aisle, the men on the other.

Strangely, it isn't uncommon for theater architects to forget dressing rooms. My husband tells of the time he was touring in the Midwest in the same period, the early twenties. A small-town theater where his company was playing had no dressing rooms at all. Actors were expected to change in an open area in the basement. A request for a partition was met with astonishment.

"What's the matter?" the manager asked. "Aren't the actors speaking?"

While we were in Chicago, the legendary Mary Garden invited me to join her at a matinee performance of Strauss's *Salomé* by the Chicago Opera Company. Mary Garden had made that role her own. A new prima donna was making her debut as Salomé that day. Mary Garden's box was conspicuously located in the center of the first circle. As the last note of the young soprano's first aria was dying away, Mary leaned out of her box and began clapping vigorously, her bracelets and bangles creating so much noise that everyone turned to stare. She was reminding everyone that *the* Salomé was present.

I have noted that there are actors—and politicians—who can't abide competition from the young. Until they breathe their last, they must be centerstage.

I had almost forgotten that I was under personal contract to Brady until he sent word that he was sending me a new play, *Chains*, by Jules Eckert Goodman. Brady notified me that we would rehearse *Chains* at once while still playing *Fashions for Men* and would open the Goodman play in Chicago in four weeks, the night after closing the Molnar play.

Fortunately I liked *Chains*, since Brady hadn't consulted me in advance. I plunged into a demanding schedule of rehearsals all day and performances at night, every night, after which we rehearsed again. Brady stood at the back of the theater, a cigar clenched in his teeth, and bellowed orders at us. The tension he produced was exhausting.

The day of the opening of *Chains* I hurried back to our apartment from the dress rehearsal and threw myself on my bed. Mother pulled up a chair and began rubbing my feet.

"Mother, what are you doing?"

She informed me, "Rested feet will do more for you than a few minutes' sleep."

For the next fifteen minutes, rubbing my feet and speaking to me in her gentle voice, she hypnotized me into a state of blissful relaxation.

The play was received with a glorious ovation. Brady joined us for a curtain call and made an unfortunate speech. An ardent booster of American productions, he resented the attention foreign companies were receiving. He poked fun at one, the Moscow Art Theater, that was playing in New York at the time. The audience found his remarks in bad taste. When he finished there was a resounding silence except from his associate, Al Woods, who loyally applauded alone.

The critics were kind to me, though one of them, Ashton Stevens of the *Herald Examiner*, said he wished he'd left the theater at the end of the second act. He added:

> . . . the production is worth looking at for the intelligence and
> alluring acting of young Miss Gahagan who, despite her brief

year in the theater, needs only a play as good as her part is here in the second act to become in fact one of our First Actresses.

Sheppard Butler wrote in the Chicago *Tribune:*

GLIMPSES OF RARE ACTING . . .
. . . this new actress named Helen Gahagan picked up Mr. Goodman's play of *Chains* and, as the saying is, walked off with it. . . . This, I should say, was acting with brains.

A *Tribune* reporter came to interview me. Like most stories about me at that time, the aspect of my parents' opposition to my career played a large part in the article that appeared in the paper. I was also asked about marriage, as all adult single women were in that era. I responded by declaring that I was not interested in traditional marriage. I added that if I found myself in the position of becoming an unwed mother, I would on no account force the gentleman to marry me. Father must have reeled.

Chains played to full houses so the producers decided to extend the run. We were crushed. We had been looking forward eagerly to a break after weeks of playing nine performances a week.

I went to the producers and asked to have Sundays off. They refused but I didn't give up. Having practiced all my life in arguments with my father and brothers, I wasn't timorous about dealing with stubborn men. After my father, all men were a snap. I demanded that the cast have one day of rest and the producers yielded.

A newspaper account of the historic victory appeared a few days later:

FEMALE OF SPECIES WINS AT PLAYHOUSE
Miss Helen Gahagan has accomplished singlehandedly what all the Equity forces and the reformers (men) couldn't bring to pass —to wit, so far as she is concerned, no Sunday performances in Chicago.
It hasn't been done in Chicago before for anyone less than a star. It was a dangerous precedent and it meant losing money. But Miss Gahagan . . . stood her ground. The managers hesitated and were lost.

Brady and I decided, more or less amicably, that we needed a month's vacation before *Chains* opened in New York. Overjoyed,

I decided to go to Hungary and meet Ferenc Molnar and the Paula on whom the character I played in *Fashions for Men* was based.

Mother, Walter, then thirteen, and I sailed on the *Conte Rossa*. To my surprise Lilli refused to go with us. We went directly from Naples, where the ship docked, to Florence. I was sitting in Hall IX of the Uffizi Palace, my head thrown back, immersed in the beauty of the ceiling, when someone sat beside me.

"Why don't you wear makeup?" a voice said.

I turned to face Stark Young, a New York drama critic I knew slightly. "Beauty is an asset for an actress," he went on. "It shouldn't worry you when critics write about your looks."

We chatted and Young pointed out how Botticelli conveyed emotion in the way he posed his figures and even in the drape of their clothes. I was grateful for his perceptions. We became friends and I owe him much for sound advice on the visual aspects of acting.

On the train to Budapest, Mother and I encountered a persistent Hungarian, an impressive-looking gentleman who shared our compartment. Learning that we hoped to meet Molnar, he grew excited and said he would arrange it but Molnar was not in Budapest. He was taking a cure at some spa and would return soon.

He introduced himself to us as Dr. Barczi and insisted on taking charge of our luggage and escorting us to our hotel, the Dune Palota Ritz. The staff leaped to our side when they saw him, bowing and scraping in deference. We learned that Istvan Barczi had been the mayor of Budapest during the days of the Austro-Hungarian Empire. After the war he served in the cabinet. He was also enormously wealthy.

We were invited to dine with Dr. Barczi at his home. Mother dressed oddly in a formal gown and heavy walking shoes.

"Mother," I said, "surely you aren't going to wear those brogues?"

"Why not?" she replied. "Dr. Barczi is certain to walk us up and down some hills between here and Buda."

I complained until she reluctantly changed into evening slippers. Dr. Barczi called for us promptly in a huge limousine and all went well until we reached the Buda hills. He ordered the driver to stop the car and turned to us. We could appreciate the view of the city only if we saw it from the summit of Castle Hill, he explained, a short walk from the car.

When he turned to help Mother out, she said firmly, "Thank you, Dr. Barczi, but I don't walk up hills. I'll wait here."

Mother had tiny, delicate feet. She didn't walk anywhere without proper walking shoes, not even to see Budapest to advantage.

Our guide to Budapest was Dr. Alexandro Marton, Molnar's lawyer and agent, a playbroker who had attended a New York performance of *Fashions for Men* and had come backstage to say kind things about my acting. Dr. Marton invited us to his home where we met his sons, Andrew, called "Bundi," and George, known as "Gyuni," and his daughter Elizabeth, whom the family called "Butzi." All three later were connected with theater on both sides of the Atlantic. Elizabeth became a playbroker like her father, George a producer and Andrew a motion-picture director. All three also became close friends of Melvyn's and mine.

The conversation at dinner that first night turned to the idol of the Hungarian theater, Oscar Beregi, a man so handsome that women fainted for love of him. Dr. Marton teased me that I would not be able to resist Beregi; I retorted that I certainly wouldn't succumb.

The Martons served a surprise dessert in our honor after the six-course dinner—a platter of corn on the cob, which they judged to be an American treat. The Martons, raised to regard corn as fit only for cattle feed, politely joined us in forcing down an ear each. We assured them that it was delicious.

I attended a Beregi matinee the next day with Dr. Marton, who brought along a bottle of smelling salts. I had no need of them but Oscar Beregi was indeed an astoundingly good-looking man. Afterward, in his dressing room, we stared at one another. Since neither spoke the other's language, we were silent. Oscar proved to have a disconcerting wooing technique. He took my hand and held it passionately, his eyes full on me with a burning expression. I cringed and tried to pull away. Turning to Dr. Marton, I found him smiling with satisfaction. I suggested we leave, finding it somewhat difficult to breath.

"Of course." He grinned.

Molnar was expected back in Budapest in two days but we planned to stay only two days more. Dr. Marton was disappointed but said I would have time at least to visit the famous Hungarian theater club, the Feszik. He invited me to go with him, his wife and Erno Szep, a beloved Hungarian poet. *Szep* is the Hungarian word for beautiful; though Erno was a tiny, ugly man, it suited him perfectly.

Szep was courageous. After the Communist government took over his country years later, he was among a group of intellectuals invited to meetings where the Soviet establishment attempted to win them over. At the end of the speaker's description of the wonders of communism, he asked if there were any questions. Szep stood up and said:

"Yes. Tell me where the hell is the door."

On the evening appointed for my visit to the Club Feszik I was waiting outside the hotel for Dr. Marton when a carriage drawn by four magnificent horses came clattering down the street. A man I recognized slightly as a fellow guest of the hotel was driving. He asked me in English if I would care to have a ride. I refused politely, explaining that I was awaiting friends.

"Not even just around the corner? It won't take five minutes."

I couldn't resist. I jumped up beside him on the high driver's seat and we started off precipitously. As we turned the last corner the carriage splashed through a mud puddle.

"Oh dear," I exclaimed. "I must change. My dress is covered with spots."

He leered at me. "You have only one spot, my dear," he said, his eyes fixed on my lap, "and it's divine."

I froze. Sheltered as I was, I had never before encountered lewdness. Without speaking I jumped down, dashed heedlessly in front of the horses and ran into the hotel. While changing I told Mother we would be leaving Budapest at once, without waiting to see Molnar. Mother agreed readily. She was always willing to go in a direction that took her closer to home.

Club Feszik turned out to be crowded with lively people. Hungarians are great talkers and love to table-hop, kissing the hands of the women and embracing the men. I was surrounded by actors and playwrights who wanted to know about American theater. At midnight, as we prepared to leave, there was a hush. All eyes turned to the door as a portly middle-aged man entered with a group of people.

Dr. Marton was delighted. "It's Molnar," he told me. "You'll meet him after all, Helen." Szep escorted me to the table where Molnar sat and made the introduction, explaining that I was the actress who had played Paula in the American production of Molnar's play.

Molnar extended his hand but didn't rise or speak. The cold silence stretched interminably. Wretched with embarrassment, I whispered to Szep:

"Take me away . . . please."

Butzi Marton once told me of another example of Molnar's rudeness. Soon after Molnar came to New York to live, a friend approached him in a restaurant and said he wanted to introduce the young man with him, an American playwright who admired the Hungarian's work. Molnar didn't even look up from his soup.

"I'm not meeting any new friends," he said. "I don't have time to keep up with the old ones."

The next morning Mother, Walter and I prepared to leave Budapest. I was in the lobby, surrounded by our luggage, when someone touched my arm. Turning, I looked into the face of Oscar Beregi, wearing his swooning-with-passion expression. He picked up my hand, kissed it lingeringly, and continued to hold it while breathing heavily, his hot eyes on mine.

I pulled away as Mother and Walter arrived but he followed me to the hotel bus, heading a procession of hotel manager and staff, all bowing to us and staring at him. As the bus pulled away I sank back in relief. Just in time, I thought. The Hungarians are much too intense for me.

As our ship passed the Statue of Liberty it slowed to allow health officials to come on board from a tender. They brought with them a note for Mother. Father wanted us to know that Lillian was engaged to Robert Walker, Jr. She wasn't returning to college and Father had agreed to a fall wedding.

I was annoyed. It was clear now why Lilli hadn't come to Europe with us.

"What a silly thing for her to do at her age," I grumbled. Lilli was twenty-one. "That's what comes of playing with all those dolls."

Rehearsals for *Chains* began immediately. We opened in September and the play was well received. As we settled in for a long run I found my days packed with preparations for Lilli's wedding. Since the reception was to be held at our house, Mother decided to redecorate and refurbish from top to bottom.

Furniture went out to be recovered and new draperies were ordered for every room, even Father's, though he loathed curtained windows. Our family dressmaker, Louella Hollenbeck, took up permanent residence on the third floor. In the kitchen, Mother and Aunt Mary spent hours making the wedding cake.

That year was also a presidential election year. Our family always voted Republican but Calvin Coolidge didn't appeal to me. I told Mother I didn't have time to vote. She was indignant.

"There's more to life than acting," she told me crossly. "Voting is a privilege, Helen, and you'll take time to do it." I obeyed, chastened.

Since I was the acknowledged "straightener-upper" in the family, I was assigned the task of making rooms neat the day before the wedding. I started with the debris in the boys' rooms, awash in books, and when I finished I took a book with a catchy title to read later.

Mother warned me to stay out of Father's room where the new draperies had just been hung. She concluded the curtains were provocation enough without also straightening his books and papers. But the temptation to complete my job was too strong and I recklessly cleared his tables of books and papers. Inadvertently I left behind the book I had carried from the boys' rooms.

When Father came home that evening we waited uneasily for him to go up to his room. We stood at the bottom of the stairs when he did, braced for his reaction. It was violent.

"Who had the effrontery to move my books?" he thundered. He glowered at us from the top of the stairs. "*Who hung those damned curtains?*" He brandished a book. "And who left this insulting tract?"

It was the book I had left behind in error. When we saw the title we were convulsed. It was *How to Make a Home Happy*.

At dinner later, when we had recovered our composure, Mother assured him the curtains would be taken down as soon as the wedding was over.

The next morning the house buzzed with caterers, maids, florists, and Gahagans. Lilli was unusually quiet. When she and Robert cut the ten-tier cake, she looked beautiful beyond compare. Soon afterward she changed, laughingly threw her bouquet to a friend, and was gone.

The family gathered in the living room that evening. We sat together in silence, each lost in thought. Even the boys had nothing to say. Mother broke the stillness.

"To bed," she said gently, and kissed us all 'round. We followed her upstairs slowly, one by one.

I couldn't sleep. I walked back and forth in the rooms Father had built for Lilli and me when we reached our teens. I couldn't believe that we would never share them again. I stood in front of the cold fireplace trying to imagine the house without her cheerful sweetness. I knelt by my bed, wondering why I felt so sad. The pain of separation was as acute as when my cousin Walter died.

I fell asleep in a praying position and dreamed that I was falling through space—alone. An Emily Dickinson poem describes how I felt that night, the one that begins, "I felt a funeral in my brain. . . ."

That winter Eleanora Duse performed in New York in a repertoire of tragedies written for her by her lover Gabriele D'Annunzio. Once again critics fell to arguing who was the world's greatest actress—Duse or Sarah Bernhardt. I saw them both. When Bernhardt made the last of her many farewell tours of America she was no longer young. She had lost a leg, her face was garishly painted and she wore a red wig. Her voice was a magnificent instrument but she failed to move me.

Duse, on the other hand, played without makeup. I attended every matinee performance she gave. I couldn't understand Italian well enough to know what she was saying sometimes, but for me Eleanora Duse was the consummate actress, not to be compared with anyone. I can still see her small figure with arms extended in a moving gesture of entreaty and I can hear her voice in a final soliloquy which began softly, softly, and built to an orchestral climax of mourning that filled the large auditorium.

I longed for plays that would give me such scope. The parts I had been playing cramped me. Was there no audience for tragedy in the New York commercial theater?

Colgate Baker, critic and playwright, compared me to Duse. He wrote:

> Helen Gahagan, an acting prodigy . . . has a peculiar mentality. Her motivation in everything she does is different from that of every other actress I have ever met. The actual truth is this motivation is precisely the same as that of the great Duse, and it is the secret of the success of them both . . . a consuming love of art, a worship of individual ideals that transcends everything else. . . .

At the close of *Chains* Brady gave me a copy of C. M. S. McLellan's play *Leah Kleschna*. The title role had been played twenty years earlier by Minnie Maddern Fiske, a famous performance. The play was old-fashioned and dreary but Brady was eager to do a revival. I decided not to oppose him; I owe Leah to Brady.

He assembled an all-star cast which included a Broadway favorite, Lowell Sherman, and brought Jessie Bonstelle from Detroit, where she was manager, director and star in her own stock company, to direct.

William Faversham, a matinee idol of the nineties, also was in the cast of *Leah Kleschna*. He was a charming man, and still handsome, but possessed of a wicked temper. During an intermission one night his angry voice drew us all out of our dressing rooms. We found him with a whip in hand about to lash his black dresser. When he saw us staring at him he went into his dressing room and shut the door.

Lowell Sherman walked through rehearsals with total disregard for the rest of us, giving no indication of how he would speak the lines or what he would do while speaking them. On opening night, in the midst of an important scene with me, he stretched himself out on the sofa and emphasized and punctuated his lines with leg exercises, upstaging me totally.

Faversham unnerved us all by forgetting his lines on opening night. To cover, he walked up and down the stage, shooting his cuffs and glaring at me with contempt and disdain as though I were to blame. I whispered his lines to him but he couldn't, or wouldn't, pick them up. There was nothing I could do but keep on talking.

Despite all the unpleasant surprises, the opening night audience loved *Leah Kleschna* and cheered us to the rafters. Brady was dragged in front of the curtain to make a speech in response to deafening applause that one critic wrote "would not be still until he appeared." He thanked the audience but said he wouldn't make a speech; he had promised Gladys George that he wouldn't. In truth he was apoplectic about our eccentric performance and didn't trust himself to open his mouth.

When I read the reviews much later I was caught by something Heywood Broun said about me, that "the sleeping script heard the voice of an actress." He added:

> Helen Gahagan touched her lips to this preposterous and discarded melodrama and for an act it was a play. Indeed, while she spoke there was a pulse . . .

Dreary or not, *Leah* was a hit in New York and Chicago, where we had a long run. During our stay in Chicago I spent a good deal of time with one of the cast, Arnold Daly, an aging actor of great renown. We used to walk along Michigan Avenue every morning, talking about the theater we both loved.

Once, while we were sitting on a lakeside bench discussing how dramatic scenes should be played, he shifted from a conversational tone and began to act a tragic scene. I was enthralled. When he broke off, he commented that audiences will feel suffering more deeply if the actor doesn't give the relief of tears. Tragedy, we agreed, should be played dry.

"You've been compared to Ethel Barrymore," Daly told me. "You must guard against becoming a handkerchief actress."

On January 13, 1927, Arnold Daly burned to death in a fire in his apartment. When I read his obituaries I learned for the first time that Daly had introduced George Bernard Shaw's plays to New York, beginning with *Candida* in 1905. New York audiences didn't like Shaw at first, but Daly believed in him and persisted. The New York *Times* paid tribute to his contribution to the theater in an editorial in which it said:

> Daly was just the man for the moment. He had youth, verve, and dash, a kind of intellectual bumptiousness; and all this, together with a slightly Irish and rather attractive accent, made him seem almost the personal agent and spokesman for the incredible Mr. Shaw. . . . Shaw has long since become the food of babes and flappers, but he was strong meat in 1905, and in introducing him —and, by so doing, the intellectual drama that followed and more or less imitated him—Arnold Daly was a pioneer.

On hearing of Daly's death, George Bernard Shaw is said to have quipped, "Spontaneous combustion sometimes occurs." Lawrence Langner, who wrote a book about Shaw, was as distressed to hear of it as I was. Shaw explained to him that he said it in order to attract attention that Daly's death otherwise wouldn't have commanded.

Shaw was quite mistaken. There is no record that his gross remark was in any way responsible for the generous coverage Arnold Daly received.

At the end of *Leah*'s run, I had an opportunity to do a twenty-two-scene, two-character play in an experimental theater in Provincetown. I jumped at the chance though the salary was almost nonexistent. The play was Walter Hasenclever's *Beyond* and it was treated to a superb set by Robert Edmond Jones, who created magic with his ingenious lighting of the tiny stage.

The critics came to see *Beyond* and were divided. Robert Littell in *The New Republic* called it "intolerably ponderous and stupid" but *Theater Arts* magazine praised it for its portrayal of "the naked truth." R. Dana Skinner of *Commonweal* reported that I had "achieved a dramatic masterpiece" and wrote that the play was "one of those bold and beautiful experiments that of itself sums up the entire mission of the little theatre movement."

Brady didn't come to the opening but turned up for the final performance of our six-week run. He was scathing. He wanted to know if I actually enjoyed playing for peanuts in a cellar that held two hundred people. Chewing his cigar, he announced that he had a new script for me and I was to begin rehearsals at once.

With that, he wheeled out of my dressing room and slammed the door with such force that he almost knocked down the shaky wall.

The script waiting for me was *The Sapphire Ring* by a Hungarian, Laszlo Lakatos, whom I had met in Budapest. It was a disaster but I remember it fondly because it marked the beginning of a new understanding between Father and me.

It happened at the end of the brief run in New York. Father and the twins called for me backstage. When I had changed I looked for Father and found him sitting in the semidarkness with Frederick standing silently beside him. Around them stagehands were busy striking the scenery, but there was a stillness and sadness about Father that caught my heart.

I had seen that look only once before, in Vermont. He had arrived for a weekend visit and we greeted him boisterously and then set off in all directions. I happened to linger behind the others and turned to look at him, sitting alone on the porch. There was something forlorn about him that shocked me. I slowly went back and sat beside him. Was it possible that Father was feeling abandoned? Was he a lonely man, despite all the bluster? He was the strength of our family, its foundation, and yet I felt sorry for him. It was very strange and confusing.

That night in the theater he had that look of loneliness again and I could see that Frederick felt it too. Our ride home to Brooklyn was subdued. When we arrived we kissed one another good night, all of us touched by Father's remoteness, and went to bed. The next morning at breakfast Father said casually:

"I build bridges, Helen. You build character. I see very little difference."

There were no more lectures about finishing my education, or about the ignominy of acting. The long struggle between us was ended.

That winter I played in a teacup comedy with fragile charm, *Enchanted April,* written by an Englishwoman under the *nom de plume* Elizabeth. I remember that period better for the family events. Lillian gave birth to a son and Father decided that she and Robert should live closer to us. He dispatched Mother to find a suitable house on Park Slope, which she quickly did. Father bought it and Bob, Lilli and little Robert setted into their new home.

Frederick then announced that he was going to elope with Alice Gerli. Alice and I were girlhood friends and the family knew her well. We were pleased but amazed by his announcement.

"Fritz," I protested, "elopements are supposed to be secret."

He explained that Alice's father, Joseph Gerli, a silk importer, was a pillar of St. Patrick's. The couple wanted to avoid the elaborate church wedding he would arrange. Frederick assured us that the Gerlis would be informed of the elopement in advance. They were delighted to welcome him into their family, which consisted entirely of daughters, Alice, Agatha and Evelyn.

The next play offered me was by a new English playwright, John Van Druten. It was *Young Woodley*, the story of a friendship between a student and a headmaster's young wife, set in an English boarding school. The part of Laura, the wife, was secondary to that of the headmaster but I was determined to play it despite Brady's objections. Van Druten had only sketched in the role but I saw Laura as a real person and I knew I could flesh her out.

Since rehearsals didn't begin for four weeks, there was time for me and Mother to sail to Italy. After an hour at sea, as always happened, my frivolous side, the part of me most like Lilli, took over. When abroad, I found time for male attention and showed a marked tendency to become engaged to Italians, a rashness regretted the moment I returned home. Twice I broke the engagements by cable soon after docking.

Van Druten's play opened at the Belmont Theatre a few doors away from Brady's Playhouse and was a big hit. A few weeks after the run began I stepped out on stage one night and couldn't remember my opening line. I stumbled along, improvising my part, unable to recollect even the substructure I had invented to play Laura. Bits and pieces came to me and somehow I got through it.

At home that night I tried not to think about it. I was afraid to look at a script because I thought it might confuse me further. I *never* had to look at a script once rehearsals began. I would just have to hope that it would not happen again.

On stage the next night, I forgot my lines again. I lived through the same nightmare, astonished that no one seemed to notice.

I was too frightened to tell anyone. Dressing hurriedly the next morning I took the subway to New York to see our family physician, Dr. Leo Stieglitz, who had known me all my life. I loved his office, which was lined with books, photographs by his relative Alfred Stieglitz and flower paintings by Alfred's celebrated wife, Georgia O'Keeffe. I began to feel better.

Leo asked how many plays I had done in the past few years. He wanted to know if I was still commuting from Brooklyn to Broadway. He asked about my symptoms and I told him I was menstruating every two weeks. He looked grave.

"You should be in bed, Helen. You're physically exhausted. You have a remarkable constitution but you have one dangerous weakness. Your body doesn't tell you when you are tired, so you never know when you should stop and rest. You've gone beyond the limits of your strength."

He prescribed one day a week in bed for the rest of my life. His regime proved unworkable but I did fall into the habit of climbing into bed whenever possible, at any time of the day. If I neglected for any sustained length of time to do that, disaster followed.

That night I felt confident that everything would be fine. Instead it was worse. As I lifted my hand to knock on the living-room door of the boys' dormitory and make my first entrance, the entire play vanished from my memory.

I wanted to scream, "Pull the curtain!" My impulse was to run off the stage and keep running. As panic swept over me, I braced myself. What was I afraid of? I had only to turn to the audience and say, "I'm sorry, I can't go on," and the stagehands would lower the curtain. It was not the end of the world.

In that instant, my head cleared. I knew my lines and everyone else's as well. There were lasting benefits from that harrowing experience. Fear of failure never again devastated me. I had faced the dragon and slain it. It had no power over me anymore.

I was twenty-six and there was much speculation about my single state. My obvious passion for the theater was often explanation enough. Anne Randolph of the Boston *Post* wrote:

> The most intrepid interviewers, male or female, would not think of asking her when she is to marry, her views on romance, and so forth, because they would surmise from the general tone of her conversation that such things are in rather poor taste, which means she has no time for anything but her work.

I seemed to have been conditioned in the tradition of the male Gahagans, who adhered to Father's view that failure was a sign of weakness. If a Gahagan didn't do well, we all felt, there was something the matter with the Gahagan. We were all full of energy and capable of working twenty-four-hour shifts, which we took to be normal when in pursuit of some goal.

Toward the end of the run of *Young Woodley*, Maestro Giuseppe Bamboschek, one of the conductors of the Metropolitan Opera Company, telephoned to ask if I was still serious about studying voice. He was a friend of Mother's and a frequent visitor to the house. Once she had asked him to hear me sing. There followed a sort of audition in which I sang "la-la-la" to the music of a favorite aria in *Madame Butterfly*, after which the maestro clapped his hands and said, "Well! We must find you a *teacher*, a good one. You mustn't work with just anyone or you'll spoil your voice. If I come across someone suitable, I'll let you know."

On the telephone he said he had just the person. Madame Sophia Cehanovska, one of the greatest voice teachers in Russia, was living in New York, a refugee from the Communist revolution. He learned of her when her son, George Cehanovsky, a baritone, auditioned and was accepted at the Met.

Madame Cehanovska lived in a brownstone just off Central Park, One West Eighty-sixth Street. Her son George opened the door to me and I liked him at once. He had an open, friendly face and proved to be one of the kindest, gentlest people I've ever known.

He and his mother lived on the first floor of the building and their living quarters were also her studio. He showed me into the parlor and said his mother would join me in a moment. I looked around. There was nothing in the room but a grand piano and a few chairs—no rugs, no pictures, no ornaments.

Madame Cehanovska entered from the far door. She was short, no taller than my mother, broad-shouldered, rather square in build, and gray-haired, with large dark, expressive eyes. She wore a strange dress of some soft material that appeared crudely home-made, as though she had taken a large piece of cloth, cut a hole in it for her head, and roughly basted the side seams.

I later learned that was exactly how she made her studio dresses. They were simple and comfortable. She didn't care how they looked.

She gestured for me to be seated and took a straight chair opposite.

"Maestro Bamboschek tells me you are an actress."

"Yes."

"And now you want to sing?"

"I would like to study with you."

"Why? Do you want to be a singer?"

"No, but I would like to study for the pleasure of singing."

"Have you ever taken singing lessons?"

"Yes, in my teens."

She grunted disapproval. "That is too bad," she said. I looked at her questioningly. She didn't elaborate.

"Why did you stop?" she asked.

"I was told I was a mezzo. If so, I didn't want to sing. I want to sing contralto."

She got up abruptly and went to the piano and played a few bars. She was completely at home with the piano. They merged; they were one. I hadn't known what to expect but I found I trusted the authority of this small, sixtyish woman. I would have obeyed instantly if she had asked me to stand on my head. She took me up and down two octaves, singing single notes, striking a

chord and ordering me to sing. She stopped as suddenly as she
had begun, looked at me severely and said:

"You are not a mezzo. You are not a contralto. There is nothing you can do of contralto. You are a soprano. When do you
want to begin?"

"Tomorrow, Madame, if possible."

"Come at twelve. We will start with breathing. Voice is
breath. Good-bye then, until tomorrow."

I hesitated. "Madame Cehanovska, may I come three times a
week on days when I don't have matinees?"

She smiled at me for the first time. "We'll see," she promised.

We began with breathing exercises. My diaphragm ached as I
could feel my rib cage expanding daily. Madame was pleased.

"If at the end of an opera the singer's diaphragm is tired, that's
good," she said. "It means the singer is supporting the voice properly. If the throat is tired, that is very bad."

As I began to improve my breathing, Madame had me sing single tones on one breath. She wanted me to feel the physical relationship between breathing and tone production. When she was
satisfied that I had it, we moved to scales.

I wasn't a novice at projecting my voice. On stage I tried to
speak from the diaphragm, though I didn't always succeed. I
winced to see the effort it took Glenn Hunter, my costar in
Young Woodley, to make his voice heard in the theater. He
spoke from the top part of his lungs and by the end of each performance the strain caused the glands of his neck to stand out
and made his voice hoarse.

In three months I could reach and sustain high C, the top tone
for a lyric dramatic soprano. I brought my father to meet Madame, the miracle-worker. I think she was impressed by his formality. Father always wore a cutaway coat in the afternoon.

Young Woodley closed for a two-month break that summer,
with plans to tour in the fall. I notified Madame that I would
spend the summer in Europe with Mother but wanted to resume
lessons when I returned. I still didn't plan on a singing career but
I was enjoying the experience of developing my voice.

Lilli's family was growing. She had a second son and she
dropped in to visit the family several times a day. When Mother

and I started making our travel plans, Lilli looked wistful. Father decided she should go with us. We made arrangements for people to look after Bob and the two boys, and left together. Most of that trip was spent in Venice, where Mother went on a buying spree at Alessandro Olivetti's while Lilli and I swam at the Lido and strolled over the bridges.

On our return I toured with *Young Woodley* for a few weeks and then returned to New York to rehearse Sir Arthur Wing Pinero's *Trelawney of the 'Wells'* produced by my new manager, George Tyler. When my contract with Brady was finished, I wanted to work with someone more reasonable. Tyler cast me in the part of Rose, which had been played by Ethel Barrymore when the play first opened on Broadway, and by Laurette Taylor in the first revival of the play.

We opened in January of 1927 in Washington to raves. Lee Sommers wrote of it this way:

> Washington last evening showed itself more than eager to storm the National Theater to get a look at the greatest galaxy of stars ever assembled. President and Mrs. Coolidge were most notable of all the notables in the first-night audience. How Mr. Tyler ever collected such a cast is likely to set theatrical scribes to wondering centuries hence.
>
> Headed by the dean of the American stage, John Drew, we find this peerless ensemble composed of such folks as John E. Kellard, Estelle Winwood, Helen Gahagan, Peggy Wood, Henrietta Crosman, Otto Kruger, J. M. Kerrigan, Effie Shannon, Eric Dressler, Frieda Inescort, Lawrence d'Orsay, Mrs. Thomas Wiffen, O. P. Heggie, and a few young people who haven't as yet obtained stardom. It is as though he gathered all Broadway, past and present, for the revival of Pinero's famous comedy of stage life.

Trelawney's huge, high-cost cast required Tyler to fix the top ticket price at nine dollars, though a front-row seat at a musical then cost only four-fifty. Audiences packed the theater anyway.

When we brought it in to New York, I resumed voice lessons with Madame Cehanovska. At her bidding, George purchased the score of *Cavalleria Rusticana* for me. I wasn't allowed to sing it. She played the score on the piano and I followed it, counting to myself. When it called for Santuzza's voice, I played her music, with one finger, in the treble end of the piano. Madame wanted me to be thoroughly familiar with the opera before I opened my mouth.

I was absorbed in working with Madame but it never crossed my mind that I had embarked on one of the most demanding of careers. My intensity led me to the edge of exhaustion. Once I sank down beside my mother and rested my head on her knee, complaining, "Why do I drive myself so?"

Mother didn't reply. She patted my head comfortingly.

At the end of the limited New York engagement of *Trelawney*, George Tyler sent us out on an extended tour of the United States and Canada. He hired a private Pullman car for his cast, with a drawing room for each of us. Our car would be attached to a train bearing a dining car and the sleeping car where the *Trelawney* retinue of wardrobe staff, dressers, managers and others traveled. Despite the expensive ticket, we played to standing-room-only audiences everywhere.

The week we played Detroit, my dear friend Harry Wagstaff Gribble was also in Detroit with a production of *Cherry Pie*, an informal revue he put together and directed.

Harry invited me to attend a cast party for *Cherry Pie*. He collected me at the theater and took me to a small nightclub on the second floor of a downtown building. I was unprepared for the discovery that many of the people in the company were black. The company was mixed, something highly unusual in theater at that time.

I had never met a black person socially. I was appalled to find myself unaccustomedly awkward and self-conscious. As I sat there, miserable, Harry asked me to dance. I was aghast. If I danced with him I might be expected to dance with one of the blacks. I said quickly, "No thanks, Harry. I'm not dancing this evening."

The lyricist of the revue, Carroll Carroll, a black man, got to his feet. He said pointedly, "Will you dance with *me*, Miss Gahagan?"

I could not refuse. We circled the floor once and he led me

back to my seat. He said kindly, "Thank you, Miss Gahagan. I appreciate what that cost you."

I waited a decent interval and then asked Harry to take me to my hotel. I was ashamed of my feelings. I hadn't been taught prejudice against blacks, or any minority, but apparently I had picked it up unknowingly. I lay awake a long time that night appreciating for the first time the humiliation that black people endured.

Religious discrimination was more familiar to me. In my teens one of my two closest friends was Helene Wittenberg, whom I met on our first trip to Europe. Helene went to boarding school when she was sixteen. Mrs. Wittenberg asked me to visit them on Helene's first weekend home. She told me that Helene was so unhappy she wanted to leave the school. Her mother hoped that she would confide in me and we could get to the bottom of it.

Helene spilled the source of her misery the first night we were together. The girls at her school snubbed her because she was Jewish. I was furious equally at them and at Helene. "And so you're going to let them drive you from the school," I said to her angrily. "Are you ashamed of being Jewish?" She shook her head, though later she was to admit that I had guessed right. "Then you must stay," I continued. "Stand up to them. Show them you're proud of your heritage."

My response that night was to be repeated throughout my life whenever I encountered someone submitting to prejudice. People must fight back. Discrimination won't go away if it isn't confronted; instead, it feeds on meekness. When I entered politics I was active in the fight for minority rights and often encountered the bigots in the opposition, but prejudice never upset me more than the submissiveness of its victims.

The morning after Harry's party, Henry Ford's secretary telephoned to say that Mr. Ford would see me Friday afternoon. I had called his Dearborn office before leaving New York, asking for an appointment during the Detroit run of *Trelawney*. I wanted to request money from him to start an experimental theater.

Arriving at the main office building in Dearborn, I was told that Mr. Ford hadn't yet returned to his office. The receptionist asked me to wait in the lounge. Men came to chat, one by one. I suspected I was being examined. The fourth one took me upstairs to meet the man who put the country on wheels.

Henry Ford's chin worried me. By the set of it I could see there was no use asking him for a donation. He made that clear from the start. The first thing he said to me was that he didn't believe in giving people money—it only alienated them. I hastily led the conversation in other directions and when he saw that I wouldn't be asking for money, he became almost genial.

When our chat ended, his production manager showed me through the plant and I witnessed the magical assembly line. I was so fascinated that I was almost late for the theater. During the drive from Dearborn I groaned that I hadn't been able to ask for money despite Ford's parsimonious chin. I recognized, ruefully, that I probably wasn't cut out to be a fund-raiser. I put aside the dream of starting my own experimental theater.

The Ford family attended the last performance of *Trelawney*, after which the cast of sixteen stars went to the Jessie Bonstelle Theater where Jessie and her repertory company were giving us a closing-night party.

After a week crowded with activities, I was deeply tired. I wanted to make an appearance for politeness' sake and go back to our hotel. We had an early call for the morning's departure from Detroit.

Three years later, the young leading man of Jessie's company chided me for my behavior that night. He had seen me in *Young Woodley* and looked forward to talking with me. Instead I shook hands all around, paying no special attention to anyone, and disappeared. The disappointed actor was Melvyn Douglas.

John Drew's magnificent career was to end with *Trelawney of the 'Wells.'* The first and second acts of a matinee had gone off as usual. In the intermission before the third act, I heard excited voices coming from the floor below. I opened my dressing-room door and saw the assistant manager running upstairs two at a time. He told me Mr. Drew had suffered a slight stroke and couldn't speak. O. P. Heggie would replace him in the next scene. George Tyler had had the foresight to arrange for Heggie to un-

derstudy the role in the event that the aging John Drew, then
seventy-four, became ill on the tour.

I ran down the stairs to Drew's dressing room. Backstage people were clustered around his prone form, trying to assure him
that everything was all right. When they told him that Heggie
would go on for him, Drew shook his head emphatically.

"Mr. Drew doesn't want Heggie to replace him," I said.

Drew fixed his eyes on me desperately and nodded rapidly in
agreement.

"He wants to play the next scene himself," I ventured.

More nods.

Drew played the role of Sir William, an aged and decrepit
man. The infirmities of the character served to cover Drew's own
disabilities. He was almost blind and needed a cane to feel for ob-
structions in his path. He moved around the stage easily only because he had memorized the fixed placement of the furniture.

The scene in which he appeared in the third act required him,
as Sir William, to call on Rose Trelawney, me, in the rooming
house where Rose and the other actors live. Mrs. Mossop, owner
of the house, brings Sir William to Rose's room. I greet him at
the door.

John Drew could not speak but his legs were not affected by
the stroke. He made his entrance and I took his arm and guided
him downstage to the wicker theater basket on which he always
sat for the dialogue that followed. I spoke my lines and then his,
prefacing his with "I suppose you think, Sir William . . ." or
"Perhaps, Sir William, you'd like to say that . . ." or "I suppose
you hope, sir . . ." Then I would pause and he would shake his
head in agreement.

Here and there, when it seemed necessary to keep the story line
intelligible, I would cut or add a line. It worked. We managed
the scene.

John Drew sat imposingly on the dress basket, both hands on
the head of his cane, the perfect Sir William of Pinero's play.
The audience didn't detect that anything had happened between
the second and third act, and didn't learn until later that they
were witnessing the historic last appearance of the dean of
America's theater.

As I took his arm, assisting him to rise from the basket, he found voice to whisper, "Sweet, sweet, sweet." Those were the last words John Drew spoke on the stage and I cherish them.

At the end of the *Trelawney* tour in the spring of 1927, I asked Madame if I could work with her through the summer. She explained that she already had plans to visit her beloved daughter Vera, in Bad Reichenhall, Germany, but I was welcome to go along. Bad Reichenhall is a health spa, or *Kurort*, in the Black Forest, famous for its baths, medicinal waters and pure, pine-scented air.

Mother, Walter, Madame and I sailed for Europe together. We left Walter in Paris, from which he set off on a Mediterranean tour with a tutor, while we continued to Bad Reichenhall. Mother and I took rooms in a modest pension across from a studio where I rented a spacious room with a piano. There I worked every day for the next six weeks on the score of *Cavalleria*, beginning at seven in the morning, breaking for a two-hour lesson with Madame at eleven and then a quick lunch, after which I went back to work.

At four I stopped for tea, which Mother, Madame, Vera and I took at a restaurant some distance into the forest. Walking more rapidly than the others, I would stride heedless of the beautiful forest, memorizing the libretto of *Cavalleria*, my pockets stuffed with notes on the most difficult parts.

While we ate huge sandwiches and delicious rich cakes, I continued to study. Once Vera lost patience with me and snatched my notes. "Can't you forget opera for at least an hour?" she demanded.

It wasn't easy for me to forget *Cavalleria* even in my sleep. I would waken in the night hearing the music and lie awake for hours going over every note of Santuzza's scenes.

Two days after Vera's outburst, Mother arrived at lunch with an armful of Agatha Christie's mystery novels, the only books in English she could find in the town. She gave me a lecture on moderation, as she had done so many times in my childhood. There was nothing moderate in the way I was studying, she said. I should read a mystery every night before going to sleep. It would wash my mind of music and give me a better rest. As with most of Mother's ideas, it worked.

However, that concentrated immersion in music made it possible for me to achieve my goal. Before we left Germany I had the pure joy of standing at the piano, singing the entire Santuzza role to Madame's rich accompaniment. She could make a single piano sound like a full orchestra.

The sheer pleasure of mastering that role convinced me that I should switch careers.

Mother was pleased, since her idea of a real career always had been singing, but Madame's reaction was surprising. She was startled and worried. She pointed out that I was a star on Broadway. Was I sure that I wanted to give it up for an unknown path?

I was, but my five-year contract with George Tyler had four years to run. I had a cable from him saying he had bought my next play. It was cast, the scenery was ordered, and rehearsals would start the day after my ship docked in New York.

I went to him as soon as we arrived home. I begged to be released from my contract. He was thunderstruck. We argued for two hours. Most of what he said started with, "Do you know . . ."

Did I know how much study was required to become a professional singer?

Did I know that I must sing in many languages? I spoke German, as he knew, but I would also have to be fluent in Italian and French. Did I know that?

Did I know that the streets were strewn with disappointed opera singers who couldn't find work?

He ended with, Did I know that I could be rich and famous in the plays he would produce for me, instead of grubbing in a studio trying to learn to sing?

To all I answered, "Mr. Tyler, I'm sorry, really sorry. But my mind is made up. I must go on studying singing."

He gave up. "Go then," he said. "Leave the theater to kitchen mechanics."

I was weak with gratitude. "If you ever need me," I promised. "I'll come back and act for you for nothing."

I determined to continue working as concentratedly as I had in

Germany. To that end I would have to stop commuting from Brooklyn to New York on drafty subways that might hurt my voice. I sadly made the decision, at twenty-eight, that I would have to leave home.

Madame and George had moved to a more spacious location at Forty-nine West Eighty-ninth Street, where her studio could be separate from their living quarters. George's career at the Metropolitan Opera was assured. The early days, when they first arrived in New York and he sang for their supper in a Russian restaurant, were over. He was to set a record at the Met, singing there for nearly forty years, seventy-eight different roles in seven languages.

George and Madame lived on the first floor. To my delight, a three-room apartment on the third floor was vacant. In truth, it consisted of two and a half rooms. The half was a tiny closet containing a bath and washbasin; the toilet was down the hall. My upright Steinway from home fit into my small space. I installed a telephone to maintain communication with my family on the understanding that I would do the calling.

I started to work. Within a few days the man below was complaining about the piano, which disturbed him until late at night. The landlady insisted that I stop at six when he arrived home. I had to content myself with silent rehearsals, mouthing the words, until I fell into bed after midnight.

Madame was horrified that I often forgot to eat. She insisted that I share her one o'clock meal, which George usually prepared.

I left the brownstone only when I wanted to hear an opera at the Metropolitan that I hoped to study. One night at the opera George introduced me to a Czechoslovakian member of the Met, Pavel Ludikar. He knew I was an actress and asked why I was trying to sing.

I answered with a shrug, "Who can say why one wants to sing?"

That was the beginning of a warm friendship. He told me he was anxious to hear my *Tosca*, the new role I was studying, one well suited to my training as an actress.

George Tyler phoned several months after I had begun to work on my voice. He was producing Sardou's *Diplomacy* with an all-star cast that included Frances Starr, Margaret Anglin, Jacob Ben-Ami and Charles Coburn. The English actress he'd engaged to play Countess Zika was ill and couldn't leave London. He needed me desperately. *Diplomacy* was already in rehearsal. Would I play Zika?

I replied, "Yes, of course. I'll do it for nothing." He told me not to be silly and to get down to the theater at once.

"I'm going back to Broadway to my old job," I told Madame gloomily.

I hoped that *Diplomacy* would have a limited run in New York and then close. Unfortunately Tyler had other plans. The success of the play exceeded his highest hopes and he arranged an extensive tour of the States and Canada. Since I was accepting no salary and wanted to conserve my savings for opera lessons, costumes, wigs and travel, I didn't take a dresser with me, an economy that worked out well except on those nights when our train left an hour after the curtain came down. Still, I was glad to do it because it relieved some of the guilt I felt about breaking my contract with Tyler.

That was in 1928. Much later, when Tyler needed money to cover frightful losses in an ill-fated production of *Macbeth*, I lent him five thousand dollars from my fast-shrinking savings. He promised to pay it back but he died soon after, destitute. I never expected it anyway. I owed him that for letting me out of my contract so gracefully.

When I could, during the tour of *Diplomacy*, I rented a room with a piano so I could practice. In Des Moines I used space in a music store. Unaware one afternoon that I had been working five hours instead of one, I emerged from my cubicle to find the store dark and deserted. I screamed. A night watchman came running and let me out, saving me from causing a cancellation of a *Diplomacy* performance. I had no understudy.

The last week of the tour we played Albany. Margaret Anglin and I had dressing rooms opposite each other across a narrow hall. I could not avoid hearing the stage door man knock on opening night to say that someone wanted to see her. Margaret answered that she never saw anyone before a performance.

The doorman returned. "The man says he is your cousin and he must see you."

This time everyone heard her irritated reply, "I don't care who he is. I wouldn't see God himself before an opening night performance!"

Charles Coburn and I were alone on stage in the second act. I was seated in an armchair center stage, facing the audience, and Charles was pacing in front of me.

In the middle of our scene a well-dressed man came rushing down the aisle. I couldn't believe my eyes. He stood at the rail of the orchestra pit and addressed me. He demanded that I get Margaret Anglin at once.

The audience accepted this extraordinary interruption as part of the play. No one moved. I thought, this is Margaret's cousin. I was afraid that he would reveal some intimate family matter if I started a conversation with him so I remained silent. I kept my eyes on his, my expression calm, hoping he would collect himself. I prayed the stagehands would drop the curtain.

Coburn walked to the footlights and demanded in a pompous tone:

"My good man, what do you want?"

Coburn's patronizing manner infuriated Margaret's cousin. He whipped a revolver out of his pocket, pointed it at me, and shouted, "Will you go get Margaret Anglin!"

A man seated on the aisle was the first to react. He jumped up and knocked the stranger's arm in the air. The gun flew out of his hand as they wrestled for it. The curtain slowly, mercifully, descended.

Backstage was in an uproar. I was shaking so violently I couldn't stand or speak. Nevertheless, fifteen minutes later the curtain rose and the play continued as though nothing had happened.

We learned afterward that the strange man was no relative of Margaret's. He was a madman so violent that it took four men to remove him from the theater. He was the author of anonymous letters that Margaret, Frances and I had been receiving throughout the tour, letters full of ravings that we should give up our licentious ways and commit our lives to Jesus. Police found in his possession ticket stubs for every train we'd taken during our entire tour. He had been with us all the way, a bomb waiting to explode.

His wealthy family took him away and provided institutional care.

That spring of 1928 George Cehanovsky went on tour with the Met, while Madame and I went to Brooklyn to live for a few weeks. Father listened to my morning lessons and had misgivings. My voice was not as fine as my mother's.

"You're right, Mr. Gahagan," Madame agreed. "Mrs. Gahagan is a lyric soprano. Her voice is naturally placed, one of the most beautiful I have ever heard. Helen is a lyric dramatic soprano. Her voice must be placed. When I do that, you'll be satisfied."

Father continued to be skeptical. He didn't believe I would succeed as an opera singer. He wasn't alone in that. My former associates in theater, Elizabeth Grimball, Harry Wagstaff Gribble and George Tyler, never stopped urging me to stop wasting my time; I belonged on the Broadway stage. Mother alone never wavered in her support.

As for me, I loved studying with the demanding Madame Cehanovska. If I made a mess of things, well, I could live with it. I owned my life.

We returned to the brownstone and I plunged into *Tosca*. One day I told Pavel Ludikar that I thought I was ready. He heard me sing and was enthusiastic. He told me he would play Scarpia when I made my debut. I was enchanted. Pavel's Scarpia was so magnificent it often was compared to that of Antonio Scotti. He urged me to sing with him in the Prague Opera, where he was a great favorite, as soon as the Met season ended.

Madame agreed, though I had been studying only two years, a short time to prepare for a major role in opera. We would appear in the opera house in Ostrava, the steel center of Czechoslovakia. Madame instructed us to spend the next four weeks working on the *mise-en-scène*, the physical movements we would make onstage.

We sailed in March, stopping in Paris to have my costumes made. When we reached Ostrava I learned that the opera company would sing *Tosca* in Czech, while Pavel and I sang in the

original Italian. I thought it strange but apparently the citizens of
Ostrava were accustomed to the arrangement.

Another oddity was that the company did without a director.
The cast was so familiar with the opera that only one rehearsal
was scheduled. Pavel and the rest of the company walked through
it comfortably but I was left to improvise. To my distress, the
tenor who played my lover was a full head shorter than I. To
avoid looking ridiculous, I managed to keep my distance whenever possible.

Madame paid no attention to my movements, concentrating on
my singing. She pronounced herself satisfied.

During the second act that night, the tenor ran up the steps
leading to a parapet that circled the prison roof, something he
hadn't done in rehearsal. I planted myself at the bottom of the
stairs so that he was forced to sing from the steps above me, concealing the disparity in our height.

I was happy with the performance. I was showered with congratulations from Pavel, the conductor and other members of the
company. I had just collapsed in my dressing room with a
satisfied sigh when the door was flung open. Madame stood there,
eyes blazing. She spat at me:

"My work was perfect but yours, *great actress*, was second-rate.
What did you think you were doing in the second act?"

I cringed. I had never seen her like this. As she slammed out of
the room, she said with a sneer, "What was Ludikar doing anyway when he was supposed to be working on the *mise-en-scène*
with you? Making love?"

In truth Pavel had spent almost no time at all showing me how
I should move. He assumed that a cursory description of how he
would move and what the tenor usually did would suffice for
someone with my stage experience. Instead we spent the time together listening to Mozart operas, Pavel's favorites. He was trying
to persuade me to switch from Italian to German so we could
sing them together.

I wept most of the night and awoke with fresh tears on my
face. All day I sat in my room, still crying, working out in my
mind, scene by scene, how I would move during my second performance of *Tosca* that evening.

Madame sent for me around four o'clock. She saw at once that I had been weeping. She looked at me sharply and said:

"Sing middle doh."

"I can't."

"You have a performance tonight. Sing."

Obediently I sang my exercises. When I finished she said, more gently, "Now, go and prepare yourself."

Despite the pain of the preceding twenty hours, I suddenly felt marvelous in the middle of a second-act duet with Pavel. Pure ecstasy swept over me. I felt sublimely at ease. The orchestra seemed an extension of me, of my voice. I felt weightless; a sense of elation swept over me. This was what I had been searching for, this *unity*. I had never found it in the theater, never found it anywhere.

Madame didn't come backstage. Pavel walked me to the hotel while I babbled my thanks for making such bliss possible.

Madame was waiting for me.

"You sang well and your acting was better," she told me coldly. "The day after tomorrow you will start work with Sasha Balaban." Sasha was Alexander Balaban, a singer married to Madame's adored daughter Vera. "Sasha is not only one of the first baritones of the Graz opera in Austria but he is also the opera's *régisseur*," Madame continued. "I don't like him much but he's a good musician, a good singer, and a gifted *régisseur*. You can learn stage movement from him."

I accepted all this in silence. Her voice softened and she added, "You must never again be thrown off your performance because of other singers. You must be as sure of what you will do as you are of what you will sing."

Sasha and Vera were in Bad Reichenhall. When I met him I knew we would get along well. As he outlined how our lessons would go, I became excited. Here clearly was someone with impressive command of opera staging. I couldn't wait to begin. In my enthusiasm I leaned toward him and seized his hand in my usual demonstrative way, thanking him for agreeing to work with me.

After lunch Sasha and Vera went to their room and Madame began to stroll the grounds in front of our pension. I started to join her but she whirled about, gave me a look of purest hatred, and made a gesture of spitting at my feet. With that she rushed indoors. I was transfixed. I realized she thought I had been flirting with her daughter's husband.

Wounded, I walked through the streets of Bad Reichenhall and found myself on the path leading through the forest to the restaurant we had visited so often two summers before. I passed it and kept climbing the mountain until the trees ended and I found scrub bushes, rocks, and edelweiss.

Blinded by tears, I began plucking the fragile edelweiss, only half aware of what I was doing. I remembered that Madame loved edelweiss and the thought led me to consider her difficult life. Before the Russian Revolution, she had been married to Vincent Cehanovsky, director of the Imperial Bank of St. Petersburg. They lived in luxury in a twenty-four-room apartment above the bank and Madame taught voice at the Imperial Conservatory. Vera, a promising young singer, had been taught by her mother, who was so gifted that the St. Petersburg Opera Company would call on her to replace a prima donna in an emergency. Madame could sing any opera in the repertory.

Madame's husband fell gravely ill just as fighting broke out between the rebels and the troops of the czar. Sophia was preoccupied with nursing him and paid little attention to the sounds of riot in the streets. One day her maid announced that she would not be working for her anymore.

Madame said, "You're leaving?"

The maid said, "No, you are. This apartment is now mine. The workers have taken over."

Madame was able to get permission to remain until her weakened husband was well enough to move. Vera and her husband fled Russia and Madame and Vincent moved into a tiny, shabby set of rooms where she supported them by giving voice lessons around the clock. Two and a half years later, he died.

George Cehanovsky was her adopted son. George was an officer in the Imperial Navy, serving on the *Aurora*, the very ship where in 1917 the February Revolution began with a mutiny in the harbor of Petrograd. When the fighting ended he came to St. Petersburg determined to train for opera. He set his heart on studying with the famed Madame Cehanovska but she refused him. One of her star pupils intervened on his behalf.

"If you take George he can be counted on to help you when you need him," Madame was told. "Of that I'm certain."

George became her pupil and soon learned that Madame's daughter and son-in-law were safe in Constantinople, then seething with White Russian refugees. One night Madame packed everything she could into two small bags and left St. Petersburg. She made her way to Constantinople and found her daughter simply by asking directions to the opera house. Sasha and Vera were running it. George followed and it was agreed that he and Madame should go to the United States. Madame was anxious about Vera's future. She wanted to make herself financially secure in order to help her.

George and Madame sailed from Constantinople in November, 1922, and arrived penniless in New York. Madame's reputation, however, was well known in musical circles dominated by ex-Europeans. On the crossing alone she signed up two pupils. George called Madame "Zolota," which means "Little Gold Piece." Her musicianship was indeed a gold piece.

I had suspected for some time that Madame worked in order to send money to Vera. She was obsessed with the notion that Vera might be reduced to poverty as she had been. Her reaction to my warmth at meeting Sasha was another expression of her love for her daughter. She feared I would develop a relationship with Sasha that would hurt Vera.

I rose from the rock where I had been sitting and took the bouquet of edelweiss to Madame. I handed it to her without a word. She accepted it, smiled, and said, "Thank you, Helen."

Sasha was indeed a marvelous teacher. When Madame and I sailed for New York a month later, I felt ready for new roles. That winter I learned Puccini's *Manon Lescaut* and Verdi's *Aïda*. The following summer it was arranged that I would sing both with Pavel in Ostrava.

We did the Puccini in July and were scheduled to perform in *Aïda* in September. The first opera went extremely well and I was full of confidence as I rehearsed *Aïda*. Madame, however, was dissatisfied with my Paris-made costumes. She said they wouldn't do and proceeded to take them apart and remake them. As a result I was obliged to sing in rehearsal wearing a partial costume, with a naked midriff and bare legs.

Two days later I had a heavy cold. We sent for mustard plasters, the trusted cure, and I went to bed to consume quantities of hot tea with honey and lemon. Wanting to make sure the mustard plasters would be effective, I left them on all night. The next morning when I removed them, I was horrified to find that my chest and back were covered with small blisters. I threw on my robe and ran to Madame's room.

"You left them on all night?"

"Yes."

"Sing middle doh."

My voice was clear.

She grunted approval. "Better blisters than no voice."

She took a needle, sterilized it over a burning match, and punctured every blister. Then she covered the burned area with clean towels soaked in mineral oil and sent me to bed, where I continued to drink hot tea with honey and lemon.

At six that evening I smeared myself from head to toe with the brown makeup required for Aïda and put on my costume. The mustard plasters and Madame's needle had saved the day.

Many American singers found it difficult to make an impression in European opera companies, but reviews of my performances had been wonderful. The intendant of the Moravia-Silesia Theatre was kind enough to write, "Thank you for the wonderful moments you gave us, moments of rare beauty. . . ."

Madame and I returned to Bad Reichenhall where I was to give a concert. The night before, on July 25, 1929, I wrote Mother telling her everything on my mind, as I always did. I said that I was tired and anxious, that I had learned seven or eight times as many songs as I needed, that my name was on posters all over town but I doubted that an unknown American would fill the 1,000-seat concert hall. I had purchased one hundred tickets myself and distributed them around to ensure that a few seats would be occupied.

My plans for the next few weeks were uncertain but it appeared that a demand was growing for the American soprano who spoke and sang in German and could do Italian opera. I would be singing *Tosca* in Salzburg in August and maybe *Aïda* in Berlin in September. I hoped to be back in New York in October.

I inquired about Father's health. He hadn't been feeling well. He had been working hard because the Gahagan Company was immersed in dredging contracts, mostly for railways such as the New York–Massachusetts–New Jersey–Long Island Railroad Company, the New York Central, the B&O and Lehigh Valley. Father's company did much of the hydraulic dredging and land reclamation for what became La Guardia Airport and created many of the Manhattan beaches.

To Father's distress, Mother was determined to move from our Park Slope home. She felt we needed something finer and was considering a Brooklyn mansion that neither I nor Father much liked—the windows weren't large enough.

The night of the concert in Bad Reichenhall I wore a new Paris gown. I was uncomfortable during the first half of the program, unable to draw a deep breath. Madame hurried backstage in the intermission.

"Why aren't you breathing properly?" she asked anxiously.

"I don't know," I told her. "For some reason, I can't."

"Turn around," she ordered. She pulled at the back of my dress. "No wonder," she said. "The bodice is too tight. Your rib cage can't expand."

She unbuttoned my gown from just below the top hook to my waist and pushed me in the direction of the stage. "There, and next time you order clothes remember you're a singer. Go. *Te calma.*"

Madame no longer accompanied me to every engagement. I missed my little gold piece, Zolota, but never more so than in Augsburg in Austria a few weeks later. The conductor met me in the opera house, escorted me to a small rehearsal studio, sat down at the piano and played random fragments from *Tosca*. I got the idea that he wanted me to sing whenever he played my music and so I did.

He closed the score and stood.

"Good," he said with finality. "You know *Tosca*. I know *Tosca*. There's no need for any more rehearsal. See you tomorrow night. Good luck."

The rest of my reception to the Ausgburg Opera Company was the same, chilly and curt. I was ignored by everyone, except a charming wardrobe mistress who wished me well with the tradition of a simulated spit on my shoulder and a whisper of *Hals und Beinbruch*. I later learned the reason for the freeze. I was singing the role of the company's usual prima donna, who was the mistress of the intendant.

I had acquired an agent to arrange my bookings, Walter Hofstötter. He was with me in Salzburg where I was to sing *Aïda* in three days' time. I awoke to find I had bronchitis and could scarcely speak. Walter took command of my cure. He loaded me into a cable car that carried us to the top of the highest mountain in the vicinity, where snow lay six feet deep. As the icy air stabbed my throat, I shivered and protested:

"Walter, this will kill me."

"The pure air will *cure* you," he promised. "You'll be well tomorrow morning."

He was right. My performance impressed even the sophisticated critics of Salzburg. The *Salzburger Chronik* of October 19, 1929, said of me:

> An extraordinary artist; her well-trained soprano possesses equal sureness in all registers, is of exquisite sweetness and inspiring warmth, and thrills especially in the high tones . . . accomplished, natural acting, noble gestures and convincing mimicry; in a word, acting and singing show as noble a style and line as her stage appearance.

On my way back to New York I stopped in Paris. In my bank, the Paris National City Bank, I picked up the Paris *Tribune* to check the stock quotations. Like everyone I knew, I was buying stocks on margin—that is, on credit. I couldn't believe the figures I was reading. I asked in bewilderment if I had an old edition of the paper.

"Miss Gahagan," a teller told me, "the stock market has crashed."

I lost $100,000 in stocks and all my savings from months of singing. In fact, I was deep in debt for the stocks purchased on margin, which now were worthless. I was shaken but I knew that I would survive, unlike many who committed suicide rather than face ruin. My profession is one that endures through hard times.

Mother and Father welcomed me home with a festive dinner party in the new house. My next goal was to be accepted by the Metropolitan Opera Company.

Madame and I prepared for the auditions with care that winter. Otto Kahn and Maestro Gennaro Papi of the Met granted me a preliminary audition in the opera house itself. I stood at center stage where the exquisite Bori, Scotti, Chaliapin and Alda had sung, where Geraldine Farrar had given her farewell performance and was pelted with roses. The lush tiered red velvet boxes rose empty in front of me. I opened my mouth and sang my best.

Maestro Papi later told George that I sang well but he'd heard me breathe. George defended me, saying that I was nervous and, besides, no one would be able to hear me breathe when I sang with the orchestra.

It was no use. The stock market crash had shaken even the Met. The management was facing a shortened season and feared using an unknown who might not draw the few patrons who could still afford opera tickets. The Depression had begun and the Met wasn't hiring; it was doubtful of finding work for its established singers.

A second audition was arranged by Bruno Zirato, manager of the New York Philharmonic, in Carnegie Hall before Arturo Toscanini. I awaited his verdict in an agony of suspense. The great maestro nodded and smiled. He thought my voice was good. However, there was no opening for a newcomer. "Keep on working," he consoled me.

Since I could find no work in New York, Madame and I turned again to Europe. Our plans were to spend the next two years there. Madame could live with Vera and work with me between the engagements that Walter Hofstötter assured me were available. When the financial crisis eased, we would try the Met again.

The night before sailing I was restless. I asked Father if he felt like a walk, a favorite pastime for us both. He and I and Billy were the walkers in the family. We set out, as usual, at a brisk pace. Father had taught me to stride as soon as I could stand.

I took his hand. Even when we were fighting about my career in the theater, I would hold his hand at dinner, or Mother's if I was beside her. I felt secure walking hand in hand with Father, sure of his love for us. He had shown concern when I announced I would be away for two years, but didn't try to stop me. I was thinking about my future plans when Father suddenly stopped and put his hand to his chest. I saw that he was panting.

"Father, what is it? Are you in pain?"

"No, no. It's just that you walk too fast, that's all. I have to rest a minute and get my breath."

Rest! Get his breath! Something was terribly wrong. Always, it had been Father who grumbled that I didn't walk fast enough. "Don't mince along, child," he would say. "Take a respectable step."

He warded off my look of alarm. "Don't fuss, Helen. It's nothing."

I searched his face. He seemed the same as always. Nothing appeared changed, but I knew otherwise. We slowly walked back to the house without speaking.

The next day, just before I boarded the ship, Father said, "If you don't like it over there, Helen, tell them to go to hell and come home." I grinned and hugged him tight.

I had a feeling of foreboding all that voyage, and couldn't shake it.

Vera was waiting in Paris and we went to Italy. I left Vera and Madame in comfortable quarters in Viareggio on the Ligurian Sea in June and went to Salzburg to sing Santuzza in *Cavalleria Rusticana,* my first opera. After the performance, I had a surprise. My brother William came backstage. I hadn't known he was in Europe.

Without greeting me, he demanded to know where he could find the tenor.

"Why?" I asked in amazement.

"*Why!*" he exploded. "He threw you across the stage!"

I laughed. "Oh. William, he didn't hurt me. I learned a long time ago how to fall onstage. Calm down. I'm so glad to see you."

The notices the next morning were wonderful. The *Salzburger Wacht* said:

> Helen Gahagan gave a really superior performance of Santuzza; she excelled all the expectations which followed her debut in *Tosca*.

The *Salzburger Tageszeitung* critic wrote:

> The highlight of the performance lay in the outstanding interpretation of Santuzza by Miss Gahagan . . . there was soulful penetration, with rich-toned emission of her voice, which had glowing warmth but without theatrical affectations . . .

The *Reichenhaller Morgenpost* said that I "carried the performance" and added:

> This richly endowed singer, who had her first appearance last year in *Tosca*, has made great progress . . . her voice triumphs over large spaces . . .

Billy flew to London that afternoon and I returned to Italy to resume work with Madame. I was adding two more operas to my repertoire, *La Gioconda* and *Manon Lescaut*. In July I returned to Salzburg alone to sing *Tosca*, a performance which was extravagantly praised. Walter Hofstötter was delighted. I was to repeat the role the next night in Vienna. If I did as well with the critics, he said, my future in middle Europe was assured.

In Vienna the opera was staged on an outdoor stage in a park, an enchanting setting. On this night, however, a wild wind was blowing, thrashing the trees noisily. I wasn't sure I could be heard above the gale, which several times lifted the long train of my costume straight behind me like a flag.

However, the critical reaction was all that Walter had hoped. One said my appearance was "triumphant" and another wrote of "vocal excellence, a talented actress, temperamental, beautiful, she created enthusiasm in her audience . . ."

I returned to my hotel excited by the reception I had received.

The desk clerk handed me a cable. Signed William and Frederick, it read:

IF YOU WANT TO SEE FATHER ALIVE
COME HOME AT ONCE.

In shock I dropped the cable and my handbag, whirled out of the lobby and rushed into the street. I walked for an hour or two, numb and unseeing. After a time I came to a bridge and stopped, my hand on the rail, staring into the dark water. A man touched my arm.

He said in German, "Please *Fräulein*, let me help you."

"Leave me alone," I said in despair. "Leave me alone." I began to sob.

He refused to go. He said gently, "I've been following you for an hour. Please let me help you."

I said through my tears, "Where is the cable office? I must send word home. My father is dying."

What a kind man he was. We found a cable office open at that hour only after walking what seemed like miles. I sent a cable and I suppose he paid for it, since I didn't have my handbag. Then he guided me back to the hotel and left. In the morning there was a sympathetic letter from him, unsigned. I never knew his name and I never saw him again.

I placed a transatlantic telephone call to my brothers. They told me that Father had been taken to the hospital with what seemed to be a problem with his heart. During tests it was discovered that he had advanced cancer of the windpipe. There was no hope that he could be saved, though he had been assured all was well.

I telephoned Zolota and explained what happened. Hofstötter, in despair but understanding, canceled the busy schedule he had booked for me. I was leaving on the first available ship.

It was necessary to find a plausible excuse for my sudden return if we were to maintain the fiction that Father would recover. It came to me halfway across the ocean. David Belasco had been begging me to come back from Europe and appear in a play he was producing in the fall. I cabled to ask if the offer was still open. He replied promptly: I HAVE BEEN WAITING FOR YOU.

Father didn't comment on my change of plans. I spent as much time as I could with him, chatting idly. One day he fell silent, absently stroking our black dachshund. He seemed preoccupied.

"Is Lillian unhappy?" he asked at last. "Have you noticed any tension between her and Bob?"

I was surprised. I thought Lilli and Bob Walker were getting along very well and told Father so. He accepted this assurance pensively.

It wasn't until after Father died that I learned he had been right about Lilli and Bob. Lilli confided in Mother that she was so miserable she would commit suicide if she didn't get a divorce. Mother didn't hesitate. She told Lilli to go at once to our family lawyer and start proceedings. Lilli's was the first Gahagan divorce; unfortunately, it wasn't her last.

Father put down the dachshund and walked to the window. He spoke without turning.

"Helen, I don't know why you have returned but I'm very glad you're here."

He knew. Of course he knew. How could we have believed he didn't know he was dying? Still, no one discussed his health with him; none of us referred to it. We couldn't bear to.

When I went to see David Belasco, he received me in his private apartment at the top of his theater. I found the white-haired legendary producer sitting at a large ornate desk in a room crammed with antique furniture and theater memorabilia collected over his long and distinguished career on Broadway.

Belasco had been at every one of my New York openings. A year earlier he had tried to persuade me to give up singing in Europe and star in one of his productions. Then as now, he was dressed eccentrically as a priest, which always made me feel uneasy. On this visit I wanted to find a tactful way to tell the cherubic old man I thought the play he wanted me to do, Lili Hatvany's *Tonight or Never*, was monumentally silly.

The plot concerned a great singer who could never achieve her ambition to sing at the Metropolitan because her voice was cold. She meets a man, falls in love, and loses her virginity to him. The result is a transformation in the quality of her voice. She sings an aria from *Tosca* with her heart and soul in it, and goes to the Met.

I was never intimidated by directors or producers. I decided to be blunt.

"Mr. Belasco," I said, "the plot of *Tonight or Never* is preposterous. Audiences will never accept that an opera singer can be changed by having an affair. It's going to take all your genius to make anyone sit through this nonsense. The only way it can work is if the actor who plays the man, the talent scout from the Met, is wildly attractive. Who is going to play that part?"

Belasco said, "I think I've chosen the right actor, Miss Helen. Here's a picture of Melvyn Douglas. Do you know his work?"

"No." I looked at the picture. It was of a good-looking boy.

"He's a juvenile!" I protested. "I'll never fall in love with him! No one would believe it. *I'm thirty years old.* You must get someone else."

Belasco said patiently, "Miss Helen, come back tomorrow and meet him. If you still object, I'll not insist."

The next morning I returned to Belasco's apartment. Melvyn Douglas was already there. He didn't resemble the callow picture. Here was a mature man, only half a year younger than I—tall, broad-shouldered, slender, and exceedingly handsome. His speech was cultivated, his bearing aristocratic, and his personality magnetic. Not since my cousin Walter had any man affected me as he did at first sight.

Belasco thanked Melvyn and me for coming and we chatted a while. As Melvyn turned to leave, he said, "It's a pleasure to see you again, Miss Gahagan."

I watched him go and thought, *that's the handsomest back I've ever seen.*

"Well, Miss Helen," Belasco asked. "What do you think?"

"He'll do," I managed.

"You knew him before?" Belasco asked, eyeing me shrewdly.

"I can't remember." I was wondering how I had missed noticing him.

We began rehearsals a few days later. I worked in a daze, sensitive to Melvyn's every move, always aware when he came or went. I hated to see the day's rehearsal end. Away from the theater I was obsessed with thoughts of him. My longing to be alone with him became a consuming desire.

Meanwhile I was impressed with Belasco's direction, among the best I had ever encountered. He arranged the stage for the first rehearsal with all the furniture in place. Rather than starting as I always had with bare boards and a few kitchen chairs, the entire set was there. Even the props were provided and Belasco took infinite pains to make sure we were comfortable with them.

For instance, I worked with tea and teacups in the first scene, and some books. Belasco would say, "Miss Helen, what kind of teacups do you like? What do you feel happy with in your hands?" He invited me to bring my own china, which I did, and my own books. Even the ornaments on the tables were my own, in the interests of making me feel completely at home.

On the first day he had a piano on stage because the scene opened with me and my coach working on exercises. Since I wore long dresses in the play, he insisted that I always rehearse in a long dress. By the time of the opening, I was completely at ease in a dress with a train. *Comfortable* was an important word with David Belasco; he was always asking, "Miss Helen, are you comfortable? Do you like that? What kind of couch would you be most comfortable on?"

He was doing everything possible to make me feel that the setting was really my home. I thought it an interesting approach. Some other directors have used it, but none to the extent that he did.

As rehearsals progressed I worried that Belasco was avoiding a crucial scene in the second act where I had supper with the talent scout and fell into his arms. Every day, when at Belasco's insistence I lunched in his apartment, I brought up my concern. Each time he put me off with a chuckle and the promise that we would get to the seduction scene soon.

We had only a few days of rehearsal left and the scene still had not been rehearsed. I confronted Belasco at lunch in an agitated state.

"We simply *must* do that scene at once," I said.

He replied uneasily, "Miss Helen, I'm embarrassed to ask you to play that scene the way I want it played."

I was astonished. "Embarrassed!" I said.

"Well," he explained, "you know why I wanted you for the part . . ."

"Because I can both sing and act."

"That too," he agreed, "but there are singers at the Metropolitan who are also actresses and also beautiful. But no one would believe that they are virgins. The whole play hinges on that, that the singer is a virgin and that when she is deflowered she becomes the full woman whose voice comes alive."

I considered this. "You seem to be describing the rape scene in *Tosca*, which I've played many times."

Belasco threw back his head and laughed. "You've played it, Miss Helen?"

"Of course I have," I said. "I know exactly what you want. It must look as if something is going on, but really isn't."

"That's it!" Belasco shouted.

I'd taken a small apartment on Central Park South. Frau Gaehler, who had been with our family for years in one capacity or another, came with me to New York. One weekend she made plans to spend two days in Brooklyn. It was my opportunity to be alone with Melvyn.

I asked him casually if he would mind coming to my apartment on Saturday night so we could go over some scenes together. He agreed. I couldn't wait for his arrival but when he knocked I was stricken with nervousness. To conceal my fluttering state, I was brisk. I suggested we work on the love scene which Belasco still had not rehearsed.

We worked for about two hours, after which I made coffee. Melvyn told me that he lived at Sneden's Landing on the Hudson with his parents and a five-year-old son, the child of a marriage that had failed. His father, now retired, had been a composer and concert pianist, Edouard Hesselberg, who was born in Russia. When he was seventeen, Edouard was sent to the United States by his parents to escape being drafted into the army. His parents feared that military service would ruin his hands for music.

Dr. Hesselberg's career had taken him all over the States and

Canada where he headed musical departments at universities and conservatories. In Denver he met and married Lena Shackelford, who was related to a Confederate general and whose family was scandalized by her choice. Melvyn was born on April 5, 1901, in Macon, Georgia, where his father then headed the Wesleyan College Conservatory.

As we talked, I began to relax. I found being with him as easy as if I had always known him. We had the same tastes, the same attitudes to the theater, the same appreciation of music, admired the same people, and disapproved of the same people.

Melvyn said he hated to see me go upstairs each day to lunch with Belasco.

"Why?" I asked.

"Because of his reputation with his leading ladies."

"Oh Melvyn, he's an old man."

Melvyn looked at me, amused. "That doesn't make him safe, Helen."

I changed the subject. I told Melvyn he looked more like a European than an American.

He laughed. "Mother always says Father is a foreigner. He's a Jew. I'm a Jew."

His simple "I'm a Jew" dissolved me. His easiness and quiet pride contrasted with my friend Helene's wretchedness and the time she admitted she hated being Jewish. All my reticence evaporated. I felt a rush of love. We fell into each other's arms.

Before the out-of-town opening of *Tonight or Never* I was deeply in love with Melvyn. Except for my cousin Walter, I knew I had never really loved anyone before. He knocked on my hotel room door in Washington the morning of the opening performance. When I opened it he thrust an armful of books at me.

"We can't go through life just making love," he told me. "We have to study too."

He was gone before I could explain indignantly that I too was an inveterate reader. Like my father, I fell asleep every night with a book in my hands. I closed the door thinking how much we still had to learn about each other.

The only time I ever saw Belasco lose his temper was during

the dress rehearsal that day when he began screaming at the crew. He had the best technicians in the business, extraordinary people who were respected everywhere. I couldn't bear it. I walked off the stage.

Belasco sent the manager after me. I told the manager, "Tell Mr. Belasco that I'll come back when he stops shouting at everyone."

"But he's not yelling at you," the manager said.

"I know that. Tell him he's making me nervous."

Belasco stopped at once.

We were in Baltimore, our final stop before the New York opening, when Belasco collapsed with pneumonia. Since he was seventy-seven years old, his condition was serious. He was rushed to Johns Hopkins Hospital but refused to stay. He phoned the stationmaster and had him hold our train for fifteen minutes so he could return to New York with his cast.

He was carried to his bed in the apartment above the theater, critically ill. On opening night we were told he was dying. We found a telegram pinned to the call board:

I WANT TO BE REMEMBERED TO MISS HELEN, TO THEM ALL. TELL THEM I'M SORRY NOT TO BE WITH THEM. THAT I LOVE EVERY ONE OF THEM. DAVID BELASCO.

It was so like him to think of us and be generous despite his illness. A saddened cast prepared for the first curtain. *Tonight or Never* was Belasco's first play in fifty years that he hadn't been in the theater with his actors. We were elated in the first intermission when we received word that he was rallying.

The play received a standing ovation and I made a short curtain speech, giving the audience the good news about Belasco.

The reviews pronounced the play a distinguished hit. Robert Littell wrote in the *Evening World*:

> Miss Gahagan has a powerful, well-trained voice of operatic dimensions and could make her mark as a singer if she were not also an actress of extremely high voltage.

The New York *Times* said:

> It is to be hoped that Mr. Belasco will be permitted to bring forth many more such evenings in the theater.

The *Journal* critic wrote:

> Miss Gahagan must take her place as one who was called and answered.

The *Evening Sun* said:

> Mr. Belasco has done the casting with his usual wizardry—it is worth a trip to the Belasco Theatre to hear Miss Gahagan sing.

Father came to a matinee a few days before Christmas, his first outing since his most recent stay in the hospital. He had never heard me sing on a stage. He came backstage afterward very moved. He embraced me and said, "It was beautiful, Helen. Now I know what you wanted." As he turned to leave, he told Frau Gaehler, who was acting as my dresser, "Take care of my daughter."

Just before the evening performance, I was called to the telephone. Lilli told me Father was dead. That evening he had dined on a tray in his bedroom while Mother and Billy prepared to attend the opera. They went up to say good night and found him in his chair, apparently asleep, the tray neatly placed on the table beside him.

I could not believe it. He had seemed so well only a few hours earlier.

I somehow got through the performance. I was in my dressing room when an old family friend, John Finnerty, came to see me. He'd heard about Father and he wanted to comfort me with a story about him.

It concerned the time I knew a good deal about, when Father had a row with Lilli's husband, Bob Walker, and a million-and-a-half-dollar dredge was lost. Bob was an insurance agent and had drawn up a policy for the dredge, which was being shipped to Peru. Father found it unacceptable. He wanted the dredge insured only for the time it was on the ship, while Bob's policy was for a much larger sum and insured the dredge even when it was safely in operation, which Father thought was unnecessary.

They quarreled and Father lost his temper and ordered Bob from the office. The dredge left New York Harbor the next day, uninsured, and sank in water so deep it couldn't be recovered.

It was the first and only time I ever saw Father deeply distressed over a business matter. I found him one day sitting in Mother's room in front of her fireplace, deep in thought. I tried to console him but he put me off roughly. "There's no excuse for being so stupid," he said. "I'm not concerned about what the loss of the dredge means to me but what it could mean to you children."

That night, while my grief at Father's death was still fresh, John Finnerty told me the rest of the story. It seemed that Father was co-owner of the dredge with the Lackawanna Railway. Typically, there was no scrap of paper to show that Father had undertaken to be responsible for the dredge's safety. The railway's board of directors held an emergency meeting. As they were discussing the matter, a clerk announced that Walter Gahagan was outside.

Father entered the room with his usual dignity. "Gentlemen," he said, "I expected to find you here this morning. Here is my personal I.O.U. I will make good your share of the dredge."

At home I found the family gathered around Mother in the living room. No one wept. It was painful for us all that Father had died alone, but knowing that the end was gentle was comforting. After a time Walter arrived from Princeton and joined the circle. We were quiet together a long while and then the boys painfully began to discuss funeral arrangements. We went upstairs to Father.

Sitting beside him, holding his cold hand, I felt better. I wished I had found the right moment to tell Father that I was in love and have him meet Melvyn. I considered the future without my father. There would be no more telephone calls from him after each performance, wanting to know how it went and if I was all right; I would no longer have his strength, advice and treasured encouragement.

The boys chose a bronze casket and Father lay in the living room with flowers piled around him. We were overwhelmed with bouquets, some of which arrived unsigned, addressed simply to "My Friend." Family and business associates sent huge floral arrangements, but there were touching bouquets as well from unexpected sources—the nuns in the convent down the street, for instance, a newsstand operator, and a tailor.

The funeral service was conducted in our home. Father hadn't wanted a religious service and Mother respected his wishes. We sat in a fragrant garden of flowers through a spare formality without eulogies. Out of deference to Mother, who was dry-eyed, no one cried.

Mother didn't allow herself to show her bottomless grief until two years later when Uncle George died. Though she had never been particularly fond of him, she wept for days. We appreciated that our uncle's death had broken through the dam she had built against her sorrow over losing her husband.

At the end of the brief service the lid was placed on the coffin, shutting Father away. Mother rose, left the room, and slowly climbed the stairs, followed by the family. We waited until the house was empty of guests and then came downstairs, dressed for travel. Father's body was going by train to Troy, Ohio, to be buried in the family plot.

William, Frederick, Walter, Uncle George and Robert lifted the casket and carried it from the house. I watched as the procession of cars left the driveway. I had to remain in New York for that night's performance of *Tonight or Never*.

Two months after Father's death I told Mother about Melvyn. She seemed disinterested as I told her I was in love but sat up sharply when I said I planned to be married.

"To whom?" she asked, looking concerned.

"I told you," I said. "To Melvyn Douglas."

She was aghast. "Your leading man? But you don't know him!"

"I do know him, Mother, and I love him. We're going to be married or, if you prefer, we'll live together. I must tell you, though, that we'll live together openly."

"Live with him," she snapped, and went to her room.

At three in the morning, she wakened me.

"Helen, it was wicked of me to say what I did. Of course you must marry Melvyn Douglas. There's no reason why a marriage to an actor shouldn't be happy."

A getting-acquainted period followed. I visited Melvyn's family in Sneden's Landing and felt at home with them at once. Dr.

Hesselberg played and I envied Melvyn growing up with such a magnificent musician in the house. Melvyn came to Brooklyn with me and captivated Mother totally. Even the twins were impressed. William and Frederick assured me it would be a lasting marriage because Melvyn was the first suitor I'd ever had who didn't figuratively sit at my feet.

Melvyn's style, however, did not prepare him for the noisy, assertive, abrupt Gahagans. He is reserved, soft-spoken and exceedingly polite. It was some time before he felt comfortable with my voluble, demonstrative family.

Soon after the opening of *Tonight or Never*, Sam Goldwyn bought the movie rights to the play. Gloria Swanson was signed to play my role and Goldwyn asked Melvyn to star opposite her, offering him a five-year contract. I was delighted that Melvyn, a relatively unknown actor, would have the opportunity to play opposite Gloria Swanson, then one of the biggest stars in Hollywood, but I was against the five-year contract. It would mean that he would have to give up the Broadway stage, which I considered a superior place for an actor to work and develop.

Melvyn's New York career, in fact, was dazzling. He'd just completed a three-year contract with William A. Brady during which he'd played opposite some of our finest actresses, such as Grace George, Fay Bainter, Alice Brady, Mary Nash and Laura Hope Crews.

I pointed out to him that if he lived on the West Coast he would be cutting all ties with the New York theater. Even worse, the five-year contract meant that he couldn't choose his own films but would have to do whatever Goldwyn wanted. He might wind up playing in trash.

Melvyn wouldn't be moved. He said he couldn't pass up a guaranteed income for the next five years.

I exploded. "You're going to accept the contract just because of the money?" I exclaimed, "That's madness!"

Melvyn said quietly, "Helen, I must think of the money. I have responsibilities." Melvyn was supporting his parents and his son.

We had been about to announce our engagement but I was having second thoughts about it. I kept to myself, brooding. Marrying Melvyn meant that I too would be separated from the New

York stage and from Madame Cehanovska. Either Melvyn and I would live apart much of the time or I would be isolated on the West Coast.

Melvyn made no demand on me, quietly waiting for my decision. In the end I concluded that I could commute from California from time to time. His five-year contract didn't necessarily bind me too. We would work it out somehow. I was helplessly in love with him. We would *have* to work it out.

We announced the engagement. The next day an actress friend congratulated me. "The way you two play the love scene in the second act, getting married is the only decent thing you could do."

The next night David Belasco was well enough to attend a performance of *Tonight or Never*, his 375th production. A horde of reporters and photographers was present for the celebration. Belasco was greeted by a standing ovation that lasted a full ten minutes as the Grand Old Man was welcomed back to his theater. After the play the cast and staff gathered in the Green Room, where I presented Belasco with a silver cup filled with violets. The cup was inscribed: *To David Belasco from the Company and the Staff of* Tonight or Never.

As we posed for pictures, Belasco whispered to me, a mischievous expression on his wrinkled face, "Am I not the best caster in the whole world, Miss Helen?"

Douglas Gilbert of the New York *World-Telegram* wrote a fine account of the sentimental event. It read:

DAVID BELASCO STARS IN A PLAY WITHIN A PLAY:
HE'S BACK ON BROADWAY FOR "TONIGHT OR NEVER"

Producer's First Gaze Upon
Helen Gahagan's Success

A less blasé and intimate Broadway paused last night to witness its most auspicious seasonal opening: a play within a play; a bit of backstage drama impromptu and vivid—David Belasco in his greatest production—the return of the 76-year-old producer and dramatist to his own theater after a bed-ridden four months of pneumonia and pleurisy. . . . And then Helen Gahagan kissed him emphatically a score of times, and Ferdinand Gottschalk, that seasoned artist-trouper of the old Belasco school, wept on his shoulder, and Melvyn Douglas, who plays the lover-lead, blushed like an understudy going on at five minutes' notice.

It was great theater, and you could see the old master respond —"Certainly I can stand up for the pictures. Tell 'em to set up their cameras"—the coolest actor of his company. . . .

"They used to do these things in the old days"—one caught a phrase here and there—"I thought those days had gone, these kindnesses, these so awfully friendly gestures. We used to be such comrades. Right here in this Green Room too. Why, I remember . . ."

And so help me, the handkerchief, mellowed, lavender-scented, hanging from the glass-enclosed frame of Adelaide Neilson as Desdemona on the wall, fluttered and waved.

Melvyn and I decided to be married on April 5, 1931, Melvyn's thirtieth birthday. That year it fell on Easter Sunday. The night before the wedding a *Time* magazine reporter interviewed Belasco and the account appeared in the April 13 issue. Belasco was asked about me and Melvyn and said:

"It was love at first sight. I've seen many romances in the theater but none so fine, so old-fashioned, so honest . . . I make it a rule to bring together my future hero and heroine before I make my selection . . . I can't explain it, but I can sense how they will play together in each other's arms, or kiss each other . . ."

The reporter added:

> Surprised theater folk waited to see if Helen Gahagan would be starred in another Belasco play, for tradition dictates that any Belasco leading lady who marries automatically leaves his service. Examples: Leslie Carter, Blanche Bates, Frances Starr, Katharine Cornell, Mary Ellis, Lenore Ulric.

We will never know if the tradition would have held true in my case. Dear David Belasco died shortly after Melvyn and I were married.

I slept at home the night before the wedding, which was to take place in our living room in Brooklyn. I awoke that morning wondering if I would feel changed the next day. I had made all the other transitions in my life without a pang of concern. I had dreamed of being an actress for so many years that it felt natural and right when I finally reached Broadway. The move to singing opera required no adjustment either because I had been able to imagine accurately what that life would be like. But I had never imagined being a wife.

The thought that one day I would commit myself to live all my life with one person had never crossed my mind. Being single and occasionally engaged—I was engaged to someone when I met Melvyn—had seemed to me an ideal arrangement.

I was aware that Melvyn also was uneasy. The distress of his first marriage left him uncertain about venturing into a second.

As I prepared for the ceremony my brothers kept interrupting with bulletins about the size of the press corps assembling on our lawn, insisting on interviews. Finally, for the sake of peace, I was persuaded to grant a press conference.

I told the reporters truthfully, "I would rather go through six opening nights than to be married just once."

As the questions poured on me, I said pointedly, "I'll never be dressed in time for the wedding . . . ," but the hint was ignored. I was asked about our honeymoon plans and replied that we didn't have any, we were still playing in *Tonight or Never*, but "when the opportunity for our honeymoon comes up we won't just go to some hotel and sit around all dressed up. We will go to China or Africa or Egypt or maybe take a walking tour through Ireland."

Someone asked if I would keep my name. I said that I would. I was superstitious about that. "Of course I'll be a good wife in the sense of what wifehood means," I explained, "but I'll always be Helen Gahagan. I'll keep the good old Irish name. I was born Helen Gahagan and I'll die Helen Gahagan."

I was reminded that Brady had wanted me to change it because he thought no one would be able to pronounce it. I had refused him flatly. He also had objected to Melvyn's name, Hesselberg, which he complained wouldn't fit on a theater marquee. Melvyn obligingly took his grandmother's maiden name, Douglas.

At five to six that day I stood at the head of the stairs with the Reverend Dr. S. Parkes Cadman, pastor of the Central Congressional Church. At precisely six, as I was about to take my first step down the stairs, the minister whispered to me, apparently with Lilli in mind, "I hope this one takes."

Struggling with my temper at the untimely cynicism, and clutching Melvyn's enormous bouquet of gardenias and lilies of the valley for protection, I gathered up my train and went down the stairs. Lilli, my matron of honor, followed. Melvyn was waiting below under a bridal bower of smilax, white sweet peas and more gardenias, a creation designed by William. William was giving me away, an honor he claimed because he was older than Frederick by five minutes.

As I walked down the aisle between our guests, fifty on each side, I kept my eyes fixed on Melvyn standing next to his best man, his brother George. He looked wonderful. I kept my composure during the ceremony though I was quivering with emotion.

Supper was served on small tables in the living room and the adjoining dining room. Champagne toasts were offered and then Dr. Hesselberg and George Cehanovsky gave a brilliant concert.

I had insisted, against Melvyn's grave doubts, that we spend our first married night in my own room. I hate sleeping in impersonal hotels. I assured Melvyn that he wouldn't be surrounded by Gahagans. Lilli and Frederick would be in their own homes and Walter would return to Princeton. That left only Mother and William in the house, a contendable number.

I had underestimated my affectionate family. The next morning the entire clan trooped up to the third floor to wish us good morning. It was years before Melvyn recovered from the shock.

That night in the Belasco, friends and friends of friends packed the house. To our intense embarrassment, they howled with approval during our love scenes. After the final curtain, backstage was bedlam. Everyone, it seemed, had brought a bottle of champagne. Melvyn's eyes met mine desperately. Would we ever be alone?

When the play finally ended its successful run, I went to Cleveland where I sang *Cavalleria Rusticana*. Melvyn and Madame came with me. They got along famously. Melvyn was thinking of training his voice in case he was required to sing in the movies. A few years later he did sing in a film with Grace Moore. George Cehanovsky said, "Even when he hummed it was good."

Then Melvyn and I sailed for Europe on our delayed honeymoon, motoring along the Riviera for a lazy and lovely three weeks.

On our return we encountered a family crisis. William, always the frailer and more anxious of the twins, had suffered a nervous breakdown during his year in Peru, where the stress of supervising the dredging of Lima's harbor had proved too much for him. Frederick had taken command of the family business, W. H. Gahagan Incorporated, Contracting Engineers. Father's old partner, Alfred Liebmann, was asking to be bought out. He had confidence in Frederick's leadership but he too was feeling the tension of a company that had to estimate bids on huge, complicated civil engineering contracts that would take years to complete. With the uncertain economics of the Depression, Liebmann had no enthusiasm for such dangerous gambles. Besides, he was an old man; he and Father had been partners for sixty years.

The family held a conference and agreed there was no choice but to buy out Liebmann ourselves. We instructed Fritz to do whatever he thought necessary to keep the company going in order to protect Father's good name and ensure the jobs of engineers and skilled workers who had been with Gahagan for a generation and more.

Liebmann had 125 shares with an estimated total value of $350,000. The company didn't have enough money to buy him out, so a contract was drawn up under which we promised to pay off the debt in installments. Father died intestate. Under the law, Mother inherited a third of the company and his children two thirds. The family discussed various alternatives and decided that no Gahagan would draw any money from the company, except as salaried employees, until Liebmann was paid in full.

In order to protect Mother, Frederick proposed that she sign her third interest over to the company, in exchange for which she could be paid a monthly sum for life. As for Walter, who was still in school, Frederick undertook to pay his expenses. I was fine, having been financially independent for ten years.

This left Lilli, who had no profession. Determined to support herself after her divorce, she went out to look for a job. She found one in Macy's department store, a haven during the

Depression for ladies in suddenly reduced circumstances. After a winter in Macy's, she followed me into the theater and appeared in summer stock, once playing my role in *Tonight or Never*. I asked her if she found it difficult.

"Not at all," she told me blithely. "I just copied everything you did."

Frederick took her aside. He said if her former husband, Bob Walker, could make a lot of money as an insurance agent, Lilli was a certain success. She studied, took the required examination, and passed with flying colors. A large insurance firm Father had used willingly took her on under an unusually advantageous arrangement whereby she could keep a share of premiums from policies she secured for the company.

She went into business with Peggy Mosley, a school friend of both of us from college, and both thrived as insurance brokers. Lilli wanted to live in New York and persuaded Mother to share a handsome apartment with her there.

Meanwhile Melvyn and I had moved to California. Our first evening in Los Angeles, we ate at Musso and Frank's. Afterward we stood on Hollywood Boulevard and looked up and down at the dreariness. Frances Starr hadn't exaggerated when she said that Hollywood Boulevard resembled a movie set built to collapse the moment the stage manager cried, "Strike it!"

I had tried to prepare myself for Hollywood's tawdriness but a wave of desolation swept over me. I buried my head in Melvyn's shoulder. His arms tightened around me understandingly. I knew he felt as I did, and probably worse. He faced five years in this celebration of bad taste.

Sam Goldwyn had arranged for us to stay in the Hollywood Roosevelt Hotel. As soon as I opened my eyes the next morning I called Barney Glazer. Barney had directed Molnar's *Fashions for Men* on Broadway but was now in California. I wailed, "Where does one live out here?"

"There are only two places one *can* live," he told me. "Beverly Hills or Malibu."

Melvyn and I agreed there were only two places we would *never* live—Beverly Hills and Malibu.

We settled in the San Fernando Valley in an isolated house

surrounded by treeless brown hills. The only green to be seen anywhere was the small patch of lawn around our house. I expected
camels to loom over the horizon. Happily there were a swimming
pool and tennis court, which promised hours of healthful exercise.
The property's main asset, I felt, was the hedge of pink cabbage
roses that bloomed day in and day out, a comfort to my eyes that
ached for Vermont.

The first night among the brown hills, Melvyn awoke to find
me gone from bed. He called and got no answer. He searched the
house, upstairs and down, but I was nowhere to be found. Out of
the kitchen window he got a glimpse of a white-clad figure in the
garden.

"Helen," he called, "what's the matter? What are you doing
out there in your nightgown, and *barefoot!*"

Contritely, I explained that I loved to walk in the night air. In
Vermont whenever I was sleepless I would throw on a robe, run
downstairs barefoot, and amble around under the night sky until
I felt sleepy. During an influenza epidemic at boarding school, I
was found one night wandering in the garden in my nightdress, ill
and delirious.

The more I explained that strolling in a dark garden was a
habit of mine, the more depressed Melvyn looked. His bride was
certainly an odd one.

I love to be outside in the country air at night. A few years ago,
only six weeks after my radical mastectomy, we were in Vermont
at Cliff Mull. Melvyn had gone to bed but it was a beautiful
night and I felt it was the perfect time to water the flowers in
what we euphemistically call the garden.

I must explain that in the years since my childhood Cliff Mull
has become a Gahagan family compound. That night the former
carriage house down the slope was occupied by Lilli's grand-
daughter Noelle and my brother Walter's daughter Gaycita. The
carriage house, which Father had rebuilt to house two automobiles and the chauffeur's quarters, had been remodeled by Lilli's
son Herbert, a painter and sculptor who spends most of his time
in Italy. His daughter, Noelle, takes care of it for him.

Noelle and Gaycita were looking after a friend's German shepherd but the dog and I hadn't met. Hearing me in the garden

and taking me for an intruder, the dog leaped out of the darkness
and began to bite me. I screamed for help and Gaycita and Melvyn came running, but not before my white peignoir was spat-
tered with blood from several cuts. With Gaycita's help, Melvyn
bathed and dressed my wounds, shaking his head with dismay
and disapproval.

Settling into our San Fernando Valley house, I placed an ad in
a newspaper and hired the first likely-sounding couple who
telephoned in reply, sight unseen. Shortly after they arrived and
unpacked, I gave instructions about dinner and sweeping the
patio and went with Melvyn to downtown Los Angeles to buy a
piano. I intended to keep working on my voice. Madame Cehanovska was concerned that it would lose conditioning quickly. She
disapproved of the move to California but pointed out philo-
sophically that my voice training hadn't been entirely in vain,
since it got me the part in *Tonight or Never*—and Melvyn.

We bought a fine Steinway from Edwin Lester, who agreed to
have it delivered the next day. Lester went from selling pianos to
producing Franz Lehar's *The Merry Widow*, in which I starred a
few years later, and today heads the Los Angeles Civic Opera
Company.

Melvyn and I were home by seven. The new houseman informed us that dinner was ready. We seated ourselves in the dining room and waited a rather long time. When our meal came, it
was a shock. The houseman placed in front of me a platter bearing a charred chicken split down the middle and spread-eagled.

"Here's your chicken," he announced, and left.

We were speechless. There wasn't a sound from the kitchen.

"What did you tell the cook we would have for dinner,
Helen?" Melvyn asked with interest.

"I said we'd have chicken for dinner."

"Well," he said and grinned, "that's what we have—chicken."

Melvyn instructed me to fire them at once. I protested that I
had never done such a thing in my life. I didn't think that
Mother had ever fired anyone. I couldn't do it. Melvyn was firm
and pushed me in the direction of the silent kitchen.

The cook explained that she had worked in a diner and her
husband was a garage mechanic. They answered the ad because

they thought it would be pleasant to work in the country. On our way to a restaurant for dinner, Melvyn and I dropped them off at a bus stop.

Filming on Sam Goldwyn's production of *Tonight or Never* hadn't begun but Melvyn was required at the studio every day because of a mustache. Goldwyn had decided that Melvyn should grow one to make him appear older but couldn't make up his mind about what shape of mustache Melvyn should have. Accordingly, every day makeup people glued mustaches to his upper lip and each was photographed. Goldwyn then made his decision and Melvyn grew the mustache to order.

I worked at the piano all day in Melvyn's absence but found it difficult to concentrate. I was overwhelmed with loneliness and homesickness in that isolated, empty house so far from Mother, Lilli, the boys, Madame, the New York theater, my friends. I looked forward eagerly to the weekends when Melvyn would be home. We would play tennis by day and host a small but growing circle of friends in the evening. Often I entertained with a mini-concert, accompanied by my friend Eleanor Remick Warren, a composer and fine pianist.

I'd brought with me to California a pair of Pekingese dogs given me by Lilli on the opening night of *Tonight or Never*. I thought them silly animals at first but before the play closed I had become attached to them and brought them with me to the theater every night.

They had one lamentable habit, that of following me everywhere. On more than one occasion they appeared onstage with me for the curtain calls. Their loyal affection was a comfort during the long bleak days in that dusty landscape until, unhappily, they pursued our car one day as Melvyn and I drove off. Both were killed in the traffic.

I was so desolated by their loss that Melvyn planned a diversion. He had one week before filming would begin so he suggested a drive through Southern California. As we were crossing the Mojave Desert we were caught in a sudden, violent windstorm. The power of the gale was terrifying. Though we were in a heavy Cadillac, we wondered if the car could remain upright against such forces.

Moments later, as we huddled inside, choking in the fine dust that came through invisible cracks, the car was blown up a small hill and along the road, coming to rest near some forlorn wooden shacks. Melvyn lurched into the howling wind and knocked heavily with both fists. The door opened a crack and a disembodied hand beckoned us in.

When the storm ended as abruptly as it had begun, we resumed our journey, part of which took us across Death Valley. The experience in the storm and the starkness of the desert left a deep impression on me that was to influence my political career profoundly. I had come from a part of the country where the earth was moist, rich, and embracing. California, in contrast, struck me as harsh and unforgiving. As the daughter of a civil engineer, I knew that water often can be moved to where it is needed. I wondered if any effort was being made to establish reclamation projects to bring California's dry soil to life.

Politician

Melvyn began work at the studio on *Tonight or Never*. By coincidence, I was preparing for a production of the play myself. Homer Curran, a California producer, asked me to appear in *Tonight or Never* in his theaters in Los Angeles and San Francisco. I agreed, grateful for the opportunity to be active.

The only way to travel from our remote home in the Valley to rehearsals in Los Angeles was by car. Melvyn bought me a Pierce-Arrow limousine, an exceedingly thoughtful gesture. He hoped it would remind me of being chauffeured to the New York theater in Father's Pierce-Arrow. I appreciated his kindness deeply. I made the journey each day curled up in the roomy comfort of the limousine's rear seat with all the blinds drawn so I wouldn't have to see that I was in California.

It was 1932, a presidential election year. The incumbent, Herbert Hoover, was being challenged by a former governor of New York State, Franklin Delano Roosevelt, a Democrat many Republicans regarded as dangerously radical. Unemployment and poverty were sweeping the country in what was to be known as the Great Depression. Both men promised Americans prosperity.

Anxious to follow the campaign, I had a radio installed in my dressing room. On days when either candidate was scheduled to make a radio address, I would arrange to arrive at the theater in time to hear it. The lineups outside kitchens dispensing free soup astonished me. California papers wrote angry stories about jobless people pouring into the state looking for handouts. What was going on?

The Gahagan company, I knew, was struggling to survive. William was in Peru supervising dredging there while Frederick ran the Brooklyn headquarters. One day an outstanding engineer

applied to him for a job. Frederick told him with regret that he
couldn't afford to hire him. The man said he would work for
nothing; he couldn't bear to be idle. Frederick then confessed
that senior Gahagan engineers hadn't been paid for a month.
They would never believe that an engineer of that man's stature
would work for no wages.

I looked for signs in the political speeches that someone knew
how to put the country together. I'd always believed that problems could be solved, but what was happening in America was so
appalling I wondered if anyone could fix it.

I planned to vote Republican as Gahagans had for four generations, but nothing Hoover said reassured me. On the other hand,
Franklin Delano Roosevelt promised something he called a New
Deal—a snappy phrase—but was vague about what it meant and
how he would improve anything. I waited for either of them to
be more specific.

By the end of the campaign I knew I couldn't vote for Hoover.
Franklin Roosevelt wasn't much better. His arrogant self-assur-
ance put me off. I resolved not to vote at all.

When I heard Roosevelt's brilliant inaugural address I wished I
had voted Democrat. The ringing words put heart in the country.
He said:

> This great nation will endure as it has endured; will revive and
> prosper. So, first of all, let me assert my firm belief that the only
> thing we have to fear is fear itself—nameless, unreasoning,
> unjustified terror which paralyzes needed efforts to convert retreat
> into advance.

Like many others, my confidence in the White House was restored during the first few months of Roosevelt's administration,
as the creative ideas of the New Deal began to emerge. I was convinced we had a President aware of what was wrong and what to
do about it.

On the night of a dinner party in Pasadena, I decided to join
the Democratic party. All the guests were Republicans and they
talked of little else than their hatred of Roosevelt. They called his
New Deal "socialism" and said insulting things about his family,
his wife and his appearance. The answer to unemployment wasn't

Blue Eagle (N.R.A.) job creation, they said, but a toughly administered dole.

I thought they were callous. People need dignity and a feeling of self-worth. Except for those unable to work, a handout is no substitute for a job. If the group at that dinner party was representative of Republicans, it was time I stopped voting Republican.

My family was shocked. Mother associated Democrats with the unsavory politics of Tammany Hall. Frederick teased me unmercifully, holding me personally responsible for everything the Democrats did, as in "I see where *your Democrats* . . ." Billy was incredulous. Only Lilli took my aberration in stride. She thought everything I did was wonderful. She became a Democrat too.

Marriage with Melvyn was going along swimmingly, despite the fact we saw one another only on Sundays. He left early for the studio and came home in the evening, by which time I was putting on my makeup in the theater. Still, we richly enjoyed the time we spent together. I finally found courage to tell him I hated cigarettes. My friends had been wondering when I would break the news to Melvyn, a smoker, that I couldn't abide them. He cut down sharply.

One day he had news. Sam Goldwyn was sending him to New York to make a film as soon as work on *Tonight or Never* was completed. I asked what the film was about. He said he didn't know. It didn't matter because under the terms of his contract he had no choice but to do as Goldwyn wanted.

This was what I had been dreading. A bad part or a poor script could ruin his career. My heart sank.

The next morning I watched him shave. When he turned to kiss me, he found tears on my face. He thought I was crying because I hated California.

"Are you that unhappy, my dear?" he asked tenderly.

I didn't answer. I couldn't tell him that I feared for his future. After he left I consoled myself with the thought that Melvyn could aways return to the stage if his movie career ended.

Melvyn was waiting for me when I returned from the theater that night.

"I asked Goldwyn to release me from my contract when I finish the New York picture," he told me. "Sam said he might."

I threw my arms around him in joy and begged for details. Winning an argument with Sam Goldwyn, particularly about a contract, was almost unknown in Hollywood. Melvyn had shown rare courage and toughness. My heart was full of love for this remarkable man.

Melvyn went East and I longed to be with him. Instead I was opening in San Francisco in a week in a revival of *Trelawney of the 'Wells.'* It was an astonishing hit. My dressing room was filled with flowers every night and people cheered every curtain call.

One Sunday afternoon I had the bliss of singing with the San Francisco Opera Company. Madame had gone to Milan to live with Vera, but Lilli was in the audience and afterward joined me at a cast party. I was presented with a precious memento of the event, a framed concert program signed by everyone connected with the performance.

The following summer I sang *Aïda* in the Polo Grounds in New York to mark the tenth anniversary of its open-air musical season. It was a glorious occasion and I was well received. I couldn't avoid seeing signs that the Depression still lay heavily on the land. The concert was a benefit for two charitable organizations that were trying to cope with the misery of the children of the poor.

My brother Walter had graduated from Princeton and was preparing to go into law school at Columbia. Despite everything Father and the twins had done, Walter steadfastly refused to consider going into the family firm. He said before Father died that it would be like working for three fathers. Walter was having a marvelous time at school, getting top marks while also being a football star. In fact he made the United States Olympic football team that year.

On my return to California in July of 1932 I went immediately into rehearsals for Jerome Kern's *The Cat and the Fiddle*. At six-thirty one morning Melvyn and I were awakened by a phone call from Walter, who was in California to play football and had borrowed Melvyn's new Cadillac the night before to take Betty

Furness dancing. To his horror, the car was stolen from a night club parking lot.

The car was recovered eventually but Walter never forgot the grace with which Melvyn received the news so early in the morning. Melvyn, as my family was learning, has an infinite capacity for kindness.

I was in San Francisco playing a return engagement of *The Cat and the Fiddle*. Melvyn expected to join me but telephoned to say he was ill with influenza. A few nights later he turned up in my dressing room, so ill he could barely stand. He had persuaded a friend to drive him up from L.A. despite the fact that he still had a raging fever.

Several weeks of convalescence followed. As soon as he was able, Melvyn and I took a stroll through beautiful Golden Gate Park, one of the loveliest parks anywhere—and man-made on a bed of sand. We sat on a park bench, basking in the sun. Melvyn said in a casual tone:

"Would you like to go around the world?"

I sat up in delight. "I'd love it!" I exclaimed. "When did you get such a wonderful idea!"

He grinned. "Last night the foghorns in the harbor kept me awake for hours. It came to me that we should get on a ship and sail away."

"When do we start?"

"As soon as *The Cat and the Fiddle* closes," Melvyn said. "If it ever does."

It was a perfect time for the trip. I had saved a respectable amount of money from my theater engagements and Melvyn's two films had provided him with a nest egg as well, and Goldwyn had just released him.

We left Wilmington Harbor in Los Angeles, bound for France by way of the Panama Canal. Our ship was a cargo boat that would make several stops to take on coffee beans. Coming into the harbor at Costa Rica, the captain misjudged the tide and the ship rammed the dock. The gash in the bow was above the waterline and, after making a temporary repair, the captain assured us it would be safe to continue on to Panama.

I was on deck watching the loading of coffee beans when the

fragrant smell began to overwhelm me. Feeling nauseated, I left Melvyn and went to the other side of the boat to escape it. When we reached Panama the captain said the ship would be in drydock for a week for repairs. Melvyn and I took the opportunity to drive through a dense, forbidding tropical jungle to visit my cousin Sarah, who was married to a U. S. Army captain, John Evans, stationed on the Atlantic coast of Panama.

I was struck by the contrast in the sumptuous style of living the American garrison enjoyed compared to the destitute condition of black Panamanians. My cousin seemed to take for granted the luxurious facilities the army provided.

We boarded the mended cargo boat and sailed across the Atlantic. On the open sea my nausea returned. I blamed the thick, greasy sauce the cook spread liberally over everything. To Melvyn's consternation, I restricted my diet to potatoes and seltzer water.

"You must see a doctor when we get to Paris," he told me.

I told him I would be all right once we reached Paris. We would dine in my favorite restaurant and my appetite would return. As I predicted, I wolfed down *gigot de mouton* in Paris and seemed my old self. We made a quick trip to Rome to visit Melvyn's parents and his son, Gregory, and finally searched out a doctor only two days before our ship was due to leave for Port Said.

The doctor examined me in silence. When I had dressed and joined Melvyn in his office, the doctor looked at Melvyn and said gravely:

"Your wife, monsieur, is pregnant."

I laughed, incredulous. Both men looked at me disapprovingly.

Melvyn said, "Well, this means we can't continue our trip."

"What trip, monsieur?" asked the doctor.

"We are on our way around the world."

"Impossible!" the doctor cried. He gave us a list of dire predictions.

I shook my head impatiently, unbelieving. The doctor protested for a time and then subsided, seeing my determination. He gave me a prescription to control nausea. It hadn't been the greasy cooking after all.

Melvyn announced that we would take the first available ship home. He went to change our tickets but returned quite upset. It would cost us more to go back to the States direct than to continue around the world. "That settles it," I said. "We'll never have such a chance again. Let's keep on."

Indeed it was a rare time to be traveling. Our tickets around the world with unlimited stopovers had cost $750 apiece.

Melvyn agreed but his expression was worried. As soon as we boarded the Dutch ship at Marseilles and were out of the harbor I threw the nausea pills overboard.

"Now that I know what's the matter with me," I told Melvyn cheerfully, "I won't be needing them."

Because a trunk of my clothes had been left behind at Marseilles, we stayed longer than we intended in Cairo waiting for it, giving us time to cruise the Suez Canal and visit Palestine. We crossed the Sinai by train, transfixed by the empty white desert broken only by an occasional Arab on a camel, followed docilely by his wife on foot in a dusty black abaya.

Our first sight of the Holy Land at sunset was heavenly. Melvyn, whose grandparents had escaped the Russian pogrom in Odessa in 1871, was deeply moved when we visited the Wailing Wall. He had not been raised in the Jewish faith but he felt his ancestors in his blood. He said the emotion was like being hit by a tidal wave. That afternoon we purchased an Old Testament and read it together, seated on the curb outside the book store.

We drove forty miles to Tel Aviv through arid countryside where only a few stunted, twisted olive trees grew. This was the land that would be reclaimed by the Jewish pioneers, Halutzim. The next time we saw it, the countryside was lush with orchards.

In 1933 Tel Aviv was a bustling town of schools, libraries, colleges, banks, shops, small factories, hotels, temples and sidewalk cafés. We were impressed that there was no jail and that policemen went unarmed. One evening we saw the famed Habima Theater group perform in an outdoor arena. The performance was in Hebrew but though we couldn't follow the plot there was no mistaking their talent.

In Port Said we boarded a Dutch ship to sail the Red Sea to Ceylon. The voyage was memorable for my discovery of how much liquor the Dutch can consume. I'd been exposed to very lit-

tle drinking. Father had a beer now and then, and Mother served
wine and champagne to guests, but other than that our home was
abstemious. I was unnerved by the noise in the corridor outside
our stateroom every night as tipplers reeled off to bed.

After Ceylon we went to Bali, where Dan Totheroh had alerted
friends of his, Katherine and Jack Merchon. They were dancers
who had fallen in love with Bali five years earlier. They insisted
we move into their home by the sea where every morning
Katherine dispensed simple remedies in a clinic she maintained in
the garden. She explained that the Dutch colonial government
charged a staggering price for medicine so she started importing a
supply to help almost penniless natives.

The Merchons had a young houseboy, Murda. Katherine told
me that after they bought the house Murda continued to come
every day to take water from her well. She tried to make him understand he was trespassing. When she said the well belonged to
her, he was incredulous.

"No one can own water," he told her earnestly.

Katherine accepted that Murda was right, especially after she
discovered that the Dutch charged an exorbitant sum for fresh
water. From that time on, she was generous with her well.

Katie took me to see a Balinese healer named Ide Bagus Made,
a tall, gaunt man. He startled me by seizing my wrist and staring
intently into my face. In Malay he told Katherine that I was
pregnant. We were both surprised; my figure showed no sign of
it.

"Ask him if I'll be home in time for the baby's birth," I instructed her.

His answer, *nyonya one*, meant yes. He offered to perform a
ceremony that would protect my pregnancy if I would return the
next day. I readily agreed. Katie warned me that the ceremony
was powerful; many women faint during Ide Bagus Made's rites.

The healer began the next day by giving me a tiny amulet the
size of my little finger, which he said I should wear constantly
until the baby was born. Well into the ceremony he put his
mouth to my forehead and said some words I didn't understand.
A force like a powerful electric shock surged through me. I had to

concentrate fiercely to keep from passing out. Katie later explained he was talking to the baby.

I wasn't sick a single day of the trip from then on. I wore the amulet always until the hour I went to the hospital to give birth, when mysteriously it disappeared.

The Balinese taught me a trick that I later used in Congress. If a Balinese is oppressed by someone, the solution is mentally to discard the offender. Imagine the person has disappeared from the face of the earth and carry on. When I came to the time when I could not bear a Southern bigot, Congressman John Rankin, I caused him to stop existing for me. The tactic worked so well that I could pass him in the hall and literally not see him.

Just before we left Bali, Katherine and Jack Merchon adopted Murda. When war broke out in the Pacific they gave him their estate and returned to the United States. Later they learned that the Japanese killed Murda. They have never gone back to Bali.

When the United States was involved in the war in Vietnam, I often thought about the durable, stable, generous villages of Bali where the Balinese culture has survived centuries of colonial rule. Vietnamese villages with similar heritages were destroyed by us in that tragic war.

Our next port of call was Hong Kong where friends of Melvyn's aunt launched us on a tour of the island and a series of delicious but overwhelming sixteen-course meals. To my consternation, my normally courteous husband got up in the middle of dinner and stretched out on a bench nearby. I carried on, chatting and eating, in the hope that our Chinese hosts would think mid-meal naps were normal in America.

When we left I could see that he was extremely ill. His guess was malaria, a hunch confirmed when our ship reached Shanghai. A doctor there dosed him with a vile-tasting medicine which he said would make Melvyn feel worse at first. Eventually it would work, he assured us, and Melvyn would never have malaria again.

The next few weeks were a horror. Melvyn was in a cycle of fevers as high as 105 degrees which caused him to sweat profusely, followed by a plunge into shivering chills requiring piles of blankets. A Chinese servant, called the night coolie, sat outside our bedroom door and helped me nurse him, bringing basins of soapy water so I could bathe Melvyn until the fever broke, helping me to change the sopping sheets, and then assisting with the mountain of blankets needed for the next part of the cycle.

Melvyn lost twenty-five pounds during the ordeal. As promised, he never had malaria again, not even when he served in the India-Burma-China theater during World War II.

As soon as Melvyn was on his feet we were taken in tow by Clara and Arthur Sowerby. Arthur was a remarkable man, born in China to missionaries, fluent in Mandarin and several other dialects, a collector of flora and fauna that he later catalogued in the Smithsonian. The Sowerbys were childless and lived in a rambling one-story house with a huge kennel filled with dogs they adored.

The Sowerbys were our knowledgeable guides to the fascinating city of Shanghai, which not long before had been bombed by the Japanese, an ominous prelude to the war in the Pacific. Night after night we attended performances by Mei Lan-fang, considered to be China's greatest living actor, and marveled at the grace with which he played the women's roles for which he was famous.

We were invited to tea, where we met a number of Chinese intellectuals, including Dr. Hu Shih, later chancellor of the University of Peking and in 1938 ambassador to the U.S., the author Lin Yutang, and Mei Lan-fang. Another guest, known as Cassandra, described in the *Chinese Critic* what happened when I asked Mei to teach me some of the gestures he used on stage:

> "And how," asked Helen Gahagan, turning excited eyes on Mei Lan-fang (it was between a dish of mushrooms steaming in a luscious dark sauce and a heavenly soup made inside a melon), "how," she asked, "does the woman on the Chinese stage show that someone is distasteful to her, you know, the get-away-from-me sort of thing?"
>
> Like a fluttering wing, Mei's pale hand wavered for an instant at the rim of the table, then with the sharpness of an engraving he made the exquisite and eloquent gesture, his shoulders and head obliquely drawn to one side, as the hand darted inside the sleeve, which was flung toward and then was swept away from the distasteful one with an air of complete dismissal.
>
> "But," cried Miss Gahagan, "we have a convention in our theater almost like that, and in the old days, isn't it true Melvyn? (she raised inquiring eyebrows at her husband who nodded in

confirmation) in the old days when women wore enormous skirts with slight trains, they would draw away disdainfully, gather the billowing skirt in one hand and swish, swish, sweep it toward and away from the scorned one. Like this."

Whereupon she made such a dramatic gesture that she almost upset the chef d'oeuvre, which arrived just at that instant, the hollowed melon like a great jade bowl, and inside the lotus bud chicken, the mushrooms, green vegetables and ham arranged in an ingenious platter.

On a breathlessly hot day we journeyed to Peking by train. Though temperatures hovered around 110 degrees we could not resist visiting the wonders of the Forbidden City and the astounding Great Wall which, years later, was the only man-made structure clearly visible to astronauts on the moon, and the Summer Palace.

When we mentioned meeting the renowned Mei Lan-fang, we were told that Mei was only China's second-greatest actor. Peking's Wang Chow Loh was the finest actor in China but he perfomed rarely, and only as he felt like it, giving his fans but a few hours' notice.

Luckily he decided to perform while we were there. Friends got us tickets and we sat in a stifling hall where attendants threw hot towels on request so that members of the audience could wipe their sweating faces. I put up my arm and caught one, discovering that the towels were deliciously refreshing.

Wang Chow Loh arrived on stage, electrifying the audience. He moved with the power of Feodor Chaliapin, was as handsome and graceful as John Barrymore, and could clown as an equal to Charles Chaplin. If there was anyone else on stage with him, I don't remember it.

Before we left Shanghai we had a somber discussion with the Sowerbys about the danger of a Japanese invasion. Arthur shrugged, "It may come, but neither Clara nor I will leave the dogs."

I never saw Clara again. After the bombing of Pearl Harbor they were taken prisoner. She died in a Japanese prison camp. Arthur survived, a broken man. Later I had the pleasure of introducing a special bill in the House of Representatives which made it possible for him to come to Washington where he completed the cataloguing of his fine collection.

Melvyn and I were welcomed to Osaka by a young business acquaintance of the Gerlis, my brother Frederick's in-laws. We found our European-style hotel ugly and asked if the man could recommend a Japanese hotel.

He looked at me as if he couldn't believe what he heard.

"You want to stay in a Japanese hotel? They are *very* different."

"I'm sure they must be," I replied, "and that's why we'd like to stay in one."

We went by train to nearby Kyoto the next morning and took a taxi to our Japanese hotel. A smiling, bowing line of women in kimonos greeted us at the door. We were led to a tiny room furnished only with a small chest on which there was a single tiger lily in an elegant vase. This room opened onto a larger room with two glass walls overlooking a lovely garden. I saw no beds, no closets, not even a hook.

The escort said a bath was being prepared for us. Twenty minutes later a woman appeared to escort us to a door she opened. Gesturing us through, she closed it behind us. We saw no sign of a shower or bath. Melvyn opened a second door and found a large wooden tub filled with steaming water, around which were arranged small wooden stools and tables bearing soap, sponges and brushes. On one wall were shower heads.

We deduced that we were to soap and shower ourselves first and then soak in the wooden tub. We dropped our robes and began. The door opened and a man, naked except for a loincloth, entered. I prepared to scream but he approached me in a composed, businesslike manner and started sociably to wash my back.

I pleaded to Melvyn to make him leave but Melvyn was hugely amused. When the man finished tending to us, he withdrew. I soaked a long time in the tub, apprehensive about what would happen next.

When we returned from dinner that night, a box spring and mattress had been arranged on the floor with a mosquito netting draped above it. We started to undress. The door opened and a half-dozen women came into the room and began helping Melvyn off with his clothes.

"Helen, get them away from me!" he cried.

I beamed and said sweetly that I was enjoying myself. "Relax," I advised him.

One afternoon in Tokyo we were stopped on the street by men asking for Melvyn's autograph. A sizable crowd gathered around him, obviously awed to see a living movie star. One of Melvyn's pictures was playing in Tokyo.

I tossed and turned that night in an irritable mood. I realized that I was offended that Melvyn's fans had pushed me aside with indifference. I decided I would have to face my jealous feelings. What did I want? An actor husband who wasn't a success? Would that make me happy? No. I loved Melvyn and wanted what was best for him. He had his career and I had mine.

I thought it through. There would be times again when he would be center stage and I would be pushed into the wings, and times when the positions would be reversed. That was the kind of marriage I had wanted, and that's what I got. Our careers were separate and the audiences were not the same. If I resolved not to let being temporarily eclipsed bother me, we would survive.

On the long crossing of the Pacific, I used the pool on our liner vigorously every day. The sight of me, roundly pregnant, made the captain anxious. He didn't relish the prospect of having a delivery at sea. "Please, *please*, Mrs. Douglas, come out," he would call. "It really isn't safe for you to swim so much."

When we stepped off the ship in San Francisco after more than eight months' absence, Melvyn and I looked like two plucked chickens. He had never regained the shocking weight loss he suffered during his bout of malaria and, despite my obviously pregnant middle, the rest of me was matchsticks.

Melvyn started work at once on a new film, *Counsellor-At-Law*, with John Barrymore and I telephoned Mother with the good news about the baby. Frau Gaehler arrived by train a week later to take care of me and a few days after that, Lilli banged on the door of our apartment in the Château Élysée in Los Angeles. We fell into each other's arms with cries of joy.

"Lilli, why didn't you let me know you were coming?" I demanded.

"Couldn't," she replied. "Came by bus. It was cheaper than the train."

"Where are your bags?"

"In a private house next door."

"Lilli!"

"Well, from the way you described the apartment I guessed there wouldn't be room for me. I see I was right. When I told the woman next door who you are and why I have to be with you, she gave me a room."

That night Lilli went to bed early, exhausted from the long bus trip, and Melvyn and I entertained two friends for bridge, Robert and Bea Greig, actors we had known in New York. We'd been playing cards for about an hour when I heard a faint sound overhead. I looked up to see the chandelier swaying.

I pointed to it and asked curiously, "What's causing that?"

"Earthquake!" Bob shouted. "Stand in the doorways!"

Bob and Bea stood in one doorway and Melvyn pulled me into another, unaccountably placing his hand over my mouth. Later he explained that he did so in order to prevent hysterics. When the entire building began to sway, we knew we would have to get out. After a few minutes of near-panic, we found the emergency stairs. Frau Gaehler, who had been out, met us in the lobby. Lilli, whom nothing less than an earthquake could waken, came running in her nightclothes from the house next door. Together we rushed into the street crowded with frightened people.

It was early morning before the earth stopped heaving. We waited in tense silence to make certain the tremors were over and then cheered with relief and embraced all around. For five minutes, everyone loved everyone else. We walked Bob and Bea back to their car and my darling sister to her temporary home. Melvyn and I went to bed, but couldn't sleep. My labor had begun.

On October 7, 1933, I was in the Pasadena Hospital. Melvyn read aloud a newspaper account of the earthquake the night before and tenderly asked if there was anything he could do for me.

"Yes," I said, "I'd like an ice-cream soda."

Melvyn and Lilli stayed with me all day, holding my hand

through the labor spasms. I insisted on walking to the delivery room rather than being wheeled like a slab of meat on a table. Melvyn obtained permission to stay with me in the delivery room while Lilli waited down the hall.

The last thing I remember is being impatient. "This is taking too long," I told the nurses. "I'm going back to my room."

It was morning when I opened my eyes. Melvyn and Lilli were still with me. Melvyn kissed me and whispered:

"We have a beautiful seven-and-a-half-pound baby boy, Helen."

When I opened my eyes a second time, Melvyn placed the infant beside me.

A second earthquake greeted the baby and me on our homecoming but this time the tremors weren't so strong as to drive us into the street. Still, they were alarming. I was finding California's chronically unsafe environment a lot to get accustomed to.

The hard birth had weakened me and I convalesced for some weeks, reading plays sent to me from New York. They were all awful. Then Dan Totheroh brought me his play, *Moor Born*, which was all about the Brontë family. I loved the part of Emily Brontë on sight but Dan warned me that several Broadway producers had turned down the play. They considered it too somber for audiences.

"I'll peddle it myself when I get to New York," I promised him. "This play is wonderful."

Melvyn and Lilli left for New York, where Melvyn was to begin rehearsals for Jesse Lynch Williams' play *No More Ladies*, directed by my old friend Harry Wagstaff Gribble. Five weeks later Frau Gaehler and I followed with the baby, who still had only two thirds of his name, Gahagan Douglas. We were waiting for inspiration for his first name.

We stayed a few weeks in Brooklyn with Mother, who was still living in the new house. Lilli had moved in with her after the divorce. Her oldest son, Bobby, at his father's insistence was with him, but the two younger ones lived with her. Frederick and Alice were a few doors away with their children. We had a joyful family reunion and then Melvyn, Frau Gaehler, the baby and I

moved to a New York apartment. We finally had agreed on a
name for our son, Peter.

The apartment wasn't particularly attractive but it was handy
to the theater. I spent my days taking Dan's play, *Moor Born*,
from one producer to another. I was turned down everywhere
until finally I persuaded George Bushar and John Tuerk to do the
play on condition that I would take only the Equity minimum
salary. Melvyn agreed to direct for no pay at all.

Melvyn put together a splendid cast. Frances Starr played
Charlotte Brontë, Edith Barrett played Anne, and Glenn Anders
had the role of the brother, Branwell Brontë. All of them unselfishly accepted Equity minimum pay. Like us, they found the
play strong and compelling and believed it would find an audience. We kept the running costs as low as possible.

Dan's play needed a small, intimate theater. The Belmont, a
few doors east of Brady's Playhouse, was ideal. We took it though
it meant that the total take, even if we sold out every performance, would bring in only enough money to break even or a little better.

Melvyn proved to be one of the finest directors I had ever
known. I've never understood why he didn't do more of it. As directors who work with him have found when seeking his suggestions, his ideas about a production invariably have insight and inspiration.

Melvyn knew exactly what *Moor Born* needed to come alive.
His direction was masterful in bringing out values that Dan
Totheroh had only sketched. I found him precise about what he
wanted, patient, polite and unhurried. He also was a perfectionist
who insisted on repeating a scene again and again until he was
satisfied.

From the first day, we rehearsed against the recorded background sound of winds wailing over the moors. I complained that
it was getting on my nerves and asked if we could be free of it for
just a week while we concentrated on our parts. Melvyn refused.

"The winds are an integral part of the play, something the
Brontës had to live with," he explained. "You'll have to get used
to them, as they did."

Certainly in *Moor Born* he got more out of me that I could

have done by myself. I would have made Emily Brontë softer but
he kept cutting away, cutting away. At home after the rehearsal,
he continued to work with me. He was especially tough about the
scene where Branwell, who is mortally ill, returns home drunk
from his nightly visit to the local tavern and sinks to his knees in
front of his sisters. Emily rises, strides to her brother and lifts
him up, crying, "Not on your knees, Branwell, not on your knees!
Stand up to it! *Stand up to it!*"

Melvyn thought I put too much compassion into the line. He
insisted that I bring out the power of Emily's plea to Branwell,
who had not managed to face life, that he must stand up and
confront death.

"Darling," Melvyn would say, "you've got it in you. You've
got to be tougher."

And he was right. He had that capacity as a director to get
more from every performer. In this he resembled Madame Cehanovska. She never cared what she said about my shortcomings or
about how tired I was becoming as she made me repeat something over and over. And I never resented it. Good strong direction never humiliated me, as it did some. The only direction I de-
test is the indecisive kind, or incompetence.

My favorite director is someone who takes a hard line and
knows exactly what he wants. Melvyn was like that; David
Belasco was like that.

Moor Born was an artistic success. Brontë enthusiasts flocked
to the Belmont for the six weeks of our limited run and poured
backstage afterward to tell us how moved they'd been. Sometimes
it seemed that the entire audience of the tiny theater was trying
to get into our dressing rooms to congratulate us.

In a review of *Moor Born*, Stark Young wrote:

> Miss Gahagan is one of the very few people on our stage who
> could have had most of the perennial banal or flaunting things
> written for it. Perhaps she should have accepted them; perhaps
> not. At any rate she deserves not a better [play] but a better-writ-
> ten role for her return.

In short, the critics didn't like *Moor Born*. We were disappointed but still it was worth doing. I would rather have had my
six weeks as Emily Brontë than star for a year in a hit.

Melvyn and I determined that we would appear together in a play the following season. For weeks we read plays, looking for something interesting with two evenly balanced parts. Unable to find something we both wanted, we asked Dan Totheroh and George O'Neil to write a play for us.

They began in the summer of 1934 and Melvyn and I returned to Los Angeles. He was to appear in four films in a row, all released in 1935, and I had the lead in Maxwell Anderson's *Mary of Scotland*, which played in San Francisco and Los Angeles.

My reviews were marvelous. Claude A. La Belle wrote in the San Francisco *News*:

> Helen Gahagan was a lovely, intelligent and sympathetic Mary. Almost never out of key with the general tone of the play, there were a half dozen times when she rose to tremendous dramatic heights . . . she is as graceful with her hands as any actress I know . . .

The San Francisco *Chronicle*'s George C. Warren commented:

> In the title role, Helen Gahagan's sensitive, inspired performance, rising to great power in scenes of high dramatic quality, made this "saucy lass and a keen one" an unforgettable figure.

Variety declared:

> Miss Gahagan—she's a fav here through several other swell performances—does a showmanly job of her title role . . .

The Los Angeles reviews were also raves. The *Examiner* declared that I was "radiant in personality and truly gifted as an actress," and Eleanor Barnes of the *Daily News* wrote:

> Helen Gahagan, whose beauty is fragile, whose voice is stirring, and who is indeed a "ladybird" with a "saucy" manner, last night achieved glowing recognition before an ermined audience for her performance in the title role.

In the spring Melvyn and I returned to New York to begin work on the play Totheroh and O'Neil had created for us, *Mother Lode*. Set on the West Coast in the 1860s and 1870s when silver was being mined in the Comstock Lode, it concerned a visionary pioneer (Melvyn) and an itinerant singer (me). To reproduce San Francisco at a time when it was a brawling mining camp, we needed a huge cast, lavish costumes and a number of elaborate sets.

Melvyn and I recklessly invested our savings in order to ensure that *Mother Lode* was mounted in the style it deserved. Unfortunately, the Group Theatre was producing *Gold Eagle Guy*, a play set in the identical period, which opened at the same time as *Mother Lode*. The Group Theatre production was a tighter, better-written play. Critic John Anderson was quite right when he wrote:

> *Gold Eagle Guy* does the trick and does it with tricky completeness. *Mother Lode* is merely a dramatic echo of *Gold Eagle Guy*, not actually, of course, but in the sense that Dan Totheroh and George O'Neil, both infatuated with Americana, have thumbed over the same material so recently presented in the new play by the Group Theatre. . . .

George O'Neil, a poet, and Dan Totheroh, a native Californian whose family crossed the country with a mule train, were indeed infatuated with Americana. Melvyn and I had loved *Mother Lode*, which Melvyn directed as well as starring with me, but we had been unhappy with some parts of the script. At our request, Dan and George made many revisions—but not enough.

We closed in two weeks. Melvyn and I lost our savings.

Fortuitously, I received a handsome movie offer that would bail me out. Merian C. Cooper, an RKO producer, wired from California to ask if I would play the title role in a film of H. Rider Haggard's *She*. I had loved the classic when I read it in my teens, so I accepted without seeing the script.

Melvyn stayed in New York to play opposite Violet Heming in Louis Bromfield's *De Luxe*, while I boarded a train to California with Peter, Frau Gaehler and my school friend Alis de Sola. I was disconcerted that Alis and I received a stream of mash notes from amorous fellow passengers.

"No one ever did that to me before," I told Alis. "I think you must give people the eye."

I knew she didn't, of course. Alis used to fret that there must be something wrong with her. Men were always making passes.

She was perplexed that she overtly did nothing to give the impression she would welcome advances and yet constantly was propositioned, while I habitually greeted people, men and women, with warm, spontaneous hugs and never had a pass. She said I had a distant look that protected me.

I was unaware of the liberties that screenwriters and producers take with even famous books. The script for *She* was appalling. I told Merian Cooper that he was wasting his money having a trained actress play the part. The lead had been reduced to a paper-thin, superficial role. I told him that the film couldn't possibly succeed because it would affront everyone who loved the Haggard book.

Cooper laughed and patted my hand condescendingly. He said he would worry about the reception of the movie. All I had to do was act.

I appealed to Alis to see what she could do to improve the script. She discovered that some twelve writers had taken a run at putting it together. There was nothing she could do to change it. Very kindly she came to my dressing room during the filming and together we rewrote my lines, keeping the cues so the other actors wouldn't be thrown. We managed to eliminate much of the drivel but the overall script remained atrocious.

I knew on the first day that motion pictures were not for me. Even still cameras make me uneasy and self-conscious, and I found I couldn't relax at all in front of film cameras. I detested having a makeup artist constantly at my side, fussing with my face and hair. The rhythms of film-making distracted my concentration. I fumed at the long, debilitating waits for lights and cameras to be adjusted, and then the suddenness of turning on the required intense emotion.

I felt that everything I did in *She* was out of my control. The director, the cameramen and the technicians ran the show. I was a puppet. I missed the audience. Without one, I ran without batteries. There is a flow of energy between a theater audience and a live performance. The actor works to hold attention and the vitality required to succeed keeps the actor in a state of creative tension, night after night.

There was a swarm of spectators idly watching the filming, but they weren't an audience. They would loiter and then make off on urgent mysterious errands. It wasn't possible to relate to them or to engross them. Like everyone else associated with the film— except me—they were technicians.

The effects for *She* were done by the same woman who did *King Kong* and they were quite spectacular. There is one impressive scene involving fire when my costar Randolph Scott wakes up. Another scene required me to descend some stairs, lit from behind, in a diaphanous gown made of several layers of chiffon. The director was dissatisfied with the dress and kept stripping away the layers until I was down to the last one. The crew gaped and Alis said she could see my pores but I was impervious. I was just waiting for the ordeal to end.

Meanwhile I couldn't adjust in the proper Hollywood style to the stream of fan magazine writers who came for interviews. They generally found me in bed in our Château Élysée apartment, trying to protect myself against my fatal tendency to become exhausted without warning. Once, to the astonishment of Alis who happened to drop in, I received a number of writers while wearing curlers in my hair and cold cream smeared all over my face.

"Oh, Helen," Alis said, and collapsed into a chair laughing. She said I had no idea what a shock it was to the press, which was accustomed to movie queens greeting them in satin and mink.

Melvyn returned to Los Angeles in time to be with me for the first preview of *She*. The movie was no better than I expected. I was surprised that people seemed to enjoy it. Melvyn said that I had got the knack of reducing my performance to suit the camera, which magnified facial expressions that stage actors were accustomed to doing somewhat broadly. Still, *She* was by no means a hit. It fell in the indeterminate category somewhere between flop and success.

It was shown across the country in a double booking with another Merian Cooper production, *Ben Hur*, which pulled in audiences. From time to time it appeared after that in scattered theaters. To my embarrassment it turned up in the Los Angeles area in 1950 when I was campaigning for the Senate, and then it dropped out of sight.

In the early sixties I had a letter from film producer Raymond Rohauer asking my help in finding a print of *She*. RKO didn't have one nor, apparently, did anyone else. He had been informed that the original negative had been destroyed and hoped I had a print. I didn't.

He wrote again in 1973. After an eight-and-a-half-year search, his persistence had been rewarded. He'd just acquired world rights to the original RKO film. He said it was just as absorbing as he'd remembered it in 1936. He planned to release it in the United States and abroad. He said flattering things about my performance and hoped I would help promote the reissue.

I'm afraid I wasn't very cooperative. I was no more eager to promote it in the seventies than I had been in the thirties. I was curious to know why Rohauer had been so anxious to track down the film. He told me it was listed among the fifty classic movies of all time. I was stunned.

She appeared in a few small theaters in New York City and then was given a gala reception in Radio City Music Hall during its 1976 Art Deco Week. That same year it was shown in a Paris film festival. The following year, when it appeared in Los Angeles, the Los Angeles *Times* critic wrote:

> One of the true rarities amidst the County Museum of Art's massive RKO retrospective is the long-unseen 1935 version of H. Rider Haggard's *She* . . . starring Helen Gahagan and Randolph Scott. . . . Replete with monumental sets designed in a kind of Art Deco Barbaric and a thundering, ominous Max Steiner score, *She* today seems at once terrifically corny yet almost engaging and finally amazingly poignant, thanks to Miss Gahagan. . . . Miss Gahagan's imperious ruler is not a Maria Montez-style Queen of Atlantis. She is in fact a tragic figure, cursed with her "burden of immortality." . . . Fortunately, Miss Gahagan, in her film debut after a notable career in the theater and opera, was nonetheless able to make human and vulnerable the monstrous She. That *She* remains compelling in its tragic conception of eternal youth is due virtually to Miss Gahagan's eloquence and intelligence.

Many films live on deservedly. *Ninotchka*, with Greta Garbo and Melvyn, is one of them. It richly deserves to be seen by new generations. But *She?* It's a mystery to me that anyone would consider it a classic.

I retired from the movie business permanently. Alis liked to explain that I simply didn't know what to do with junk. Melvyn, a more deliberate actor who could find something worthwhile in almost any part, was to have great success in film. That year he did *She Married Her Boss* with Claudette Colbert and his career took off.

I returned gratefully to the stage. I played the lead in *The Merry Widow* in the Los Angeles Philharmonic Auditorium, in what was the first of a popular series of light operas. The engagement was a joy from beginning to end. Audiences adored it. We took it to San Francisco to more adulation. Critics spoke of "magic," and said I had scored "one of the most notable personal hits of many seasons." It was balm to my damaged self-esteem after *She.*

Madame Cehanovska was back in America and with George came to the Coast to see me. I urged them to move to California. George could find work in films, I said, and I would be thrilled to resume studying with Zolota again. To my delight, they agreed. Madame and I worked on Puccini operas, widening my repertoire, but I also concentrated on polishing the operas I knew well. If I could do *Tosca* with the San Francisco Opera Company, a respected company, it might be the opening that would lead to the Met.

To our great sorrow, the *Tosca* engagement fell through at the last minute, for reasons beyond our control.

I continued to shuttle back and forth between California and New York. When *The Merry Widow* closed, I appeared on Broadway with Clifton Webb in the Theatre Guild's production of *And Stars Remain,* by Julius and Philip Epstein.

Unfortunately it was the poorest Guild comedy production in an otherwise long and distinguished chain of hits. The Guild hierarchy attended rehearsals, stopping us every few minutes to change a line. They would all laugh heartily at their own wit with each revision, but neither Clifton nor I could see any improvement. The original Epstein script had merit but the daily improvisations by the management made it increasingly dreary.

I telephoned Melvyn from Pittsburgh, where we opened our run. I told him that I didn't want to come into New York with the play. Melvyn told me to be calm. He would fly to Pittsburgh and see if it was as bad as I said. He was sure I was wrong.

After the performance he came backstage. I said, "Well?"

"Let's get out of the theater," he answered. "Take off your makeup and we'll walk a little."

We walked in silence until I could bear it no longer.

"Melvyn, please tell me what you think of it. I'm embarrassed to be on stage in that mess!"

"No wonder," he said. "It's even worse than you thought. But you mustn't leave it."

I stopped, amazed. "*Why not?*" I wailed.

"It's a Guild production," he explained. "It'll be accepted. Stop worrying."

Melvyn was right. *And Stars Remain* was accepted by the critics and public alike. I have never understood why.

On my return to Los Angeles I took Mother and Herbert, Lilli's second son, with me. I thought it would be a good change for Herbert and I hoped that he and Peter would become friends. We were renting a large, old-fashioned house on Rossmore Street that had a lovely garden, and there was plenty of room.

Melvyn's parents also decided to move to California. Melvyn found them a small housekeeping apartment, which they adored. With so many relatives about, our small son Peter was in seventh heaven. For a change I wasn't working and could be with him every day when my voice exercises were done.

Before long Melvyn's father required an operation to remove polyps in his nose. It was a simple procedure but he died of a heart attack on the operating table. Melvyn was shocked and distraught. To help his grief-stricken mother in that terrible time, we arranged for her to live with us for a while.

Billy drove to Los Angeles to visit and pick up Mother. On the return trip, they had a serious car accident. Both were thrown out of the car onto a pile of rocks. William's right ear was almost severed and Mother's back suffered a frightful wound.

I flew to Yellowstone and arranged for their removal from the hospital there to Los Angeles by train. Two nurses met the stretchers at the station. Both patients were taken by ambulance to the hospital, where Billy's ear was sewn back. He was able to fly home soon afterward, but Mother's recovery was slow. For a month, until her strength returned, she stayed with us.

It made a full, busy household. At the same time I had an opportunity I welcomed. The San Francisco Opera Company wanted me to sing Puccini's *Suor Angelica*. While I studied the role, Melvyn commissioned the brilliant sculptor Isamu Noguchi to do a bust of me.

Noguchi was then a young man whose great career was just beginning. He required a month of sittings but they worked out well for us both. I studied *Suor Angelica* and he studied me. We both concentrated intently on what we were doing, and each did not disturb the other. The silence and sense of tranquil communication is a memory I cherish. He is not only a genius but a richly humane man with no sharp edges.

Melvyn was awed by the completed bust. He said to me, "It looks like you now. It looks like pictures of your grandmother. It will probably look like you when you're old."

When I was ill forty years later he used to look at me sleeping and then go into the living room and stand before the Noguchi bust. It was as he had predicted, he told me; I still looked like the sculpture.

My performance in *Suor Angelica* was well received. The San Francisco *News* of December 3, 1935, said of it:

> That particular dynamic quality which causes Miss Gahagan to dominate every scene in which she appears on the dramatic stage was no less compelling in the opera setting. Her voice proved clean and dramatic, of graceful, vibrant timbre.

The *Examiner* said I scored "a personal success," the *Bulletin* spoke of a voice which "evinced careful and intelligent training, dramatic in quality and beautifully intoned," and the *Chronicle* predicted my debut in opera would "lead to greater successes."

I was encouraged to concentrate on preparing myself for the career in opera I wanted so much. At the end of a year of hard work, I was ready to try another tour in Europe. Walter Hofstötter, manager of my previous tours, was happy at the news. He told me that I was remembered fondly in Middle European concert halls.

Unlike opera, which I loved, concerts were a strain. I found it an ordeal to walk out on a bare stage under glaring lights to sing with a single piano for accompaniment. The relationship between a singer and accompanist is a close, mutually dependent one. I didn't want to work with someone I didn't know. I cabled Walter that I was bringing Sanford Schlussel with me.

Walter cabled back that he'd already engaged a pianist, Fritz Kuba, an Austrian. It would be insulting to bring an American pianist, he said.

I had an ugly suspicion that Hofstötter didn't want Schlussel because he was Jewish. Melvyn thought I might be right. We both had been disturbed at stories of rising anti-Semitism in Germany. I cabled Walter that I wouldn't sing in Germany. If Jews weren't welcome there, I wouldn't go.

I was booked to sail in March, 1937, on the fastest liner ever built at that time, the luxurious *Queen Mary*. The day before I was to fly to New York to board the ship, Melvyn surprised me by announcing that he was coming along. He had studied his schedule. By booking passage on the *Queen Mary* both ways, he would be back in California to start work on a new film, *That Certain Age*, and still have time for a day and a half in Paris with me.

It was an expensive, romantic plan. We sailed together on what I calculated was my twenty-ninth Atlantic crossing and had a rapturous few hours in Paris, after which he caught the boat train to Cherbourg and I caught another train for Salzburg.

Smiling Walter Hofstötter was waiting on the station platform, dressed as usual in his Alpine leather shorts and a small, tight woolen jacket. Beside him was Fritz Kuba, the Austrian hired as my accompanist. Walter was his usual relaxed and friendly self, but I found Fritz chilly and severe.

Kuba and I began work the next morning. My trepidation had been unnecessary. We worked as smoothly as if we had been touring together all our professional lives. We spent a week preparing my programs, which included for the first time some charming songs by Joseph Marx, an Austrian considered by his countrymen second only to Richard Strauss.

Dr. Marx, hearing that I planned to sing his songs in the Salzburg Festival series, sent an invitation to visit him in Vienna if I was stopping there on my way to Prague for my first concert. When Walter learned of it he was delighted. He said when Dr. Marx heard me sing he might offer to accompany me in Salzburg and perhaps even in Munich.

"Munich!" I cried. "But I told you not to make any bookings for me in Germany!"

Walter looked shamefaced. "It was necessary," he told me. "You must have Munich notices before singing in Salzburg. It is very important."

I asked if he had booked me elsewhere in Germany. "Yes," he confessed, "in Bad Reichenhall."

His explanation was that I would need a rest between the Munich and Salzburg engagements. What better place for it than the Bad Reichenhall *Kurort* I loved so much, where I would have an entire week. He had booked only one concert there, on the grounds that I might as well sing while I was resting.

Much as I disliked the prospect of singing in Hitler's Germany, I could see Walter's reasoning.

In Vienna I called on Joseph Marx, a friendly, outgoing man who put me at ease at once. He was a big, heavyset, sleepy-looking person with a shock of gray hair. His drowsiness vanished the instant he sat down at the piano. Some composers aren't great musicians but Dr. Marx was brilliant. I sang for him joyfully for an hour, after which he rose, kissed my hand and asked if he could accompany me at the Salzburg Festival.

Fritz Kuba was waiting for me in the lobby of my hotel with bad news. The director of concerts in Prague would not accept him. He had sent word that a Czech pianist would accompany me. I was annoyed that I would have to rehearse all over again with a strange musician, and baffled. What did this mean? What did the Czechs have against an Austrian?

In Prague the director greeted me with another pronouncement. He said I must change my program. He didn't want me to sing any German lieder.

I replied that I couldn't make any substitutions. Why was he asking such a thing?

His manner was cold. "If you sing German lieder in a Czech concert hall, there might be a riot," he told me. I gaped. He went on, with rising choler, "Why do you, an American, want to sing German songs anyway? You should be singing American songs."

I dug in my heels and refused to make any changes. His voice grew louder.

"You're also singing the songs of the modern composer Joseph Marx," he said. "He's an *Austrian!* Czechs don't trust Germans *or* Austrians. They are the same. They are all Germans." I would not budge.

I couldn't believe the director. An audience of music lovers would not hold Brahms, Schumann and Marx responsible for the Nazi movement. I was calm and controlled as I went through the program, which may have had a pacifying effect on the audience. In any case, the admiring reviews the next day seemed to belie the director's forebodings.

The next concerts in Budapest, Innsbruck and Scheveningen also passed without incident. I was scoring a hit everywhere. When Kuba and I flew to Bad Reichenhall, Lilli joined us. She'd been in England visiting the family of her new fiancé, a British journalist who later was killed early in World War II.

Lilli and I were awakened every morning by the sound of gunfire. The first time I heard it I sat bolt upright in bed. Lilli, who hated Germans, told me it was Hitler's army training the local reserves for war. When Walter Hofstötter arrived in Bad Reichenhall he laughed and said Lilli was mistaken. We were hearing only the guns of hunters. I didn't believe him, but it was also hard to accept that Germany was again preparing to wage a war in Europe.

In Munich an old friend, a Dutch woman, was waiting in the hotel lobby to see me. She had come from Holland to hear my concert that night. It was stuffy in the hotel, she said. Did I want to visit with her while we walked outside?

As soon as we were on the street, her voice dropped to a whisper.

"It isn't safe to speak freely indoors," she said. "Nazi informers are everywhere."

I was chilled as she went on to tell me that German munitions factories were working around the clock again. Hitler was giving speeches all over Germany, working people to a frenzy with his demagoguery, ranting about the Fatherland and the superiority of the pure German Aryan.

"He *hypnotizes* people," she said. "In Holland we can see where all this is leading, but the Germans are enthralled by him."

I told her about my experience in Prague. She nodded.

"Of course," she said. "The Czechs believe that Hitler and the Austrians are planning to invade Czechoslovakia."

That night I included a group of songs by three modern German composers who were in the audience. They came backstage afterward to thank me. Hofstötter was enthusiastic about the reviews of the Munich concert, which he said were exactly what I needed to carry me to triumph in Salzburg.

The *Völkischer Beobachter* of July 26, 1937, said:

> The artistic revelations which come from beyond the sea used to be rare ones. So much the more, an artistic accomplishment such as offered by Helen Gahagan . . . deserves our admiring recognition. . . . The shining soprano of the Irish-born [*sic*] American is extremely changeable in its shadings of expression. Her emotional grasp of the words inspires her to mimic passion. . . . Helen Gahagan could calm the resounding applause only by encores.

The *Münchner Neuests Nachrichter* the next day commented:

> The Bayrischen Hof has been the scene of quite an unusual artistic success: Helen Gahagan gave a song recital in the German language which resulted in an applause of the audience in increasing intensity from the first to the last bar. The young artist herself is of an extraordinary appearance; she owns an enchanting voice, the charm of which no one can escape.

The *Abendblatt München* a week later said:

> With her song recital in the Bayrischen Hof, the American soprano Helen Gahagan received great applause. You find here a young temperamental artist who knows how to influence us in

her favor by her originality and power of her voice, as well as by
her musical ability and her very remarkable art of performance. . . . The rendition was remarkable and significant for her
genuine enthusiasm for German songs and the care and almost
flawless clearness of pronunciation of the German text by the artist.

Just as Lilli and I were leaving Munich, there was a disquieting
incident. I went to a bank to exchange my German marks for
French or American currency and was informed that it wasn't
permitted. I protested. The teller leaned across the counter, fixed
me with a look of loathing, and told me to get out.

In Salzburg my concert at the Mozarteum Festival was a huge
success. Joseph Marx, as he had promised, accompanied me for
part of the program. Hofstötter brought me the reviews the next
morning in a jubilant mood. They were raves about my command
of German, my "radiant soprano" and "beautiful carrying voice."

Later that day I received word that Dr. Kerber, director of the
Salzburg Festival, wanted to see me. Dr. Kerber was a very
influential man in the music world because he was also intendant
of the Vienna Opera House. Walter and I were excited at the
possibility that Kerber meant to invite me to sing in Vienna, one
of the three or four opera houses in the world where a singer
must be invited in order to be considered first-rank.

A critic I knew slightly, a friend of Joseph Marx, called soon
after. He wanted me to meet someone interesting. He was so
pressing about it that I agreed to fix a time an hour after my appointment with Kerber. In case I was delayed, I dispatched Lilli
to the coffeehouse to explain my absence.

Only slightly late, I almost danced down the street. Kerber
wanted me to sing *Tosca* in the 1938 season of the Vienna Opera
Company. In fact, I had signed the contract.

The coffeehouse was crowded and it was some time before I
spotted Lilli sitting at a table with a stranger. I wondered where
the critic was. I sat down and the stranger, an Englishman, excused himself to speak to someone who had just entered. I started
to bubble over with my wonderful news, but Lilli's distraught expression stopped me.

"When he comes back, let him talk," she whispered, taking a fierce grip on my arm. "You won't believe what he's been telling me unless you hear it yourself. Here he comes. Let him do the talking."

The Englishman plunged into his topic almost at once.

"Do you know what's the matter with the world, Miss Gahagan?"

"No," I answered dutifully.

"The Jews," he said.

He went on with the Nazi propaganda about a Jewish conspiracy that was familiar from the rantings of Hitler and Goebbels. Then he leaned toward me conspiratorially. He said I could be a great help to Germany, since I was a respected American. I could keep my ears open when I returned home and look out for people who felt sympathetic to the Nazi cause. Aryans such as we, he continued, had a duty to defend the superior race against Jews.

Because of Lilli's warning, I had tried to maintain a noncommittal expression in order to encourage him to continue. I could bear it no longer. My flashing eyes made him pause. He saw my mood and the meeting broke up quickly.

In fact, I couldn't speak. My tongue was dry in my mouth. The thought came to me, full-blown, that I would not sing in the Vienna Opera House after all. I would never sing in Germany again.

I thought I was going to be ill. The man was a friend of charming Dr. Marx. Was Joseph Marx a Nazi? Was Walter Hofstötter a Nazi? Someone obviously thought that an American woman who spoke and sang in German would support Hitler. Who was behind the effort to recruit me for the Nazi cause? I felt betrayed.

Lilli and I sat there a long time, too shaken to trust our legs. The world was mad.

Gratefully, I remembered that Lilli and I were leaving Salzburg the next day for Paris. I wished we could avoid having dinner that night with Walter Hofstötter.

Walter could talk of nothing but the contract to sing in Vienna, which he promised would lead to recognition that I was one of the foremost sopranos in the world. I scarcely heard him.

Halfway through the meal I excused myself and went to sit in the restaurant's garden. The room seemed stifling; Salzburg seemed stifling. I was overwhelmed by horror and a premonition of disaster.

Something more happened before we left Salzburg. Walter was in our train compartment, bidding us good-bye, when the conductor entered. He asked for our tickets and as we were hunting in our handbags for them he glanced at Walter and said sharply, "*Steh auf!*" Walter jumped to his feet at once and stood at attention.

Lilli and I did not speak for some time after the train left the station. I was stricken by the evidence that Walter was involved in some way with military training. Lilli broke the numb silence.

"I really don't like the Germans," she mused. "I wish you'd sing French songs."

I smiled at her. At the moment I didn't want to discuss Germans or German music with Lilli, a hopeless francophile. I was thinking of Walter, an Austrian, and remembering the words of the Prague director: "Austrians and Germans are the same. They are all Germans."

Melvyn was making a film on the Metro-Goldwyn-Mayer lot and couldn't meet my plane in Los Angeles. I went directly from the airport to the studio and found him in his dressing room. I slammed the door and announced:

"I'm not going back. I'm not going to sing *Tosca* in Vienna."

Melvyn looked at me calmly. "Does that decision prevent you from greeting me?" he asked politely.

I rushed into his arms and wept.

It was painful to turn my back on all that I had worked so hard to achieve in music, but I had no choice. I could not go back into that environment of oppression. Melvyn and I talked until the early hours of the morning. He had been following newspaper stories of the events in Germany and had come independently to the conclusion that Hitler was preparing for war.

He told me that during his return passage on the *Queen Mary* a few months earlier he had sat at the captain's table with a group of American businessmen from the Midwest. One night a conversation about U.S. politics ended with agreement, except for

Left, the Gahagan home on Lincoln Place in Brooklyn's Park Slope. Cousin Walter Clyde lived next door.

Right, with sister Lilli (right), at age thirteen. *(Otto Sarony Studios)*

Left, as Tosca, 1928.

Right, with Warburton Gamble in *Tonight or Never* at the Belasco Theatre in 1930. *(White Studios)*

Above, as a bride, April 5, 1931. Below left, with Melvyn on the around-the-world trip of 1932. Below right, in *Mary of Scotland*, 1934.

With Eleanor Roosevelt and Melvyn, touring a Farm Security Administration Camp in 1939. *(Western History Collections, University of Oklahoma)*

Hollywood's "Declaration of Independence." Film stars sign a petition to observe an economic boycott of Nazi Germany, circa 1939. Left to right, they are Claude Rains, Paul Muni, Edward G. Robinson, Arthur Hornblow, Jr., Helen Gahagan, John Garfield, Gloria Stuart, James Cagney, Groucho Marx, Aline MacMahon, Henry Fonda and Gale Sondergaard. Seated are Myrna Loy, Melvyn Douglas and Carl Laemmle.

him, that Roosevelt was evil. One man referred to the President as "that son-of-a-bitch in the White House," and another said, "What we need in America is an Adolf Hitler."

What concerned me, I told Melvyn, was the passivity I had encountered in Germany and Austria. People accepted Hitler's message of hate against the Jews without protest. There was no evidence that anyone was outraged by the racism.

Deeply troubled, I tried to concentrate on a marvelous opportunity that had been presented to me. I had been invited to sing in the massive Hollywood Bowl with the renowned Fritz Reiner conducting the orchestra. I regretted that I had sent Reiner an all-German program, but it was too late to change it. The orchestra already had been rehearsed in a number of songs by Joseph Marx and an aria by Carl Maria von Weber.

I woke on the morning of my debut in the Hollywood Bowl with no voice. There had been no warning of a sore throat or any other symptom, but I could scarcely speak. I gargled with hot water, hung my head over a steam kettle, and drank quantities of hot tea and lemon. None of the traditional cures made the slightest difference.

I had never canceled a concert. Somehow I always managed to summon enough voice to get through. This time it would be impossible.

I notified Mrs. Leland Atherton Irish of the Southern California Symphony Association, sponsors of the concert, that her soprano was nearly voiceless. Mrs. Irish immediately found two replacements, my friend George Cehanovsky and a tenor, Mario Chamlee, a man I didn't know. To my dismay, she instructed me to make an appearance anyway.

She announced to the huge audience that I was unable to sing but would come out and take a bow. I felt ridiculous, decked out in the formal gown I had planned to wear for the concert, bowing and smiling to the polite applause of the confused audience.

Critic Isabel Morse Jones of the Los Angeles *Times* began her review the next day with this paragraph:

> The Hollywood Bowl Concert last night was a doleful affair. Helen Gahagan, indisposed and unable to sing, came on the plat-

form only to bow and acknowledge a floral display that reached half across the stage and only served to emphasize the disappointment of the audience.

I realize now that I lost my voice that night because I didn't want to sing German songs.

Melvyn and I joined the Anti-Nazi League, the only organization in California that was speaking out against Hitler. For me it was not a dispassionate decision. I agonized over it. I had loved Germany most of my life. I spoke the language and sang the songs; I had lived for months at a time in Germany where people had been kind to me; many Germans were friends with whom I corresponded. I did not join the Anti-Nazi League lightly, but neither could I passively accept the monstrous activities of Adolf Hitler.

Melvyn and I received hate mail from people who scrawled obscenities about the Jews and threats against us. We became aware that California had a number of Nazi sympathizers. Alis de Sola wrote me from New York that the streets of Yorkville, where many German-Americans lived, were thronged nightly with brown-shirted Bundists singing the *Horst Wessel*.

Joining the Anti-Nazi League wasn't enough for Melvyn. He began speaking against Hitler all over California. He was one of the first movie stars to take an active part in politics. Almost overnight he was recognized as one of the most influential supporters in the state of Franklin Delano Roosevelt's efforts to arouse Americans to the danger of developments within Germany. In a period that was profoundly isolationist, it was unusual for anyone to claim that events in Europe had any importance for Americans.

I had delayed cutting my commitments in Europe in order to make certain that it was not an impulse I would regret. Now I was sure. I cabled Walter Hofstötter to cancel all my engagements, including the contract with the Vienna Opera Company.

While I was in Europe, Melvyn made the decision that we were spending so much time in California that we should buy a house, rather than continue to pay rent. On my return he showed me a house he had in mind. I didn't care for it but I loved the neighborhood, a location high in the hills known as the Outpost.

We bought a large lot, almost three acres, and commissioned a talented architect, Roland Coates, to design us a house. We learned of Coates through some new friends that I was finding most dear, Helen and Remsen Bird. Knowing the cultivated Birds and their circle of artists, scholars and scientists had changed my opinion of California. All was not tackiness. He was president of Occidental College, which he had built into a prestigious center of learning.

Every morning Remsen rose at six, ahead of Helen, and painted a morning salutation for her, a Daumier-style drawing illustrating an event of the previous day or something they planned to do together. When she opened her eyes the first thing she saw each day was an amusing sketch at the foot of her bed.

The Birds were registered Republicans but strong supporters of Franklin Roosevelt. Such was their urbanity and grace that they numbered staunch Republicans and Democrats among their closest friends. Then, as now, that's quite a trick. Helen's avocation was singing and she worked diligently at improving her sweet voice.

To my joy, I discovered I was pregnant again. Construction of the new house high above Hollywood and the prospect of a new baby filled our lives but not to the exclusion of our concern over events in Europe. In 1936 Hitler had taken back the Rhineland Germany lost in World War I and the world had not protested. In 1938 he remilitarized the Rhine, a clear threat to Holland, Belgium and France, but still few spoke against him. In March 1938 his storm-troopers marched into Austria and were welcomed with flowers and a cheering multitude.

We were sick at heart. The Austrian Chancellor, Kurt von Schuschnigg, resigned in outrage but Europe appeared to tolerate this further expansion of Hitler's Germany. I realized that if I had kept my contract with the Vienna Opera Company, I would have been caught in the Nazi occupation.

The U. S. Neutrality Act of 1935 banned the shipment of American arms to any belligerent, which meant that the United States was helpless to send aid to Britain and other countries who were awaiting the inevitable confrontation with Nazi Germany's aggression. William Allen White, the distinguished Republican

editor of the award-winning Emporia *Gazette* in Kansas, formed
an organization aimed at freeing America to help the threatened
nations of Europe. The formal title of his group was the Non-Par-
tisan Committee for Peace Through the Revision of the Neutrality Act, but generally it was called the William Allen White
Committee.

Melvyn was active in forming a California branch. He invited
Clark Eichelberger, Director of the League of Nations Association and chairman of the American Union for Concerted Peace
Efforts, to address a blue-ribbon gathering of movie stars, directors, writers and producers. The group, which met at the home of
Edward G. Robinson, included Claude Rains, Paul Muni, John
Garfield, James Cagney, Groucho Marx, Henry Fonda and Myrna
Loy, all of whom were among the fifty-six who signed a petition
calling for the economic boycott of Germany. It was the intention of Melvyn and other Committee members to circulate the
petition throughout the states until the objective of twenty million signatures was achieved.

Melvyn's efforts to win support in California for Roosevelt's
foreign policy stirred up the moribund Democratic party on the
West Coast. The state government had been headed by Republicans for forty-five years. In 1938 the Democrats had a strong
challenger to throw against the incumbent, Robert C. Merriam.
He was Culbert L. Olson, an esteemed spokesman for liberal
causes who had served in Washington as U. S. Assistant Attorney
General and in the state senate of Utah before moving to California, where he was elected to the state senate.

That summer Melvyn threw himself into helping Olson's campaign for governor. He was one of those who arranged a meeting
at the home of Miriam Hopkins, where the Studio Committee
for Democratic Liberal Action was launched. The first objective
was to elect Culbert Olson governor of California. The Committee issued a letter, which Melvyn signed, urging notables in the
movie industry to help.

Louis B. Mayer, head of the MGM studio where Melvyn was
working, was affronted. Mayer was a devoted Republican, vice-
chairman of the California Republican Committee, who four
years earlier had personally solicited contributions to the party

from his contract employees. Many were intimidated and donated generously rather than risk Mayer's wrath. They happily supported the Olson campaign in order to even the score at last.

Olson won the primary handily. He asked Melvyn to head his campaign organization in Southern California and Melvyn agreed. California is such an enormous state that both political parties require twin organizations to cover it properly, one in the north and one in the south.

Meanwhile I was roundly pregnant and finishing a concert tour. The final performance before the baby's arrival was in Toronto. I was sitting in my dressing room waiting for my call when the theater manager knocked. He wanted to wish me well, he said. As he was leaving he turned to me with a puzzled expression.

"Ah, Miss Gahagan, I must say that you're a larger woman than I expected."

I blurted, "No wonder. I'm about to have a baby."

During the concert, in the middle of a cycle of melting love songs by Schumann, the *Dichterliebe*, the baby began to kick violently. For a wild moment I wondered if my child intended to be born on the stage. Perhaps the baby objected to being squeezed when I drew a deep breath.

I was in a flustered state at the reception that followed the concert. My host flopped down on the sofa beside me, startling me. "Please," I cried to him and the room at large, "you're crowding me and *crushing my baby!*"

On the plane to California the next morning I thought blissfully that I had nothing more to do but relax and wait for the baby Melvyn and I hoped would be a girl. The next four weeks were happy ones. I decorated, then redecorated, then decorated again the bassinet that would hold the infant. I purchased a wardrobe of tiny dresses and dreamed over them.

My assistant was Evelyn Chavoor, a striking-looking young woman of Assyrian descent with black hair and huge dark eyes, whose father delivered fruit and vegetables to our door every Saturday morning. Evelyn was a teenager still in college but came willingly to give me a hand on weekends. She could do anything. Once she filled in when the nurse for our active four-year-old son

Peter was indisposed; on another occasion she helped the cook prepare food for a dinner party and then assisted in serving.

Good-natured, bright and possessed of dignified authority, she was the first stranger to come into the Douglas household since our marriage who didn't seem a stranger. Melvyn felt as I did about her. Watching her play with young Peter one day, he suggested that I hire Evelyn to look after the new baby.

When my labor began, Melvyn came with me to the Pasadena Hospital and didn't leave my side through the long hours of birth contractions. When I opened my eyes he was leaning over me with a huge grin.

"Helen," he said, "we have a beautiful little girl with a head of blond hair." It was August 14, 1938, and we called our daughter Mary Helen, my names in reverse.

Two weeks later we moved into our new house, even though painters and carpenters were still putting on finishing touches. Evelyn took Mary Helen to the home of friends while Melvyn, Peter and I struggled to get settled. Walter Pick, my cousin, had become an invaluable part of the household, acting as our secretary and everything else.

The house was perfect. Roland Coates, the architect, had understood perfectly my obsession for large windows everywhere and plentiful access to the outdoors. One-story and rambling in the style described as Early California Ranch, it was made of wood painted a pale gray with white shutters and trim. A wide porch outside the living room afforded a view of the city and, on a clear day, the Pacific Ocean. On the opposite side of the living room were french doors opening on a covered terrace beside a swimming pool.

The servants' quarters were at one end of the house with the kitchen, pantry and laundry room and the children's wing at the other. Melvyn and I had two large bedrooms, mine as large as our spacious living room, with adjoining baths. Melvyn's opened onto a small patio and mine onto a larger patio beside the pool.

Roland Coates also had designed an office for us that could be used as a spare guest room. To my delight, there were windows on three walls and a floor-to-ceiling bookcase on the other. He even designed the furniture, including a dream of a desk that could be worked at from either side, and wonderfully comfortable chairs with the lamps perfectly positioned for reading or working at night.

The details were beautiful. The floors were pegged planks, the doors hand-carved, the paneling and stairs the work of superb carpenters. The cost seemed prohibitive in that period: $55,000.

I whirled through the rooms, giving instructions to the furniture movers and calling out for Melvyn to come and see this or that wonderful part. I caught sight of his expression, which was less than enthusiastic, and paused.

"What's wrong?" I asked.

"This," he groaned, waving a hand at the expanse of living room. "Did it have to be so large? It's big enough for a camp of gypsies."

Melvyn had been so busy at the studio by day and running Olson's campaign in every spare moment that he had left the decisions about the house to me. I saw no reason why we shouldn't have rooms as large as we liked, so they tended to expand with each consultation with the architect.

"Melvyn, darling," I said, full of concern, "why didn't you tell me you wanted the living room and my bedroom smaller?"

He groaned. My distaste for small, choked rooms was a family legend. I once had declared that I would be perfectly at home in the Louvre. "Are you sure these rooms are large enough?" he inquired.

Walter Pick prepared to put my theatrical papers in the new office files but I decided to sort them first. I sat on the patio, engrossed for hours, discarding duplicates of playbills, chuckling over reviews, sinking into nostalgia. Melvyn suggested that I rest and finish another day but I was anxious to get it done in one big effort.

That night I lay awake in agony with back pains. A cool autumn breeze blowing in the open window caused my aching back muscles to go into spasms. The pain was so severe that I was taken to the hospital. After I spent several hours on a heated table, the muscles unknotted but it was a few days before I was strong enough to return home.

I have a high tolerance for pain but the problem with my back

was excruciating. Like labor, the cramps came in waves that built
to livid torment. Bouts of it were to plague me about every six
months for the rest of my life, each time requiring hospi-
talization.

Distracted by the new baby and my alarming back problem, I
saw very little of what Melvyn was doing to help elect Culbert
Olson. Melvyn was traveling all over Southern California, drawing immense crowds curious to see a movie star, people who went
away impressed with his arguments about Olson and Franklin
Roosevelt's New Deal. As support began to build, the Democrats
scented victory; after forty-five years in power, the Republicans
looked beatable.

Harold Ickes, Roosevelt's Secretary of the Interior, came to
California to campaign for Olson. That was one of the two political meetings I attended and I admired Ickes on sight. I went to
the other at Melvyn's urging. He wanted me to hear young Jerry
Voorhis, a newly elected U.S. congressman already marked for a
great political career. Voorhis was rich and handsome and brainy,
a Yale graduate who spent his fortune on a school for orphans
near Pomona. Voorhis reduced himself to pennilessness for that
school, and in 1936 when he was elected to the House of Representatives he drove to Washington in a battered secondhand car
and then worked eighteen-hour days for the New Deal, earning
himself the nickname of "Kid Atlas."

Like Ickes, Voorhis was capable of documented argument in
support of Roosevelt's social welfare and conservation policies.
What they said rang true for me and for a large number of others
in California. Culbert Olson was elected governor of California.

I went with Melvyn to Sacramento to attend the jubilant
inauguration. The capital was crowded with Democrats celebrating the new regime. I found the pace exhausting and announced that I needed sleep. Someone had a better idea, a stimu-
lant. I took a Dexamyl pill for the first and last time in my life. I
thought the effects would never wear off.

Leading Democrats gave Melvyn a good deal of the credit for
Olson's victory. Interior Secretary Harold Ickes held a luncheon
in Washington in Melvyn's honor and introduced him to the
party's inner circle, who formed such a high opinion of his judg-

ment and influence that after that he was consulted regularly about political issues in California.

One of the issues Melvyn knew at first hand concerned the migration of tenant farmers to California from the dust bowls of Texas, Oklahoma, Arkansas and Missouri. "Tractored out" by landowners switching to mechanized farming, or else driven out because drought and winds had blown away the topsoil, they piled their belongings on top of decrepit automobiles and drove west looking for work until they fetched up in California.

John Steinbeck later immortalized those desperate thousands in *The Grapes of Wrath* but the first reaction in California was to pretend that such people didn't exist. Radio and newspapers, the media of the day, simply ignored them or referred to them as a minor nuisance. The fact was, as Melvyn and I saw for ourselves, that the countryside all over California was dotted with shacks built by destitute families, some of them in roadside ditches. Men and women could get seasonal employment at extremely low wages but when the harvest was in or the seeding was done they were ordered to move on, often at the end of a sheriff's gun.

Sometimes the subject of the "Okies" would be raised at a dinner party. Melvyn and I listened in astonishment to people making comfortable statements about how the situation was exaggerated or that the migrants should stop being so lazy and dirty. Though an estimated six thousand were pouring into California *every month*, there was an entrenched aversion to recognizing that a problem existed.

One of the few to respond was John Steinbeck, who formed a committee to provide aid. Melvyn had a call from someone on the Steinbeck Committee asking for the use of our patio for a meeting.

We agreed although Melvyn was working at the studio that day and I was confined to bed, still weak from my ordeal with the back spasms. Walter Pick acted as host on our behalf as the committee assembled on the patio just outside my bedroom.

After an hour or so, he came in to see me. "Helen, you really must come and listen to what they're saying," he told me, very upset. "My God, those poor migrants are suffering from pellagra! They're starving!"

I put on some clothes and went out the door, standing at the back of the meeting to listen to tales of personally witnessed horror and the indifference of the state authorities. I could not know it then, and did not realize it until years later, but when I left my bed that afternoon I took my first step into politics.

Some days later the Steinbeck Committee asked Melvyn to join in a discussion of a proposal to give a Christmas party for the deprived children of the migrants. I went along just to be with him, with no intention of becoming involved. There I heard about the Farm Security Administration Camps that Roosevelt had built in California, fenced-in sites where families could pitch their tents and have access to plumbing, laundry facilities and other sanitary services. Someone reported that these camps were inadequate to the need. All of them were packed to capacity, with hundreds more migrants camped beyond the fence.

One such camp was the Shafter Federal Farm Security Camp near Arvin, administered by Laurence Hewes from a federal office in San Francisco. The meeting arranged to ask Hewes for permission to give the party there. After much discussion about the overwhelming numbers involved, it was agreed that children from the families living outside the camp should be included in the Christmas party as well.

One speaker after another pointed out that enormous quantities of food and toys would be needed. Where would it all come from? I grew impatient.

"Why do there have to be so many problems?" I interrupted. "It doesn't matter whether there are two thousand children at the party or three thousand, or however many. It's *Christmas*. Go to toy manufacturers and food wholesalers and tell them what we need. I'm sure you'll get it."

For a moment no one spoke. Then someone suggested mildly, "Why don't you do it?"

I had no choice but to agree. I went home and started telephoning at once, first drafting a number of our friends to help. The response was heartwarming. Word of the plight of the migrants had reached more people in California than any of us had realized. The generosity of California wholesalers exceeded even my confident expectations. It took an army of us, all of our friends and all of the Steinbeck Committee, just to transport the food and gifts to the camp.

The Christmas party was a model of smooth organization despite the staggering problem of feeding more than two thousand hungry children and their parents. There was a pathetic docility about the families patiently waiting their turn to eat. We served them picnic-style out of doors and then the children lined up to enter the main camp building to select a toy from the heaped-up tables.

Konrad Bercovici, one of our friends who had come to help, suggested that we explore the camp while the gifts were being distributed. We passed along rows of tents built on concrete platforms and encountered a man and woman standing silently, both of them dressed in rags and with faces stamped with poverty and despair. I was stunned by this intimate confrontation with the human calamity of the forced migration. We tried to speak to them but they were too shy to reply. I left them to their privacy but I was shaken.

When I was invited to become the chairman of the Steinbeck Committee, I accepted. What made me do it? I was haunted by the memory of those bewildered children lined up to receive a single Christmas toy, and the emptiness in the drained faces of that couple.

I had to do what I could. One part of my responsibility as chairman of the Steinbeck Committee, as I saw it, was to become better informed. I wrote to the Department of Agriculture for information about migrants. In the weeks that followed, I read every word in the bundles of reports that arrived. I also toured the Shafter camp again, asking about the work of the Farm Extension Service and clinics that functioned in each camp.

The problem was complex. The migrants were descended from settlers who had worked single-crop farms, usually cotton or corn, that quickly depleted the soil. Too poor to allow the land to lie fallow, and often illiterate and without any knowledge of crop rotation, they allowed their farms to become less and less productive. Some had never seen running water. Few knew the rudiments of hygiene or nutrition. After my first tour of the camp I returned home with a raging case of impetigo.

The camp program not only provided food, hygiene and shelter but also had imaginative activities aimed at improving self-sufficiency. Men were instructed in modern agriculture and given government loans to help them purchase land and a line of credit to buy seed and equipment. Women learned how to make mattresses out of cotton stuffing, plentiful at that time, and how to preserve vegetables and fruit for the winter. I sometimes thought that the symbol of the camps should have been a pressure cooker.

I'd like to digress to say that the government's investment was sound financially, as well as being a humane response to an American disaster. The new farmers made good. The rate of return on government loans was impressively high. In World War II the farms operated by once-migrant families provided a substantial proportion of the food that fed our nation and our allies.

After the war, when I was a frequent visitor to veterans' hospitals, I met a young soldier who told me that he was the son of a dust bowl family. He remembered me from the children's Christmas party and said he joined the army with pride. He wanted to help his country because when he needed it, his country had helped him.

In the aftermath of that Christmas party, however, I had encountered intense resistance to everything the government and private citizens were trying to do to help the migrants. Most of the animosity came from the big growers in the areas near the Farm Security Camps. They hated Franklin Roosevelt anyway but especially detested his decent and practical efforts to relieve the misery of the migrants.

Every request for help was met with a curt refusal. The growers were fearful that the migrants would form permanent communities and join unions. To avoid that, the growers employed Mexicans, contract laborers paid little more than slaves, who were packed shoulder to shoulder into trucks, dumped into the California fields to work brutal hours until the harvest was in and then returned across the border.

Importing labor was cheap, and besides, it meant that the growers didn't pay taxes for such services as schools and health clinics. The big growers used every method they could, including force, to get the migrants to move on. The government camps were therefore considered an outrage because they symbolized permanency.

I reasoned that once people knew the truth about the camps there would be broad support for the government's programs that would offset the powerful lobbying the growers had mounted. I went all over the state describing the destitution of the migrants and the benefits of the Farm Security Camps. Once I even traveled to Washington, D.C., at my own expense as always, to address an audience to bolster support for the program.

After each talk people asked what they could do to help. I told them, "Everything." The migrants needed jobs with decent wages, household equipment, clothing. I suppose I drew on my experience as an actress to put across my appeal, but the facts and firsthand reports that I brought to each audience needed little embellishment.

People began telling me that I should be the next national committeewoman for the Democratic party. I had never heard of a national committeewoman so I arranged a pleased expression on my face and answered evasively.

One aspect of the work of the Steinbeck Committee concerned establishing a farmworkers' union to provide migrants with better working conditions and a fair wage. I agreed enthusiastically with that objective (which again won me no friends among the growers) because I saw it as necessary for the rehabilitation of the migrants as sanitary housing and food.

The Steinbeck Committee met early in 1939 to consider a welcome problem. The response to my speeches had been an overwhelming amount of donated clothing, most of it sweaters and shoes that were desperately needed. We discussed what to do with the deluge of gifts. My recommendation was that we distribute the clothing in the camps on the basis of need. Three members of the Committee had another plan. They had been active in the fund raising to hire union organizers and they urged that we distribute the clothing from the union offices instead.

I objected, commenting that the tactic would be coercive. The word "coercive" inflamed the three unionists and a heated argument followed. I said it was unconscionable to use the donations given in good faith as a lure to get migrants to join the union. I agreed that the migrants would benefit from a good union, but joining should be a free choice. We must not attach any strings to the gifts of clothing that Californians were donating. Our job was to provide unconditional help to people in want.

The three were not persuaded but I was sure that the rest of the Committee was with me. Ignoring the furious faces of my opponents, I called for the vote. The decision was to send the clothing to the camps. My education in politics had begun.

Later I went with Melvyn to Washington, where we were invited to a party in the home of Dorothy McAllister, director of the women's division of the Democratic National Committee. John L. Lewis, founder of the CIO, was there. I told him I wasn't sure about some of the people in the union movement in California.

"Are they all they should be," I asked, "or are some of them communists?"

He assured me they were all loyal Americans. It was reported to me later that after I moved to another part of the room Lewis snapped, "Mrs. Douglas wants me to turn every union man upside down to see if a Communist card falls out of his pocket."

Though my work for the Steinbeck Committee was tiring and expensive, since I paid office and travel costs myself, it had many personal rewards, not the least of which was the opportunity to meet some of the most distinguished Americans of the day. Several of them were in attendance at the first speech for the migrants that I gave, at Mills College in Oakland.

There I met Paul Schuster Taylor, who became a friend for life. Paul Taylor, a professor of economics and a social scientist, had taken a leave of absence from the University of California to help the migrants. With Dorothea Lange, a young photographer who shared his concern, he set off on a thousand-mile fact-finding tour of ditchbank settlements, pea-pickers' tents and sheds on the edges of cotton fields, during which Dorothea took the pictures that caused Edward Steichen to describe her as "without doubt our greatest documentary photographer."

Her most famous photo, that of a gaunt woman holding a baby on her lap with two wan children clinging to her sides, was believed to be responsible for congressional approval of Roosevelt's bill to establish the Farm Security Camps program in California. After Dorothea and Paul were married in 1935, Paul was commissioned by the federal government to study the problems of farmers in the states from which the migrants had come.

From then on, his consuming concern was reclamation of the land by means of federal water-diversion schemes. He introduced me to the 1902 Reclamation Act, which limited the supply of cheap federal irrigation water to small farm units of no more than 160 acres. Taylor passionately believed that the subsidized water should not go to the owners of large farms, which some described as "socialism for the rich."

Another remarkable person in the audience at Mills College that evening was the world-renowned educator and civil libertarian, Dr. Alexander Meiklejohn, the former president of Amherst College. In 1926, while professor of philosophy at the University of Wisconsin, Alex had established the celebrated Experimental College, which formulated and tested improvements in methods of teaching undergraduates in the liberal arts. It would take another generation before his improved methods, based on a higher level of participation and self-reliance, became widely adopted.

Alex Meiklejohn and his wife Helen Everett, an economist, moved to San Francisco in the mid-thirties at the request of civic leaders and established there the School for Social Research, whose style was based on the methods introduced at the Experimental College. Helen and Alex brought some of their faculty to hear me and they too became my lifelong friends.

Two of them were Myer Cohen and his wife Elizabeth. She headed the WPA theater program in Northern California and he was an authority on the United States Supreme Court. In 1937 Harper and Row published Myer's book, *Selected Supreme Court Decisions*, a seminal guide to the direction the court was taking and its consequences. He used it in his classroom, and this was the first time that legal material had been applied to the study of social change.

With the Cohens and Meiklejohns was Charles Hogan, known as "Hogo" to his wide circle of admiring friends. Hogo had been a professor of philosophy and was active in the San Francisco branch of the American Civil Liberties Union. When I first met him he was helping Alexander Meiklejohn conduct the first study of housing conditions in San Francisco's Chinatown. Hogo later was our first ambassador to the United Nations.

We were drawn together by our common concern for the migrants. We gave one another comfort in a time when much of California was still indulging in denial that a problem existed. As Laurence Hewes wrote later in "Boxcar in the Sand," we wondered "why the appearance of these ragged, starving people in California aroused so much hostility, so little humanity."

Hewes could never fathom it, nor could we. The Farm Security Camps were giving people security, roots and hope but they were under constant siege from powerful groups who insisted they were at the least unnecessary—and breeding grounds for communists as well.

Those of us who knew otherwise clung together in our fight to save and extend such New Deal programs. One of our heroes was Henry Wallace, who with Norman Thomas and Harold Ickes was an architect of the positive-minded New Deal. Wallace, a man with his roots in the farmers' world, made an enormously valuable contribution to America when he developed several strains of hybrid corn that were superior to any grown previously in the Midwest. His reputation as an agrarian authority led him straight to Roosevelt, who appointed him Secretary of Agriculture. Wallace's decency and the soundness of the creative programs he designed for small-farm operators won him the passionate loyalty of disadvantaged rural people all over America.

Melvyn and I had a phone call one day from Aubrey Williams, head of the National Youth Administration, who was making one of his regular inspection trips to the West Coast. He wanted to hear about what we were doing, about both my work with the Steinbeck Committee and Melvyn's activities on the California State Welfare Board. We had a pleasant exchange and as he was leaving he said, "On your next trip to Washington, I'm sure Mrs. Roosevelt will want to meet you."

We were startled that he could be so certain of the inclinations of the President's wife. He explained that he acted as a sort of talent scout for Mrs. Roosevelt. Because her husband was unable to move around the country easily, she had taken on the responsibility of collecting people who possessed the grass-roots information he needed. At that time she was only beginning to travel around the nation herself, so Aubrey Williams and others were watching out for people involved in community enterprises that the President should know about.

We were certainly in that category, Aubrey told us. Mrs. Roosevelt was already intrigued by reports of our involvements because it was unusual for actors to be political and social activists.

Mrs. Roosevelt's training as an information gatherer for her husband began soon after he was stricken with polio in 1921. After that he was restricted to a wheelchair, or else wore painful, heavy leg braces. His first inclination was to quit political life but she was one of those who urged him to continue. The arrangement between them was that Mrs. Roosevelt, an intensely shy woman, would have to make herself aware of what was happening in the Democratic party and among the voters, and bring reports to her husband.

He trained her to ask useful questions and to be observant. When he was elected governor of New York State by a huge majority, he would tour the state by car, stopping at factories and schools and the like. Mrs. Roosevelt would get out and visit the building on his behalf, acting as his eyes and ears, and bring him a detailed report.

After he was elected President of the United States in 1932, she was compelled to become the most visible First Lady in American history in order to continue to perform that fact-finding function. Since he couldn't travel without revealing the extent of his physical helplessness, which he was reluctant to do, she took to the road on his behalf.

When she was in Washington she arranged nightly dinner parties to which she invited obscure experts in some emerging area of public concern, or little-known specialists from a government bureau, or people Aubrey Williams advised her about. To this mix she always added several members of the large Roosevelt clan and the President's chief aide, Harry Hopkins, who lived at the White House.

The dinners were so relaxed and gracious that it was possible to be unaware that the President of the United States was doing his homework.

A few weeks after Aubrey's visit to California, Melvyn and I were in Washington. Soon after checking into our hotel we received a note signed by Mrs. Roosevelt asking us to have tea with her the next day, dine with the President that evening and sleep overnight in the White House. The invitation informed us that a White House car would pick us up at a designated hour.

The moment we walked through the doors of the White House we were struck by the emotional impact of our country's history all around us. This building had known Jefferson and Lincoln, had echoed to the distant sound of Confederate cannon, had felt the fire of the British invasion in the War of 1812. My throat stung and I found my eyes full of tears.

We were shown to a small elevator just off the main entrance. On the second floor we were escorted to a bedroom suite opposite the President's study, the suite later occupied by the King and Queen of England. An usher came to take us to Mrs. Roosevelt. We followed him, awestruck, down a long gallery and behind tall screens at the end of it, where Mrs. Roosevelt had created an intimate sitting room for her private entertaining.

She rose to greet us with that smile that warmed everyone. I felt at home at once.

She served us tea and our friendship began. In the years to come, we would breakfast there many, many times.

The First Lady already was familiar to me, as she was to most Americans. She was beginning to pop up everywhere. She not only tirelessly attended sod-turnings, ribbon-cuttings and wreath-layings, but she wrote a daily newspaper column, "My Day," which was a popular and powerful vehicle for informing the country about New Deal programs. In addition, she had written an autobiography, *This Is My Story*, and like her husband, whose "Fireside Chats" on radio were informal reports to the nation, she frequently made broadcasts.

I knew and admired the positions she took on the grave issues of the day, but nothing I'd read or heard prepared me for meeting her in the White House.

In fact, that was my second meeting with her. In 1929, when my father was a director of the Manufacturers Trust Company, later known as Manufacturers Hanover, his organization sponsored a luncheon for some worthy charity. I was one of the celebrities, as the invitations put it, seated at the head table. Next to me was Mrs. Roosevelt, wife of the governor who had sent his regrets and delegated her to attend in his place.

She gave a brief speech reasonably well. We carried on a somewhat strained conversation because I found her self-conscious and ill at ease. She kept me at arm's length with a certain cool reserve, but even so I was impressed with her air of simplicity. There was nothing affected or pretentious about her and nothing she said was evasive or empty.

That quality of simplicity was very evident as we sat down to tea with her that first hour in the White House, but now I found her vastly changed by the six years she had been First Lady. She had developed assurance and poise and obviously no longer found it an effort to make conversation with strangers. Despite the fact that her entire person was imbued with soft but unmistakable authority—in the more than twenty years of a close friendship, it never occurred to either of us that I should call her Eleanor—she had a disarming quality of directness that dissolved all nervousness in the people she met.

Melvyn and I were impressed with her questions about California politics, the State Welfare Board and the condition of the migrants. She already had an astonishing amount of accurate information. Her penetrating questions revealed an awareness of the state's problems and attitudes. As we talked, no detail of what we said escaped her. Her curiosity was insatiable and we found ourselves gaining new perspective as we described what was happening.

I suggested that she see the Farm Security Camps for herself the next time she visited California. She readily agreed.

At dinner that evening we met the President. Franklin Roosevelt was already seated when we arrived in the family dining room. Mrs. Roosevelt presented us and he looked up with an open, dazzling smile that I found very moving. I sat on his right at a crowded table and he turned his full attention on me. Like his wife, there was magic in him. We talked earnestly and naturally.

Mrs. Roosevelt presided with the easy good manners instilled in her from childhood. She was the one who always guided the general conversation and drew out the quietest guests. Even the President followed her lead. Though she was in complete command of the table, she managed at all times to focus attention on her husband. Her manner with him was at once intimate, informal, natural and deeply respectful. Though she addressed him as Franklin, there was no question of her deference to the office he held.

She knew what she was doing. She was fully aware every minute that she was a catalyst who could bring disparate and necessary bits of information about the country to her husband's attention in this effortless way and thereby exert a profound influence on the direction the White House was taking.

Shortly after that evening, the President appointed me to the National Advisory Committee of the WPA. WPA programs were job-creation programs designed to combat the country's record-breaking level of unemployment. Imaginative and varied, they produced a legacy of good works, public buildings, parks, land reclamation and other worthy projects Americans enjoy today.

One of my favorites was the Toy Loan Library, which hired people to repair donated toys. The only overhead was their modest WPA salaries. All the used toys and the materials to repair them were donated to the Library. Factories regularly gave paint, wire and fabrics that were seconds. The rebuilt toys, often stronger and better-looking than new, were stocked in the Toy Loan Libraries where poor children could come and borrow them. If the child returned the doll or truck in good condition on the agreed-upon date, he or she could select another toy.

I had something to do with that program and I admired it prodigiously. Making use of what otherwise would have been discarded, it provided lovely toys to children who otherwise would have had none and taught them to respect the toys. At the same time it kept large numbers of people usefully occupied and off the relief rolls.

When Mrs. Roosevelt announced that she was coming to California I wrote immediately to ask her to stay with us. Melvyn and I arranged to hire an airplane to take her to the San Joaquin Valley where she could see the migrants firsthand without losing too much time from her schedule. I wanted her to see the people living in hovels along the roadside in order to compare their plight with the comparative comfort of those in the Farm Security Camps.

Mrs. Roosevelt replied that she would be delighted to accept our invitation. She said she would be traveling with her secretary, Malvina Thompson, known as Tommy to us all. Tommy gave her life to helping Mrs. Roosevelt. One of her contributions, cheerfully and excellently done, was to prepare the daily "My Day" columns for Mrs. Roosevelt to edit.

Melvyn decided we would give my room and bath to Mrs. Roosevelt and his room and bath to Tommy. We moved into Peter's room and he went to his uncle's. It was a sort of musical beds but Peter didn't find it humorous at all. He complained that his little sister, Mary Helen, was remaining in her crib but he was being sent away. We readily understood his feelings and promised that he would meet Mrs. Roosevelt.

Los Angeles had a holiday feeling on the day of Mrs. Roosevelt's arrival. Her visits seemed to do that to communities everywhere—perk them up and make them feel important. We met her plane. She came down the stairs briskly and strode rapidly toward us with the gait of an inveterate walker. I noticed that she wore comfortable shoes; it would have been difficult to imagine her traveling the world in high heels. In my mind's eye I see her still, walking with grace and assurance, smiling and eager, her eyes fixed on me as though I were the one person in all the world that she couldn't wait to see.

She greeted us and got into the car, her manner clearly indicating that we should move off at once. I quickly learned that when Mrs. Roosevelt was ready to go anywhere, she went. If someone was supposed to accompany her and wasn't ready on the dot, that person would have to find transportation to follow her or pass up the trip; Mrs. Roosevelt wouldn't wait one second for anyone.

Her pace was the result of a packed schedule. If she made herself ten minutes late for any appointment, she would be late for every appointment the rest of the day. Even when she left the White House, there was no difference. She was still pressed for time and she hated keeping people waiting.

In some wonderful way Mrs. Roosevelt seemed perfectly at home in our house and not at all a visitor. Perhaps it was because she brought none of the usual traveler's luggage of fatigue and leftover things to do. When she was with you, she was wholly with you. She gave the impression of having been nowhere else and having no plans to leave for anywhere else. You had her total attention; she was fully *there*.

As arranged, Melvyn and I took Mrs. Roosevelt by plane to the Bakersfield airport in the Tehachapis, where we were met by Laurence Hewes, regional director of the Farm Security Camps program. Mrs. Roosevelt, Tommy, Melvyn, Larry and I piled into two cars and were driven through the Valley.

The day was unforgettable. Soon after we started, Mrs. Roosevelt spotted a cluster of makeshift shacks constructed of old boards, tarpaper and tin cans pounded flat, one of the ditchbank communities that were commonplace in California then.

"Stop the car, please," she asked, and with that she was out and walking quickly across the fields toward some migrants doing chores. I followed at a trot. One of the bent figures straightened to see who was approaching and recognized her at once. He greeted her with hand outstretched and a beam on his face.

"Oh, Mrs. Roosevelt, you've come to see us," he said. He seemed to accept as a natural event of American life that the wife of the President of the United States would be standing in a mucky field chatting with him. After a few minutes Mrs. Roosevelt turned and made for one of the shacks. The man tried to stop her.

"Please don't go in there," he called. "My wife and children are sick with the raisin's." Migrants called all skin rashes "raisin's." I learned that in this case he meant chicken pox.

"It doesn't matter," she flung over her shoulder, and in she went. Larry Hewes wilted. Melvyn and I looked at one another in consternation. We had wanted Mrs. Roosevelt to meet the migrants but we hadn't figured on exposing her to contagious diseases. She soon popped out of the shack and got back into the car without comment.

We drove on through the San Joaquin Valley in the direction of Visalia, past the tin-sided huts of the squatters on every side and followed by a parade of newspaper photographers and reporters.

When we reached the first Farm Security Camp a reporter asked Mrs. Roosevelt if she didn't agree that *The Grapes of Wrath* was an exaggeration.

She replied evenly, "I have never believed that *The Grapes of Wrath* was an exaggeration."

At the camp where migrants could live for ten cents a day with access to toilets, running water, food, health services and training for a healthier, productive life, Mrs. Roosevelt was surrounded by refugees from America's dust bowl. Like the man in the field, they seemed to find it unremarkable that she would visit them. Though she was without protection and hundreds of people were packed in a circle around her, they gave way politely to enable her to move freely and there were no unpleasant incidents.

Mrs. Roosevelt also had promised to hear the National Youth Administration orchestra. To make it easier for her, I arranged for the concert to take place on our patio. Governor Olson attended, along with other state officials, the administrator of California's NYA program, and leaders of the women's division of the Democratic party.

On the night of the scheduled speech which had brought Mrs. Roosevelt to California, we were filled with apprehension. Feeling against the New Deal and against her personally ran very high in the state where many of the power brokers were committed Republicans. Early that evening we heard rumors that an attempt would be made on her life.

We found a huge crowd massed around the entrance of the Philharmonic Auditorium where she was to speak. She had to push through them alone in order to reach the stage door, with me in her determined wake. At that time there was never any security protection for a President's wife; no other President's wife had ventured out of the White House as she did.

The audience, packed to the walls of the auditorium, clearly was hostile. They received her speech coldly, waiting for the question period. After a series of rude, abrasive questions which she fended with dignity, one man rose and asked coolly:

"Mrs. Roosevelt, do you think you husband's being a cripple has affected his mind?"

People gasped aloud. The auditorium was breathlessly still. With perfect calm, Mrs. Roosevelt took the silence and held it. Then she answered in a tone devoid of anger, resentment or defensiveness.

"Yes," she said evenly, "my husband's illness *has* affected him. How could it be otherwise? One couldn't suffer as he has suffered and fail to be touched by it. Suffering has made him more responsive to the suffering of his fellow man."

When the ordeal was over, I hurried backstage. I found Mrs. Roosevelt ready to leave by the stage exit she had entered.

"No, no," I called to her. "Not that way, Mrs. Roosevelt. The passage outside is filled with people. We'll take you out another way."

She didn't appear to hear me. She continued with unbroken stride and in a moment was in the middle of the crowded corridor.

"Please, Mrs. Roosevelt," I shouted, genuinely frightened for her safety. "*Come back!*"

She turned briefly to look at me. "Come along, Helen," she said pleasantly, and plunged into the crowd. To my relief, people moved aside, their faces stony, and allowed her through.

Some of the opposition to her was coming from Democrats who were outraged at the announcement that Franklin Roosevelt intended to run for an unprecedented third term. With Europe obviously moving toward war in that summer of 1939, Roosevelt concluded that his experienced leadership would be needed in the White House. The Democratic party was split. John Nance Garner, the Vice-President, wanted the nomination and he was supported by James A. Farley, national chairman of the party, and Cordell Hull, Roosevelt's Secretary of State.

Democrats all over the country organized for Garner, trying to load state delegations with people who would vote against Roosevelt at the Democratic National Convention scheduled for Chicago in August. Those of us who supported the New Deal and Roosevelt's foreign policy of helping Britain rallied in his support.

Governor Olson met in San Francisco with Harold Ickes, who remained loyal to Roosevelt. At a lengthy session which Melvyn attended, pro-New Deal Democrats selected a strong slate for the California delegation, all of them people who would not waver in voting for Roosevelt. Melvyn was named to the slate, the first movie actor ever considered as a state delegate to a presidential nominating convention. I was named as his alternate, I think to ensure that Melvyn got to the convention. Ellis Patterson, California's lieutenant governor, was nominated to head the slate.

In the weeks that followed, Melvyn worked unceasingly to persuade Democrats to reject the Garner supporters and elect the New Deal slate. I was told again and again that Melvyn was one of the most effective campaigners the party had ever seen. In the end he helped bring about a victory. By a large margin, California picked the pro-Roosevelt delegation.

Melvyn was committed to working on a film on the day that the train carrying the California delegation left for Chicago. It was decided that I would travel with them by train and he would follow by plane when he was free.

Just before leaving for Chicago, I attended a dinner party given by George Creel, a prominent and highly influential California Democrat. He took me aside for an earnest conversation about allowing my name to stand for nomination as national committeewoman. I still hadn't discovered what a national committeewoman did but I nodded agreeably to everything he said.

During the three days that the train traveled to Chicago, I was approached many times by people urging me to stand for the office of national committeewoman. Still ignorant of the structure of the Democratic party, I continued to be noncommittal. After a time it appeared that people thought I had consented to do it. I resolved to find out at once what a national committeewoman was.

I spent an evening with my friend Dorothy McAllister, director of the women's division of the Democratic National Committee, and she enlightened me. She explained that Democrats made an effort to have women share key positions with men. Of all the *unpaid* honorary posts in the party, the title of national committeewoman was the most prized. It required the holder, at her own expense, to travel around the state addressing women Democrats to inform them about the party's national and international policies. The incumbent had to have a proven record of loyalty to the party, ability to speak well in public—and money.

Just before the opening ceremonies at which I was to sing the national anthem, Melvyn arrived. I had time only to give him a brief, confused account of the possibility I would stand for the office of national committeewoman. Soon afterward a number of labor leaders sought him out. They said that I seemed to get around the state a good deal and I was well liked. Did he think I would stand for the office of national committeewoman?

Melvyn, knowing my independent mind, was amused that they had approached him. "Better ask Helen," he advised them.

The California caucus met and elected me national committeewoman. One other woman, Mrs. Mattison Boyd Jones, someone I didn't know, was also nominated but lost by fifteen votes to my twenty-nine. She never forgave me for defeating her. I later learned that she had been working for years for that position. I wasn't very happy with the result myself. What had I let myself in for?

At the hotel afterward Melvyn and I threw outselves on the bed and didn't speak for a long time. We were both worried.

The next day the newspapers were sympathetic about Mrs. Mattison Boyd Jones's defeat, describing her as a "very intellectual lady and experienced in politics." My opponent made a scathing explanation to the press, saying, "When it comes to competing with glamorous young movie stars in a delegation composed of forty men and four women—the result was inevitable."

The Democratic National Convention nominated Franklin Roosevelt as the party's candidate for President and, to my delight, chose popular Henry A. Wallace as his running mate.

A few weeks afterward, California Democrats held their state convention in Sacramento. Because of our 50–50 law in the state, the convention elects not only a state chairman, always a man, but also two state vice-chairmen who are women, one for Northern California and one for Southern California. Male chairmen alternate, one term coming from the southern part of the state and the next from the north.

That year the convention bogged down in a long, bitter wrangle before electing William Malone as state chairman. Somehow in the confusion the election of two women vice-chairmen was overlooked until it was too late. A hastily prepared resolution was passed, authorizing Malone to pick his own two vice-chairmen.

The next day I had a telephone call from Malone. He was abrupt with me. He announced that he was coming to Los Angeles and expected me to be at home for his visit.

Two days later he was seated opposite me in my drawing room. He began by telling me that he was the new state chairman and that this was a very powerful position in the party. I said that I knew of his election and I offered congratulations. That established, he went straight to the point.

"Mrs. Douglas, I have decided to name you as my vice-chairman," he said.

I wasn't sure that I had heard him right. "You can't do that," I said. "I'm already fully occupied as national committeewoman."

"That's the point!" he declared, in a manner which indicated I was a very bright child. "And now you're *the* state vice-chairman!"

"Of the north *and* the south?" I said incredulously.

"Right. You see, I'll be much too occupied with all I have to do as chairman to go running all over the state talking to three different women. Furthermore there's no need to have two women as my vice-chairmen. One is plenty. In fact, one is plenty for all three jobs, and it's going to be you."

"Mr. Malone," I began, "I don't have the time—"

He cut me off. "That's no problem. I don't want you to do anything anyway."

I kept my temper and thanked him coldly for the honor. I said I would have to decline. He rose.

"You can't decline," he said flatly. "I'm naming you, and that's all there is to it. Good day."

The next morning California newspapers carried my picture and the story of my appointment as vice-chairman of the state Democratic organization in the north and the south. I fumed. Malone had taken me for a lightweight who would be passive in the position and take no initiatives on my own. He had made a grievous error. I was a political novice but I'd learned at my mother's knee the importance of women in the political process.

I visited the Los Angeles Democratic headquarters to get my bearings. I was directed to a tiny back room, the headquarters of the women's division. It had the general appearance of long disuse. By good fortune Leisa Bronson, an astute woman who had been one of Jerry Voorhis' key campaigners, happened to be there that day.

I had two questions. Did the women's division have its own office in each of the two areas? No, she told me; women shared space with the men. Did women finance their own operations? No again. Except for two annual teas, one in the north and one in the south, the women's division raised no money for itself but relied instead on a grant from the men. In fact, she added, funds raised at the teas were split evenly with the men.

Leisa gave me a list of the most active women in the two districts and I left, much wiser.

Accustomed as I was to associating women's independence with financial independence, my first political decision was to make the women's division economically self-sufficient. We would raise our own money to support our administrative costs and we would establish our own, separate offices. I had no intention of working in that cramped back room.

I went out and rented a good-looking office in the heart of Los Angeles, paying the rent myself. I also hired an experienced executive secretary to work full-time.

From the day that I took over, the women's division financed itself, raised its own money, and organized an education program that reached every corner of the state. My premise was that if democracy is to work, voters must be informed. People can't choose intelligently between candidates until they understand the issues. I assumed that women wanted to know what was going on just as much as men did. To help me I drew on a core group of women who had never been active before in politics any more than I had. They were academics, civic leaders, professional women, community workers. Though they were neophytes in politics, they were sophisticated, disciplined women.

We weren't afraid of anybody. We all felt we had an important job to do. We were there to make sure that California supported Roosevelt's policies and we were determined not to be stopped or cowed by anyone.

I discovered that one of my responsibilities as national committeewoman was to play a part in the patronage system which has oiled the wheels of politics since human history began. I made it clear that I was not interested in pork-barrel politics. I would not go along with political payoffs to unqualified people as a reward for their contribution to the party. That kind of payoff isn't good for the country and in the end it doesn't serve the interests of any political party either. I would recommend only men and women who had outstanding qualifications for the vacant post.

Word spread quickly that the women's division had its own headquarters in Los Angeles and that I would be available in it from eleven until three every weekday. A steady stream of women came to see me. They had the same story: the Democratic party used them for manual labor—stuffing envelopes and making coffee, spending tedious hours on the telephone—and yet the men never consulted them on their views or considered them for appointment to influential positions. The women saw me as someone who might do something about it.

I had approximately the same story for every one of them. I explained that I was raised in a household of dominating males, a father and two older brothers, and I learned early that men guard their authority over women jealously. As for politics, they sincerely believe public life to be a male bailiwick. They reason that men have been running the country for the past two hundred years and are meant to continue to do so for centuries to come.

In short, men never would share power with women willingly. If we wanted it, we would have to take it.

My strategy required a great deal of dedicated preparation. For the two years that I would be national committeewoman and vice-chairman in both Northern and Southern California, I wanted to activate women to educate themselves about domestic and foreign affairs.

"We get the facts and we'll decide what we think the government should be doing," I explained. "Then we'll be prepared to ask tough questions of anyone aspiring to political office. If they can't answer, or they propose something with which we disagree, we won't support them. There's no advantage in Democratic women working to replace know-nothing Republicans with know-nothing Democrats."

Dorothy McAllister and her assistant, May Thompson Evans, had prepared an excellent series of pamphlets describing Franklin Roosevelt's New Deal programs and their effectiveness. For a start, I ordered batches of them to be sent to Democratic women all over the state.

In September 1939 Hitler invaded Poland. Melvyn and I heard the news on the radio. Two days later, with Poland crumbling, Britain and France declared war. Our worst fears were realized. I wept. Then the cynical pact between Germany and the Soviet was signed and Russia invaded Poland from the east. The news from the front was ghastly; it was a bloodbath.

Melvyn and I were among the many Americans who felt that American interests were best served by helping the Allies defend the democratic countries of Europe against the aggression of dictators. If Hitler couldn't be stopped in Europe, it wasn't likely that America would escape attack as soon as Germany consolidated its gains. Most Californians, however, felt removed by geography and interest from what was happening in Europe. The squabbles of foreigners, they maintained, were none of our business.

I planned a campaign to make women in the party better informed about the stake Americans had in the outcome of the war in Europe. It consisted of seminars all over the state at which women would hear the facts of the situation. As a teaching tool, I decided we would need pamphlets on Roosevelt's foreign policy of the caliber of those prepared by Dorothy McAllister on domestic issues.

I needed help. I made an appointment with a brilliant, scholarly woman, Mrs. Malbone Graham, regional director of the American Association of University Women. I explained to her that Leisa Bronson, whom she knew, was my adviser on domestic affairs. I needed someone with an equal grasp of the international scene to assist me in designing a foreign affairs program.

Mrs. Graham had just the person, Esther Murray, who headed the foreign policy division of the Association of University Women. She added that she wasn't certain of Esther's politics. It was possible that she wasn't a Democrat.

"I'm not recruiting Democrats," I told her. "I'm recruiting knowledgeable women who support Franklin Roosevelt's foreign policies."

Mrs. Graham arranged for me to sit next to Esther Murray at a luncheon so that I could judge for myself whether she was suitable. Within a few minutes of talking to her I knew that she was exactly what I wanted. She was informed, articulate, and as concerned as I was about Americans who opposed the gestures of support Roosevelt was making to Britain. I asked her if she would work with me to explain the issues to Democratic women.

She looked shocked. "I couldn't be active in politics," she said with an element of disdain. "I'm just not the type."

I wasn't going to let her get away with that. I said heatedly, "What's wrong with trying to get people elected who will support Roosevelt? Don't you care who goes to Congress? Is it enough for you to read about the mess in Europe and wring your hands because so many Americans don't understand the issues? Don't you want to have a voice in what our government does?"

We finished lunch with bruised feelings on both sides. She came to me a few days later. "I've thought over what you said," she told me gamely, "and I've decided that you're right. I'm ready to go to work. What do you want me to do first?"

She'd already begun. She showed me some maps of Europe illustrating the spread of Nazi Germany. She'd prepared them herself as visual aids for our presentations.

In November 1939 the Soviet Union invaded the small and peaceful country of Finland. Melvyn, a prominent member of the Motion Picture Democratic Committee, which had strong leftist

leanings, prepared a toughly worded resolution condemning the
Soviet for the aggression. Philip Dunne, a friend of Melvyn's who
wrote the screenplay for such films as *How Green Was My Valley* and *The Robe* and directed *Ten North Frederick*, also had
drafted a resolution of censure. The two men therefore collaborated on a jointly presented motion. After a bitter debate, the majority of Committee members voted against the Douglas-Dunne
Resolution.

Melvyn and Philip promptly resigned. Aggression is aggression
is aggression. It seemed to them inconsistent to condemn Germany's invasion of a peaceful neighbor but to find excuses when
Russia did the same.

Esther Murray and I redoubled our efforts. The seminars were
a great success, drawing throngs of women who were delighted to
be taken seriously. Esther and I made a fine team except that we
shared one failing: neither of us could read a road map. Almost
invariably we arrived at our destination looking very harried and
exactly one half hour late.

I realized as soon as I began to work in the Los Angeles office I
had created that the volume of activities I was undertaking in the
southern part of the state would make it impossible for me to do
a proper job in the north. If Malone could appoint me sum-
marily, I reasoned I could do the same. I had to unload my responsibility in the north or else I would never see my family—and
our household had grown with the addition of Gregory, Melvyn's
sixteen-year-old son by his first marriage.

The two women I knew best in San Francisco where the northern district was administered were Julia Porter and Catherine
Bauer. Neither had any experience in party politics but both supported Roosevelt to the hilt. Catherine was a disciplined professional with national recognition for her creative concepts about
community planning. She was married to a distinguished academic, William Wurster, who headed the School of Architecture
at the University of California at Berkeley after holding the same
post at Harvard. Julia Porter had just finished a term as president
of the San Francisco League of Women Voters and had a solid
background in national and international issues. Between the two

of them, Catherine and Julia knew almost every influential woman in the northern part of the state.

Both were intrigued by the task I outlined, that of making women aware of what was happening in the country and abroad. I promised them complete autonomy if they would share the job of co-chairman for the north but I had a recommendation that I put forth strongly. I had discovered that it was the habit in the Democratic party to include minority members—blacks, Mexicans, Asiatics, and so on—only in meetings in large public halls. Any time the meeting took place in a private home, only the white elite was invited. I urged Catherine and Julia to stop such discrimination. As I knew they would, they agreed at once.

My friendship with Catherine went back to my days in New York when we both were still single. That night at dinner in her home I regaled her with the story of my encounter with William Malone. She roared with laughter and I knew her heavenly sense of humor would guarantee the success of the partnership between Malone and my northern substitutes.

The first divisional meeting in the south under my chairmanship was to be held in a huge, lavish home in Long Beach. As I instructed, invitations were sent to *all* Democrats to attend. A week before the event, the woman who had provided the house called me in great distress. She told me that people in Long Beach were up in arms about black people coming to the meeting. Her voice rose to a hysterical pitch as she went on to say that leading male Democrats had announced they wouldn't attend unless black people were barred.

"What should I do?" she wailed.

"Nothing," I said.

"But if the men won't come," she asked, "*how can we have a meeting?*"

"We'll simply have it without them," I told her calmly. "In fact, the meeting will be a great success whether they come or not. I'm bringing two busloads from Los Angeles myself. Cheer up. If you stand firm, those Long Beach men will change their minds."

As I predicted, the meeting went smoothly. It wasn't long before it was accepted as natural that all minorities would be pres-

ent wherever Democrats met. I had almost forgotten the uproar
the first occasion provoked until the day of our first annual fund-
raising tea, which was held in our home. The governor and other
state and municipal officials were invited, along with two thousand other Democrats. One phoned me to ask if she could bring
out-of-town guests, some Democrats from Georgia, and I readily
agreed.

Almost the first to arrive were three carloads of black people,
one of them an enormous woman weighing over three hundred
pounds. My plan was to receive guests on the front steps and
show them into the house, through which they would proceed to
the spacious patio where tea was served. These first guests, however, either confused or plain tired, sat down in the living room
instead.

I paid little attention, busily welcoming the waves of Democrats who were climbing out of their cars. In a little while the
woman with the Georgians in tow made her arrival. The Georgians said they were thrilled to death to meet a movie star and exclaimed about the handsomeness of my husband and our house
with an equal degree of rapture. Eventually they went inside,
where the first sight to greet them was a room full of black people. They were back on the porch in a twinkling, explaining that
they had something else pressing to do.

"Please don't apologize," I said sweetly. "There's no need. I
know perfectly well why you're leaving. I want you to appreciate
that this is a tea for the Democratic party and in California we
welcome *all* registered Democrats at such events."

My experience with the migrant workers had shown me that
there is no substitute for first-hand observation. At a time when a
housing bill was before the Los Angeles City Council, I organized
a bus tour of the slums. Observation of the lamentable housing
conditions brought home the need for decent low-cost housing as
no orator ever could.

While I was launching my women's division programs, Melvyn
was active in the presidential election, giving speeches all over
America in support of Franklin Roosevelt. At the President's
request, he made one quick trip to Texas to speak on behalf of a

promising young New Deal congressman, Lyndon Baines Johnson. Johnson was a comer, Melvyn told me, a charming man with a quiet air of authority that already had won him the friendship of fellow Texan Sam Rayburn, the congressman most directly responsible for steering New Deal legislation through the House.

I too was drawn into the campaign. Despite my many commitments in California to get the women's division moving, I crossed the country many times and gave a total of 168 speeches for Roosevelt and other New Deal Democrats, paying my own expenses as Melvyn did his.

When the election returns were in that November, California women delivered votes at a time when the divided Democrats needed them most. The Roosevelt-Wallace ticket swept the state, and the country.

I was finding political speaking very different from anything else I had ever done on a public stage. After a play or a concert, people who approached me always talked about my performance —how well I did, how lovely I looked, and so on. But after a campaign speech the embarrassing preoccupation with me didn't happen. Talk afterward was about the issues I had raised; people were drawn to me because they wanted to discuss matters of enormous importance.

I found that kind of contact with strangers vastly more satisfying than flattery had been. For the first time I understood something about my Grandmother Hannah, that participating in current events must have been deeply gratifying for her. There was an excitement and relevance about politics that singing and acting lacked.

The Steinbeck Committee was preparing for its second Christmas party for children of migrants, this time in a Farm Security Camp in the Imperial Valley, home of some of the most hostile farmers in the state. I determined to make an effort to win their sympathy. I reasoned that they would not be able to resist the appeal of destitute children at Christmas and perhaps this beginning would lead to acceptance of the adults as well.

I was shocked by the ruthless rejection I met everywhere. The growers were incensed particularly because the Steinbeck Committee was inviting children from miles around, the needier ones who were suffering in the primitive ditchbank shacks. They believed it was part of a plot to stir up dissension against them.

I retorted angrily that I was willing to cancel the party and inform the press that the rich farmers were opposed to a party for impoverished children. They looked at one another uneasily. They suggested that I meet with local clergymen, which I was happy to do. To my dismay, the clergymen were as antagonistic as the growers. They put me through an ordeal of cold questioning for almost three hours, and then one of them sneered:

"I see, Mrs. Douglas, you're just a do-gooder, a Lady Bountiful."

With some asperity I asked, "Do you *Christian* gentlemen want me to cancel this party for children? If so, I will. And I will tell everyone why the party can't take place."

They replied that they hadn't intended any such thing. I asked if they would feel better if a sheriff and deputies attended to make certain that the party didn't lead to an assault on the neighbors.

"Since it's a party for children," I added sarcastically, "I hope the lawmen will keep their guns out of sight." With which, the nasty session broke up.

To offset some of the rumors of rabble-rousing that were being spread by the growers, I issued an open invitation to local citizens to attend the party if they wished. We planned to follow the same plan at the Brawley Farm Security Camp as had proved so effective at Shafter the year before. Food was served from long tables out of doors and families ate picnic-style on the grass. Inside the main building, we heaped toys on a row of tables end to end. I was told that many of the children had never owned a manufactured toy in their lives and I had a qualm that the situation might get out of hand.

Steinbeck Committee volunteers took their places behind the toy tables, ready to hand each child the desired one, and I stood outside the door to keep order in the line of children quietly waiting. We allowed the first children inside and then the line stopped. I rushed in to see what was wrong. Children were standing in front of the tables staring glassy-eyed at the mounds of dolls, trucks, musical toys, games and other favorite children's toys. None had chosen anything.

My friend Gladys Robinson, wife of actor Edward G. Robinson, was entreating the first child to select a toy. The child didn't move or speak. Gladys held up a gorgeously dressed Shirley Temple doll.

"Would you like this?" she asked.

No response.

She picked up a xylophone with keys the colors of the rainbow. "Do you want this?"

The child looked miserable but didn't move or speak.

It was the same with the next child, and the next, and the next. One of the volunteers lost her temper.

"What's going on here?" she snapped at me. "These children don't want anything."

"No," I replied, understanding dawning, "they want everything."

It was a feast of riches before a starving man; they were in agony because picking one toy meant losing all the others. I instructed the volunteers to make the choice for the children on the basis of gender and age and hunch, and simply distribute the toys as they saw fit. From then on we kept the line moving in a happy, orderly way. Children went in one door and emerged a few minutes later, clutching a lovely toy, from another.

The national committee of the Democratic party met in Washington that spring. Mrs. Roosevelt invited me to stay at the White House and put me in the Lincoln Room next to Lorena Hickok. She knew we'd like each other at once, and we did.

Lorena Hickok, known as "Hick" to all her friends, was a reporter for Associated Press who was assigned in 1928 to cover Franklin Roosevelt's successful campaign for governor of New York. She met Mrs. Roosevelt then but their friendship really bloomed when Hick covered the 1932 presidential election. In her stories she described Mrs. Roosevelt as the "sleeper" in the campaign and predicted that a Roosevelt victory would bring a very unusual First Lady to the White House.

"I remember puffing, panting, and perspiring as I followed her through a cornfield somewhere in Nebraska or Iowa," Hick told me. "She moved swiftly, coolly and as easily as though she were accustomed to striding through a cornfield every day of her life. With despair I watched her glide nimbly through a barbed wire fence into an adjacent pasture."

After the election, Hick suggested to Mrs. Roosevelt that she should hold regular press conferences just as her husband did. The President agreed and Mrs. Roosevelt stopped protesting when it was pointed out to her that every major newspaper and news service would then have to hire women reporters. They wouldn't dare ignore the First Lady, and women journalists therefore would advance in status. At that time almost all women reporters covered only teas and fashion. Mrs. Roosevelt made two rules: no men reporters at her press conferences and no political questions.

On March 6, 1932, two days after the inauguration, Mrs. Roosevelt held the first press conference ever given by the wife of a President.

Hick meanwhile came to the conclusion that she would have to leave the Associated Press. She found the Roosevelts such remarkable people that she could no longer report impartially about their activities. Harry Hopkins invited her to work with him as his confidential adviser in the office of Federal Relief Aministration, a sensitive position that required Hick to travel around the country assessing the effectiveness and errors of New Deal welfare programs.

I found the White House very subdued during that visit early in 1940. The throngs of blacks, union leaders, young liberals and spunky women who brought the President news of grass-roots movements were gone. We dined quietly and afterward the President, Mrs. Roosevelt and I viewed a film in a makeshift screening room set up in the wide corridor on the second floor.

When it was over Mrs. Roosevelt excused herself and left me alone with Franklin Roosevelt. He seemed tired and depressed. I had misgivings about adding more to his burden but I was full of concern that programs for migrant people weren't expanding to meet the need. I asked his permission to tell him the story of the Christmas toys and the deprived children who found it impossible to make a choice. I said that we must do more to help those people.

"Surely, Mr. President," I said, "we can't abandon those children?"

His eyes filled with tears. His voice broke as he answered, "Don't tell me any more, Helen. You and Eleanor, you must stop ganging up on me. There are some things we can't do now . . . we just *can't*."

I knew it was the truth. New Deal programs were beginning to be rolled back as America put its resources elsewhere in order to respond to the worsening situation in Europe. On May 10 that year, Nazi Germany's tanks pounded across the borders of Belgium and the Netherlands. The next day they were in France, sweeping around the concrete bunkers of the Maginot Line that we had been promised were impregnable. By the end of the month British troops were evacuated from the port of Dunkirk by pleasure boats able to shuttle across a miraculously calm English Channel. A few weeks later we saw newsreel footage of Hitler dancing a jig as France signed the surrender.

Benito Mussolini, fascist dictator of Italy, picked that moment to exercise his function as Hitler's ally. Italy declared war on Britain.

The world awaited Germany's invasion fleet but Hitler paused to soften up resistance by bombing British cities. That September the Battle of Britain was fought in the skies as a handful of Royal Air Force fighter pilots struggled to defend their island.

My cousin Walter Pick wrote to my friend Alis de Sola in October to explain to her why Melvyn hadn't found time to comment on a new play she had written. Walter wrote:

> . . . if you could see us these days you would think you were in Grand Central Station at the rush hour or, if you prefer, take Times Square on New Year's Eve. It is a madhouse. When Melvyn isn't at the studio, he is either writing campaign speeches or making them—ditto for Helen. . . . Besides having three telephones ringing constantly, two typewriters going at a great rate, a continuous stream of telegraph boys and people to interview, the

elements managed to provide an earthquake of no little proportions and a brushfire, the limits of which were in doubt for some hours. . . .

In December 1940, with Britain still holding out though London burned every night under German bombers, Herbert Agar telephoned. Agar was active in Wendell Willkie's Fight for Freedom Committee, which was attempting to gain support in America for sending aid to Britain. He wanted Melvyn to establish a branch in Los Angeles. Melvyn agreed at once, despite my protests that he was already overloaded with work at the studio, on the State Welfare Board, and in the campaigns.

I wrote Alis:

> Melvyn is nearly crazy with work. I don't know how he is going to keep on in politics and be a movie actor as well. It seems to me to be too heavy a schedule for anyone.

One month later Melvyn was not only the most active member of the Fight for Freedom branch in California, he was its director.

Those of us who believed that the United States had a moral responsibility and a self-interest stake in helping Britain were opposed by the America First Committee, the most powerful isolationist group in the country, whose success rested in considerable part on the popularity of its most notable recruit, Charles Lindbergh, the appealing hero of the world's first solo transatlantic flight.

That winter Lindbergh was in great demand as a speaker. His radio broadcast in 1939 advising Americans to stay out of the European war had been printed in full in the New York *Times* and the *Herald Tribune* and his arguments were being repeated everywhere, particularly his declaration: "We must not permit our sentiment, our pity, our personal feelings of sympathy to obscure the issue, to affect our children's lives. We must be as impersonal as a surgeon with his knife. . . ."

Congress was considering Roosevelt's Lend-Lease Bill to give Britain fifty overage destroyers to protect vital convoys from Canada in return for establishing American naval bases in strategic parts of the British Empire. Lindbergh appeared before a congressional committee examining the legislation and said:

"Personally, I do not believe that England is in a position to win the war." He recommended that the United States keep its hands clean in order to be in the position of a neutral when it came time to negotiate the peace.

Despite the strong lobby of the America Firsters, the mood of such groups as the Fight for Freedom Committee prevailed. On March 11, 1941, Congress approved the Lend-Lease Bill. With the barriers to direct help for Britain removed, American automobile plants geared up and in an astonishingly short time were turning out five hundred airplanes a day.

Only recently did I learn how the miracle was accomplished. In Victor Reuther's book *The Brothers Reuther*, I found this account of that period when Walter Reuther was head of the United Auto Workers Union at General Motors:

> Months before Hitler's armies marched eastward into Poland, Walter and I had had a conversation with Ben Blackwood, a trusted aide in the General Motors department and himself a skilled toolmaker, about Roosevelt's call for aid to Britain and the kind of help America was best equipped to give. . . . As toolmakers we knew it would be many years before American industries turning out civilian goods could be tooled to produce weapons in any quantity. But, as Walter said . . . a plane was made of steel and aluminum like other vehicles, and its component parts could be manufactured by essentially the same kind of machines and machine tools that stamp out the parts of an automobile. . . . A careful survey taken by Ben Blackwood and me in GM plants all over the country corroborated Walter's hypothesis and became the basis of his proposal for the "500 planes a day" program, to be undertaken by the automotive industry.

Philip Murray, president of the CIO, submitted the proposal to Roosevelt on December 20, 1940. Roosevelt sent it to William S. Knudsen, then a co-director of GM's production team, with a note: "I do not know if you have seen all of this. It is well worth our while, I think, to give a great deal of attention to this proposal."

Thanks to the farsightedness of such men as Reuther and

Roosevelt, America was ready to respond when Britain was in peril. I knew Walter Reuther well and always considered him one of this country's greatest statesmen, but it wasn't until I read his brother's history of the UAW that I appreciated what a valuable man he was, and why the President and Mrs. Roosevelt held him in such high esteem.

In September 1941 Franklin Roosevelt and Charles Lindbergh were scheduled to give major addresses on the same night. More than seven thousand people had packed a theater in Des Moines to hear the "Lone Eagle" speak against American intervention. Roosevelt was speaking on a radio network and the Des Moines organizers decided to allow the audience to listen to the broadcast before Lindbergh spoke.

To the consternation of America Firsters, Roosevelt's speech was punctuated eleven times with cheers, while Lindbergh several times provoked boos. When Lindbergh revealed the depth of his anti-Semitism, warning the country of the danger of Jewish "ownership and influence in our motion pictures, our press, our radio, and our government . . ." his credibility vanished.

In California the women's division I headed was making startling gains in winning votes for Roosevelt Democrats. When the party had an impressive national convention of Democratic women, I was inspired to try the same tactic on a regional basis. I threw myself into preparations for a two-day conference that would send voters to the polling booths in a mood to throw out the Republicans and fill Congress with Roosevelt supporters.

We invited registered Democrats from eleven western states to attend the sessions in Los Angeles and all but took over the Ambassador Hotel. We advertised that the most notable figures in the Democratic party would be in attendance, and we delivered. Edward J. Flynn, national chairman, and vice-chairman Gladys Tillet agreed to attend, and Governor Culbert Olson lent the support of his office.

Lorena Hickok, who was secretary of the Democratic National Committee at that time, was a tower of strength on my behalf in Washington. At her suggestion I included Mrs. Mattison Boyd Jones, the woman I had defeated for the job as national committeewoman, in a prominent place in the program. Hick, an astute politician, also sent me names of influential Democrats who would be gratified to be invited to one of the dinner parties I planned to give in our home.

Leisa Bronson worked hard to organize the conference on behalf of Southern California and Julia Porter and Catherine Bauer drummed up interest in the northern part of the state. Bill Malone, who had come to realize that women could tip the scales in an election, put his considerable power at our disposal. To gain the widest possible audience for the issues we would be discussing, there was an intense effort made to contact newspapers and radio stations. We wanted coverage before, during and after the conference.

Melvyn and I gave two dinner parties. The first was on the eve of the conference, September 11, and the second on closing night, September 13. We invited one hundred and ten guests to the first and slightly more to the other. Both affairs were formal, sit-down dinners and both went off smoothly, thanks to Alma Hermann and her staff.

Alma was a superb caterer who became a friend and generous supporter. She came into my life when Melvyn and I attended a dinner party given by Herbert Marshall and were astonished that the food served to some seventy people was not only delicious but *hot*. When I asked who was the magician in the kitchen, Herbert introduced me to Alma. After that I never had any qualms about entertaining as many people as our house could hold.

We established the tone of the conference at that kickoff dinner. Melvyn and I gave a reading of Stephen Vincent Benét's powerful poem *Listen to the People*. Sprinkled among the dazzled Democrats were some of our friends in the industry, Edward G. Robinson, Joan Bennett, Herbert Marshall, Douglas Fairbanks, Jr., Bette Davis and Walter Wanger.

The highlight of the conference on the first day was a banquet at which Secretary of Agriculture Claude Wickard spoke, after which Edward J. Flynn and R. J. Reynolds, national treasurer of the Democratic party, said a few words. Seated in the banquet hall were a number of California farmers, who came in response to hand-written invitations I sent, using a list supplied me from the Department of Agriculture.

We had a luncheon on the second day to honor Mary Norton, the outstanding congresswoman from New Jersey who was chairman of the House Labor Committee, and Gladys Tillet. This time I wrote personal invitations to every labor leader in California asking them to the luncheon.

I was particularly proud of the program that followed the luncheon, which presented a panel discussion of U.S. foreign policy —and every foreign expert was a woman. Twelve university and college professors received hand-written invitations from me to join us for that session.

The hard work paid off handsomely. Eight hundred women registered for the conference, and national radio carried the panel discussion on foreign policy. I was grateful for the cooperation we received from the Ambassador Hotel, which gave us free such extras as conference rooms where Secretary Wickard could confer privately with farmers and Mary Norton could talk with union leaders. When our blue-ribbon guest list proved too large to be accommodated at one head table, the hotel ingeniously arranged three tiers of head tables to seat them all.

We did it inexpensively too, even for 1941's low prices. Banquet tickets were $2.58 each, including tax; the Norton luncheon cost $1.29 and a sumptuous working breakfast was $1.03.

The result was a triumph. Mary Norton's impassioned speech asking labor to support Roosevelt's policies led to resolutions by the AFL, CIO and Railroad Brotherhood in favor of the White House's stands.

Lorena Hickok wrote to Eleanor Roosevelt about the conference. Her letter, which is preserved in the Roosevelt Library in Hyde Park, comments on the remarks Ed Flynn made at the first-day banquet. Hick wrote:

> . . . the conference has been a thrilling success. . . . Ed Flynn's answer to Lindbergh when he spoke at the banquet was the best speech I've ever heard in my life. . . .

I had a letter from a Colorado delegate, Lucille Beck, who said:

> I have attended three [conferences] in recent years, and it was very much the best Democratic Women's Division Conference I

ever attended. . . . If the wheels creaked underneath, there certainly was no evidence of it to the visitors. . . .

Esther Murray, my cohort in spreading the word about our foreign policy to women all over the state, recently spoke very kindly of my contribution during that period. She said, "No other person came close to the influence of this dynamic, devoted and selfless woman on the political structure of California.

"No money was provided by the party organization, who tolerated women as a troublesome minority. So Helen gave of her own, helped others with money-raising projects, and financed the opening of an office staffed with at least one full-time secretary.

"Activity was the word—educational activity. So it was that anti-Roosevelt congressmen began to fall by the wayside. California became an overwhelmingly Democratic state and Helen Gahagan Douglas remained the most loved and respected of its leaders.

"She was certainly the most effective woman in the Democratic party. There are those who felt she was the most effective *person* in the party."

I include Esther's comments at the risk of appearing immodest because they describe what was happening in the state at that time. Women were on the move and we were making an impact.

As we prepared for the congressional elections, early indications were that Republicans would take many seats away from Democrats. Predictions were that Roosevelt would face a hostile Congress in 1942.

I went to Sacramento for the state convention, where I was the keynote speaker. Later the convention unanimously reelected me state vice-chairman. What was interesting that weekend was what I suspect was a clever attempt by Harry Bridges, radical leader of the longshoremen's union, to compromise and discredit me. I believe he sicced onto me the handsomest man I had ever seen who hung at my elbow everywhere I went. That night he kept phoning my room, begging to see me. I suspected, correctly I still believe, that the plan was for someone to burst into the room and catch us in bed together.

I was having none of it. On the last day of the convention, the man gave up. He scarcely spoke to me. I suppose I had injured his pride and his reputation as a lady-killer. They'd sent him out to get me and he had failed. It was the only time in my career that anyone tried that particular tactic against me.

I threw myself into campaigning for the candidates the women's division was endorsing. "There's never going to be any Republican trend out here," I told reporters. "This state is going Democratic, and no one knows it better than Governor Olson."

When Californians went to the polling booths that November, they showed that the once Republican state was now solidly Democrat. In contrast to elsewhere in the country, where there were Democratic losses, in California we took four seats away from Republicans. The women's division glowed with pride.

Meanwhile it was painful to see the havoc in Works Progress Administration programs as the result of budget cuts. One of the early casualties was WPA theater, which had given Orson Welles his start. It was followed by the cancellation of almost all the cultural activities which had flowered under WPA and the National Youth Authority. California had two WPA symphony orchestras, one in the north under Leopold Stokowski and one in the south. The northern one survived the ax but the one in the south was scheduled to disappear.

On a Sunday morning, December 7, 1941, the entire orchestra from Southern California arrived on my doorstep bearing instruments. The musicians had come to plead with me to intercede on their behalf with the President. In the middle of the unhappy discussion I was interrupted by a telephone call. I returned to the living room with dreadful news.

"I'm sorry," I said. "There'll be no more NYA orchestras for a while—in Southern California or anywhere else. We've just been attacked at Pearl Harbor by the Japanese."

The musicians rose slowly, gathering up the cellos and flutes and horns they had brought with them. They moved like sleepwalkers and silently went out of the door.

Like all Americans that day, I felt that my life was no longer quite my own. Melvyn left at once for Washington, where he volunteered to work without pay in the Arts Division of the Office of Civilian Defense which was mobilizing actors, directors, producers, writers, composers and technicians to make films to help the war effort.

President Roosevelt appointed me co-chairman of civilian defense for Southern California. Our responsibility was to train women how to react to an enemy bombing attack or a landing on the coast. Every day I worked long hours in the State Building in Los Angeles organizing civilian programs such as conserving food and other material that would be needed by our armed forces.

The West Coast fully expected a Japanese attack, though the extent of the damage to the American fleet wasn't admitted at that time. All we knew was that the unthinkable had occurred: the enemy, temporarily at any rate, was stronger than the United States.

Californians of Japanese origin were the objects of hysterical accusations of being spies and there was talk of putting them all in internment camps. This issue, I believe, was one of the many over which Governor Olson disagreed with his attorney general, Earl Warren, who quietly was coming to the conclusion that he would run for governor himself in the next election.

I talked to Harold Ickes many times on the telephone. Harold was distressed at the tide of sentiment against Japanese-Americans and felt it did loyal citizens a grave disservice. For myself, I was of two minds about the proposed evacuation of all people of Japanese descent who lived on the West Coast. I disagreed with those who declared that they were a fifth column who would turn against their adopted country if Japan attacked, but I was concerned for their safety if they remained in their communities. Insults and beatings were beginning to occur and I feared we could have mob violence against the peaceful Japanese-Americans.

In the end, in an infamous act of injustice, the Japanese were herded inland. My younger brother, Walter Gahagan, later was in a position to influence their fate. Walter, a brilliant graduate of Columbia Law School in 1935, was launched on what promised to be an extraordinary career in law. From the prestigious New York law firm of Hughes, Shurman & Dwight, he had moved to the post of assistant U. S. Attorney for the southern district of New York. While in this position, he was selected by the

U. S. Attorney General to conduct the investigation of the judiciary which led to the trial of Judge J. Warren Davis, at which
Walter was the U. S. Government's chief prosecutor.

Walter joined the army in 1942 with the rank of major and immediately was attached to the General Staff. After the victory in
Europe he was one of two officers assigned the task of deciding
what was to be done with the "dangerous Japanese" still confined
in prison villages. Many authorities believed they should be allowed only restricted movement.

Walter, asked to evaluate the risk to America, spent two and a
half months studying the files on Nisei-Americans and then
visited the camps. He inspected the homes the escorting officers
wanted to show him but he also insisted on seeing homes not on
the tour. In one of these he found a tiny Japanese-American
woman—"about five-foot-one," Walter said sarcastically, "and
very dangerous"—who showed him pictures of her husband and
brother, both in U. S. Army uniforms, and the walls hung with
gold, silver and bronze stars that the two men had won in an all-
Japanese regiment that had been earning more citations than any
other regiment in the history of the United States.

Walter put in a strong recommendation that the Japanese-
Americans were no threat and should be released without restric-
tions. Happily, his recommendation was followed and he was
given a commendation for it.

At the time of the panic after Pearl Harbor I couldn't make up
my mind about the enforced evacuation. I insisted on visiting the
camps to assure myself that the housing arrangements were humane, which they were. I never did believe that the Nisei were a
threat to the safety of Americans, but I thought Americans were
a threat to *their* safety and was relieved to have them out of the
reach of racists.

Civilian defense headquarters one day received notice that the
United States was running short of aluminum necessary for building airplanes. I was asked to notify patriotic Americans to donate
aluminum pots and pans to the war effort. My heart sank. Our
spanking new house was fully equipped with brand-new aluminum cookware of the finest quality.

We placed a huge container in front of the Los Angeles City Hall and invited Californians to donate their pots and pans. My lovely cookware was the first into the bin.

Melvyn was so busy with the OCD in Washington that he was able to come home only twice, once when I was sick with a strep throat, and another time when he spent two days helping us move into a charming new beach house in Carmel. Living on our savings as we were, I reasoned that in a pinch we could rent the big house in the Outpost and live in the small airy house near the Carmel Mission.

I made one trip to Washington with a special purpose in mind. Again, I stayed at the White House. Mrs. Roosevelt arranged for me to speak to the President early in the morning before his work day started. I waited for him in the living room on the second floor. When he was wheeled in from the bedroom, he looked exhausted. Before speaking he put his face in his hands and rubbed hard, as though he could wipe away fatigue that way; then, throwing back his head, he gave me a reassuring smile and a cheery, "Good morning, Helen."

I hated to bother him. I considered apologizing and backing out, but I knew he would have no patience if I had cold feet. I plunged into what I had come to say.

"Mr. President, I'm speaking to you as national committee-woman. We hear that you are considering Edwin Pauley as your new Under Secretary of the Navy. We in California urge you not to do it. He's an oilman and we believe his oil interests make him an unsuitable choice."

The President seemed to sag. He listened while I described Pauley's connection with such oilmen as J. B. Elliott but gave no indication of what he was thinking. When I was finished, he thanked me with great courtesy and said he would consider what I had said.

I returned to California, where our household had grown. In addition to Peter, Mary Helen, and Melvyn's son Gregory, we now had Melvyn's widowed mother living with us. Walter Pick helped relieve the load of office work as I tried to spend as much time as I could with the children to make up for Melvyn's absence.

Melvyn wasn't satisfied that his contribution to the war effort
was enough. In the hothouse of Washington politics, he found
that our friendship with the White House could be a liability.
Though he was working as a volunteer, there was an undercurrent
of resentment in some places and accusations that he had received his position because of favoritism.

Melvyn was forty-one years old but he enlisted as a private in
the army. He was sworn in on December 6, 1942, as he put it "at
a special ceremony set up to beat an automatic exemption from
service for men over forty." He refused a commission in order to
avoid any implication that he had exploited his friendship with
the President.

Melvyn was in good physical condition but the training was designed for robust teenagers, not men older than forty. One evening he phoned to tell me he'd been on a simulated forced march
with a fully loaded backpack, at the end of which he was ordered
to climb a steep hill. He got through the ordeal but told me wryly
that if there had been an enemy at the top of the hill he
wouldn't have had the strength to lift his gun.

After basic training he was sent to the School for Special Services in Lexington, Virginia. I visited him there for a happy reunion and then hurried to New York to see my family. Mother
had written that Frederick didn't look well.

He was in bed when Mother and I arrived to see him in his
apartment. We found him on the telephone to the office, trying
to keep in touch with the family business despite his illness. His
appearance was shocking. I couldn't believe that anyone could
lose so much weight in the year since I'd seen him.

I made a wretched effort at light conversation, since he made
it clear he didn't want to talk about his mysterious ailment. I asked
if he went to the office much.

"It depends," he replied carefully. "Some days I do . . . some
days I don't."

Before Melvyn finished his training in Lexington, Frederick
was dead of leukemia at forty-three.

After the funeral his wife Alice read a letter he had written to
us all a few months earlier. He had entrusted it to his doctor with

instructions that it be given to Alice after his death. I don't have it before me, but the essence of the letter was this:

> The doctors are not to blame for my death. I have leukemia. There is no medical cure for cancer of the blood. The doctors have done all they can to make me comfortable. I asked them not to inform any member of the Gerli or Gahagan families that I was going to die. I saw no reason why the last months of my life should be made torturous for those I love.

The family gathered after the funeral to discuss the fate of the Gahagan Construction Corporation. William had done what he could to help run the company but each time he exposed himself to the pressure he found it was too much. If the company was to survive, our youngest Gahagan, Walter, would have to come to the rescue.

Walter, handsome in his uniform as a General Staff major, had served first with General Hugh Drum of the 1st Army and had been transferred to the Eastern Defense Command under General Grunert.

Taking over the company was absolutely the last thing that Walter wanted to do. He loved law and had demonstrated that he had prospects to be U. S. Attorney General or a partner in a famous law firm. His only contact with the business was as the "smiled-on brother," as he put it. Besides, he was in the army.

Also, the company was in terrible shape. Father's fortune had been almost destroyed in the stock market crash and ensuing Depression. At one time he had held $2,500,000 in stock in the Manufacturers Trust but in 1931, when he died, shares that had been worth $285 apiece had dropped to $15. During the thirties Frederick had been forced to give up Father's extensive land holdings on Long Island because he couldn't pay the taxes. In fact, we hadn't yet paid our debt to Liebmann.

Walter studied the situation and found it a disaster. The company had contracts for dredging what would be Idlewild Airport, later John F. Kennedy Airport, but the work wasn't completed. Our dredge *Peru* in the Panama Canal area hadn't been overhauled in three years and would need expensive renovation estimated to cost $300,000. Another dredge, *Nebraska*, was at Bos-

ton's Logan Airport. One of the most powerful dredges on the
eastern seaboard, it unfortunately was operated by electricity
which couldn't always be made available at dredging sites.

We had a shipyard at Washington, North Carolina, which was
building thirty wooden oil barges, but was in some difficulty. And
the company owed almost a million dollars in taxes.

Walter said that taking over the company would be like a
widow in India climbing on the funeral pyre; he would be consumed. In the end he was persuaded to try to save the company
out of concern for the staff. There were three vice-presidents and
several other engineers who had joined the company twenty-five
to forty years ago and were still working for Gahagan. If we dissolved the company, it would be difficult for them to relocate.

Walter went to see his general and explained the problem. The
general immediately said, "Of course you can be released from
military service. Your company is engaged in building projects
that are vital to the war effort."

"You don't understand, sir," Walter said. "I want to do both. I
want to stay in the army and I want to be president of Gahagan
Construction, and I think I can do both in good conscience."

Which he did. Under Walter's direction the company gradually emerged from its debts. He proved to be a superb gambler.
Moving the company's meager resources wholly into dredging, he
opened an office in Boston and made a liaison with the powerful
Byrne Organization in Washington. Lillian and I remained self-
sufficient but the company did pay William for the consultation
services he was able to provide, and Walter took over Mother's
care. Mother was living in a handsome apartment at Park Avenue
and Fifty-fourth Street in New York.

When I returned to California after Frederick's death I had a
request to meet with Jessie Terry. Jessie was a black woman, a respected leader of the black community and an ardent Democrat.
A few days earlier in her home she had presided at a meeting of
black leaders who were concerned that Roosevelt's executive order
prohibiting racial discrimination in defense plants and shipyards
was being ignored in California. The decision of the meeting was
to ask me to use my connection with the White House to bring
the matter to the President's attention.

I got in touch with Mrs. Roosevelt at once. The result was that a second executive order was issued and the plants and shipyards were forced to comply. For the first time, black Americans had equal job opportunity.

Melvyn graduated from training with the rank of first lieutenant and was assigned to the India-Burma-China theater as director of the Entertainment Production Unit. He was to demonstrate great foresight and initiative in recognizing the importance of entertainment for the morale of soldiers and airmen far from home. He planned the extensive USO camp show program in that theater and for almost three years tirelessly toured bases to learn the local conditions and problems.

The night before Melvyn sailed for India, our friends Lola and Jack Leighter drove me and our son Peter to join Melvyn for dinner at a hotel near the naval base. Gregory was away at school and we decided Mary Helen was too young for the trip.

Peter held his father's hand throughout dinner but didn't cry, not even when we hugged Melvyn good-bye. On the way home, our nine-year-old flung himself on the floor of the car and sobbed his heart out. As for me, I was in a state of agony and loss—and fear. Melvyn was going into the Pacific theater at a time when the Japanese army and navy were triumphing in every battle.

Melvyn was under no illusions that the war would be over quickly. He left me with his savings, some $18,000, which we knew would not stretch very far. I determined not to touch them at all. I still had some money of my own. But it would take major economizing to get through. On the day after he sailed I gave our five household help two weeks' notice, keeping only the gardener to maintain the outside appearance of the house. I began to do the cooking and cleaning myself and discovered that I was mildly competent at both.

Melvyn's brother George and his family were having a difficult time finding accommodation in Los Angeles, which was jammed with war workers and the families of servicemen. I invited him, his wife Sarah, and their two children, Marvin and Mona Rita, to move in with me, Grandmother Lena, Gregory (who was soon to join the Merchant Marine), Peter, Mary Helen, and two dogs, a

Doberman pinscher and an Irish setter. Their arrival helped fill
the gap that Melvyn left.

Reporters who came to interview me about my political activities found the chaos unnerving, but the bustle seemed natural to
me. Whenever it got too much, I went for a long walk in the
mountains or else dropped over to visit such good friends as
Orson Welles and his wife Rita Hayworth.

I was seeing a lot of Lillian Ford, a tiny dynamo who was married to Thomas F. Ford and was responsible in good part for his
phenomenal success in representing the Fourteenth District in
Congress for the preceding twelve years. One day Lillian asked
when I planned to return to the theater. I was surprised by the
question. I really hadn't thought about acting or singing for a
long time. I told her that I would give it some consideration
when I finished my terms as national committeewoman and state
vice-chairman.

She eyed me shrewdly.

"You're hooked, Helen," she told me after a moment. "You
might as well do something really important and run for
Congress."

"Never," I assured her flatly.

Soon after, Tom Ford approached me. He was feeling his years,
he said, and wanted to retire that year. He was so indiscreet as to
tell a reporter, "I'm fed up associating with nitwits."

Out of loyalty to the party, however, he didn't want to have his
seat taken by a Republican or a right-wing Democrat who
wouldn't support Roosevelt.

"If you'll run in my place," he said, "I can retire with a clear
conscience. You and I see eye to eye on causes and I know you're
a fighter."

"I couldn't bear it," I told him. "I just couldn't bear it."

"What do you mean?" he asked.

I explained, "I've sat in the gallery of the House of Representatives and listened to the discussions. They're *boring*. You're
asking me to sit and listen to that tedium day after day? I'd go
stark raving mad!"

"Helen, if someone's dull and long-winded, you just walk off
the floor. You don't have to stay there and listen to it."

"You know I wouldn't do that, Tom," I said. "No, I'm sorry. It's out of the question. I simply won't run for Congress."

He was becoming exasperated. "Listen to reason," he told me sternly. "You've *got* to do it. The President has to have people he can depend on in Congress. We must make sure his programs are supported. If you don't run, the Fourteenth might be represented by someone who will work to defeat White House bills."

I continued to refuse. Tom mentioned my reluctance to Franklin Roosevelt, who wrote urging me to change my mind so that Tom could retire.

Mrs. Roosevelt happened to be in California to give a lecture. She said to me, "I know Franklin has asked you to run, Helen, and we'd both like to have you in Washington, but don't do it unless you're certain that you can be elected."

I couldn't make up my mind. Esther Murray and I were sitting in the women's division office with only a week remaining before the deadline to file. The phone in the outer office kept ringing as friends called to urge me to do it, and also not to do it. Phil Connelly, chairman of the extreme-left Industrial Union Council, CIO, in Los Angeles, a man rumored to be a communist, was waiting to see me.

I wished he would go away. I knew why he was there. He wanted to persuade me to run in my own congressional district, the Fifteenth, which took in most of Hollywood. John Costello, a conservative Democrat, was solidly entrenched there and I was certain to lose the nomination. Connelly didn't want me in Washington because he knew I wasn't an uncritical supporter of labor. We'd clashed before over issues where I judged labor was being unreasonable and he'd discovered that I didn't automatically condemn management and I didn't automatically applaud the union. That wasn't the kind of person he wanted to see in Congress.

I was torn with misgivings. What would it mean to the children if I accepted? With Melvyn away, they needed their only parent on the job. What would happen to my career as an actress and singer? Madame Cehanovska already was furious at the mention of Eleanor Roosevelt, who she believed had lured me from

greatness on the opera stage. Could I retrain myself after a few
years in Congress?

My secretary said that Tom Ford was on the telephone. I told
him about Connelly waiting to demand that I run in the Fifteenth District and Tom lost his temper.

"Let me talk to that (unprintable)" he shouted. Connelly used
the phone in my office. I heard him say that he wouldn't support
me if I ran in the Fourteenth Congressional District. There was a
long silence at our end of the line while Tom Ford loudly
denounced Connelly's character and motives. He ended with a
bellow I could hear plainly:

"Helen Gahagan Douglas will be elected no matter what you
do!"

When Connelly hung up, red-faced, I knew what I would do. I
picked up my handbag. There was no time to lose; I was going to
file.

When I arrived at City Hall I found the corridors crowded
with reporters. When they saw me, they flocked to ask what I was
doing there. I replied that I was filing to run for House of Representatives for the Fourteenth District. A few of them expressed
surprise. How could I run in the Fourteenth? they asked. I lived
in the Fifteenth. I smiled, kept my silence, and filed for the Fourteenth.

One reporter had a hunch that I probably knew what I was
doing. He suggested that they investigate further before they
wrote a story that I had made a naïve mistake. In fact, odd as it
may seem, it was perfectly legitimate for me to file in a district in
which I didn't live. No California law forbid it. Several other
states also had this gap in regulation. In the early days of the
New Deal, New York's Fiorello LaGuardia ran and was elected in
a district in which he didn't reside.

Susie Clifton, a key member of the campaign that made Culbert Olson governor of California, went with me to file my
papers. As I was filling out the forms, Susie asked Benny Hite,
the registrar of voters, whether the Roosevelt delegation had yet
qualified for the ballot. When he replied that nothing had been
filed to date, she was aghast.

In 1944 the procedure for getting presidential candidates on the ballot was for delegates supporting that candidate to register themselves accordingly in advance. As Susie and I drove back to the women's division office, she told me what Hite had said. Immediately I called Bill Malone, who told me casually that he hadn't been able to get things moving in the Los Angeles area.

With a week before the deadline to register, I managed to get petitions printed, circulated and signed in sufficient quantities to qualify the Roosevelt delegation for the ballot. Susie worked day and night with some women who volunteered to help, culling the registration lists against the signatures on the petition in order to be certain that they qualified. If we had not gotten on the ball, as Susie put it, the Roosevelt delegation for the 1944 convention might not have been on the ballot.

Evelyn Chavoor had been in Washington working as a secretary in the Treasury Department. To my delight she recently had been transferred to Los Angeles. She submitted her resignation the day after I filed. She told me she was coming to work with me on the campaign. I protested that she had a promising career with Treasury, but she was determined.

"Very well, Evie," I said, hugging her. "When I'm elected we'll go to Washington together."

Because Tom Ford was so admired in his district, he had needed very little help from the women's division to get reelected. Consequently I knew almost nothing about it beyond its boundaries and general composition. Traditionally Democratic, it took in much of Los Angeles and most of the ghettos, rich and poor, of that varied city. One boundary ran north and south from City Hall, along Wilshire Boulevard beyond the Ambassador Hotel and middle- and upper-class homes. Some small industries were located in another part of the district, which had pockets of Mexicans, Italians, Chinese, Greeks, and the largest concentration of blacks west of Chicago. It also included a forlorn Skid Row where derelicts slept in alleys littered with empty shaving-lotion bottles.

The probable Republican opponent was considered weak. William D. Campbell had run three times against Ford and each time had been defeated by a decisive margin. For that reason the nomination as the Democratic candidate was a plum that brought a swarm of important Democrats, all men, to fight for the candidacy. I faced six other Democrats, plus Phil Connelly's active opposition and an anti-woman tradition in the state, which hadn't sent a woman to Congress since the 1920s. I'm skipping ahead, but it interested me that California didn't send a second woman to Congress for another twenty years. In a forty-year span, I was the only member of my sex elected in that huge state.

Tom gave me his superb campaign team, which consisted of Ed and Ruth Lybeck. Ed, a former newspaperman, handled the strategy and public relations aspect of the campaign, and Ruth was an incomparable organizer. Between them they had run all six of Tom Ford's campaigns with silky efficiency. The third member of the team was Tom's California secretary, Florence Reynolds.

I already knew them all. Ed was laconic and taciturn, a man steeped in political skepticism, while Ruth and Florence were warm and outgoing. Between the three of them, they knew everything there was to know about the Fourteenth District.

The Los Angeles *Times*, the most powerful newspaper in the state, immediately opposed my nomination. Editorials accused me of being in cahoots with the radical Political Action Committee of the CIO. I was either described weakly as an "idealist," with the strong suggestion that I was muddleheaded, or as a "radical." My friendship with Henry Wallace, whose New Dealism struck conservatives as more than "pinko," also made me suspect, despite the fact that Henry Wallace was Vice-President of the United States and probably would be Roosevelt's running mate in the presidential elections again that year.

John Baumgartner, a powerful Republican on the Board of Supervisors and a friend of Tom Ford's, agreed to be honorary chairman of my campaign, which startled those who were trying to paint me as a communist sympathizer. I always suspected that John secretly liked the New Deal.

The only advice Tom Ford gave me concerned black voters. He urged me to stay out of black neighborhoods. If blacks wanted to talk to me, I should arrange for them to visit the campaign office.

I had no intention of following his recommendation. It was inconsistent for me to visit every part of the district but the black ghetto. Tom conceded that it was all right to address meetings in black community halls, but I shouldn't walk in the streets or go into homes.

"It will demean you," he said. "Voters won't respect you if you mingle with blacks."

My view was that I demeaned the office I was aspiring to if I didn't treat black voters exactly as I did white. Ruth Lybeck agreed to accompany me on walks through the black neighborhoods, up one side of main street and down the other, in and out of stores and soda fountains, along the side streets and, where Ruth knew the families, into homes for a cup of coffee.

Florence Reynolds called me early one morning to say that a delegation of black men was waiting to see me in Tom's office. I hurried there and found the room crowded. A spokesman began:

"Well, we're supporting you in this election, Mrs. Douglas."

I thanked them.

"How much do you plan to give us for voting for you?" the man asked in a businesslike tone.

"Nothing," I replied. I went on to say that I hoped to be their representative in Washington but if I bought their support, I would be embarrassed to speak for them.

"If you don't pay us, we'll vote for someone who will," I was told.

"That's for you to decide," I said, rising to my feet. "It's up to you."

Word of the strange meeting spread quickly. A few days later the real leaders of the black community visited me, offering support with no strings attached. They were impressed by my record while a member of the WPA advisory committee, where I had been forceful in insisting on equal opportunity for blacks, and for the stand I had taken in the women's division in ending discrimination against blacks at the social gatherings of Democrats. They remembered as well meeting in my home when Jessie Terry told me that shipyards and war plants were not hiring blacks. It added up, they told me, to a creditable record of supporting minorities.

The first request for me to give a campaign speech came to my home rather than through the campaign office. I was asked to address a meeting the next night at ten and I was given an address in downtown Los Angeles. Evie Chavoor insisted on going with me. When we arrived at the designated place, we both thought we had made a mistake. We were outside a dingy bar.

Evie went in to investigate while I waited in the car. In a moment she was back with an incredulous expression on her face.

"Yes," she said. "This is the right place. They're expecting you."

It was Phil Connelly's work, I knew. He hoped to discourage me by bringing me to an almost deserted, dark part of the city at a late hour of the night. I determined to show him that I couldn't be intimidated.

The bar was packed with men, many of whom were not sober enough to listen to a political speech. Nevertheless I pushed my way through to the bar, turned my back to it, and surveyed the room until I had silence. Taking a deep breath, I began. Within a few minutes, I was interrupted with a rude question. I answered politely and went on. The same man interrupted again, and again. I concluded he was either drunk or Connelly's plant.

I banged on the bar and in the most powerful voice I could muster shouted:

"*Keep still!* I didn't come down here at this hour of the night to be heckled. Be quiet or get out."

He was too startled to argue and I was allowed to finish my remarks in peace. I left to scattered applause.

As a result of that ugliness, I acquired an unofficial bodyguard. Three young men, calling themselves—inevitably—the Three Musketeers, took it upon themselves to consult my schedule daily. Whenever I was planning to speak in a neighborhood they considered questionable, they followed in a car and stayed with me until I left.

The second request for me to give a speech also looked like Phil Connelly's handiwork. I was asked to address a Sunday afternoon gathering in Skid Row. Coming so early in the election, it seemed suspicious to such veteran campaigners as the Lybecks. Ed announced he was coming with me.

On the way to the run-down theater where the speech would take place, Ed drilled me on what the audience would want to hear. There was only one issue, he said. The men were interested in a proposed pension plan and I would be wasting my breath if I talked about anything else. I thanked him for the advice.

The meeting could have taken place in a flophouse. I saw before me a ragged collection of bruised and lethargic old men dressed in castoffs. I was the only woman present.

I spoke for almost an hour and not about the Townsend pension plan. Instead I told those winos about the Tennessee Valley Authority and how important water was for the reclamation of the American desert. I explained that I realized the audience was interested in pensions, but I wanted them to know about another government program that perhaps they hadn't heard much about.

The meeting went well. The men seemed to enjoy hearing about the TVA and what federal water was doing for the small farmer. Going home, Ed Lybeck said not a word for the entire forty-five minutes. We were in the driveway of my house before he opened his mouth.

"Well, you're different," he said with a sigh. "Maybe your way will work too."

To my mind, campaigning should be educational for the candidate and the voters. Elections must be used to discuss bread-and-butter issues of the day, but they are also opportunities to inform the electorate about long-range programs and developing situations that have a complex background. Regional matters are important, of course, but candidates for the U. S. Congress should provide a broader picture of national and international policies.

I was never sure whether my speech in Skid Row was so painful that Ed Lybeck couldn't bear ever to listen to another, or whether he decided I was able to take care of myself. In either event, he never again accompanied me when I was going to give an address.

Phil Connelly's position as head of the Los Angeles Industrial Union Council was a powerful one. As he had promised, he did what he could to work against me. I found it ironic that this alleged communist was fighting against my candidacy on the one side, claiming that I was too sympathetic to the right, while my Democratic opponents on the other side were berating me for being too far left.

Nevertheless labor had supported me in the vote for national committeewoman and most unions continued to be in my corner despite Connelly. Sidney Hillman, who headed the CIO's Political Action Committee, came to California and asked Connelly why he was stirring up so much trouble for me.

"She's a silk-stocking candidate," Connelly told him. "She shouldn't be running in a poor people's district."

"Roosevelt was a silk-stocking candidate too," Hillman retorted. "And he put silk stockings on all of you."

Three weeks before the primary, Ruth Lybeck sent out women volunteers to crisscross the Fourteenth District. From the list in the registrar's office, they were provided with the name of every Democrat. As much as they were able, they visited every Democrat in the district, called the person by name, and reminded the household of the date of the primary. For those who needed it, we offered transportation to and from the polls. Each canvasser distributed my campaign literature and had been briefed on my positions in order to be able to answer any questions at the door about what I stood for.

Ruth suggested that it would encourage the canvassers if I would do some of the list myself on the first day of the blitz. For four years as head of the women's division I'd been stressing that every voter should receive a personal visit, but this was my first chance to make such a canvass on my own behalf.

To my surprise, I found I was almost paralyzed with fear and embarrassment. It was worse than an opening night to walk up to a stranger's door, knock, and introduce myself. Summoning all my courage, I drove to the first address on my list. The Democrat was mowing his front lawn. The conversation went like this:

"Good morning, Mr. Bryant."

No reply.

"Beautiful day."

No reply.

"You know, of course, that Tom Ford isn't running this time."

The man came to life. He stopped pushing the lawn mower and whirled on me.

"Yes!" he shouted. "And now we're going to get something *worse!*"

I wilted and sat in my car for some minutes before I recovered enough to push on to the next address.

I had a letter that buoyed my flagging spirits. On White House stationery it read:

> Tom Ford has just told me that you are going to run for Congress in his place. I do not need to tell you how much I have always thought of Tom Ford, but if he has to leave the Congress I can ask nothing better than to have you in his place.
>
> My best wishes to you and Melvyn,
>
> As ever yours,
Franklin Roosevelt

A peculiarity of California elections was that congressional candidates cross-filed, offering themselves to both Democrats and Republicans. The oddity allowed a disgruntled Republican to register a protest against his or her party by voting for a Democrat in the Republican primary, but more often the cross-filing simply confused the voters. Candidates who maintained a low profile about party affiliation could be mistaken by careless voters of one or the other party as one of their own.

In keeping with the local tradition I had cross-filed but it wasn't possible that many Republicans could have taken me for a member of the Grand Old Party, not with Mrs. Roosevelt writing about me in "My Day" and the visibility of my activities in the women's division. Nevertheless, on July 15, 1944, the date of the California primaries, I almost won the Republican nomination. I did win, by a decisive margin, the Democratic primary over my six male opponents.

Almost immediately afterward I was on my way to Chicago for the national convention of the Democratic party. With the Allied landings in France only a few weeks old, we Democrats were making history by nominating Franklin Roosevelt to run for a fourth term. The President looked exhausted in newspaper photographs, with dark circles etched deep in his drawn face, but it was unthinkable that the country should change leaders with victory in Europe so close.

In addition to singing the national anthem at the opening of the convention, I was also scheduled to address the delegates. I suspected that this distinction owed something to the announcement from the Republicans that their glamorous rookie congresswoman, Clare Boothe Luce, would be the keynote speaker at their national convention.

Newspaper headline writers were intrigued. One Chicago paper ran a story with the banner: HELEN VS. CLARE: TORCH VS. ICICLE. A press conference was arranged for me, at which attention was paid to my hat ("It's too large for the photographers—would you mind removing it?"), my knees, which were revealed when I sat down in my narrow skirt, and the color of my eyes (blue). Someone asked pertly what I would be wearing when I addressed the convention.

Only a few questions dealt seriously with my political views. One was about women, to which I replied:

> An army of forty-eight million have benefited directly under the New Deal. I do not know whether these women call themselves Democrats or Republicans. I only know that their government under Roosevelt has reached out to lighten their burdens and brighten their lives.

I also said:

> Women are doing everything of an emergency nature that they have been asked to do to help win the war . . . [after the war] it will be as necessary for them to support themselves as it is for men to support themselves.

Some papers noted that I predicted there would be racial problems in industrialized cities such as Los Angeles and Detroit after the war when veterans and blacks competed for scarce jobs.

Toward the end of the press conference someone asked about my so-called "rivalry" with Clare Boothe Luce. Heads bent over notebooks as I answered, "I don't like fencing. I have the greatest respect for Mrs. Luce."

That summer the Republicans chose as their presidential candidate Thomas E. Dewey, the dapper lawyer who was governor of New York. The Democrats, of course, named Roosevelt. To my consternation, it appeared even before the convention began that renomination of Henry Wallace as the vice-presidential candidate was by no means certain. There was a strong wind of conservatism blowing; the mood of the country was swinging away from the New Deal.

I told fellow delegates from California that if they didn't support Henry Wallace on the first ballot, I was going back to Brooklyn.

Alben Barkley, the loyal Democrat who was Senate leader, was often mentioned as a successor to Wallace and then it seemed possible that southerner Jimmy Byrnes would get it. James A. Farley, former Postmaster General and still a power broker in the party, was opposed to Roosevelt's fourth term and as a consolation prize wanted to dump Wallace. He worked first for Barkley and then for Byrnes, and then was asked to go along with the compromise choice who was emerging, Harry Truman, a senator from Missouri. Truman, an unknown until a few months before when he had caught the public fancy with his vigor on a Senate investigating committee that exposed a million-dollar bungle in the awarding of war contracts, was emerging as acceptable to moderates, New Dealers and labor.

Farley fanned himself with his hat. "I'm through hustling," he told reporters. "I'll just sit this one out."

Truman, an unprepossessing man blinking behind his spectacles, got the nomination as Vice-President. I wept with disappointment at Wallace's humiliation.

Afterward I sought out Mrs. Roosevelt and asked what had happened. She said she didn't know. She appeared as bewildered and hurt as I was.

My speech was well-received by those who heard it. Many later commented on its unfortunate position at the end of a long, tiring day when many delegates were near collapse from fatigue, and more than a few had succumbed to the comforts of alcohol.

I said, in part:

> The Democratic party is the true conservative party. We have conserved hope and ambition in the hearts of our people.
> We are the conservative party. We have conserved the skills of their hands. We have husbanded our natural resources. We have saved millions of homes and farms from foreclosure and conserved the family stake in democracy.

We have rescued banks and trust companies, insured crops and people's savings. We have built schools. We have checked the flooding rivers and turned them into power.

We have begun a program to free men and women from the constant nagging fear of unemployment, sickness, accident—and the dread of an insecure old age.

We have turned a once isolated, flood-ravished, poverty-stricken valley, the home of four and a half million people, into what is now a productive, happy place to live—the Tennessee River Valley.

We have replanted the forest, refertilized the soil. Ours is the conservative party. . . .

I hurried back to California to campaign in the Fourteenth District, a relative snap after the hard work of winning the primary. The women's division proved itself in that election, sending four new Democrats to Washington in 1944, all of them Roosevelt Democrats. One of them was me. I beat the Republican candidate by two votes to one.

We women Democrats had organized ourselves well, we were well-informed, and we were ready to take on anyone in a debate about the issues. By turning out to support the Democrat of our choice, we could create a landslide. And that's just what we did.

Immediately after my election, newspapers took up the theme that had been created in Chicago and spoke of the coming "battle of the glamor queens" between me and Clare Boothe Luce. We were two of the nine women in the House of Representatives in the Seventy-ninth Congress and there were none in the Senate. Unlike the other seven, however, Mrs. Luce and I both were associated with the Broadway stage and both of us mingled with what was regarded as high society.

For reporters short of real news, it was a simple day's work to speculate that we would claw one another. The implication was that we were frivolous, vacuous women rather than serious, committed politicians. I was determined to clear the air of such insulting innuendo as soon as I possibly could.

Melvyn read of my victory in an army newspaper. I hadn't mentioned in my letters to him that I was running for Congress because I didn't want him to be anxious about me through the six months of the campaign. He wrote a jubilant letter of congratulations with concern between the lines for my health and well-being in an undertaking he knew I would conduct at full tilt.

I found another tenant for our big house in the Outpost, closed up the Carmel place and packed our belongings in a car. Mother and Lilli agreed to have Mary Helen stay with them in Mother's apartment and some friends in California took Peter in until I could send for him. I didn't want the children with me until I found a suitable house and school for them.

Evie Chavoor and my friend Jarmilla Marton joined me for the long drive across the country to Washington. We set off, the springs of the car sagging with our luggage. We had one stopover planned, a visit in Tennessee with Helen and David Lilienthal, who had promised me a tour of the TVA project that David headed.

One morning Evelyn, seated in the back seat, looked up from a newspaper she was reading.

"Helen," she said, "did you know you're listed as one of the ten best-dressed women in America?"

We all howled. I hadn't bought any new clothes since Melvyn joined the army. My best outfit, a black velvet suit, was made from a costume I wore in *Mary of Scotland*.

On the day before we reached Tennessee, I cracked a cap on a front tooth while eating lunch. The cap conceals a baby tooth that is unsightly but is as secure as a second tooth. What to do? I couldn't arrive in the House of Representatives with a gap in the front of my mouth. I telephoned David and explained the problem, asking if he could arrange for a dentist to see me the next day, a Sunday. Somehow David managed to find a dentist kind enough to help me. I had the cap replaced, toured the TVA site, and was in Washington a day later to be sworn in with a broad smile.

Sam Rayburn, courtly Speaker of the House, greeted me, along with Majority Leader John W. McCormack. I wondered if I dared ask the Speaker if he was supporting my hope to be named to the House Foreign Affairs Committee, a powerful, elite congressional committee not normally available to a first-term congressman.

The Foreign Affairs Committee was the one in which I was

most interested, however, and for which I felt suited after four
years with Esther Murray teaching California women about U.S.
foreign policy. I had mentioned my preference to Tom Ford, who
passed the word along to Sam Rayburn. Most of the California
delegates also supported me, though the veterans among them
warned me that appointment to the Foreign Affairs Committee
was a plum beyond the reach of a newcomer.

To my great joy, the Ways and Means Committee announced
a few days later that Helen Gahagan Douglas was a member of
the Foreign Affairs Committee. Among those who came to congratulate me for this singular honor was a lanky Texas congressman, Lyndon Baines Johnson. He told me he had a special
reason to be glad for me because Melvyn had campaigned for him
early in his career. It was a bond between us that began a rich
and helpful friendship.

My appointment was confirmed the next day, January 16, 1945.
I went at once to pay my respects to the chairman of the Foreign
Affairs Committee, Sol Bloom, a man I hadn't met. The Foreign
Affairs Committee was housed in a suite of three rooms on the
floor directly above the House of Representatives. There was an
outer office for secretaries and clerks, the chairman's private corner
office, and a large committee room dominated by an oval table
that could accommodate all twenty-five members of the committee.

Republicans and Democrats faced one another across the table,
which was ample enough to allow witnesses to sit with us while
testifying. The arrangement provided an atmosphere of intimacy
and cooperation without sacrificing dignity. I much prefer it to
modern committee rooms which are laid out in inquisition style,
the committee arranged on a raised platform while the witnesses
testify below from something vaguely resembling a docket.

The Foreign Affairs Committee of the Seventy-ninth Congress
was composed of seasoned legislators who were among the best in
either party. On the Republican side were Charles A. Eaton of
New Jersey, John M. Vorys of Ohio, Walter Judd of Minnesota,
Frances Bolton of Ohio, Edith Rogers of Massachusetts, Robert
Chiperfield of Illinois, Karl Mundt of South Dakota, Bartel Jonkman of Michigan, James Wadsworth of New York, Charles

Gerlach of Pennsylvania, Lawrence Smith of Wisconsin and Chester Merrow of New Hampshire.

Besides Sol Bloom of New York and myself, the Democrats were Luther Johnson of Texas, John Kee of West Virginia, James Richards of South Carolina, Joseph Pfeifer of New York, Pete Jarman of Alabama, W. O. Burgin of North Carolina, Wirt Courtney of Tennessee, Thomas Gordon of Illinois, Emily Taft Douglas of Illinois, James W. Trimble of Arkansas, Joseph Ryter of Connecticut and Daniel Flood of Pennsylvania.

John Vorys of Ohio was a conscientious member and had important things to say, but he was possessed of a maddeningly slow delivery. To keep myself from snapping at him to get to the point or, worse, throwing my briefcase at him, I started to smoke.

The women of the Washington press corps have an established custom of giving a party at the beginning of each congressional session to mingle with new and seated congresswomen. I looked forward to the opportunity to put an end to irresponsible stories that Clare Boothe Luce and I were feuding.

At dinner I sat to the right of the president of the press corps and Clare sat on her left. I was the first one introduced and asked to speak.

I stood for a long moment considering what I would say, looking from one reporter to the next. Then I began.

"We're in a war," I said. "My husband is overseas. I will be in Washington with our two small children. I came here to support our country's war effort and to do what I can in Congress to help bring the fighting to a successful end as soon as possible. I'm not here for petty quarrels or a competition with anyone, and certainly not with Clare Boothe Luce."

Clare jumped to her feet at once, leaned across the distance between us, and extended her hand. We shook, grinning. That put an end to stories about "the battle of the glamor queens."

I was assigned an office in the Cannon Building, known as "the old building" because members of the House of Representatives also occupied the Longworth Building which was only ten years old. My space was two rooms on the ground floor, and I loved it for its high ceilings and tall windows with a view of a strip of green lawn and the handsome Library of Congress across the way.

The outer office was furnished with three large desks, a long worktable, a few comfortable chairs and a bank of file cabinets. My inner office was equipped with an enormous desk and a swivel chair for me, and a black leather couch and deep armchairs. Even when seniority permitted me to advance to space in "the new building," I stayed where I was.

Most congressmen found that two secretaries, or even one, were sufficient but I had three. From the day I arrived and arranged my photos of the Roosevelts, Melvyn and the children on my desk, all of them were overworked. We received mail not only from the sorely troubled minorities in my Fourteenth District but from people all over California who saw me as the friend of underdogs. In addition, women of California were accustomed to looking to me for leadership in certain situations, and they continued to do so.

Evelyn Chavoor was my right hand, so tuned to me and my reactions that she could and did handle routine correspondence exactly as I would have. We also had an experienced woman from Alabama who showed great efficiency and tact. The third person was hired on the recommendation of Tom Ford and Congressman Emanuel Celler, chairman of the Judiciary Committee, who told me that she had executive ability and would coordinate the office.

I thought privately that I should hire a black secretary. A good proportion of Fourteenth District residents who voted for me were black and I felt that fact should be recognized in the composition of my office staff. I decided I was too new in Congress to take such a step. While there were two black women secretaries on the Hill, both worked for black congressmen. A white congressman had not hired a black secretary in all the history of the United States. I decided I should give Congress an opportunity to know me as a reasoned person before doing something that southerners, at least, would view as outrageous.

My sister Lillian Gahagan Walker came to Washington to help me find a house. I warned her that it would have to be inexpensive. The rent from our big house in California went to pay the mortgage, the gardener's salary, and the rent on the apartment in which Melvyn's mother lived. I would have to support myself and the children out of my $12,000 annual salary as a congressman and the allotment I received as the wife of a U. S. Army officer.

Lilli located a good-looking four-bedroom house in Chevy Chase, Maryland. I asked Evie to live in the spare room so that her small salary wouldn't have to be stretched by the high cost of Washington apartments.

As soon as Evie and I were settled, I sent for the children, Peter, eleven, and Mary Helen, then six. Since their school was only two blocks from where we lived, Evie and I would drop them off every morning on our way to the office. Peter escorted his sister home for lunch provided by Roxie, a motherly, resourceful housekeeper and cook for whom I thanked my lucky stars.

The first week Mary Helen was in Washington, she managed to reach me by telephone while I was attending a session in the House. I thought this a remarkable achievement for someone in Grade One. She simply asked the operator to connect her to the House of Representatives. The operator asked, "Republican or Democrat?" Mary Helen thought a moment and replied confidently, "The Roosevelt side,"—and was put straight through.

Soon after my new office staff began to function, it was apparent that the executive secretary so warmly recommended was inadequate for the workload. I let her go and appointed Evie Chavoor as my executive assistant. Evelyn was reluctant to take the responsibility, protesting that she didn't know her way around Congress well enough, but I overrode her objections.

Two weeks later, on a Sunday, I was working at home on what would prove to be only an installment in a non-ending series of battles to defend the Reclamation Act against a lobby determined to get rid of the 160-acre limitation on publicly irrigated land holdings. I had been talking to my friend Arthur "Tex" Goldschmidt, head of the Power Division in Ickes' Department of the Interior, who gave me some information I needed as ammunition for the debate the next day.

As I put down the telephone, Evie came into my study and collapsed into a chair. "I can't do it," she wailed. "I can't straighten this mess out."

I knew what she meant. The tangle in our files and correspondence left by the departed executive secretary dominated our
lives. Evelyn, a perfectionist, was frustrated in her efforts to sort
out the chaos while at the same time keeping abreast of the daily
onslaught of fresh mail to answer.

I pleaded with her to be patient. She was trying to accomplish
too much too quickly. She shook her head and announced that
she was quitting.

"Don't do that," I said quickly. "There's one other way out."

"What's that?" she said without interest.

"You don't have to be a failure," I told her brightly. "You can
always commit suicide."

She jumped as though I'd thrown a bucket of ice water on her.
After the first horrified gasp, she began to laugh helplessly. "You
win, Helen," she said, climbing to her feet. "I'll go back at it."

Lyndon Johnson came around to see how my office was run.
He draped his long frame in one of my easy chairs and listened as
I explained that Evie and I started by planning the day and taking care of urgent matters. At ten I rushed through the connecting tunnel to the Foreign Affairs Committee sessions. At noon I
was in the House to answer "present" when my name was called.
Afternoons were spent in Congress where members met as Committee of the Whole to discuss and vote on bills. No committee,
however pressing its concerns, was allowed to meet afternoons unless given permission by the Speaker.

I checked the legislative calendar and noted upcoming debate.
Bills with which I was unfamiliar were earmarked for research
and reflection so that I could vote on them responsibly and explain my position when asked. At the end of the day I signed letters spread out on the long table in the outer office and took
home the file of letters requiring my attention. That night I did
homework on pending legislation and answered my mail.

I was fussy about the use of the congressional frank. No letter
went out of my office without a stamp if it could be construed
even remotely as personal.

Lyndon nodded in approval and then asked if I would like to
see how his office was run.

"There isn't any office like it in Congress, I'm sure of that," he
told me with satisfaction.

His efficiency astounded me, since his offhand manner gave little hint of the technocrat lurking beneath. In one aspect it was indeed unique. Lyndon had perfected a system whereby his staff seemed to know of every birth, every graduation, every wedding, every death in his district. His constituents would get a hand-signed note from Lyndon marking the occasion, a practice that made him so loved that a raft of infant Texans had been named for him. Lyndon loved to show a sheaf of pictures of children whose first names were Lyndon, Baines, Johnson, or all three.

I was struck by the paternalism inherent in the effort. Lyndon, in the tradition of *noblesse oblige*, was being kind to the less fortunate. On the other hand, I couldn't help but be impressed by the pride he took in the affection he received and how much he seemed to need evidence of it.

As in all congregations of human beings, there was an elite within the elite of Congress. Lyndon Johnson effortlessly belonged to it. He didn't have as much seniority as others who made the wheels run behind the scenes, but he certainly belonged with them. Everyone knew that he knew what was going to happen and what would make it happen. The friendship of Sam Rayburn, who lunched with him almost daily, had much to do with it but there was also Lyndon's own presence, which exuded the unmistakable air of the keeper of the keys.

Lyndon wasn't one of those indifferent congressmen who didn't make a point of being present when an important bill came to the floor. He was always there. Congress was his field of operation week after week and he couldn't be tempted away to give speeches across the country when important legislation was being considered.

However, he rarely spoke in the House and he spent little time listening to others speak. His style was to vote and leave, loping off the floor with great long strides. If he did remain he looked the picture of boredom, slumped in his seat, eyes half closed. Then, suddenly, restlessness would seize him and he would leap to his feet all energy, stride to whisper something to a colleague here and a colleague there, and leave—taking something out of the room with him.

He had an explosive side that I saw when I traveled one time

to New York with Lyndon and his wife, Lady Bird. We were
shown into a hotel suite but Lyndon told us to keep our coats on;
it wasn't the one he'd ordered. He got on the phone to the desk
and his display of temper was so violent and unexpected that I
was shocked for days afterward. I couldn't believe that anyone
would get so out of hand over the small matter of a mistake in ac-
commodations.

Over the years I knew him, I came to understand that tendency to abrupt rage. I think Lyndon, who never admitted to fatigue, was simply exhausted. He behaved the same whether he
was tired or not, but when his resources were gone and he
couldn't go full steam anymore, his inner state was betrayed by
the suddenness of his fury. Later I wondered if he hadn't driven
himself to the limit of his capacity over the war in Vietnam, making it difficult for him to see it for what it was.

Representative Matthew Mansfield Neely of West Virginia
came to see me one day in March 1945. He was introducing a bill
in the Senate proposing that the United States establish and fund
a center where the best scientists would be brought together to
work toward a cure for cancer. He wanted me to sponsor the bill
in the House of Representatives while he put it before the Senate.

Cancer research appeared to be getting nowhere. Neely wanted
legislation to "authorize and request the President to undertake
to mobilize at some convenient place in the United States an adequate number of the world's outstanding experts and coordinate
and utilize their services in the supreme endeavor to discover the
means of curing and preventing cancer."

Neely was a respected man and many of us fought hard for his
bill but it never got past the committee stage. I buttonholed
members of Congress on its behalf, not only in the Seventy-ninth
Congress but also in the Eightieth Congress where we rein-
troduced it, this time pointing out that an argument could be
made that the United States, which had just created the world's
most terrible weapon, the H-bomb, should put equal resources to
curing the world's most terrible disease.

We failed to convince Congress. No one was interested in
mounting an expensive program to beat cancer. In the years since,

we have made some progress in determining contributing causes but we still haven't learned how to cure cancer. I have wondered if a concentrated effort such as Neely and I pressed for in 1945 and 1947 would not have yielded a breakthrough.

I was asked recently to testify before Congressman Claude Pepper's Committee on Cancer Research. I was too ill from a recurrence of cancer to travel to Washington at that time so it was arranged that I deliver my statement over a telephone hookup. Unfortunately the connection failed after I delivered the first paragraph.

The committee, above all else, needed publicity for its worthy work, so I gave a copy of my statement to Edith Evans Asbury of the New York *Times*. I mailed Claude Pepper a copy for the Congressional Record.

The following are some excerpts from that statement:

> I've had some experience with terminal cancer. My father, a brother and my only sister died of it. There is a great need now for expanded cancer research because the number of people suffering from it is growing. The majority of patients that contract it may be over sixty, but I assure you from my personal observation in Memorial Hospital that the number of young and middle-aged suffering from cancer is increasing rapidly. Nor are little children spared.
>
> Cancer research is expensive. Laboratory equipment is expensive. Living out the time allotted to terminal cancer patients is also expensive and harrowing for the families who don't have the money or time to properly care for a loved one who has reached the stage where science can do no more to arrest the spread of the cancer.
>
> Science has made advances. Those of us who have cancer live longer. But doctors still don't know how to prevent cells from going wild and multiplying. They still don't know what it will take to make the cells again normal.
>
> Representative Neely and I hoped that our bill at the time we introduced it would compensate in a small way for that introduction of the atomic bomb in the affairs of men. It never got out of the Foreign Affairs Committee.

Jim Patton, former president of the National Farmers Union with whom I had worked for many years to improve conditions

for farm laborers, wrote me a note on July 9, 1979, a few days
after the New York *Times* story. He said:

> You have always been a great fighter for people and for justice. I
> have such fond memories of you during our work on the WPA
> Advisory Board on Community Arts Projects. I was so happy to
> have you at our National Farmers Union convention at Saint
> Paul. I am so sorry about your fight with cancer. My love and
> deep respect. Also my everlasting thanks to you for all you have
> done.
>
>   Jim.

The failure of the Neely-Douglas cancer bill was an instructive
lesson in dealing with disappointment and frustration in office,
but I was also experiencing another congressional hazard: lobbies.
American citizens have a right and a responsibility to lobby
congressmen and petition Congress over matters of concern. I respect the process because it is central to democracy, but I found
it has an ugly side.

One illustration of pernicious lobbying occurred while I was
still finding my way around Congress. After a long, tiring day in
the House, I found a delegation waiting in my office to see me. It
was led by Harry Bridges, the militant West Coast head of the
longshoremen's union. He had no appointment and he brought
so many men with him that my staff had no room to work.

Bridges was making the rounds of the California delegation in
Congress and it seemed it was my turn. He took a chair in front
of my desk and did all the talking. He ordered me, in so many
words, to support a certain piece of legislation. I replied in a level
tone that I hadn't studied the bill thoroughly as yet but expected
that I would oppose it.

Bridges glared at me. "In that case," he snapped, "the longshoremen won't support you in the next election."

I glared at him. "That's your privilege, Mr. Bridges. You can
oppose me if you choose. It has no bearing on my decision in this
matter."

Bridges rose and led his group out of my office. The last to
leave the room hesitated at the door, turned and said quietly:

"Mrs. Douglas, we're sorry. Some of us knew better than to threaten you in this way. I apologize."

On another occasion representatives of the Railroad Brotherhood came to my office. They were lobbying for a bill the railway companies wanted in the hope, I suspected, of sweeter negotiations at the bargaining table.

"I can tell you right now that I think the company has no right to that land," I informed the delegation. "I won't be voting for this bill."

They were a good deal more polite about my refusal than Harry Bridges had been. One of them sighed, "Well, we had to come. We were assigned this wing of offices, but we knew we wouldn't be able to change your mind if you didn't like the bill."

Some lobbying came in waves. Every time reciprocal trade agreements came before the House, for instance, we could be certain that delegations would arrive. Once it was California nut growers who wanted me to introduce an amendment forbidding the importation of nuts. I told them I couldn't do that. If exceptions are made in one case in reciprocal trade agreements, the entire fabric begins to unravel. It ends up with other countries making exceptions directed at American exports. I think they saw my point but they went away very discouraged with me.

Years later a freshman congressman stopped me one day in the corridor just as I was entering the House. He asked how I was going to vote on the trade agreement bill we would be discussing that day. I told him. He shook his head. The California nut growers, he said, wanted him to introduce a bill banning imported nuts. He didn't know what to do; they represented a lot of votes and his majority hadn't been very decisive.

I told him I couldn't advise him; he would have to decide for himself. With the lobbies, we were on our own to cut a course that could embrace conscience or survival, but not always both at once.

That spring of 1945 President Roosevelt reported in person to the combined Senate and House of Representatives on those aspects of the Yalta agreement that it was prudent to reveal. He had met with Winston Churchill of Britain and Joseph Stalin of the Soviet in the Crimea to redraw the map of Europe.

When I saw the President, I was appalled at his haggard appearance. For the first time he had not been able to tolerate the iron harness that kept him on his feet for such public occasions, but was brought into the chamber in his wheelchair. I learned that he was in agony from the long plane trip during which he was strapped into an Air Force bucket seat.

As the double doors closed behind him after his address, I had a premonition that I would never see him again. I left the chamber and ran down the hall to a back staircase I knew he would have to pass on his return to the White House. When he came into view, I called out:

"Good-bye, Mr. President!"

He looked up, smiled, nodded his head, and waved.

A few days later I was flying to Milwaukee to address a Democratic party fund-raising dinner. Over the intercom, the captain paged the flight attendant. She emerged from the flight cabin moments later and went down the aisle, saying a few words to passengers on either side. I assumed it had something to do with the turbulence we were experiencing and felt concern that we would be diverted to another landing field and I would miss my speaking date.

When she reached me, she said, "The President is dead."

I cried out, "No! No!" and tried to stand, forgetting I was buckled in. I clenched my hands and tried not to cry. My eyes fell on a magazine I had been reading, a leading newsmagazine that usually was critical of the Roosevelts. My memory flashed to an evening when I had cocktails in the President's sitting room before dinner with a group of his family and friends. The President picked up an edition of the newsmagazine and read aloud a vitriolic criticism of himself. When he finished he threw back his head and roared with genuine laughter, exclaiming:

"Isn't that *wonderful!*"

I wondered when we again would have a President in the White House who could laugh at himself.

Andrew Biemiller, a member of the House of Representatives, met me at the Milwaukee airport with some other Wisconsin Democrats. We huddled together in mutual grief. We felt rudderless in a storm. Who was Harry Truman anyway? None of us knew much about him.

President Roosevelt's body was brought back to the capital and weeping mourners lined Washington's broad avenues to watch the cortege pass. I called on Mrs. Roosevelt at the White House and found her calm and gracious, a marvel of strength and self-control.

After the funeral, Lyndon Johnson asked me to come to one of his offices. He had them scattered all over the capital, but this was his most private one. We sat there sorrowing together, exchanging stories about Roosevelt, sometimes laughing at funny incidents we remembered. Roosevelt was Lyndon's inspiration, perhaps his model.

Roosevelt died on April 12, 1945, only weeks after the war in Europe ended. Germany signed papers of unconditional surrender and the boys began to come home, many of them to be issued tropical uniforms in preparation for more fighting against Japan. Melvyn was sent home on leave and we fell into one another's arms. We were together in New York for the victory celebrations in Times Square that August as Japan surrendered. Few of the celebrants cared that victory had been achieved as the result of a terrible new weapon, the atom bombs dropped on Hiroshima and Nagasaki.

Our California friends Jack and Lola Leighter were with us. Lola cheered along with the rest but she confessed she was troubled. She kept saying:

"We shouldn't have dropped those bombs."

Melvyn waited five months for the overloaded discharge machinery to release him. Meanwhile in Washington everyone was talking about the frightful weapon that had ended the war in the Pacific. Pictures of the devastation appeared and there was no way to protect children from awareness of its power. Little Mary Helen had nightmares for weeks. She'd run into my room and hurl herself into bed with me, crying, "Mother, the bomb won't drop on us tonight, will it?"

My good friend William O. Douglas of the U.S. Supreme Court told me that one of his children had the same reaction. I was beginning to share Lola's anguish about the bomb, despite

my realization that it was responsible for the fact that Melvyn
was home and safe.

When Congress resumed in the fall of 1945 I made a speech in
the House touching on my concern. I said:

Mr. Speaker, mixed with my feelings of elation on August 14
that we had come finally to the end of the war was a feeling of
stupefaction. . . . I realized that we had come to the end of one
age and that we were witnessing the birth of another because of
the smashing of the atom and the release of atomic energy.

Now I know that is true. We cannot retrace our steps, whether
we like it or not. This new age demands of us an entirely new
concept of our responsibilities toward one another. These responsibilities must be based fundamentally on a fully Christian, moral
attitude.

Now, more than ever before, is the time for all of us to read
our Bible to live by the principles found within the Golden Rule
. . . the first order of business of this Congress and the peoples
of the world is the question of the survival of mankind.

Melvyn had returned to the States on detached service in order
to select men and materials for the company he had created in
the Pacific theater to produce soldier shows with GI talent.
While waiting to be demobilized after V-J day, he coproduced a
revue, *Call Me Mister*, which was about army life and became
the first big musical hit of the postwar period. He took an apartment in New York and we commuted as frequently as our hectic
schedules permitted.

Melvyn had signed a five-year contract with MGM some two
years before Pearl Harbor. He was heartily sick of appearing in
films of uncertain quality over which he had no control, and intended to become a free agent as soon as his contract expired. By
his calculation, that time had arrived. MGM, however, had something he had signed before leaving for Burma which stipulated
that the five years were not calendar years but years before the
camera.

MGM took Melvyn to court, claiming he owed them about
three years of films. Melvyn retained a bright lawyer who had experience working with the Screen Actors Guild. The lawyer used
an ancient piece of legislation, the California Peonage Law,

which had been drawn up to protect illiterate Mexican farm workers from exploitation. It stated that no laborer could be bound by a contract that he didn't understand when signing. Melvyn's lawyer maintained that Melvyn was in such a hurry to leave for active service that he hadn't appreciated what MGM's bit of paper was about—which was true. The judge ruled in Melvyn's favor. MGM threatened to appeal the decision but cooler heads pointed out that the public would not sympathize with a studio imposing forced labor on a man who had served his country for three years.

Melvyn and MGM struck a compromise by which Melvyn would make one more picture of their choice and then would be rid of his obligation.

He was startled and not very pleased to learn that I had sold our house in Carmel for exactly what we had paid for it. I took that step soon after moving to Washington. Friends in California wrote me that the house would need a new roof, a repair I thought was unjustified in a building only a few years old. I put it on the market and it went quickly. That area now is completely built up and the property, I suppose, is worth rubies.

Since our big house in the Outpost was still rented, Melvyn took space elsewhere while making films. The children went to California to live with their father. By putting them in private schools in Los Angeles, from which they went home to him on weekends, Melvyn was able to manage. The arrangement wasn't perfect for any of us but it was the best we could do given our commitments.

That fall the Daughters of the American Revolution refused to allow Marian Anderson to sing in Constitution Hall, which they operated tax-free under a federal exemption. They took no pains to conceal the reason for their rejection, which was that Marian Anderson was black.

In Congress a few days later I read quotes from Thomas Jefferson and cited the fact that my Grandmother Hannah had been a proud member of the DAR. I went on:

> But this pride is meaningless if the spirit and word is lost. It is not easy to be free men, for to be free you must afford freedom

to your neighbor, regardless of race, color, creed or national origin, and that, sometimes, for some, is very difficult.

Freedom is not won on the battlefields. The chance for freedom is won there. The final battle is won or lost in our hearts and minds. . . . We cannot legislate equality but we can legislate, as free men, equal opportunity for all.

I introduced a bill to condition the tax exemption the DAR enjoyed on their not denying commercial use of Constitution Hall by reason of race, creed, color or national origin.

Harry Truman and the Seventy-ninth Congress were faced with portentous decisions about what America should do with its alarming new atomic power. The military was mounting a strong campaign to take control of all atomic power development, which many of us thought was a dangerous direction in which to go. The magnitude of the destructive potential of the H-bomb made it imperative, I thought, that it be under international control. The United Nations seemed to me the appropriate agency. It was yet to hold its first session, so its role in world affairs was unclear, but I had high hopes for its potential to settle differences between nations peaceably and put an end to war. I said in Congress:

The air needs to be cleared of suspicion and doubt and fear. . . . What we need now in the world is friends.

I was impressed with something Walter Lippmann, respected observer of the political scene, wrote in his syndicated column:

It would be dangerous in the highest degree to suppose we were keeping the secret [of the bomb] if in fact we are not. For that could only give us, as it has already given many, a false sense of security and a false sense of our own power.

Amen, I thought. That false sense of security could lead us straight back into isolationism.

I was still in my office around six one evening when Dr. Robert Lamb, a scholar who was a consultant with the steelworkers' union, dropped in to see me. He wanted to know if I was aware that the Military Affairs Committee had sent the Johnson-May bill (by Senator Edwin Johnson and Representative Andrew

May) to be printed, ending a very brief hearing on its contro-versial clauses that put control of atomic power into the hands of the military. It proposed an authority that would be responsible to no one, not even the President.

"Mrs. Douglas," he said. "I thought you should know about it at once. The public hasn't had a chance to be heard on that bill."

I sent for a copy and read it carefully. The wording was clear. Congress was preparing to put control of atomic power solely into the hands of the American military establishment. What would that message be to the world, already nervous that one nation had a bomb that could flatten a city?

I telephoned my brother Walter Gahagan to say that I was coming to New York at once and needed to see him on an urgent matter. I asked him to collect some of his lawyer friends who had expertise about constitutional and legislative matters.

Walter and a distinguished group of legal authorities greeted me in his apartment. Some were from the office of the U. S. At-torney and others from Walter's former firm, Hughes, Shurman & Dwight. I gave them a copy of the Johnson-May bill and told them it was on its way into legislation after only cursory public hearings.

They discussed the provisions while I waited in the next room. After a long time, Walter came for me. The lawyers had agreed that a decision of such magnitude should not be reached in near-secrecy.

I caught a late plane back to Washington. The next day, fortu-nately a Saturday, was spent in my office. Evie Chavoor helped me contact key newspapers across the country. I spoke to editors, publishers, and everyone else who would listen, telling them that a copy of the Johnson-May bill was in the mail to them. Since it had received little public airing, they probably were unfamiliar with its provisions. If, on reading it, they agreed with me that the Military Affairs Committee must recall the bill and reopen public hearings, would they publicize that opinion in their editorials?

The response cut across party lines. American newspapers, Democratic *and* Republican, thundered their outrage that such a drastic step was being considered without adequate consultation.

They succeeded in forcing the Military Affairs Committee to recall the bill and hear more testimony.

I later learned that those who advocated military control of
atomic power were well aware that an informed public might be
aroused against them. The bill therefore was being sneaked
through expertly in order to have it become law before Americans
woke up to what had happened.

James R. Newman came to see me when he learned who was
responsible for the campaign to inform the press. Jim Newman
was author of a four-volume work, *The World of Mathematics*,
which made mathematics not only intelligible to laymen but also
delightful. He was moving into a similar translator's position between the incomprehensibility of atomic power and the American
public. As counsel to the new Senate committee established to review atomic power legislation, the Special Committee on Atomic
Energy, he became the link between the scientists and the rest of
us.

Jim Newman and I went out to lunch and over three hours of
replenishing our coffee too many times, I learned from the best
teacher in the country what atomic power was all about. Newman
was obsessed by concern that whoever had the bomb would also
acquire world dominance, which he believed presented grave risks
for keeping the peace. Like me, he hoped to see an international
tribunal administer the development of atomic power for the
benefit of all nations.

The possibility that the military would control atomic power
created an uproar in the scientific community. Physicists turned
up everywhere urging that control remain in civilian hands. It was
coming home to a lot of us that when America split the atom, the
world was changed. The old diplomatic games of big cats stalking
one another were no longer feasible, not if one of those big cats
could destroy the earth.

Jim Newman was tireless in arranging for scientists to meet
with influential congressmen to tell them what atomic power
could do. My office became the center of operations. We cleared
the long table in the outer room and turned it over to the visiting
scientists. They spent hours there drafting press releases, background papers and memos for legislators.

Tris Coffin, Washington reporter for CBS, covered the hearings before the Special Committee. He said that behind door 457 in the Senate "a fantastic new world was taking place." He described in taut prose what happened when Rear Admiral William R. Purnell, the navy's expert on atom bombs, testified and shocked the world by saying the next war would last about thirty minutes.

Purnell also said something that grabbed my attention—*that any other nation could build the bomb*. America had been in a hurry, he explained. Scientists who worked on the atom bomb project hadn't stopped to consider alternate ways of reaching their various objectives. In fact, there could be shortcuts that we hadn't noticed.

"Any nation may find these shortcuts," he explained casually in the committee room dense with silence.

Robert J. Oppenheimer, the physicist described as "the father of the atom bomb," also testified that week in October 1945. He supported Purnell's statements. The atom bomb team had "taken a tree ripe with fruit and shaken it hard," he said. That same tree was available to scientists everywhere.

"You cannot keep the atom secret," he went on. "The immediate problem, it seems to me, is to get confidence among the nations, not force them apart by trying to build up a great secret."

Senator William Fulbright of Arkansas, great libertarian, asked Oppenheimer:

"Could our forty million people be wiped out in one attack?"

"I'm afraid that is true."

Fulbright considered. "That is a compelling reason why we must undertake some other means of defense," he said heavily. "I feel the only way is through government opposition to nationalism. Governments must agree to some world system of control."

I read into the Congressional Record a statement of principles signed by six hundred scientists who met in Philadelphia in those critical months. It declared:

> . . . the use of atomic power must be controlled by a world authority . . . it is imperative that we have the good will of all nations, for it must be realized that we are dealing with a deadly

challenge to civilization itself. We believe that international control is technically possible and feasible. . . . It is our hope that the bomb will be a great force for world cooperation and peace.

We won our fight against the Johnson-May bill. It was defeated and a new bill, sponsored in the House of Representatives by me and in the Senate by Brien McMahon, who had chaired the Special Committee on Atomic Energy, was introduced. Its official name was S.1717 but I am proud that it is better known as the McMahon-Douglas bill by which atomic power was placed in civilian control.

On July 18, 1946, I spoke in support of the bill in the House of Representatives, saying:

> To me, S.1717 is the most important piece of legislation to come before Congress. Having discovered how to harness the source of the sun's energy, we must now control that knowledge if we are to live to use it.
>
> The controls must be such that they function for peace and express the will for peace. This is what this bill, S.1717, seeks to do. . . .
>
> We have heard much discussion on the floor. Unfortunately, we have heard little discussion about what is actually in the bill. In view of what has been said on the floor, I want to stress the security aspect of this bill. . . .
>
> A half-dozen people on the floor keep getting up and saying, "Everybody wants to give away the secret of the bomb." I do not know to whom they refer—I heard no one make such a statement on the floor of this House. . . .
>
> Mr. Chairman, security is divided into three parts. There is the temporary security to be found by guarding the secrets of the technological aspects of the making of the bomb which we now possess and which at present nobody else possesses. . . .
>
> [Secondly], at the moment we lead the world in science, so that any bill which we write to protect ourselves must provide for the greatest possible development in science and nuclear fission. We must see that we do not cripple ourselves. We must see to it that we do not lose our preeminent place in science because if we do, we are not working toward security but instead are building a scientific Maginot Line which will be as fatal to us, if we do not secure peace in the world, as the Maginot Line was to France.
>
> Thirdly, everyone agrees, including the President, the Secretary

of War, the Chief of Staff, Mr. Vandenberg, and Mr. Connally, who have just come back from Europe, that the only completely sure, enduring protection which we have against atomic energy being used for destructive purposes in the future is peace. . . .

Therefore, the third aspect of security is a strong and harmonious United Nations, international control of atomic energy, and national control of atomic energy [for] peace. We must not write any piece of legislation which will . . . impede the program which Mr. Baruch is presenting to the nations of the world at this moment for the international control of atomic energy.

If we do, we set ourselves off on a war program and the end of that no one can see. We should not concern ourselves only with the fire-engine aspects of atomic energy.

If we do, we will not have protected ourselves. We [shall] have been absolutely foolhardy. . . . One cannot legislate in a vacuum on atomic energy. There are certain facts of which one must be aware if we are to have any security, if we are to have any of the benefits of this cosmic force.

What are these facts?

To get the facts the Senate committee spent six long months asking questions—going to school, studying with the nation's foremost scientists, with the foremost civilian and military leaders in the country. . . . I have only time here to give a brief synopsis from the Senate findings:

One, the atomic bomb is a weapon of appalling destructiveness. . . .

Two, other countries of the world will be able to make atomic bombs. . . .

Three, no real military defense against the atomic bomb has been devised and none is in sight. The destructiveness of atomic bombs is so engulfing that any defense which is not literally airtight will not protect our country against devastation.

Four, the secrets which we hold are matters of science and engineering that other nations can and will discover. In large part, they are secrets of nature, and the book of nature is open to careful, painstaking readers the world over. We can give ourselves a certain temporary protection by retaining the secrets we now have. But that protection grows weaker day by day . . . our research must be vigorously encouraged, supported, and pursued if we are to maintain our place among other nations, to say nothing of retaining our advantage.

Five, the peacetime benefits of atomic energy promise to be

great indeed, particularly in medicine, biology and many branches of research. These benefits are immediate in their promise but will require extended and unfettered development for full realization. The vast possibilities of utilizing atomic energy as a source of power depend on (1) further research and development, and (2) study of the economic and international implications of the establishment of plants producing and using fissionable material.

In this connection, the point has been repeatedly emphasized that plants which produce power also produce material which constitutes the explosive element of bombs. This fact raises domestic and international issues of profound significance. In other words, people can be producing power for seemingly peaceful purposes while they are actually preparing to destroy you. That is why international controls are necessary.

Six, military control of atomic energy development, though necessary and useful during the war, is a form of direction to which scientists in peace time will not willingly submit. The continuation of such control probably will discourage further development and research. And on that development depends not only peaceful progress, but the maintenance of a position in the military arts essential to the national defense.

On the other hand, the armed services are entitled . . . to have a voice in protecting the military secrets of atomic weapons. . . . Since the only real solution to the whole problem lies in continued world peace, legislation should be directed in specific terms toward that end and should contain a practical expression of our desire for international cooperation.

The McMahon-Douglas bill ran into heavy opposition in both the House and Senate. Most of the amendments were directed to imposing an element of military control. I spoke against them all vigorously, saying on one occasion:

The bill without amendments covers all the situations in the field of atomic energy that we now know anything about. There should be no amendments at all, since we can't improve the bill intelligently at this time.

If the military amendments are passed, the entire concept of the bill will be destroyed. Having military men on the commission gives our atomic energy program a warlike character. To place them there would be a violation of our historical democratic tradition giving control of government to civilians for carrying out national policy. Military men are not the policy makers.

The President, the Secretary of War, the Secretary of the Navy, as well as Congress, the Secretary of State, the Senate, who have responsibility for forming national policy in relation to any war situation, are all civilians.

This constitutional principle is recognized in a statute of 1870, providing that military men on active duty shall not hold civilian government posts.

It was a civilian who directed the atomic bomb scientific laboratory at Los Alamos. This fact is respected by the heads of our War and Navy departments. The Chief of Staff of the Army and the Chief of Naval Operations and the Chief Executive have expressed their preference that the director of the Division of Military Application in our atom control program be a civilian.

Since those most directly concerned with our military security and who know the most about it want it this way, why should we write more military control into the bill than the heads of the military establishments themselves desire?

Both military amendments—the one providing that the director of the Division of Military Applications shall be a member of the armed forces, and the other permitting two members of the Atomic Energy Commission to be representatives of the armed forces—must be defeated. They must be defeated to remove the characteristics of militarism from this bill and to prove to the world our peaceful intent.

In the eyes of the world, we already have two strikes against us while we make our fervent protestations of peace. It was we who first dropped atomic devastation from the skies without forewarning. Therefore when we say that we will never do it again, there must be evidence of the validity of our statement.

Secondly, it is we who are experimenting with the death-dealing effects of atomic energy—its uses in war, not in peace—at the very moment that we loudly contend that atomic warfare must be outlawed. Are our contentions as loud in the ears of our neighbors as the explosions of the bombs at Bikini?

If, after dropping the bomb in the first place and experimenting with it in the second place, we put military men in charge of our atomic energy in the third place, who is going to believe that we are dedicated to the peaceful exploitation of the greatest miracle of modern man for the benefit of all mankind?

The bill before us expresses our faith in the future and our faith in each other. It does so, that is, so long as it is free from amendments which would put the precision instrument of peace into the hands of the practitioners of war.

Let us pass the bill unamended—the bill the President wants, the Secretary of State wants, the Chief of Staff wants, the bill the scientists want because they feel they can work under it.

Let's pass the bill which gives the Army and Navy full scope for the protection of our country, which gives the scientists sufficient freedom to move forward for the security and advancement of mankind, which opens the way to international understanding and which keeps in the hands of our civilian public the traditional democratic right to control civilian affairs.

Let us pass the bill unamended as our contribution to the *peace* of the world.

The McMahon-Douglas bill, without the pernicious amendments, passed into law on July 30, 1946, almost exactly a year after the *Enola Gay* dropped the bomb on Hiroshima. President Truman signed the Atomic Energy Act "designed to control and develop the forces harnessed in this unparalleled instrument of destruction," and Americans had atomic energy under civilian control.

Jim Newman and Byron S. Miller wrote about the dilemma of scientists in the immediate postwar period in *The Control of Atomic Energy*, published in 1948. They commented:

> The scientists were certain that by the use of fissionable materials and radioactive materials profoundly significant further discoveries in basic science would be made, which in time would produce innumerable and unpredictable technological devices and apparatus.
>
> In the immediate future, however, all they could be sure of were some limited medical applications of radioactive materials, and the utilization of atomic energy for the generation of power. It is a little disillusionary to discover, for all our progress in mastering natural phenomena, how little ability we have to predict the chain of events that an epic discovery will set in motion.
>
> The savants who so startlingly demonstrate their insight into the heart of the atom manifest only the most imperfect intuitions of the scope of the application of the power they have won, and no confidence at all in their ability to predict the social, economic and political consequences of their discovery; historians find no precedent to give us guidance, and even the indefatigable categorists in the science of sociology exhibit an unwonted reticence.

The limitation of scientists in the field of accurate prediction is as obvious today as it was in the forties right after atomic power was released for the first time. The recklessness of those who now speak of America "winning" a nuclear war reveals a sorry lack of information, humility and respect for the laws of nature and life on this planet.

Newman and Miller dedicated *The Control of Atomic Energy* to me and Senator Brien McMahon, calling us "two of the people's representatives who saw far and saw clearly." Jim added something I treasure: *For Helen, who is the best of us in heart, in spirit, in courage, in integrity, in sympathy, in forbearance, in vision, and in purpose. She evokes our love, commands our admiration and earns our fealty.*

For the rest of his short life, Jim Newman continued to urge the world to renounce nuclear weapons. His most powerful statement on that subject appeared in the Washington *Post:*

> It is best not to qualify what cannot be qualified. The attempt ends in absurdities. That the sun rises in the east, that yesterday cannot return, that man is mortal, are statements admitting of no exceptions. That a war of nuclear weapons is lunatic is in the same case. It is an uncontingent truth, beyond niggling or casuistry. One hears in our day a good deal about the dignity of the individual. This is often coupled with the suggestion that while emblems and territory and treasure are not at our stage of civilization a justifiable *casus belli,* the dignity of the individual is worth fighting for. I cherish my individuality, and I respect the individuality of others. I know that many men are not free. But it does not occur to me that I can protect my dignity, and maintain or achieve that of others, by dropping atom bombs. . . . It is difficult to believe that when men are dead dignity will endure. It will vanish when they vanish.

The Allied Commander-in-Chief, Dwight David Eisenhower, returned home a great hero. He made a report to the nation before a joint session of Congress, the Supreme Court, and the Cabinet. Speaking from a stage banked with maps of the battlegrounds, to which he directed our attention with a pointer, he cut an impressive figure.

I've forgotten who suggested it, but some senators and I decided to find out whether Eisenhower was a Democrat. In case Truman proved to be a disappointing President, as it seemed he would, General Eisenhower would be a credible candidate in 1948. I talked to fellow congressman Chet Holifield about it and we decided to pay Eisenhower a visit.

We had a pleasant chat with the general, who appeared to be neither a Democrat nor a Republican. He gave the impression that he was a man with so little interest in politics that he had made no distinction between the two parties. As we talked, his ignorance of government was embarrassingly apparent. Chet and I reached the same conclusion at the same time, without even exchanging a glance. We rose, thanked Eisenhower for his time, and left. We agreed that he wouldn't do at all as a Democratic candidate for the presidency of the United States, and that I must head off the senators at once, which I did promptly.

Roosevelt's death left some of us in Congress feeling lost. Harry Truman in his first year of office appeared a shaky and inadequate man who gave us no sense of security. Without much planning, Chet Holifield, a number of senators and I began to meet about once a month with Henry Wallace to discuss issues and pending legislation. Despite his snub by the party, Wallace had campaigned strongly for Roosevelt and Truman had named him Secretary of Commerce.

We gathered on a Sunday, always in a private dining room of the Cosmos Club, arriving around six and breaking up three or four hours later. The comradeship and flow of information at those sessions was a tonic that helped us through an unnerving postwar period when the White House and Congress were trying to sort out the mess left in the wake of World War II.

I was becoming a passionate advocate of the yet-untried United Nations. I spoke at Columbia University in January 1946 on the subject and said:

> We must live not only in our own communities but in a world community with seeing eyes and living hearts, sensitive to the yearnings and the dreams that help men to grow, sensitive to the needs that must be fulfilled if men are to be kept healthy.

I found in Henry Wallace a kindred spirit. As Edward L. and Frederick H. Schapsmeier wrote in *Prophet in Politics:*

> There was no doubt that Henry Wallace was preoccupied with developing an American foreign policy based on humanitarian principles. Only then, he believed, could lasting peace be achieved. This was the meaning of his statement to Madame Litvinov [wife of the Soviet Ambassador] that "the object of this war is to make sure that everybody in the world has the privilege of drinking a quart of milk a day." He did not think industrial nations could live in abundance, while allowing underdeveloped nations to exist in abject poverty.

Mrs. Roosevelt shared our hope that world stability could be achieved by nations talking to one another in a forum where differences could be adjusted before they became too inflamed for reason to prevail. She was as much in demand as a spokesman for liberal causes after her husband's death as she had been before. She was traveling still, exuding that quality of good nature that disarmed even Republicans who thought they hated her. Nothing about her was abrasive and she had an uncommon capacity for loyalty. After her sons were divorced, for instance, she continued to be in touch with their ex-wives.

She traveled abroad extensively, gathering information about the needs of such countries as Britain, Yugoslavia, Greece, Turkey, Lebanon, Syria, Israel, Jordan, India, Burma, Siam, Japan, Hong Kong and Indonesia. When Elliott Roosevelt visited Moscow, Stalin's greeting was, "When is your mother coming?"

Our hopes were dampened by the Soviet veto of Bernard Baruch's proposal for an international agency to control the world's fissionable materials. Communism was gaining strength in France, Italy, Turkey, Greece and Iran, where shattered industries were trying to rebuild without adequate funds, which meant that unemployment figures were high and wages low. Truman, who appeared sympathetic at first to concepts of international cooperation, began to harden his stands.

Harry Wallace disagreed openly with the militant tone that was developing in American diplomacy. He resigned as Secretary of Commerce but continued to attend our irregular meetings at the Cosmos Club.

Meanwhile I was having my problems with another member of the House of Representatives, John Rankin of Mississippi, a thin, biting man who was feared for his scathing tongue and violent accusations. Rankin also was the most outspoken of the many racists in Congress at that time.

One day right after roll call he asked permission to make an address. He described the heavy casualties that Americans had suffered in the Italian campaign and later in the Battle of the Bulge. He claimed that the cowardice of black soldiers was responsible for the deaths our forces suffered, particularly at Anzio and Cassino.

I surprised myself by hissing loudly. I'd never hissed before in my life. After the outburst I sat in fuming silence, rigid with anger, waiting for other congressmen to protest. I could see reporters leaning over the railing of the press gallery, searching the faces of congressmen below to gauge their reaction to Rankin's tirade. I hoped they hadn't detected the source of the hiss, but I was disappointed. A page came to say that reporters wanted to talk to me in the lounge.

On leaving, I passed John McCormack, the Majority Leader.

"John," I said, "did you hear me?"

He looked at me knowingly. "I heard nothing," he told me firmly.

"The press must have heard me. They're waiting to see me about something."

"Helen, you didn't hiss," he said. As I turned to go he took my arm urgently and whispered, "Remember, Rankin is a killer."

With that grim warning, I went out to face the Fourth Estate, pretending innocence in order to avoid confrontation with Rankin by that means. After the interview, unsatisfactory from their perspective, I went immediately to my office and called the armed services. I wanted reports on participation by black soldiers in the wars America had fought. I was informed that no such records existed. The military had only press clippings. I asked to see them.

Boxes arrived and were piled one on the other until they choked the outer office. They continued to come, packed not only with clippings but with various citations and battle records black units had achieved. Piles of boxes teetered in every spare corner of my office so that I had little room to move. I was being subjected to overkill.

Since it was impossible for me to sort through the material myself, I paid out of my own pocket—and I think Evie took a temporary cut in pay—so that we could hire a researcher to pull out the information I wanted. The process went on for weeks and weeks.

When I had the breakdown I asked Lorena Hickok to come to Chevy Chase over Christmas and help me draft a statement. Our routine was that I rose at four in the morning to prepare a draft of what I wanted to say and Hick joined me at nine to start typing, making suggestions to tighten up the prose or point up a statistic better as I strode back and forth, dictating.

When Congress reconvened in January 1946 after the Christmas recess, I had my strategy ready. I asked the Speaker for permission to address the House at the end of each day's session for two weeks. That way I could read the lengthy record of black soldiers into the Congressional Record for posterity while not interfering with the business of the House.

Most congressmen remained in their seats out of curiosity on the day that I began to read the address I called "The Negro Soldier." Rankin's hot temper flared as soon as he heard the title. He started to get to his feet to protest but was restrained by congressmen nearest him. Later one of them revealed what they said to control the fiery Rankin: that he could not object to what I was saying because the information came directly from the army and navy.

After reading the report into the Record, I had an extract of it printed in a pamphlet at my own expense and circulated it to black soldiers in military hospitals and black community groups. Eventually the demand exceeded my resources. I asked the military to underwrite the costs, and they did. I take pride in the fact that the pamphlet, subtitled *A Partial Record of Negro Devotion and Heroism in the Cause of Freedom, Gathered from the Files of the War and Navy Departments,* was the first in what has become a substantial amount of examination of the contribution black people have made in our war efforts.

228 A FULL LIFE

Here, as evidence, are some excerpts from my addresses that appeared in the Congressional Record of January 22, 24, 25, 28, 29, 30, 31 and February 1, 1946:

> Mr. Speaker, it is about the Negro soldier I wish to speak today. I wish to pay him the respect and to express the gratitude of the American people for his contribution in the greatest battle of all time—the battle which decided whether or not we were to remain a free people. . . .
>
> This was the most mechanical of all wars. Training had to be based on the education and experience of the average man. . . . Three-fourths of all Negroes in the armed forces came from areas in this land of the free where their people had been held down for generations, denied educations, denied the use of tools any more complicated than a hoe, denied the right to participate in self-government, denied even the right to self-respect. . . . They went into the armed forces ill-equipped, through no fault of their own, for the tremendous job required of them. But they did the job, all the same, handicap or no handicap. And they did it magnificently.
>
> Despite the Selective Service and Training Act, which established a policy of non-discrimination because of race or color in building up our Army, and in spite of improvement during the course of the war, it must not be forgotten that segregation, discrimination and race prejudice, in all its varied forms, placed an added burden on the Negro in the armed forces and dogged his footsteps from the induction center to the front line. . . .
>
> It was a mess attendant—not permitted, because he was a Negro, to train as a gunner—who manned a machine gun and fought back when the Japs strafed his ship at Pearl Harbor. For this and dragging his mortally wounded captain to safety, Dorie Miller, mess attendant first class, won the Navy Cross.
>
> In December, 1944, when the picture in Europe was dark, when our front line losses were mounting with tragic swiftness, a call was sent out for volunteer replacements from troops assigned to non-combat duty behind the lines. More than 5,000 Negroes eagerly responded. Because only privates were accepted, many non-commissioned officers offered to sacrifice their stripes for a chance to get into the fighting. Twenty-five hundred Negro soldiers were accepted, but 3,000 more were turned back because a quota for Negroes among the volunteers had been set. . . . One

of the finest tributes paid those volunteers came from Brig. Gen. Charles T. Lanham, assistant commander of the 104th Infantry Division, following the presentation of combat decorations. "I have never seen any soldiers who have performed better in combat than you," General Lanham told the Negro doughboys.

And so on, page after page, a litany of individual and collective courage recognized by medals and unit citations. Since blacks most often found themselves in service outfits, their record of achievement in building airports, bases, roads and highways under fire, in freezing cold and blazing heat, had attracted little attention. Blacks built an approach to a bridge across the Rhine under heavy German artillery fire, unable to take cover or shoot back. Negro Seabees won a commendation for building an airport on an island in the Pacific while taking Japanese bullets, and they trucked high explosives and octane gas over the Red Ball highway which was under continuous aerial bombardment.

In 1940, when the Selective Service Act was passed, there were only 4,451 Negroes in our Army, including five commissioned officers and eleven warrant officers. In February a year ago there were 690,282 Negroes in the Army. . . . Last August 495,950 Negroes were overseas. On the day of final victory in Europe, there were twenty-two Negro combat units in action on the European front.

Their valor won praise from General Eisenhower himself. I detailed what Negro units had done, from the "singing engineers" regiment, the 41st Engineers, which was the first Negro unit to land in Africa, to the 99th Pursuit Squadron, which flew 500 combat missions over Italy, and the 614th Tank Destroyer Battalion, which military historians regard as having the most brilliant record of all Negro combat units in Europe. Pinned down in one notable engagement in France, one platoon of the 614th held out though it took fifty percent casualties.

I ended, fifty-four pages later, with a mention that the first American soldier of the armored forces killed in the Pacific was a Negro, Private Robert H. Brooks, son of a sharecropper in Tennessee. The main parade ground of the armored forces at Fort Knox is named in his honor.

Rankin's dreadful temper wasn't improved by my tactic. In the weeks that followed he found opportunity every time he was on his feet to sneer at those of us who supported liberal causes, often stretching the rules of the House which forbid improper language.

One afternoon when we were debating in the House, Rankin was fulminating as usual. I was paying little attention, chatting with a few other liberal Democrats some distance from Rankin. Something caught my attention. Rankin was making a gesture in our direction and saying, "these communists." He did it again.

I jumped up. "Mr. Chairman," I said, "I demand to know if the gentleman from Mississippi is addressing me!"

Rankin stopped and glared at me. I think I was the only person in the House who ever dared to lock horns with him. It wasn't so much courage on my part as recklessness.

I said again, "I demand to know if the gentleman from Mississippi is addressing *me!*" I couldn't say "is addressing us"; I had to make it personal.

Then there was a lot of movement in the House. I saw the man to my left pushed out of his seat as Wright Patman, chairman of the Banking and Currency Committee, sat in his place beside me. There was a scuffling of feet outside. For a point of order the Speaker must be in the chair. Someone had been sent for Sam Rayburn.

Patman lowered his head and quietly advised me.

"You don't have to demand another time, Helen. Just keep standing. Rankin has to answer."

Sam Rayburn arrived and then we were in a Committee of the Whole. Right behind him was the lanky form of Lyndon Johnson, who had been in the coffee shop when he learned that "Helen is taking on Rankin!"

Lyndon came running. I was told later that he had bounded up the stairs to the chamber three at a time. Sam Rayburn banged his gavel and declared, "The gentleman from Mississippi will answer the congresswoman from California."

Rankin had resumed his speech and seemed not to have heard the Speaker. Rankin was such a fearsome man, he appeared to believe himself untouchable. Lyndon went to the podium and whispered something to Rayburn. Sam scowled and banged his gavel again. This time his voice was fierce with warning as he again ordered Rankin to answer me.

Lyndon told me afterward that what he said to Sam was, "Who runs this House, you or Rankin? Are you going to let him get away with this?"

Rankin measured Rayburn, who remained impassive. Finally he had to submit.

"I am not addressing the gentlewoman from California," he said with obvious pain.

I asked permission to set the record straight on the subject of my commitment to democracy. Rayburn granted me the right to address the House the following week.

Lorena Hickok arrived on the double to help me once more. We were polishing the last draft together on Sunday morning when Lyndon Johnson dropped by for a visit and immediately threw himself into the editing process. "What you mean is this . . . ," he suggested. "Or this." He had a knack for putting himself in the other person's situation and visualizing exactly what they meant to say or do.

He thought the speech needed more flourish at the end and proceeded to write my final paragraph. I thought his language a little picturesque but I accepted it rather than spurn the gift.

I read "My Democratic Credo" into the Congressional Record on March 26, 1946. Here are some excerpts:

> Mr. Speaker, I think we all know that communism is no real threat to the democratic institutions of our country. But the irresponsible way the term "communism" is used to falsely label the things the majority of us believe in can be very dangerous. . . .
>
> I shall talk about democracy because it is democracy that we believe in and live by—or should live by. We are interested in communism only as a system that challenges democracy. I am not afraid of that challenge.
>
> I don't think we value democracy highly enough. The great mass of American people will never exchange democracy for communism as long as democracy fulfills its promise. The best way to keep communism out of our country is to keep democracy in it— to keep constantly before our eyes and minds the achievements and the goals which we, a free people, have accomplished and intend to accomplish in the future. . . .

I am jealous for democracy. I do not like to see the things that democracy can accomplish credited to communism. . . .

I am jealous for the school system we have built under democracy, and I do not want its extension—including fair salaries for teachers, day nurseries, school lunch programs, and federal aid to education—called communism. . . .

I believe now—and I shall always believe—that this people's government is capable of self-growth, is capable of making whatever adjustments are needed in a world that has changed so greatly since the days when my great-grandfather, the Rev. William Harrison Gahagan, helped found Dayton, Ohio.

I do not claim that democracy, as we now know it, is perfect, but I know that it has the capacity to remedy its own imperfections, and I do not want to hear each remedy called communism. . . .

I think we do a disservice to democracy when we dismiss communism as the devil's handiwork. Of course, there is competition between democracy and communism in the world today. And there is no doubt in my mind that the result will continue to be the triumph of democracy in the world if we spend our energy and genius in demonstrating to the world what democracy can do. . . .

Communism was born out of hunger, slavery, illiteracy, superstition, degradation. Communism has no place in our society. We have something better.

We have democracy. Communist methods are foreign to ours. Their policies are superimposed from the top and you take it from the top whether you like it or not. Under our democratic system, programs are proposed from many sources in the community . . . the people themselves select or reject what is good for them. We do not believe that one man or a group of men can save the people. *We believe that the people save themselves.* . . .

The fear of communism in this country is not rational. That irrational fear of communism is being deliberately used in many quarters to blind us to our real problems.

The spreading of this fear is in fact propaganda for communism. I am nauseated and sick to death of the vicious and deliberate way the word "communist" has been forged into a weapon and used against those who organize and raise their voices in defense of democratic ideals. . . . Communism could successfully invade only a weakened democracy. A vigorous democracy—a democracy in which there are freedom from want, freedom from fear, freedom of religion, and freedom of speech—would never succumb to communism or any other ism.

Our fight is not against the windmill of communism in America. Rather it is against those who would make a treadmill of democracy through special privilege, bigotry and intolerance. . . . Nobody believes in free enterprise or its future more than I do. I have had all the benefits of this free enterprise system. I was bred in a family that handed down its business from father to son, a family that believed and believes today that individual initiative is the source of our economic vitality. I had every advantage and every opportunity that a child born into that kind of family would have.

It is because I know what education and opportunity and the respect of the community mean in the development of human beings that I fight for them for everyone. *I've* never been in a breadline. *I've* never had to live in a ditchbank. *I'm* not one of those millions who has never known a doctor's care. I was not one of those 200,000 women a year who give birth to their children without medical attention. . . .

But I've been in the slums of America. I've been to the ditchbank. . . .

I have seen shanty towns. . . .

I have seen children with sore eyes and swollen bellies. . . .

I have seen minorities humiliated and denied full citizenship. And I tell you that we betray the basic principle upon which this government of free people was founded unless this people's government finds a way by which all the people can live out their lives in dignity and decency. . . .

Only 10,000 persons own one-quarter of our economic resources and 75,000 persons own one-half of all the corporate stock in this country. Only 61,000 persons out of 130 million collect half the dividends. The war Franklin D. Roosevelt talked about in 1936 is still going on. It is, as he said, "a war for the survival of democracy," and the battle should not rage around the bogus issue of communism but around the real issue of monopoly, and the exploitation of people and their resources. . . .

Democracy cannot long survive when the people permit their lives to be dominated—economically or politically—by a powerful few.

We must make democracy work. We must realize the greatness that is in America. . . . We must reverse the trend to monopoly. We must enlarge the opportunities for all with our magnificent capacities for production and distribution. It is in this atmosphere of hope and freedom that we became great and shall go forward to new leadership in the world. It is in this setting that we can undertake to provide new security and well-being for all our people, rather than much for the few and little for the many. . . . There is no danger in letting people have their say. We have proved that. There is a danger when you try to stop them from saying it.

This, the most powerful nation on earth, stands today as irrefutable proof that there is no danger in a conglomerate peoples, and ideas freely expressed. In fact, out of the very conglomeration, a rich harvest, which is the growth of America, has been reaped. . . .

Tom Paine said: "Suspicion is the companion of mean souls and the bane of all good society." This is true at home and abroad, as true in 1946 as it was in 1776. And former Secretary of State and War Henry L. Stimson wrote a few days ago, "The chief lesson I have learned in a long life is that the only way to make a man trustworthy is to trust him; and the surest way to make him untrustworthy is to distrust him and show distrust. . . ."

We, the members of this body, will fail in our duty if we permit suspicion of another's purpose to divert us from our own purpose—that of making democracy function at full efficiency for our own people. . . .

Mr. Speaker, this body must always be loyal to the principles of its founders and the teachings of its fathers. It must never yield to the tyranny of bigotry. . . .

We, the members of this Congress—chosen by a free people to protect their rights and to bring to reality their hopes and faiths —are not bigots. We don't believe in name-calling. We don't agree that everyone who disagrees with us should be hunted down like a criminal, denied his civil rights, and deprived of his ability to earn a living.

I concluded with the flourishing paragraph that Lyndon Johnson had composed:

We, the members of this House, do not believe that Capitol Hill is a hill on which to kindle a fiery cross, but rather one on which to display the shining Cross which since Calvary has been to all the world the symbol of the Brotherhood of Man.

My friend William O. Douglas of the U.S. Supreme Court invited me to his home to meet Dr. James Yen, a Chinese scholar and humanitarian. Wherever Jimmy Yen traveled in the southern part of China, he planted seeds of true democracy. He taught people to read and write a basic Chinese language in order to unify the diverse linguistic groups of his vast country, and these people became teachers who fanned out through the villages, not only teaching literacy but giving the people knowledge of modern agricultural methods and training in home-industry skills.

When George C. Marshall came before the Foreign Affairs Committee, I spoke to him about the Jimmy Yen program. Marshall had been Truman's ambassador to China before he was appointed Secretary of State, so he was not unaware of it. I asked if we could fund Jimmy Yen's work under the Counterpart program by which America was selling arms to General Chiang Kai-shek to help him fight the communist rebellion led by Mao Tse-tung. The United States used the revenue from that arms sale to finance programs in China aimed at relieving some of the effects of dire poverty there.

Secretary Marshall was not receptive. I talked next to Sam Rayburn in the hope that something could be done to allow Jimmy Yen to tell Congress about his program in person. Rayburn suggested that the entire Foreign Affairs Committee meet with Jimmy Yen in the capacious private dining room of the Speaker. That way it wouldn't be an official representation before the committee.

Jimmy Yen won a number of converts at that luncheon but not enough to secure Counterpart funds for his work. At that time Congressman Walter Judd was pressing for more aid to China. His father had been a missionary there and Walter thought he knew more about the Far East than anyone else. He was always lecturing Congress on what we should be doing to stop communism there, and his solution always involved guns rather than social improvement.

On a day that a special meeting of the Foreign Affairs Committee had been called, I noticed Judd deep in conference with some strangers in the congressional dining room. They were making notes on bright yellow pads and I wondered if their activity had anything to do with the special meeting.

During the meeting, Judd distributed a sheet of yellow paper to each of us.

"What's this?" I asked.

He explained that it was an amendment to a bill that was coming up that afternoon in the House.

"I can't vote on this," I protested. "It isn't printed."

"But Helen," he pleaded, "we must vote it out of committee right now so I can have it printed in time for the debate this afternoon.

I sat back and folded my arms. "I can't vote for something scribbled on a yellow note pad," I said.

Because what he was trying to do *was* unorthodox, Judd needed unanimous consent from the committee before he could proceed. I refused flatly to cooperate.

Judd returned to his seat. He thought a moment and then wrote something on a second slip of yellow paper. He showed it to me. His amendment now included a request that U.S. Counterpart funds be used to support the grass-roots organization of Dr. James Yen. I laughed and agreed. That's how Jimmy Yen got the money he needed to carry on his wonderful work.

Congress was torn by dissension in those days over what should be done to restore the havoc that war had left in Europe. I talked to my friend Robert Carr, who was one of a three-man Reparations Commission which had toured the ravaged cities and countryside. Whole harbor installations, factories, art collections and livestock had been pillaged by the Nazis and transported to Germany. I urged that reparations to France, Belgium and Holland, which had suffered most of the thefts, should be made by Germany. I met general resistance to that suggestion not only on the Foreign Affairs Committee but in the House as well. Many felt that the lesson of World War I was that Germany should not be driven to the wall.

The workload I was carrying was beginning to tell on me. My doctors were concerned but there was little I could do about it. Evie and I brought work home to Chevy Chase every night and long after she retired I was still hard at it.

Besides skimming the leading newspapers every day, there were some journals that I felt obliged to peruse carefully. *Bulletin of*

the Atomic Scientists, published by the Educational Foundation
for Nuclear Science, founded in 1945 by Albert Einstein and
others, was one such. I also read *The New Republic* and *The Nation* and tried to keep up with the postwar spate of books which
analyzed the economy, world power relationships, international
diplomacy and the political process, especially if I respected the
writer.

I went to sleep with my mind racing and would waken in a few
hours, fully alert, to snap on the light and study government reports until I was drowsy again. To appreciate the complexities of
a housing bill, for instance, I pored over material obtained from
the Housing Administration and weighed it with a synopsis of
committee hearings on the bill, paying special attention to the arguments advanced by people who opposed it.

The next morning I would talk to a network of authorities I
trusted, listen to their views and follow their suggestions for more
reading.

When the legislation was complex and important, the Rules
Committee would allow three or four days, or even a week, for
discussion and the vote. I used the extra time to delve into the
background more deeply. Mostly, however, we had but a single
day in which to decide how we would vote and why. In such circumstances I depended heavily on specialists—friends in the
Labor Committee, for instance, and some trusted union leaders—
when a labor bill was before the House.

For the perennial struggle to save the Reclamation Bill from
the inroads of lobbyists, I relied on Arthur "Tex" Goldschmidt,
the Texan who was a special assistant to Ickes in the Department
of the Interior, and made a long telephone call to Paul Taylor in
California. For social legislation Goldschmidt's wife, Elizabeth
Wickenden, an authority on public affairs, helped me. For housing, Wright Patman, chairman of the Banking and Currency
Committee, was an expert.

I missed reading for pleasure. I couldn't remember when I had
picked up a book that didn't contain information I could use in
the House. I read always with pad and pen handy, sifting and
digesting data as I turned the pages. Most of my life I had looked
forward to the evenings with expectancy, wondering what marvel-

ous book would entertain me until I was sleepy. That was over. I always knew I would be reading government reports and I hoped that I could stay awake long enough to finish what I needed to assimilate.

There was always a pile of stuff on my desk. It pained me that no matter how late I worked, I never quite got through it all.

Melvyn and the children were in California and though we talked on the telephone a great deal I felt cut off from them. When I could get away from Washington I went to New York to see Mother at her apartment and stay with Lilli at her house on Long Island, near the ocean she loved. Lilli, I knew, was concerned that I brought with me each time a back-bending stack of work.

One Sunday when I was making notes for a speech in the House, Lilli's son Herbert Walker came into the room. Herbert is a painter and sculptor of considerable talent. He looked at me with exasperation. "Oh Helen," he said, "for godsake aren't you ever free of those papers?"

"No, I'm not," I sighed. "I always have work to do."

"Put it down for a minute, just for a minute," he ordered.

He took the papers out of my hands and led me to a bedroom where he had set up an easel on which was placed invitingly a fresh canvas. Beside it was a tempting bowl of brushes and paints. He selected a brush and handed it to me with a flourish.

"Paint!" he cried.

Once I began, I couldn't stop. I worked for four hours and produced a painting of two ducks, one flying and the other on the ground. Elizabeth Wickenden and Tex Goldschmidt have it now. Elizabeth said of it, "Those are the two you's, dear Helen. You're the duck who is taking off, and you're also the worried duck on the ground who looks up and asks, 'Where are you going? *Where are you going?*'"

That was the beginning. Little by little I became addicted. Whenever I would visit my friend Helen Fuller, former managing editor of *The New Republic*, who had retired to a cozy house not far from Washington, she would have paints waiting for me. She'd say, "Paint—but everything you paint belongs to me. You can't take it away."

When she died in 1972 I was one of the executors of her estate. On a cold, overcast day we had an auction of her things at her home on Long Mountain in Virginia. I wanted my pictures but the other executor, George Davis, said I couldn't have them. They would have to be auctioned with her other paintings, two of which were oils by Diego Rivera and another a small Renoir.

I was aghast, sitting on the auctioneer's platform where I was wrapped in blankets. I doubted that anyone would want my paintings, but my friends loyally bid on all six and carried them away. The proceeds of $28,000 went to the Rappahannock Library as Helen Fuller requested.

She was a remarkable woman. Lady Bird and Lyndon Johnson sent a telegram from Texas which was read at the memorial service. They said, "Born before her time, Helen Fuller was an advance trumpet heralding us to awareness and compassion for all people." She used to give parties for neighborhood children—not just children of people she knew, but *all* children.

In Colombia one time when I was visiting Mary Helen, I had leisure enough to paint. I propped the results up in my hotel room where hotel maids admired them greatly, so I gave them all to them. My brother's secretary once said she wished she could have one. "Nothing could be simpler," I said. "Which one do you want?" So they are scattered everywhere.

A friend of mine, antique dealer Paul Jenkins, once insisted that he have one to sell in his shop. The next time I saw him, he dropped almost $200 in my lap. Someone actually had bought the painting. Later the purchaser called me. He wanted me to settle a dispute he was having with his wife. He thought the painting, which was a rather eerie one, not at all in my usual cheery bright-hued style, depicted the beginning of the world. His wife thought it was just the opposite, the end of the world.

"Which is it?" he inquired.

I told him. It was the end of the world. The bird figures represented missiles and bombs. He told me it had a place of honor over his mantel.

In the spring of 1946 I took part in a Washington conference called Win the Peace, along with such other congressmen as Estes Kefauver, Adam Clayton Powell, Jr., John Coffee and

Charles Savage. Paul Robeson, the black singer, Mary McLeod
Bethune, chairman of the National Council of Negro Women,
and Bartley Crum, head of the Republicans for Roosevelt group
in the 1944 campaign, were among the sponsors.

In my statement to the gathering I said:

> Because of the unified efforts of everyone—government, industry,
> labor, agriculture—we won a war where everything was against us
> at the beginning except the confidence and knowledge that right
> was on our side. We can win the peace if we have the same
> unity. We cannot have this unity unless right is again on our
> side.
>
> If the peace is to be a people's peace, we shall have that right.
> It will weld us together and hold us to our goal.
>
> If the end of all our endeavors is the welfare of human beings
> at home and all over this world, we shall succeed.

When I went to Congress it was known that I was interested
in the problems of the Middle East where the infant United Nations was struggling with the conflicting claims of Jews and Pales-
tinians. Senator Robert Wagner, father of the man who became
New York's mayor, was head of the American Christian Palestine
Committee, which was made up basically of Christian clergymen
who were exercising their Christian consciences by helping Israel
gain independence. He asked me to be vice-chairman and I accepted.

I supported the migration of shattered European Jews to Israel
and the Zionist demand that Israel be created a Jewish state and
homeland. Oil played a major role in our foreign policy even then
and there was a strong lobby in Washington that argued against
recognizing Israel. Dean Acheson, Under Secretary of State, went
along with the Arabs who were opposing Israel.

I had lunch with Dean to discuss the British decision to limit
Jewish emigration to Palestine. He said the Jews always were trou-
blemakers in the world and shouldn't be encouraged. I was appalled.

Dean Acheson and I clashed on that issue and on others but
we also liked each other. Tony Freeman, who was one of our ambassadors, told me that after he and Dean appeared before the

Foreign Affairs Committee one time and were subjected to a barrage of criticism by its Republican members, Dean turned to him when they left the committee room and said, "Wasn't Helen wonderful? Wasn't she *wonderful?* The way she got the questioning back on track so diplomatically."

Still, he didn't think my views on Israel were wonderful. The Hadassah chapter in New York did, however; it announced later that I was its choice for Woman of the Year.

For a time I had, for free, some high-priced help in my office. One was Dr. Charles Hogan, my friend from California, who was between assignments for the State Department and would later spend twenty-one years as our man at the United Nations. Hogo turned up in Washington one day and said he had time to spare and wanted to work for me. He and his wife, who was a journalist, moved into my house in Chevy Chase and became valuable and overworked members of my team.

Hogo spent the war attached to the U. S. Embassy in London under Ambassador James Winant. He told me that Irish patriots who enjoyed seeing England clobbered used to leave their lights on at night so that German bombers could get a fix on London.

The other volunteer was my cousin Walter Pick, newly discharged from the navy. He resumed the secretarial and organizing jobs he'd done for me before and took a load off Evie Chavoor for a few months, and then went back to California.

The Hogans and Walter were godsends. With them around I no longer had to pay researchers to help with my congressional work. They also helped write the speeches I made around the country whenever I needed extra money to pay my office overhead. I was grateful too for college students who worked in Washington every summer as part of an internship program. Evie fitted them into the office routine nicely and I used them as my ears and eyes in congressional galleries when I couldn't follow an interesting debate myself. They were helpful, intelligent, enthusiastic young people and I loved having them around.

I was standing for reelection in the Fourteenth District that year but I couldn't seem to find the time to campaign or even to visit California. The official reason given, and it was true enough, was that President Truman had appointed me U. S. Alternate

Delegate to the General Assembly of the United Nations. Adlai Stevenson was also one of our U.S. delegation to the United Nations. The first United Nations General Assembly had met that spring in a half session in London. The second session was to convene in New York at Flushing Meadow and I threw myself into an intensive study program to prepare myself for it.

There was another reason I was unable to shuttle across the country to take an active part in my campaign. I was advised by my doctors that my heart was showing signs of the stress I was putting myself under. They urged me strongly to get rest or I would be in serious trouble. I would have to eliminate something from my schedule, either the campaign or the United Nations. Unhesitatingly, I decided not to campaign.

Ed and Ruth Lybeck and Florence Reynolds kept me informed and I did what I could to aid them in the daunting chore of electing a candidate who wasn't there. The 1946 elections promised to be difficult ones for Democrats everywhere. Since it was a non-presidential election year, the turnout would be small, which usually hurts Democrats. We also faced an electorate that was tired of us after sixteen years and seemed to be unimpressed with Harry Truman. The mood indicated that a number of Democrats would lose their seats.

Sensing victory, the Republicans threw everything they had against me in the Fourteenth District. By their analysis of the 1944 campaign, my victory came from the support of the black community. There was every reason for Republicans to believe that the blacks in the Fourteenth would continue to vote for me. My voting record on black issues was impeccable. Besides the Constitution Hall bill and my reading into the Congressional Record of the story of black military history, there were my fights for such legislation as prohibition of discrimination in employment and an anti-lynch-law bill.

When my first congressional option occurred, I appointed a black student, David Carlisle, to West Point. On another occasion I was helpful when blacks needed support for a charter to open a savings and loan association.

Blacks in my district had learned that I was ready to battle for them. In April 1945 Edith Terry sent me a telegram to tell me that her son Roger Terry was one of 101 black officers arrested in a race riot at the military base in Freeman Field, Indiana. I investigated at once and learned that the base commander, a bigot, had forbidden black officers to use the officers' club. I contacted Henry Stimson, Secretary of War, and demanded their immediate release. Henry looked into the matter and promptly sacked the commanding officer and freed the blacks.

After considering the problem, the Republicans decided to run a black man against me. They lined up Moody Staten, an army colonel with an impressive record, but Staten didn't file. Instead there was another black, Frederick M. Roberts, the first black elected to the state legislature, a popular man who had served in Sacramento for sixteen years.

I was in the hospital with heart trouble on the night of the primary when it was decided that it would be Douglas versus Roberts. As soon as I was mobile again I undertook several speaking engagements so I could pay the costs of my campaign. Because I was helping the United Jewish Fund at the time at various fundraising events to help Zionists, I had as many as thirty invitations a day asking me to speak.

Evie wrote to Ed Lybeck, who was very concerned for my health, that I was completely worn out. "Just sitting at luncheons takes a lot out of her," she said.

Lybeck and the others valiantly kept the secret of my exhaustion, though Phil Connelly, the labor leader who opposed me in 1944, thundered that I was neglecting the Fourteenth. Lybeck kept his eye on the *Sentinel*, the influential black newspaper run by Leon Washington. The editorial position wavered between me, a proven friend of the black community, and the strong appeal of Roberts, who would be the first black ever sent to the U. S. Congress by California.

Republicans imported the heavyweight champion of the world, Joe Louis, easily the most admired black in the country, to campaign against me. People in the Fourteenth District were ecstatic to see the "Brown Bomber" and turned out in droves.

The *Sentinel* endorsed Roberts just two weeks before voting day. The headline of October 24 read LET'S ELECT FRED ROBERTS and a supporting story ran for three pages urging the rejection of "Lilly-whitism" [*sic*].

I wrote Lybeck that if the black community voted for me I would feel "that I have made my first really concrete contribution since I have been in Congress." I added, "I have long felt that the oppressed had a potential for loyalty far beyond anything you or I could understand."

In another part of the state, the Twelfth District, Jerry Voorhis was being challenged by a newcomer to politics, Richard Milhous Nixon. Nixon, then thirty-three, a lawyer and navy veteran, had no background on which to draw in order to debate Jerry on the issues, especially since Jerry was a conscientious congressman who was thoroughly informed, so he was waging a vicious campaign to discredit his opponent.

Voorhis was described not long ago in the Binghamton, New York, *Sun-Bulletin* as coming "as close to being a decent human being as a person can get in politics." He had served in the Seventy-ninth Congress on the House Un-American Activities Committee, HUAC, where one of his contributions was to insist on the right of accused people to be protected from abuse. Since HUAC was not bound by the safeguards provided in normal courtroom procedures, some appalling abuses of innocent people were creeping into the tactics. Nixon maintained that Voorhis was trying to thwart the work of HUAC in order to protect communist spies.

Nixon was careful never to make such inflammatory statements himself. Possessed of superb oratorical skills, he got his message over by means of innuendo and facial expressions. His staff, however, was under no such restraint. The daughter of one of my campaign workers spent a day in the Nixon headquarters to see what was going on. She was assigned to a room filled with people using the telephones, systematically calling everyone in the district. When the person answered they would say, "Good morning. Do you know that Jerry Voorhis is a communist?" and hang up.

Nixon and other Republicans swept the nation on November 5, 1946, scattering good Democrats everywhere. Voorhis left politics, broken and discouraged, and moved to Chicago where he became active in establishing cooperative housing for low-income people. For the first time in almost thirty years, there would be a Republican majority in Congress. Even California, which had been growing into a Democratic bastion, was hit by the trend. Voorhis was only one of five Democrats who lost to Republicans.

The Fourteenth District, however, bucked the tide. Despite the attraction of sending a black to Congress, the black community remained touchingly faithful to me. With a record-smashing turnout, blacks doubled the margin of victory that I had achieved in 1944. Instead of winning by 4,000 votes, this time I won by 8,622 votes.

It was believed to be the first time that a white candidate ever carried a black district against a black candidate in a major election. I even beat Roberts in his own precinct.

A graduate student at the University of California in San Diego, Colleen M. O'Connor, working on her Ph.D. in American history, made a study of that 1946 campaign in the Fourteenth and traced the drama of that confrontation. I'm indebted to her for refreshing my memory of what happened. Preoccupied as I was with the United Nations, I was unaware of most of the details.

Adlai Stevenson and I were assigned to the Economic and Social Council of the United Nations. The major item on the agenda was the crisis involving the United Nations Relief and Rehabilitation Administration, UNRRA. Launched in 1943, UNRRA sent aid to war-ravaged countries that were being liberated by Allied armies in Europe. In the beginning the aid consisted of noncontroversial items such as food and medicine. Next the countries needed help to restore essential public services, and gradually the aid took the form of assistance to get industry and agriculture started again.

Fifty-two nations participated in UNRRA, each pledged to contribute 2 percent of its income. Since the United States was far and away the wealthiest country on earth, the American contribution was about half of the four billion fund. The United States had just announced that it planned to pull out of UNRRA, a response to the country's strong postwar isolationist trend. We all knew that if the U.S. left, UNRRA would collapse.

Governor Herbert H. Lehman, who had succeeded Franklin
Roosevelt as governor of New York, was the first head of
UNRRA. When he was forced to resign because of ill health, he
was replaced by feisty Fiorello LaGuardia, the "Little Flower,"
for twelve years the most popular mayor New York City ever had.
LaGuardia was selected in the expectation that he would be eager
to get the United States out of UNRRA.

The appointment backfired when LaGuardia went to Europe
and toured the refugee camps where more than a million stateless
people were stranded. Some seven million war refugees had been
returned to the countries of their origin but these were the ones
who couldn't, or wouldn't, go back. LaGuardia returned enthusiastically converted to keeping U.S. participation in UNRRA.

The argument being used was that UNRRA aid now was going
principly to communist nations such as Poland, the Ukraine and
Yugoslavia, and to countries where the communists were gaining
strength, Greece and Italy. I thought that was irrelevant. People
needed help and those countries fortunate enough to escape
bombings and massive refugee problems had a responsibility to assist those who had endured such depredations; it was as simple
as that.

I moved into the Hotel McAlpin in New York where the
American delegation was housed and launched a campaign to persuade State Department people and anyone else in a position of
influence that our decision to withdraw from UNRRA was mor-
ally wrong.

Alis de Sola came to visit me one day. She said she could hear
me talking as she walked down the hotel corridor past the Marine
guards posted there. It was three o'clock in the afternoon but she
found me in bed, following doctors' orders, with curlers in my
hair. I was holding a press conference for reporters from the New
York *Times,* *The New Republic* and *The Nation.*

One day the American delegation was discussing where the
United Nations should have its home. Senator Warren Austin,
head of the delegation, was in favor of accepting the offer from
the Rockefellers of free land on the East River in New York City
and some were arguing against it. I wasn't interested in the topic.
I interrupted with a plea that we refuse to accept our directive

from the State Department to withdraw the United States from UNRRA.

The room exploded. Some were for it and some against. Adlai Stevenson quietly got up and left the room. He returned a few minutes later to say that Dean Acheson was on the phone from Washington and wanted to speak to me.

Dean opened with a blast.

"Helen, what the hell are you doing?" he demanded.

"What do you mean?" I asked, though I knew at once that Adlai had tattled on me.

"You're opposing the cutoff of UNRRA. Don't you realize that we have no choice in this matter? The Administration got the Senate to support our last request for funds for UNRRA only because we promised that it would be the last. The Senate simply won't support UNRRA again and we can't ask it to."

"Dean, it's all wrong," I protested. I went on to explain my view that it was essential for UNRRA to continue to provide aid. Europe was a shambles and the United Nations had to have funds to do something about the dire conditions there.

He didn't wait for me to finish my argument. "You're not a free agent," he informed me in an icy tone. "You're at the United Nations as a delegate charged with the responsibility of carrying out U.S. policy. You can agree or disagree with that policy in Congress but not when you're at the UN. I order you to drop this campaign of yours to keep us in UNRRA. We aren't going to do it, and you have no right to keep saying that we should."

I slumped in my chair. "All right, Dean," I conceded. "But I know it's wrong."

Adlai was to address the Economic and Social Council of the UN the following day to announce the U.S. pullout. That evening he went to New Jersey to give an address so I was left to work with the advisers from the State Department on the speech he was to deliver in the UN.

It was sent to me that morning in my hotel suite. As I read it, I was shocked by the ruthless tone and tactless language. It was insulting to every nation working in UNRRA. I called the State Department and asked for a meeting. The men assembled around

five o'clock, clearly expecting that the session would be a brief formality.

"This is outrageous," I began. "If Adlai reads this speech as it
is written, the United States won't have a friend left in the
world."

Someone commented with a shrug, "What's wrong with it? It
simply says straight out that we've given plenty of help in the
past and now we're through."

"Exactly," I replied. "You've listed every bit of help we've
given, which is insulting and humiliating to the recipients.
There's a lack of compassion here. You don't say to people who
have come to you for help, 'Look, I've already given you one over-
coat, three sweaters and a bowl of soup, so that's plenty.' It just
isn't done that way."

Tyler Wood, the State Department chief at the United Nations, had written the speech. He asked me politely to point to
the parts I didn't like.

"Every line," I told him.

"So," he said gamely, "we'll go over it line by line."

We parted close to midnight. Though I was outnumbered
twenty-four to one during that seven-hour marathon of revising
the speech, I won my argument that the statement should be
courteous and considerate. We removed the offensive language
but we were left, of course, with the same bitter content: when
the present commitment to UNRRA ended, the United States
was pulling out.

UNRRA's Director General Fiorello LaGuardia opened the
session of the Economic and Social Council with a passionate description of the appalling conditions in Europe that he had
witnessed. He called for support of UNRRA. Delegates from various participating nations spoke next, all of them in favor of continuing in UNRRA. Then it was Adlai's turn; he was obliged to
do what the State Department wanted.

Fiorello headed straight for me the moment the meeting ad-
journed. His face red with anger, he brushed past Adlai and
snapped at me, "Why did you go along with this, Helen? *You
know better!*"

I did know better, but what could I say to LaGuardia? I have often wondered if I should have resigned from the delegation at that point. It wouldn't have done any good but it might have been a comfort to the nations we had abandoned to know that not all Americans agreed with our selfishness.

The withdrawal from UNRRA marked the beginning of many actions by which the United States undermined the authority and effectiveness of the United Nations. We took that small step in the wrong direction and eventually found ourselves far afield from our intention when we helped form the United Nations in the first place.

Someday we may have a Parliament of Man where each delegate will be independent to vote his or her conscience. Today the United Nations isn't remotely like that. The delegates are bound hand and foot—as I was in 1946.

I was able to help persuade Congress to fund some short-term aid projects, particularly to assist the million people still in refugee camps; *displaced persons*, we called them, or DPs. UNRRA died, as Fiorello and I knew it would. It was discontinued in Europe in 1947 and the final shipment of aid went to China in 1949. To fill the gap, the United Nations established the International Refugee Organization and set up International Refugee Year, during which all those helpless people finally were absorbed into sponsoring countries.

Other functions of UNRRA went on under various UN organizations such as the International Children's Fund and the Food and Agriculture Organization. The vacuum left by UNRRA wasn't completely filled, however. The Marshall Plan came along in 1947 to do that.

At the end of that session of the General Assembly I was invited to give a number of lectures on the structure of the United Nations. I composed what I must say was a scholarly but dull speech. I felt it was important to get around the country talking about the United Nations in order to bolster support for it that seemed to be slipping away. Because I saw the United Nations as the world's best hope for peace, I made myself available to speak on the topic for free, asking only for travel expenses when they were available and paying out of my own pocket when they weren't.

I was chairing a congressional subcommittee of the Foreign Affairs Committee devoted to examining the specialized committees that the United Nations was establishing. The post provided me with ample evidence that the United Nations had the potential to transform power relationships in the world if the major nations would cooperate.

Harry Truman knew of my opposition to hard-line American tactics. He was hearing the same message from Mrs. Roosevelt, who believed that Russia had legitimate concerns about its security and that America should be prepared to go halfway to meet those concerns.

Eleanor Roosevelt told Truman, "America's greatest need today is for a positive program to strengthen democracy rather than a negative program aimed solely at a futile attempt to stop communism without offering anything better than the strengthening of autocracy and dictatorship."

One of the states that invited me to speak about the United Nations was Texas, where the League of Women Voters wanted me to give an address in Dallas and a teachers' organization asked me to speak in Austin. Just before I was due in Texas, the state legislature, which was considering a bill to increase teachers' salaries, informed the teachers that they wouldn't get their pay increases if Helen Gagahan Douglas spoke to them. The League of Women Voters, which had lobbied for many years on behalf of the teachers, got the same message. The legislature was hot about my stands on racial integration.

Early one morning I had a call from a teacher in Dallas telling me what had happened. I assured her that I understood the situation and didn't mind canceling.

"But you must come!" she protested. "We're not going to give in to bullying. We're changing the arrangements so it will look as though someone else is sponsoring the speeches, but we want to go ahead with your talks."

Lyndon Johnson heard about it and made some telephone calls to ask friends of his to help me. He was worried that something unpleasant would happen. Lyndon's friends met me at the Dallas airport and drove me to the hotel where the meeting was held, supposedly under the auspices of a college chum of mine, Minnie

Mae Fleming. The place was packed with people, many of them, I suspected, curiosity seekers wanting a glimpse of this flaming liberal who was giving the white males of the state fits.

I'm sure they were bored to death with my lecture on the United Nations and its committees but the evening passed without incident. Then Lyndon's friends drove me to Austin, where the announcement that I was coming had drawn Democrats from all over that part of Texas. Austin didn't have a hall large enough to hold them, except for a huge church whose minister was under fire for his reactionary positions. He planned to be in Detroit that same night with some hired goons who were trying to break up a strike in the Ford plant. To show how open-minded he was, he made his church available to me.

I gave my dull speech again to a hall that was packed. The side aisles were jammed with temporary seating and more than a hundred people stood at the back. At the end of the talk, I was slammed with the meanest questions I'd heard in a long time. They went after me about communism, migrants, equality for blacks, women in politics, and the fact that my husband and children lived on the other side of the country. I'm usually at my best in such slanging matches and I enjoyed myself hugely.

Meanwhile I had asked Florence Reynolds in my Los Angeles office to find a black woman to work with me in Washington. I stipulated that the black woman must be able to hold her own on a professional basis. I knew it would do no good opening the way to hiring black secretaries if we settled for an incompetent one. Just to have a black face in my office is not what I was after. I despise that kind of appointment, which does nothing to change the hiring attitudes of whites.

After months of searching and interviewing and turning down recommendations that came from black assemblymen in the state legislature, we chose Juanita Terry. The daughter of Jessie Terry, who was one of the leaders of the black community, she came from an educated and respected family.

Florence found Juanita working in one of the government agencies in the Federal Building and asked:

"Juanita, do you want to go to Washington?"

"Sure," Juanita answered. She added that she couldn't take shorthand.

"Learn," Florence instructed her.

Juanita worked hard and mastered shorthand in record time. Evelyn Chavoor interviewed her and Juanita was hired for about $200 a month, a substantial raise from her previous salary. When they heard she was coming, even my most liberal friends in Washington were worried. "We'll work it out," I assured them.

Juanita wasn't allowed to eat in the staff cafeteria or dining room of the House of Representatives, which were segregated. I didn't notice for a while because she was so discreet. She pretended to be busy at lunchtime and would ask someone to bring her a sandwich. Since I often ate at my desk as well, I thought nothing of it.

When it dawned on me that something was wrong, I raised a storm and ended segregation. Eventually all three black secretaries in the House, Juanita and the two who worked for black congressmen, were allowed to eat with the other secretaries. I think the black congressmen had allowed the situation to go on because they were reluctant to make waves. To spare Juanita the embarrassment of sitting at a table alone, someone from the office always went to eat when she did.

Later, Paul Douglas of Illinois was the first white senator to hire a black secretary. As I had, he made a fuss about segregation until the woman was allowed into the Senate dining room.

Southern congressmen reared back in shock the first time they saw Juanita calmly working in the outer office. For a long time after they arrived in my office and shut the door I would have to answer incredulous questions about her before we could settle down to the business at hand. From that beginning, however, others in Congress gradually hired black staff and in no time no one thought anything of it.

One casualty of my introduction of integration was the southern woman in my office who had been with me for more than two years. Her behavior toward Juanita was above reproach, but working on an equal basis with a black person put more strain on her than she could bear. I think her family put pressure on her as well. In any case, she came to me with a transparently fabricated story about being needed at home and said she was quitting. I told her that I understood how difficult it had been for her and thanked her for unfailing courtesy.

I had only newly acquired the ability to be completely comfortable with black people myself. It was something that nothing in my life had prepared me for. Happily, I no longer was making gauche mistakes. Juanita grins to recall the time when I was speaking in a church filled with black people. Speaker after speaker praised me to the skies for what I had accomplished on civil rights issues. I was feeling marvelous when it came my turn to say something.

Full of joy, I spread my arms and said, "I just love the Negro people." I knew from the cold silence that fell on the crowd that I had made a frightful mistake. I kept talking and eventually they warmed to me again. Afterward Sidney Bercovici, a part-time person on my staff who later worked in Jimmy Roosevelt's office, took me aside and explained that my impulsive gesture had been taken as patronizing. I saw his point at once.

Juanita Terry told me that she never did use the shorthand skills she so painfully had acquired. Evie and I were always so busy that we had no time for dictation. We'd just thrust a letter at her and say, "Answer this," and she would.

President Truman had followed up the decision of Congress to put atomic power under civilian control by pushing through a bill that the military wanted, one which unified the army, navy and air force under the Department of Defense. For whatever reason, and some of us thought that bellicose moves by the United States were a factor, the Soviet was becoming increasingly difficult. After rejecting the Baruch plan for international control of atomic power, Stalin went on to oppose Allied plans for the unification of Germany. The Soviet also was against the establishment of a United Nations peace force, suspecting that it would be a tool of the United States.

In this worsening situation, Harry Truman proposed what was called the Truman Doctrine, a bill to provide military aid to Greece and Turkey. The reasons were complex. Britain had been pouring resources into Greece in order to support a shaky government against civil unrest. When Britain could no longer afford to do so and announced its intention to withdraw its forces, a certain balance of power in the Middle East was removed. Russia mobilized on the Turkish border, sending shock waves through the West. Turkey asked for military aid just as fighting broke out in Greece between the government and Greek communists supplied from Yugoslavia.

I didn't dispute the facts. It was quite clear that Russia was trying to expand in the Middle East and I agreed that something should be done about it. But what I believed then, and I believe today, was that Russia's military buildup on Turkey's border should have been brought to the Security Council of the United Nations where it could be put in the context of a problem for the whole world rather than a U.S.S.R.-U.S. confrontation. The United States should not have acted unilaterally. By doing so, we undermined the United Nations and created the horror that should have been avoided at all costs: America and Russia locked head to head.

Dean Acheson testified every day before the Foreign Affairs Committee in support of Truman's proposal. I tried to persuade him that the White House was making a grave mistake in sending munitions to Turkey and the beleaguered government of Greece.

Greece had suffered terribly in the war. Armies had crossed the country five times and the people fought heroically against the Germans, taking frightful casualties. Perhaps they had a right, even if some of them were communists, to establish a less autocratic government than they had known in the past.

Dean Acheson was irritated with me again. He said there was no time to go to the United Nations, which was slow-moving over matters of protocol. Besides, the Soviet was a member of the Security Council and had veto power.

I protested that there were ways around that. The Assembly could hear Turkey's complaint against the Soviet. It would be interesting to see how the countries of the world lined up. At the very least it would be a positive demonstration that world powers were conducting themselves differently now. Sending arms to Turkey was old-style, pre-atomic-bomb diplomacy. The nuclear age demanded a saner approach, that of airing grievances in the United Nations.

If we tried to frighten the Soviet, I argued, it would only make the Soviet more frightened of *us*. Belligerent Americans seem to have the notion that people in foreign countries don't mind dying, that we are the only people on earth who aren't willing to commit suicide for our country. That's false. That's blind. That's dangerous.

It takes fifteen minutes for a nuclear weapon to reach a target in the United States. *Fifteen minutes!* We live with that; it's madness.

At my urging, California Democrats passed a resolution condemning arms loans and sales to Greece and Turkey. We took a lot of heat for that because we were Democrats opposing something that a Democrat in the White House wanted. It was, in fact, the first and only time I did not support a Truman bill in Congress.

I offered amendments to the bill both in the Foreign Affairs Committee and on the floor of the House. If they had been accepted by the Republican-dominated House of Representatives, I would have voted for the bill.

One amendment was intended to protect our atomic energy program. I said on the floor of the House:

> It is frightening to think that this bill, as now written, authorizes the transfer to two such governments as those of Greece and Turkey weapons, materials and information incorporating what Congress has repeatedly and excitedly declared to be the most vital element in the bastion of our security. If there were a bill before you to give atomic bombs to Britain, I believe you would reject it out of hand. Surely materials and information which cannot be shared even with Britain and Canada—who participated in and contributed to all phases of our atomic energy development and therefore have a claim to such fruits, apart from the fact that they really know our secrets anyway—must not be entrusted to Balkan governments which are neither, to say the least, stable nor dependable.
>
> Months were spent in determining whether the chairman of the Atomic Energy Commission had sufficiently demonstrated his loyalty to our form of government, whether he sufficiently understood the principles of democracy, to make him a fit person to guard our bombs and our knowledge. We have not spent five

minutes inquiring into the beliefs of King Paul of Greece, to
whom, under this bill, the President would have the authority to
hand over anything related to atomic energy.

I put forward another amendment in Congress in May 1947,
which I began by reminding the House that I supported the principle of providing economic and military aid to both Greece and
Turkey. I went on to say:

> We propose to extend aid to Greece and I *heartily approve of
> that*. We must be very sure that this aid will produce democratic
> and sound economic results. . . . Official British, United States
> and United Nations reports clearly point to the reasons for fail-
> ure [of previous aid programs to Greece]; namely the incompe-
> tence, corruption and oppression which exists in the present
> Greek government.
>
> Terror exists in Greece today—economic and political terror.
> Terrorism from the extreme right is as oppressive as terrorism
> from the extreme left. In our opposition to communism, we must
> not make the mistake of backing remnants of corrupt and decay-
> ing systems. . . .
>
> This is the sure formula that will breed communism. . . .
>
> There is only one way to succeed. We must make it clear to
> the oppressed people of Greece that we are in profound sympa-
> thy with their legitimate aspirations for economic reform and so-
> cial rehabilitation, and that we propose to see that United States
> aid is used to create channels for the free political expression of
> those aspirations . . . Great Britain failed in her efforts to aid
> Greece. We must not fail!
>
> It was said yesterday by the gentleman from New York [Mr.
> Wadsworth] that when we defend liberty for others we de-
> fend our own liberty. I agree fully with all my heart and mind, if
> the liberty we defend for others is the same liberty we cherish for
> ourselves; and I am ready to defend that liberty abroad as well as
> at home, not just with $400,000,000 which guarantees nothing
> but a beginning, but with billions of dollars.
>
> That is evidently not the sentiment of this Congress, or it
> would have passed the International Children's Fund before this,
> and it would not have gutted the Relief Bill, the crippling of
> which will invite communism in Italy, Hungary, Austria and
> Poland.
>
> If we are going to be instrumental in the development of a

democratic world it is going to cost us something in terms of hard cash and generous treatment to the impoverished and miserable people of this earth.

With a handful of others I fought strenuously for a brief moratorium on the bill, at least before arming Turkey, in order to allow the United Nations an opportunity to demonstrate that it was capable of functioning as its founders had hoped. I pleaded this cause on the floor of the House, saying:

> It seems fairly obvious that the conditions prevailing in these two countries are not the same. Greece is in the midst of civil conflict. Turkey is not.
>
> Facts have been presented to the committee to show that Greece is in extreme need of aid. No facts have been shown to prove that Turkey is in imminent peril or in dire need of outside assistance.
>
> Turkey who at the beginning of the war had about 45 million dollars in gold has today in total gold and foreign exchange resources 245 million dollars. Two hundred and twenty-seven million of that is in gold.
>
> When we talk about aid to Turkey, we are talking about military aid—there is no evidence that economic aid is needed in Turkey or that the government of the United States expects to extend economic aid to her.
>
> We are falling into the ancient error of preparing for war without attending the issues which create war. . . .
>
> Where are the facts to buttress our decision committing the nation to so grave a step? I do not say there are no facts. I say, too, that the United Nations alone is in the position to make an impartial examination to get at the truth of Turkey's claims and make the facts available. . . . My amendment says that the United States will not do so and so unless the United Nations fails to take action within a specified period of time. There is a vast difference between steaming ahead on our own, subject to countermanding orders by the United Nations, and giving the United Nations precisely the kind of responsibility it was set up to discharge.
>
> My amendment provides that the President shall instruct the United States delegate to the United Nations to request the United Nations to study conditions in Turkey and to evaluate the contentions of the Turkey government insofar as they pur-

port to show that the national integrity of Turkey is threatened
by pressures from outside sources. . . .

The amendment allows a period of six months during which
the President of the United States is to get this train of actions
under way. If within that time the United Nations acts, presum-
ably the President will await the report before deciding on the
next step. If, on the other hand, the United Nations signifies
that it is unwilling or unable to accede to our request, the President . . . is at liberty to furnish such military assistance to Turkey as is authorized in the bill before you. . . . Let the United
Nations decide and let the United States be the leader in cham-
pioning this course.

I took pains to repeat many times that my stand should not be
construed as critical of President Truman but I felt privately that
the man from Missouri was contributing to the growing mood of
panic in the United States. The White House, the State Department and the media seemed convinced that communism was
galloping across Europe and aimed straight for the throat of the
American eagle. The perfect instrument to examine the true situation and deliver an impartial report, it seemed to me, was the
United Nations.

Congress, however, was obsessed with what orators liked to call
the Red Menace. Most congressmen were enthusiastic suporters
of the Truman Doctrine. Said Senator Edwin Johnson of Colorado, the man who had tried to give control of atomic power to
the military:

> I am going to support this bill. I do not care whether it costs
> four hundred million or four billion, as long as it will stop the
> mad rush of communism that is sweeping over Europe, the Mid-
> dle East and is making inroads in this country. We should spend
> any amount of dollars that is needed to stop this insidious
> thing. . . .

There were similar statements on every hand. Minority Leader
John McCormack declared, "May I call attention to the fact that
not only is the Near East in danger but if the communists take
over Greece, Italy is gone. . . . There are millions of Americans
of Italian blood who are hoping that Italy will be saved." Truly,

our mail from constituents indicated that Americans were reacting to the poses our leaders were striking.

Jackson of California reflected the national mood when he said, ". . . my heart is very much concerned over the Red tide of aggression which is sweeping over the earth . . ." My nemesis John Rankin piously announced, "I am the only man in either House of Congress who has stated openly that he was in favor of breaking relations with communist Russia. Do not kid yourselves, they are already making war upon us . . ."

Public attention was focused on the House Un-American Activities Committee, where J. Edgar Hoover, head of the FBI, was giving sensational testimony that the United States was inundated with traitors and communist spies. Our former ambassador to the Soviet Union, William Bullitt, increased fears when he said that the Soviets' aggression toward the United States was so intense that if they had an H-bomb they would drop it on us at once.

Rankin took that opportunity to declare his support of and trust in Harry Truman, a fellow Baptist, inviting the President to join him in "driving communism from the American soil." He appended this broadside: "If the communists take over this country there will be no Baptists in Missouri, there will be no Methodists in Mississippi, or Presbyterians in Iowa, there will be no Catholics in Louisiana or New York, there will be no Episcopalians in Virginia . . ."

Nothing could have been better designed to inflame the situation. I wondered where we were headed. Congress and the country appeared to be in the hands of demagogues.

Senator Harry Byrd of Virginia spoke for the vanishing moderates when he proposed an amendment to the Greek-Turkish aid bill that was similar to mine. He pointed out that the United States was providing copious aid directly to the Soviet Union and to satellite communist nations, an economic fact which appeared to be lost in the debate about the Red Menace. He asked sensibly, "Can we nourish communism with our left hand and crush communism with our right?"

Byrd went on to say, "Today the State Department is urging Congress to approve seventeen million dollars to Russia for the

purchase of machinery to develop new processes for aviation gaso-
line, which will result in strengthening communism, and yet at
the same time the State Department requests Congress to approve four hundred million dollars to resist communist aggression
in Greece and Turkey."

A handful of us—Harry Byrd, Jacob Javits of New York,
Arthur Vandenberg of Michigan, me, and a few others—continued to protest the bill but everything was against us. Some
congressmen sincerely believed that sending munitions to Turkey
would save American lives; many others, I suspect, realized that a
badly informed public wanted warlike gestures against Russia.

Even an amendment I offered making aid to Greece condi-
tional on such basic American principles as amnesty for political
prisoners and a promise of a free election supervised by the
United Nations was defeated resoundingly. The United States
was opposed to democracy in Greece, the birthplace of democracy! Desolate, I watched the loss of every amendment that attempted to involve the United Nations in any way, or to prevent
atomic weapons from going to Turkey.

Across the floor of the House I often caught the new congressman Richard Nixon watching me, obviously delighted that
every effort I made to change the bill failed. Lyndon Johnson was
distressed. He had no yardstick in foreign affairs as he did in domestic matters. I don't remember his discussing foreign policy
very often, though he was an important member of the House
Military Affairs Committee and, as such, was close to the thinking of the military.

I was never sure whether some of Lyndon Johnson's votes were
cast out of conviction or out of judging what Texas politics
required. It was hard to tell; he never gave any indication. He was
willing to make the compromises necessary, I believe, to stay in
Congress. In fact he made fun of those who refused to bend at all
to conditions that were stacked against them and therefore were
out of the running before they had hardly started. He wanted to
stay on top of Congress and stay in politics, so he rode out the period of passionate anticommunism without tipping his hand very
much.

He protected himself by not being serious. In conversation he

was prone to exaggeration and to a certain kind of humorous jib-
ing. Afterward, if there was any protest, he could always say that
he was just kidding.

I wasn't much aware of the new congressman from Massachusetts, John F. Kennedy, who had little to say. Our back-
grounds were somewhat alike, both of us privileged easterners of
Irish descent, but we had little to do with each other.

Eleanor Roosevelt never did approve the Greek-Turkish aid
bill, which violated her basic principles for international peace
and cooperation. Months later she wrote that communists in
Greece would never be repulsed by guns and warships; they
wanted work and prosperity.

To the horror of many of us, Harry Truman instituted a loyalty
program for all government employees. I said that the country
was accepting totalitarian practices which it professed to despise.
Even a leading anti-communist, James Wechsler, thought Truman
was creating "an artificial uproar" in order to win votes as a foe of
the Red Menace. Liberals wondered what had happened to the
First Amendment and other constitutional freedoms.

At the same time, the domestic front was shaken by rapidly rising costs. Business and industry lobbied strongly for the removal
of wartime price controls. Rent controls were under continuous
attack and I was one of those who struggled to have them retained. The removal of price controls on food had resulted in a
steep rise in the cost of food and I was determined that low-income people be protected from the double jeopardy of expensive
food and expensive shelter. I knew from my mail that salaries
weren't keeping pace with inflation; my constituents wrote that
they could barely afford to eat.

I knew I would have to be careful of my facts in order to make
a persuasive argument in a Republican Congress strongly inclined
to decontrols. I hired an economist, Lucy Kramer, who spent
weeks gathering data and weeks more putting it together in a fat
file.

I always seemed to leave the actual drafting of a speech until
the last minute. The day before I was due to speak in Congress,
Lucy, Evie, Juanita and I toiled on the first draft, and the second,
and the third.

Darkness fell and we munched on sandwiches and continued. Lucy had surveyed selected pockets of the country to determine what happened to grocery bills when price controls came off. The Labor Department had given useful information about average incomes in those regions. It was my job to put the material together in a speech that wouldn't cause waves of boredom in the House and in the press.

In order to give me a quick grasp of the situation Lucy had rounded off all percentages. Now she insisted on working each out to the exact decimal, a process that was so time-consuming that we all groaned. Still, I agreed with her; I wanted my arguments to be airtight.

Juanita brought me the second last draft page by page and I entered final revisions, after which Evie checked line by line for errors. We finished long after midnight and dragged ourselves home with aching heads. I lay awake worried that the data I had taken from charts and graphs would be stupefyingly dull. The congressional press gallery would ignore it and I would lose my valuable opportunity to gain public support.

By morning I had an idea. I sent Juanita and Evie out to a supermarket. That afternoon I walked into Congress with a metal shopping basket on my arm and displayed the basic foodstuffs they had purchased. I declared that decontrol had resulted in a 50 percent increase in the cost of bread, milk, flour, eggs, fats, meat and soap. I pointed out that corporate profits also were up: in the latter part of 1946, following a modest round of wage increases, corporate profits were running over seven billion, after taxes, higher than in 1945—after paying more in salaries. The price increases, in short, were gouging the consumer.

My speech did nothing to reimpose controls on the price of food but it contributed somewhat to the decision Congress made that year to delay removing rent controls. If food prices had spiraled so high in only nine months, it was clear that affordable housing would also be impossible for the poor and low-income people—whose numbers included thousands of veterans.

In April 1947 the United Nations formed a special committee to study the dispute between Jews and Arabs over Palestine. The committee's recommendation was to establish a Jewish state, an

Arab state and an international zone which would include the holy city of Jerusalem. The State Department, sympathetic to the Arabs and their oil, opposed partition. Harry Truman defied his State Department and ordered the United States delegation in the United Nations to vote in support of the motion.

General George Marshall, Truman's admired Secretary of State, cautioned delay and Truman accepted the advice. Instead of partition, the United States would vote for a United Nations police force to supervise the Middle East and keep the Arabs and Jews apart.

"We have been vacillating and dishonest," I protested. Eleanor Roosevelt offered to resign from the American delegation to the United Nations. Truman frantically urged her to stay and she agreed only after wringing from him reluctant permission that she would be free to speak against the White House stand.

With Arabs and Jews already fighting in Palestine, Britain withdrew and on May 14, 1948, the state of Israel was born. Truman forced the unhappy State Department to accept American recognition of the new nation.

The liberal Democrats who continued to meet for Sunday dinners at the Cosmos Club viewed the presidency of Harry Truman with mixed feelings. One evening we were discussing the 1948 nominating convention. We all felt there was no possibility that Democrats would select anyone but Truman. His domestic policies were being flattened by the Republican Congress but his bellicose foreign policies were making him popular with the nervous public.

Henry Wallace said, almost idly, "I think I'll try for the nomination."

There was an embarrassed silence. Henry Wallace had no chance against Truman. We tried tactfully to dissuade him. Henry shook his head.

"Well, I don't know," he shrugged. "I'll have to think about it. It's been proposed that I join a third party and run against the Democrats and the Republicans."

We were stunned. Wallace's statement lay on the table like a hot potato. None of us wanted to touch it. People began to make excuses that they had to leave though it was much earlier than we usually broke up. They said good night pleasantly to Henry and piled out of the door as if fleeing a bad odor.

I pulled Chet Holifield aside. "They aren't being honest," I said in consternation. "They've got to make it clear to Henry that none of us will support him if he runs for a third party. We mustn't go without telling him where we stand. It isn't fair."

Chet agreed. We waited until everyone else had gone and then I said, "Mr. Secretary, I won't support you if you head a third party. I don't think anyone here tonight will support you. I beg you to reconsider." Chet said the same. Henry Wallace looked from one to the other of us with a hurt expression.

Wallace hadn't felt the same about the Democrats after Truman's bill to send military aid to Greece and Turkey. He still believed conciliation and peaceful coexistence with the Soviet Union was possible. I hoped he was right but the portents were against it. Still, when Wallace went to Britain to meet with leading progressives I was one of 125 who signed a "scroll of greeting." Other signatories were Fiorello LaGuardia, Aubrey Williams, Elliott Roosevelt and senators Harley Kilgore, Claude Pepper and Glen Taylor.

I wondered if Henry Wallace simply had been naïve in believing that a third party could succeed. He had little experience with practical politics. His grandfather had been Theodore Roosevelt's agricultural adviser and his father served in the Cabinets of Warren Harding and Calvin Coolidge but the family was not accustomed to campaigning. Henry didn't have a sense of the futility of a third party and the fact that his good name was being used by manipulators.

Out of our old friendship, I pleaded with him to give up his plan to run on a third-party ticket. I could see that radicals of the left, many of them communists, were taking over the splinter organization. At the founding meeting of the Progressive party, a number of liberals—Frank Kingdon, a Democrat from New Jersey, and Bartley Crum among them—walked out in protest of communist domination of the organization. Trustingly, Henry Wallace didn't see it that way. Walter Reuther mourned, "I think Henry is a lost soul."

Those of us who had opposed the Greek-Turkish aid bill on the grounds that Europe needed economic and social aid rather than guns were being proved right. Without UNRRA to provide assistance, the noncommunist nations of Europe were unable to restore their economies. American industry, looking for markets, found itself with bankrupts for trading partners.

The European Recovery Program was the answer. Known as the Marshall Plan in honor of General George C. Marshall, it was a model of economic and social assistance welcomed by liberals because it was humane and by industrialists because it would restore world trade. Strategists in the State Department wondered how to sell the American public, which had been hoping for housing programs and health insurance, on pouring millions of dollars into Europe. The answer was to tout the Marshall Plan as a bulwark against communism. The line was that France and Italy would become communist unless prosperity was restored. Even Mrs. Roosevelt sadly agreed that as a tactic it was sound.

The Marshall Plan was conceived at a multinational conference in Paris in 1947. The Soviet Union opposed the scheme strongly but Marshall promised the smaller nations of Europe that the United States would help them. The Marshall Plan was brought to the Foreign Affairs Committee and we presided over lengthy public hearings, followed by hearings at which we listened to what other congressmen had to say.

Then we closed the door and contemplated the stacks of documents and transcripts we had accumulated. A clerk read the bill, line by line. Any member of the committee who wanted to make a change could suggest it at that point, and then we would debate. Out of that debate, which could last for hours, would come an amendment on which we would agree. The clerk then would read the next line. The process went on for months.

The Speaker took pity on us and allowed us to meet in the afternoons as well as the mornings. We stuck to it, while the State Department's lawyers drooped with weariness in the corner of the committee room. Attendance dropped off as one tedious week followed another. At times we had as few as four congressmen working on the bill.

I was one of the handful whose commitment never flagged. I can say with truth that I helped to write the Marshall Plan. Anyone who was willing to endure the marathon inevitably played a key role in formulating the clauses of that legislation.

It was my responsibility to round up absent committee members on the double when it was time to vote on an amendment the rest of us had painfully drafted.

I would call Sol Bloom and say, "Sol, vote's up. We have five minutes to get our people here to vote." He would then round up committee members who we knew would support the amendments I wanted. That's how we produced the Marshall Plan.

One of the others who stayed through the whole exhausting process was John Vorys of Ohio. He and I were on opposite sides of almost every issue and fought every day. On the final day's work on the bill, however, when we voted it out of committee and rose to stretch our sore muscles, Vorys came to me, put out his hand, and generously said:

"Well Helen, I admire you. I respect you. You do your work."

Another who stayed every line of the way was Judge Kee, an old, old man. He never missed a session and never left early. Despite the pressure on us by lobbyists such as industrialists who wanted special concessions, we few managed to get the bill through without any weakening amendments. It was a good bill, a very good bill.

The names of the Foreign Affairs Committee of the Eightieth Congress are worth preserving for the work on that bill alone. The Republican chairman was Charles A. Eaton of New Jersey, and other Republicans were Robert B. Chiperfield of Illinois, John M. Vorys of Ohio, Karl E. Mundt of South Dakota, Bartel J. Jonkman, Michigan, Frances P. Bolton, Ohio, Lawrence H. Smith, Wisconsin, Chester E. Merrow, New Hampshire, Walter H. Judd, Minnesota, James G. Fulton, Pennsylvania, Jacob K. Javits, New York, John Davis Lodge, Connecticut, Donald L. Jackson, California, and Franklin J. Maloney of Pennsylvania.

Democrats were Sol Bloom of New York, John Kee of West Virginia, James P. Richards, South Carolina, Joseph L. Pfeifer, New York, Pete Jarman, Alabama, Wirt Courtney, Tennessee, Thomas S. Gordon, Illinois, Mike Mansfield of Montana,

Thomas E. Morgan of Pennsylvania, William M. Colmer of Mississippi, and me.

When we brought the bill to the floor of the House I spoke about an aspect of White House strategy that concerned me. I didn't like to see the Marshall Plan sold as an anti-communist measure. I said that if there had been no such thing as communism, we should still want to give aid to the countries of Europe that were flattened by the war. We Americans were the only people in a position to give assistance and we had a moral obligation to do so.

Ironically, despite the hope many of us had that the Marshall Plan would be supported because of its decency, it succeeded in the Eightieth Congress mainly because of the Cold War. I think it was Senator Vandenberg who told Truman, "If you want to see this through, you've got to scare people to death."

The Soviet Union cooperated splendidly during the passage of the Marshall Plan by invading Czechoslovakia. The Senate, which had just destroyed UNRRA because it didn't believe in international aid, immediately voted for the Marshall Plan.

That technique of crying "wolf" when there isn't one tends to be self-defeating. The paranoia in the United States about communism was being used to discredit good programs and elevate bad ones. All legislation was sorted into two categories: either it was bad for communism, like the Marshall Plan, and therefore was a good bill, or it was good for communism like—inexplicably —food stamps, which were rejected.

I thought Harry Truman and others in power could have done a better job of educating the country about our strengths. Instead there was a certain encouragement of Red-baiting.

We should have had programs directed to a better understanding of issues. The craziness was allowed to grow unchallenged by people who knew better. It is fundamental to a democracy that voters know the facts as clearly and honestly as people in office can present them. The public makes decisions that will change the society and influence the world, so it must be properly informed.

In order to supply that vital flow of information to the Fourteenth District, which I rarely saw, I was in the habit of going to the House radio station once a week to make a report of my activities and the reasons for the stands I was taking. A record of my talk was sent to several California radio stations, which found that audiences were appreciative. When I was fighting to extend rent controls, Chester Bowles came to the studio with me and we did a joint presentation.

The worsening Cold War was creating a good deal of attention for the House Un-American Activities Committee, whose treatment of citizens dragged before it to face vaguely based charges of being communists was an affront to justice. On December 1, 1947, I introduced a bill to "guarantee the accused the right of defense before congressional committees." Though HUAC wasn't specified in the bill, it certainly was the target. In fact, it was the only committee of Congress where a witness had to be prepared to defend himself or herself and where the consequences of a poorly presented case were disgrace or prison.

Richard Nixon, a rising star on HUAC, took satisfaction in seeing that bill destroyed. Later he was the sponsor in the House of Representatives of the Mundt-Nixon bill which sought to outlaw communism and put all sympathizers of Marxism in jail.

I voted against it, pointing out that it was in violation of the Constitution. Others also spoke against it, most notably Representative Lemke, a Republican from North Dakota, who said:

> You cannot kill un-Americanism with an un-American law. . . .
> This bill violates the Constitution, and permit me to state it does
> violence to the intelligence of this Congress. It is brought in here
> for political purposes and will have political repercussions. It will
> not weaken communism, but if anything, strengthen it. It will
> drive them deeper underground.

President Truman opposed the Mundt-Nixon bill strongly in its 1948 form and again when it was introduced only slightly altered in 1950. He said:

> These measures [to protect our internal security] must be accu-
> rately devised to meet real dangers. They must not be so broad as
> to restrict our liberty unnecessarily, for that would defeat our
> own ends.

Thomas E. Dewey, who was campaigning at the time for nomination as the Republican candidate for the 1948 presidential election, was one of many Republicans who were shocked by the Mundt-Nixon bill. In May 1948 he stated:

> Stripped to its naked essentials, this [bill] is nothing but the method of Hitler and Stalin. It is thought-control borrowed from the Japanese war leadership. It is an attempt to beat down ideas with a club. It is a surrender of everything we believe in. It is a philosophy which I shall fight to the limit of my strength.

I also voted against resolutions to increase funds for the House Un-American Activities Committee. As I explained in a radio broadcast:

> I believe in the separation of the powers of government— legislative, executive, and judicial—as provided by the Constitution of the United States. That is why I have voted consistently against the Committee on Un-American Activities.
>
> Those who make the laws should not be given power to suppress opposition to those laws, or to judge citizens by headlines under the cloak of congressional immunity.
>
> We cannot protect freedom by destroying the checks and balances that have preserved it for 150 years. That will not protect freedom nor, let me add, will it preserve the prestige of the American nation in the eyes of the world.
>
> In totalitarian countries, men trade aspirations of freedom for promises of bread and security. In our democratic country, we can have bread and security and freedom for everyone. Not to understand this basic difference between democracy and totalitarianism is to fail to understand the threat of communism throughout the world. To ignore this difference is to abandon the greatest weapon in the hands of democracy, as we seek to stop the spread of communism.
>
> I believe in our American democracy.
>
> I repeat, the way to keep communism out of America is to keep democracy in it.

Richard Nixon was reported in the Washington *Star* as saying that HUAC had made "mistakes" and "deserves criticism"; but the practices of character assassination continued.

A growing number, and then an avalanche of witnesses began to protect themselves by declaring that they would not answer certain questions, or all questions, on the grounds that it might incriminate them. The Fifth Amendment of the Bill of Rights provides that Americans cannot be compelled to testify against themselves. HUAC then turned to Congress and asked that we cite such witnesses for contempt of Congress. I refused to do so because I felt HUAC was usurping the powers of the Department of Justice. A congressional committee, I felt, had no right to investigate and accuse; that was for the courts. Later, when the Supreme Court ruled that congressional committees did have constitutional authority in that field, powers that never before had been exercised, I was surprised but began to support some contempt citations.

I also supported a bill establishing equal pay for women but I was opposed to the Equal Rights Amendment to the Constitution. At that time, responsible women and women's organizations were against it. With Eleanor Roosevelt, I believed that it would be used to strip from women certain protections that the Labor Department had been able to secure with great difficulty during the war when women found jobs in munitions factories.

The argument for the ERA was that safeguards won by women, such as the one setting a limit on the weight women could be required to lift, would be extended to men as well with a consequent reduction of hernias and other ruptures. I felt otherwise. I thought employers would say to women, "You want equality? You got it. Lift that weight." So I opposed the ERA then. Now, of course, I support it ardently; times have changed.

The White House came back to Congress asking for more aid to Greece and Turkey. Since the principle of giving the United Nations the opportunity to investigate and report had been lost forever, I saw no point in objecting to it. I noted, however, that the bill was supposed to cover social and economic aid as well as military but that this objective had been lost. I said:

> [appropriated money] was earmarked for food, clothes, machines, houses, fertilizer and the many other desperately needed items for the people of Greece. But a greater part of this money

was not spent for these purposes. No; instead it was transferred to the military budget.

Bullets, not bread, was our answer to the people in Greece.

We sought to solve the Greek dilemma solely with guns—well, we have had our answer. Communism has doubled.

I tangled with Richard Nixon over a bill to allow the President the right to keep his documents secret. By one of the ironies of history, Nixon was *in favor* of forcing the President to surrender confidential files to Congress on demand. He wanted to see Truman's loyalty files. HUAC was hot on the campaign trail, getting a great amount of space in newspapers and on radio for charges that Truman's office and departments under his direction were riddled with communists.

I, on the other hand, supported Truman's position that such files were privileged. Chief Justice William Howard Taft stated, "The President is required from time to time to give Congress information on the state of the Union . . . but this does not enable Congress or either House of Congress to elicit from him confidential information which he has acquired for the purpose of enabling him to discharge his constitutional duties, if he does not deem the disclosure of such information in the public interest."

The bill passed the House but was killed by the Senate.

Serving a term in a House of Representatives dominated by the coalition between the Republican majority and a group of Southern Democrats who hated Truman's civil rights legislation proved to be discouraging. The House was near-empty when I made a second "market basket speech" to show that food costs were still rising.

A housing bill which eliminated all provision for slum clearance, public housing and urban development swept through by 319 votes to 90 despite my well-prepared arguments based on exhaustive research. The Speaker, Republican Joseph Martin, pretended he couldn't see me. I said, "Mr. Speaker, MR. SPEAKER" a dozen times, but he looked the other way.

Afterward, Juanita Terry wrote to her mother in California, "They lynched the housing bill today." Both of us sat in my office and wept.

Frustrated, furious and heartsick as I was, my determination to argue my stands on the issues only increased. When I lost, I buckled down and worked harder on the next bill. I clung to the belief that solid facts and coherent presentation would somehow be heard above the hysteria of men like Rankin, Jackson and Nixon.

I took solace in the fact that I could be extremely effective in the important Foreign Affairs Committee, where I was the fourth-ranking member and my views were treated with respect. By lobbying members to consider evidence that I had dug up, I was able to persuade them to vote for an important amendment or to block something that would cripple the bill.

A notable failure was my redwood bill. Governor Gifford Pinchot, a noted agronomist and conservationist, drafted it just before he died. The formal name for it was the National Redwoods Forest bill and Walter Reuther's United Auto Workers Union paid the research costs. Walter always took a keen interest in the good management of our resources.

UAW studies showed that the trees surrounding the redwoods acted as a natural barrier to destructively strong winds off the Pacific. Evidence was produced to show that many of the redwoods wouldn't survive unless the lumbering in the adjacent forest was conducted according to rules of prudent reforestation which are common today but which at that time were being resisted. The legislation didn't prevent lumbermen from cutting near the redwood forests, but merely required that they stop cutting the trees indiscriminately.

I could see at once that the redwoods bill had problems. For one, it concerned only one state, California, which meant that most congressmen would take little interest. For another, the bill was about conservation which was not at all popular at that time.

The lumber industry reacted with a furious lobby against the bill. They flew around Congress declaring that the government was trying to interfere with private enterprise, always a compelling argument with some legislators. I protested that they were only being asked to harvest the trees scientifically but it was in vain. Governor Pinchot was well in advance of his time and the redwoods bill was defeated.

As the time of the 1948 Democratic convention approached, it was evident that Harry Truman was going to have to fight for his nomination as the candidate for the presidency. Truman's Fair Deal, as he called it, bore too much resemblance to Roosevelt's New Deal to suit Southern Democrats, who proposed J. Strom Thurmond for the nomination. On the other hand, Truman alienated New Dealers when he dumped some of the loyal staff who had worked for Roosevelt. Another element within the party, Americans for Democratic Action, was looking for an alternative candidate.

I stood firm for Harry Truman. I had disagreed with his Greek-Turkish aid bill and other aspects of his foreign policy but the Marshall Plan was superb and his domestic policies, though thwarted by the Republican Congress, had been humane.

Henry Wallace announced his candidacy for the presidency on the third-party ticket. Feeling depressed about my old friend's decision, I encountered Lyndon Johnson who was in a jubilant mood. He told me almost gleefully how the Democrats planned to campaign against Wallace and the independent Progressive party. The plan was to spread stories that Wallace had been taken over by the communists.

Henry Wallace offered me the endorsement of his Progressives in the congressional election in the Fourteenth District. I rejected him firmly. After the Soviet aggression in Czechoslovakia, Wallace's policy of appeasement seemed to me dangerous nonsense. If I accepted his endorsement I felt it would give the impression that I approved of his declaration that the Soviet Union was not a threat to world peace, which it unquestionably was.

I had been asked to make an address at the national convention and was working on my speech when Evelyn Chavoor interrupted. She said there was a delegation of young people waiting outside to see me. They were launching a campaign to have me nominated for the vice-presidency.

I laughed and said, "That's silly."

Evie frowned at me. "This is *serious*, Helen. They've been hard at work lining up delegates. They say people are very interested in the idea of a Truman-Douglas ticket."

I told her to give them my sincere thanks but I couldn't spare time to talk with them. Some time later, influential Democrats who were highly placed in the Washington establishment took me aside. They said that the Helen Gahagan Douglas for Vice-President movement was well advanced and gaining supporters quickly.

I was genuinely astonished. The idea of a woman running on a presidential ticket had never crossed my mind. "Oh, really," I said in some confusion.

Later, word swept the Hill that Truman's choice for running mate was Alben W. Barkley, a southern senator and loyal Democrat. I thought Barkley was an excellent choice. His presence on the ticket would help us in the South so I asked my friends to stop all efforts on my behalf.

Truman ran a low-key whistle-stop campaign telling the public that his initiatives to provide civil rights, housing, fair employment practices and other needed reforms had been blocked by the Republican "do-nothing" Congress. Political experts gave him no chance against the slick campaign conducted by his Republican opponent, Thomas E. Dewey, particularly as the Republicans presented a fairly solid front while the Democrats were in disarray.

I went back to California to campaign, joining Melvyn and the children in our house in the Outpost.

Ed Lybeck found me as great a trial as ever. One time he arranged for me to speak to some workers coming off shift at the North American Aircraft Company. He hoped I would talk about lunch-box issues but instead I thought it was an excellent opportunity for me to explain the importance of retaining the 160-acre limit in the 1902 Reclamation Act.

Ed was apoplectic when he heard it. Al Meyers, who became a vital member of my campaign committee, told me that he had never seen Lybeck so angry. Al asked me curiously:

"Just why would you want to talk to factory workers about the 160-acre limitation in the Reclamation Act?"

"What was I to talk to them about?" I retorted. "Labor legislation? They know all about that. They don't know about the Reclamation Act and they should, if we're going to save the small farms in California."

I knew I would be facing another bitter fight in Congress to save that venerable Reclamation Act from big ranchers who wanted to acquire cheap, subsidized, federally irrigated land for themselves. As the daughter of a civil engineer I appreciated what reclamation projects could accomplish, but it was not an issue that most Americans knew or cared about. An election campaign was ideal for making voters aware of the need to preserve the provisions of the Act.

I had been part of a long struggle to extend the 160-acre limitation to new irrigation projects by army engineers. Harold Ickes and I conferred a hundred times over that. When one approach failed, I found that there was always another way to achieve the goal we wanted. Others in government—chiefly Arthur Goldschmidt—and out of government—particularly the redoubtable Paul Taylor—helped me with tactics and information, so I was really well informed about reclamation.

To my dismay, a number of California Democrats were being persuaded that the Reclamation Act should be changed, especially the 160-acre limitation clause. Governor Culbert Olson, whom Melvyn had worked so hard to elect, had been a liberal who favored the 160-acre limitation. It is one of the phenomena of political life that he changed on that issue. Politicians when elected tend to put on blindfolds and vote in ways they believe will get them support and campaign contributions.

If I may digress, this dependence on large private contributions is demoralizing to elected officials. We've got to put an end to it. Campaigns should be financed from tax money if we really mean to maintain a democratic system. Television and radio should be available to candidates on a fair basis without the impossible costs that are being charged today. *Common Cause* is so right in its approach to this.

Politicians aren't any more wicked than other citizens but the situation in which they are placed warps their judgment. Wealthy self-interest groups such as the oil barons or Associated Farmers have a lot of power. If you're in office, you don't want them working against you in the next election. Unless you are very deeply committed to a program, as I was to reclamation, the temptation is to make concessions and even to reverse your position.

That's essentially what must have happened to Sheridan Dow-

ney, the senior senator from California, who every year tried to
destroy the Reclamation Act. One of his most vicious tactics was
to try to have two supporters of the 160-acre limit, Michael
Straus and Richard Boke, fired from the Department of the Interior. When Ickes refused to discharge them, Downey tried to
have Congress enact a federal law to dismiss the two men.

That same year William Knowland, who was a Republican senator from California, worked *with* Downey to try to repeal the
160-acre limitation. We had managed to stop them but I knew
that when the Eighty-first Congress convened, Downey and
friends would be back on the attack. So I used every chance I
could find to talk about reclamation during my election campaign
in order to drum up support. Ed Lybeck eventually got used to it.

I faced the wrath of the Associated Farmers as a result. Because
of the redwoods bill, powerful lumber interests were against me.
I also had inflamed the oil interests because in the Seventy-ninth
and Eightieth Congress I voted against California's attempt to
gain jurisdiction over tidelands where important oil deposits had
been located.

I believe that America's coastal waters belong to all its citizens
and should be administered federally. The three states affected by
the tidelands issue—California, Texas and Louisiana—were pressing for states' rights. The oil companies were behind it, I thought,
because the state governments would be easier to deal with than
Washington. In any case, President Truman vetoed the bill giving authority to the states and the Supreme Court later supported
him. I felt vindicated for arguing against the bill but I had made
enemies of state politicians and the oil companies.

Nevertheless, Ed Lybeck assured me that there was little doubt
that I would be reelected. His long experience in political campaigns led him to predict, accurately as it turned out, that California was going Democratic in 1948.

In the nearby Twelfth District, Richard Nixon waged an interesting campaign. Jerry Voorhis had rejected all pleas to return
to the state and run against Nixon, so Nixon really had no opposition. But he was taking no chances. It was well known that he
had his eye on a seat in the Senate in 1950 and therefore needed

to stay one more term in the House of Representatives in order to be a credible candidate.

With that in mind he managed during his two years in Congress to keep it almost a secret that he was a Republican. In Frank Mankiewicz's term, he "de-partied" himself so that inattentive Democrats would think he was one of their own. The incumbent has an advantage under California's cross-filing practices because the primary ballots, which don't give affiliation, list the candidate who holds the seat as "Congressman——" In 1946 half of the congressmen up for reelection in California were nominated in both Republican and Democratic primaries. In 1948, I lost the Republican primary in a recount.

Nixon planned ahead to take advantage of the peculiarity in the electoral system. During his first term in Congress, the literature coming from his office described him only as Congressman Nixon, never as Republican Congressman Nixon. In 1948 his identification with the Republicans had been buried so successfully that one piece of campaign material bearing his smiling face was headed "My Fellow Democrats."

He was also aided in the 1948 election by the presence of the independent Progressive party. His opposition's vote was split between Stephen Zetterberg, a Democrat and lawyer with a weak following, and the third party. Nixon won the Democratic primary handily. Frank Mankiewicz, in his analysis of Nixon in *Perfectly Clear: Nixon from Whittier to Watergate*, believes that Nixon would have abandoned politics if he had lost his congressional seat.

I too faced a three-way fight in my Fourteenth District. When I refused the endorsement of Henry Wallace's Progressives, they put up a candidate against me. I knew that it would mean a loss of some labor support.

The political reporter Marquis Childs, in his syndicated column "Washington Calling," described the election this way:

> Because the prejudice against women in high office is still a factor in American politics, they just naturally have to be better than the men.
>
> I believe a statistical average of the awareness, the ability, the

intelligence of the seven women as set against the 425 men in the House would show that the ladies have an overwhelming advantage.

Two of the women members are engaged just now in extremely interesting political contests. One is Margaret Chase Smith of Maine, a Republican, and the other is Helen Gahagan Douglas of California, a Democrat.

Because she had the courage of her liberal convictions and refused to swallow the third-party line, Mrs. Douglas is in the middle of a three-way fight in her district in Los Angeles. The Wallaceites tried to make her take a stand against the European Recovery Program [the Marshall Plan] and, when she said no, they entered a third-party candidate against her.

Mrs. Douglas is running in both the Republican and Democratic primaries, which is possible under California law. At the same time, with the primaries on June 1, she is fighting on the floor of the House for the issues she considers most important.

First on this list would come inflation and the cost of living. In season and out, Mrs. Douglas has fought for some easement on the pressure that is working such hardship on millions of salaried families all over the country, and especially in her own district.

Once, she came onto the floor with a market basket full of groceries and with a sales slip showing what they cost as compared with a sales slip of a year before. It was a dramatic demonstration of what the high cost of living really means to a housewife. Mrs. Douglas was one of the little band in the House to stand up against the Mundt bill to outlaw communism in America—a bill that, in the opinion of many, would coerce all independent thought. . . . Congress would be improved, in my opinion, with a higher proportion of women members. . . .

The presidential campaign was ugly. Democrats accused Wallace of being a tool of communism as the strategy outlined by Lyndon Johnson had indicated they would. For his part, Wallace charged that Truman was responsible for the Cold War.

To some degree both sides were correct in their allegations, which made it difficult for voters to sort fact from fiction. The President did contribute substantially to escalating the Cold War with Russia, and Wallace certainly did have fanatical communists close to him.

Henry realized much later, when the war in Korea broke out, the true composition of the Progressive party. Its members repudiated him when Henry endorsed the intervention of the United Nations, at which point a disillusioned Henry Wallace promptly resigned.

Evie Chavoor and I made a visit during the campaign to some farm workers in Bakersfield who were on strike against the DiGiorgio Farms Corporation. One of the reporters in that group was a young Chet Huntley and another person with us was Louis de Anda, a World War II hero who would be described today as a male chauvinist.

De Anda told Harry Leland Mitchell, the former sharecropper who started the Southern Tenant Farmers Union, that I was the first woman he had ever met whom he considered superior to himself and other men.

"Besides," he added, "she's lovely to look at."

Republicans were so certain of victory that one newspaper even printed a headline that Thomas E. Dewey was the new President of the United States. But the experts were wrong about the diffident, spunky little man from Missouri. Harry Truman was swept back into the White House and with him a Democratic majority in the Eighty-first Congress. I won the Fourteenth District by a phenomenal 50,000 vote: my support in the black section of my district was solid.

Richard Nixon was returned to Congress from the Twelfth District and set his sights on running for the Senate in 1950. The Committee on Un-American Activities was creating the hottest news in the country with its daily accusations of espionage in high places. Nixon was to play a prominent role in HUAC's biggest catch, Alger Hiss, the brilliant adviser to the State Department who was accused by magazine editor Whittaker Chambers of carrying American secrets to the Soviet. HUAC had been desperate to land someone important for the sake of its credibility. When Alger Hiss went to jail for perjury, HUAC's importance swelled and the name of Richard Nixon was propelled into national prominence.

While that drama was taking place, I was embroiled once more in protecting the Reclamation Act from a fellow Democrat, Sheridan Downey, and his cronies in the Senate. I was also struggling with much-beleaguered Fair Employment Practices legislation, which Southern Democrats hated. At one point in the acrimonious debate I said:

> The discrepancy between American ideals and American practice—between our aims and what we actually do—creates a moral dry rot which eats away at the foundations of our democratic faith.
>
> Democracy cannot thrive in a climate of hypocrisy. Democracy cannot prosper in a land where forty million people—members of one minority group or another—are denied the basic assurance of healthy community life, the assurance that they belong, the assurance that they count, the assurance that there is one-class citizenship and that they enjoy it.
>
> Our national morality, based on our religious heritage, demands an end to discrimination rooted in bigotry. In the words of George Washington, "to bigotry, no sanction."

Despite the growing popularity of HUAC's bearpit sessions, I continued to attack it, arguing that a congressional committee was taking on itself powers that rightfully should be exercised only by the Attorney General's office, and that the civil rights of individuals pilloried by HUAC were being violated. On that issue I said in Congress:

> When accused persons have no right of appeal and when administrators can make unreviewable decisions and be answerable to no one, then basic democratic guarantees have been breached, and decisions can be capricious or vindictive.
>
> When laws are passed to allow administrators to act unchecked, a government has started on the totalitarian road in which one man can get rid of another without just cause, one group can get rid of another which differs from it, and one party can get rid of its opposition. . . .
>
> We have achieved in our country under our form of government greater liberty for the individual and a higher standard of living—in other words, greater security—than anywhere else in the world.
>
> You cannot barter security for freedom, or freedom for security. They tried to do that in Germany; they tried to do that in

Russia. I thought that was what we disliked about communism. . . .

Are we now to curtail our cherished freedoms by adopting communistic and fascistic patterns?

Once more I opposed a resolution to increase funds for HUAC. I was also against giving the maverick committee the legitimacy of permanency; I voted against making it a fixed standing committee of Congress. Richard Nixon, of course, voted for HUAC each time. A great many congressmen were discovering that their constituents admired HUAC's rough tactics and could not get enough news about its activities. Of the diminishing number still in open opposition, Senator Wayne Morse and Senator Margaret Chase Smith made fine statements on the issue.

Senator Morse made a statement to the press which was a ringing condemnation of what he called HUAC's "kangaroo court" procedures. In 1949 and 1950 it took courage to defy HUAC, which had no compunction about investigating its critics and laying charges, based on highly dubious evidence, that they were communist sympathizers.

Morse said:

The time has come when the American people at Congressional hearings should be guaranteed the rights of fair trials as provided under the Bill of Rights. This idea of ruining the reputation of people by making charges against them in Congressional hearings and not guaranteeing them the right through counsel to cross-examine those who testify against them cannot be reconciled with the constitutional guarantees of fair trial in America.

Margaret Chase Smith made a speech in the Senate which she titled "A Declaration of Conscience." In it she declared:

I think it is high time we remembered that we have sworn to uphold and defend the Constitution. I think it is high time that we remembered that the Constitution, as amended, speaks not only of freedom of speech but also of trial by jury instead of by accusation.

Despite the dissension sown in both House and Senate by HUAC, the Eighty-first Congress managed to get through important legislation. From the perspective of the Foreign Affairs Committee, nothing equaled the legislation by which the United States entered into the North Atlantic Treaty Organization, NATO. I was able to play a significant role in the committee to prevent cuts in America's commitment to provide western Europe with a defense force capable of resisting further Soviet aggression.

I said in one of the debates in the House to keep the full aid in the bill:

> I am supporting the military-aid measure which we are now considering. . . .
>
> I think it contributes to the further building of world peace— to our own national security. The main point to be made about this legislation is that it is a proposal to bring military assistance to bear in support of an undertaking of mutual defense in time of peace.
>
> Mutuality in military objectives is certainly no novelty to this nation. In the form of a direct alliance with France it was a decisive factor in the war of the American Revolution. . . .
>
> It was a decisive factor in World War I. It was the pattern of victory in World War II. Now it has entered into the American experience in peace as well as in connection with hostilities. It has been welded into the system of the American republics. It is the essential ingredient of the North Atlantic Pact.
>
> What is new about this legislation is that it brings into focus in time of peace the two elements—military assistance and mutuality of defense. It does so in a manner entirely consonant with the basic aims expressed in the United Nations Charter and with the goal of economic recovery. . . . At the end of the war the first job was to help rebuild those areas which were utterly flattened. That has been started.
>
> The fact that we must now take measures to insure peace is not discouraging. Rather, it is an acceptance of the facts as they are. The need for common defense can be a unifying force. It certainly was a compelling force in the establishment and the growth of the Union of the States which make up our country.
>
> Common defense can be a unifying force in western Europe today.
>
> In working for world peace, past experience must teach us something. The League of Nations failed because it lacked the power to stop aggression. Without an international police force

the United Nations is also powerless to maintain peace in the world. There is general agreement on this fact. We have been unable, up to now, despite efforts in that direction, to agree on a general program that would achieve universal regulation and reduction of armaments, including armed forces, under adequate safeguards to protect complying nations against violation and evasion. Because we have been unsuccessful in these efforts we, therefore, have not been able as yet to set up under the United Nations an international police force to enforce the peace.

The Foreign Affairs Committee believes, and so states in the bill before us, that we should continue to seek for agreements to provide the United Nations with armed forces as contemplated in the charter, and agreements to achieve universal control and reduction of weapons of mass destruction.

In the meantime, we can sit idly by, ignoring the potential threat of Russia, or take positive action to maintain order in the world.

The Atlantic Pact and this military-aid program go as far as possible under the present conditions.

This is a program to implement collective security. It is not an aggressive program, but a program of defense—*a program that can be a pilot program for a future world police force.*

Many liberals saw NATO instead as another step in American military expansion and a further weakening of the power of the United Nations. It could be argued that NATO escalated Cold War tensions and committed the United States to armament programs rather than disarmament programs. Henry Wallace opposed NATO vigorously and the Americans for Democratic Action complained that our first line of defense should be economic and political aid rather than guns.

I was in the group which saw NATO as a path back to United Nations principles. Eleanor Roosevelt didn't believe the pact violated the basic charter of the United Nations. Paul Douglas declared, "Our ratification of the North Atlantic Pact serves notice on the Kremlin," which is the way most Americans felt in those nervous years. I noted that Truman could not point to any evidence that the Soviet, having gobbled up Czechoslovakia, was planning another aggression but I said, "To do nothing is to sow the seeds of war. The plain facts of history demonstrate that." I was thinking of Munich.

In what I described as "the first time since I became a member of this body [Congress] I can sit relaxedly and thoroughly enjoy the discussions," the House of Representatives finally passed a good housing bill that provided shelter for low-income Americans. I don't recall that Nixon spoke even once on the issue of housing.

In Beverly Hills, the B'nai B'rith named Melvyn and me "Mr. and Mrs. American Citizen of 1949." We were delighted but I don't think either of us was in California at the time of the announcement. I was in Washington and Melvyn was touring in a play.

I was home in the summer of 1949 during a congressional recess. Paul Taylor and Dorothea Lange invited me to join them on a motor tour of reclamation projects through the northern part of the state and down to Bakersfield. We filled the car with reference books and notebooks and turned the outing into an intensive study expedition. I felt I needed to be in touch with the facts of the situation in order to deal with Sheridan Downey's next assault on the Reclamation Act.

Paul, Dorothea and I visited projects during the day, asking questions and taking down information, and that night we would discuss what we'd learn and check it against the literature we'd brought.

We talked with everyone we could—small farmers, big ranchers, reclamation officials, assemblymen, community leaders, and so on. One day we came to a town that had suffered terribly in the drought. It once had been one of the richest citrus-producing areas in the state but a long dry spell had almost wiped out the orchards. Finally reclamation water reached the area and people's livelihoods were restored.

We dropped into the local newspaper office to meet the editor. I felt I had stepped back a century. The entire operation was in a single room—his desk, the clanking typesetting machine, an ancient press, the smell of printer's ink and pulpy paper. The editor was seated at a desk on the other side of a wooden fence. He looked up, recognized me, and rushed through a swinging gate to throw his arms around me.

"Oh my dear, oh my dear," he kept saying, almost weeping. "Come upstairs with me. I want to show you something."

We went up an iron staircase and emerged on the flat roof of his office. He pointed to groves of trees stretching into the distance.

"Do you see them, do you see the orchards?" he asked. "Do you see how they're flourishing? Have you seen how big the fruit is? Well, I'll tell you that a few years ago the fruit was hard little rocks."

He told us that when the water came from the great dam for the first time, before the side canals were built, people ran out with buckets to scoop it up. They cried and they yelled and they sang, and some dropped to their knees to offer prayers of thanksgiving. They were so delirious with joy that they dumped the buckets of water over their heads.

"You've never seen such happiness," the editor told me. "That's what you did for us. Thank you, thank you."

Years later I learned that because of my obsession with reclamation projects and my insistence on talking about it every place I could, no one in California could run for county clerk without being asked where he or she stood on the water issue. People in the cities were less interested of course, but in the country water is life.

Not everything the Department of the Interior did was wonderful, but the approach was right. The basic difference between the Democratic stand on resources and the Republican one was whether there would be an overall government plan, within which private enterprise could function, or a *laissez-faire* approach that would allow companies to do as they pleased with the resource.

I never approved of nationalization of resources, as some have said. My aim was to have ecologically sound administration of a general policy that would preserve the land or water or resources for the next generations.

It wouldn't be fair to say that there were no principled people in the opposition, because there were. But the House of Representatives voted in a partisan manner on resource issues. The word would go down to support the administration, however fuzzy, if you were a Democrat and defeat it, however excellent, if you were a Republican.

Paul Taylor likes to cite the statement on reclamation that was made in 1911 by Theodore Roosevelt in a speech defending the law. Roosevelt told the Commonwealth Club:

> I wish to save the very wealthy men of this country and their advocates and upholders from the ruin that they would bring upon themselves if they were permitted to have their way. It is because I am against revolution; it is because I am against the doctrine of the extremists, of the socialists, it is because I wish to see this country of ours continue as a genuine democracy; it is because I distrust violence and disbelieve in it; it is because I wish to secure this country against ever seeing a time when the "have-nots" shall rise against the "haves"; it is because I wish to secure for our children's children the same freedom of opportunity, the same peace and order and justice that we have had in the past.

Early in 1949 the notion began to form in my mind that I should run for the Senate against Sheridan Downey and remove one of the most dedicated enemies of the Reclamation Act from Congress. I confided in a few people, among them Ed Lybeck. He was cautiously optimistic.

"You have a widespread reputation for integrity even among people who don't much like you," he wrote me. He warned that I would need lots of money because the Republicans were hungry for Downey's seat and would be spending their donations on the campaign rather than—as Lybeck put it—stealing donations as they usually did.

"Nobody's crazy about bucking a party incumbent," Ed told a Democrat who was concerned that I would split the party, "but the demand is such that Helen will probably *have* to run." Strategists in Democratic party back rooms insisted that I should wait until 1952 to run for the Senate. If I ran in 1950 to take Downey's seat away from him, the party would bleed.

As rumors spread that I was considering the Senate, Ed told people who asked about it, "If she makes up her mind to run, she'll run the hell out of the whole damned state and anybody who happens to be on the ticket will just get swept in with her. Nobody will even be paying any attention to them."

I went to Vermont to think about it with Melvyn and the children. I felt restored the moment we arrived. California always seemed to me very dry. My skin felt parched and I had to apply oil every day to keep it from flaking away. In Vermont the air is moist and I have no need of creams.

The big house on Cliff Mull was falling apart but it didn't matter. I kept running from one window to another exclaiming to Melvyn, "Look at the light! Did you ever seen anything lovelier than the light on the lake!"

Melvyn still did not love Vermont as I did. The first time he saw it after our marriage there were so many noisy Gahagans around that he felt suffocated. I could see how wretched he was, though he tried to remain his pleasant and polite self, so I took him to a favorite mountaintop where we could be alone. I prayed that when we reached the summit he would be overcome by the beauty of the scenery. I imagined wildly that he would be converted on the spot. Instead he felt, and looked, out of place.

It was a crushing disappointment for me and I thought about it with sadness over the years that we lived in California, New York and Washington. But he was beginning to appreciate the restfulness as much as I did. Ed Lybeck wrote me from California about Jimmy Roosevelt's plans to run for governor of California against Earl Warren, a scheme that seemed foolhardy to many observers. Eleanor Roosevelt and I had discussed her son's political career many times and I certainly supported him. Ed told me there was something disturbing in Jimmy's campaign office and it would be wise if I didn't tie myself too closely to whatever Jimmy planned to do.

Al Meyers, immersed in my campaign as discreetly as possible, since he was still working for the I.R.S., was trying to get a sense of the electorate. He wrote on August 19, 1949, to say that there was a lot of support for me to run against Downey. He had a suggestion for someone to work on my campaign, a movie actor who was an ardent Democrat, Ronald Reagan. "I think we would want a guy that would be a stellar attraction on his own and could make a speech to go with it."

The Roosevelt camp, Al reported, was anxious to have me run against Downey. Jimmy's supporters had conducted a secret poll which was reported to show that it would help him if I was in the Senate race. As Al put it roughly, Jimmy's people had concluded that "Helen Douglas's potential was greater than James Roosevelt's because all he had was a name he'd inherited, while she had one she'd built herself."

Ed Lybeck had a humorous comment on the deluge of mail he was receiving from people anxious to help my campaign. Many of the letters were written "in the spidery Spencerian script of a half century ago," he said. He wrote that he was convinced that I was "a lineal inheritor of the ancient liberal tradition . . . a god-damned good stubborn bull-headed proselyter for things that make sense to anybody who wasn't completely behind the door when the brains were passed out."

He was worried about money, knowing that I would not attract any big donations from oil interests, growers, or lumber barons, all of whom were devoted to Sheridan Downey. Ed thought I would need $150,000 to conduct a good campaign, a staggering sum for me to raise.

"Now you *can* win," he advised me. "You will not be a favorite; you'll be rather a long shot. But given luck and money and a hell of a lot of work, you can win. The work I am pretty sure we'll get, the luck we'll just have to keep our fingers crossed for, but for Christ's sake don't commit suicide with no dough. It's the primary you have to keep in mind; you'll be up against an incumbent who will be able to procure anything that money will buy. . . .

"Maybe you can't crucify mankind upon a cross of gold, but you can sure as hell crucify a statewide candidate upon a cross of no-gold."

Nixon vs Douglas
1950

As the time approached for me to make my decision about the California election, I went to see Harry Truman in the White House. I told him about the country's disgraceful neglect of veterans' hospitals. In the five years since the end of the war, most veterans were back in the community except for those most seriously injured, a group which included paraplegics.

The hospitals, however, had not been designed for a population of young men in wheelchairs. There was an absence of recreation and training programs for them or even such facilities as ramps for their wheelchairs. The result was that veterans were trapped inside hospitals where they appeared to be forgotten men.

When I emerged from the Oval Office the press pounced on me to ask if I intended to contest the primary against Sheridan Downey. I didn't want to tell the real purpose of my visit to the President because I didn't want to raise veterans' hopes until I was certain something was being done for them, so I invented some weak-sounding excuse for my visit.

The evasion only fueled stories that were sweeping the Hill that I would run against Downey. Bill Malone, the man who had appointed me his vice-chairman of the party in California, told me in great distress that I was causing a rift in the party. If I waited until 1952 and ran against a Republican, I could be sure of sweeping the polls, he said.

"That's not the issue, going to the Senate," I explained. "I don't care if I'm never a senator. I really don't see how all of you can sit back and let our own Democratic senator destroy a program that is essential to the well-being of the West Coast."

The point of saving the 160-acre limitation was that it protected people with small holdings who would create communities.

If the big growers could take over huge tracts of land irrigated at taxpayer expense, the valleys would be empty except for truckloads of migrant workers coming and going.

"That's not the kind of world the pioneers saw for California," I told Malone. "We have riches enough to do better. Farm workers should be living here, building schools and churches, starting towns. Someone has to take on Downey and protect the reclamation programs."

My sense of security was solid. I was never timorous about any decision once I made it. The ever-present question for me in venturing on an uncharted course was to examine alternatives from every side. By studying every choice, collecting what information was available and consulting with people I trusted, I would reach a conclusion and, that done, proceed without a qualm.

Adlai Stevenson once said that emotion drove me. I think I would agree with him. Emotion did drive me and so did the rooted values I learned from my parents. But because I was willing to learn everything I could before I made a step, I mostly kept on the right track.

On October 6, 1949, I announced myself as candidate for the Senate.

A week later Representative John Kee of West Virginia, who was chairman of the House Foreign Affairs Committee, paid a tribute to me in Congress. He said:

> The House will sustain a very real loss through the decision of Mrs. Douglas not to run for reelection to her present post, for she has become an outstanding member of the Committee on Foreign Affairs and a leader in the House of Representatives through her untiring devotion to her legislative responsibilities, and because of her thorough understanding of current fundamental problems, both foreign and domestic.
>
> The gentlewoman from California has been a member of the Foreign Affairs Committee since 1945 and is chairman of two major subcommittees. The committee's prestige has been greatly enhanced by her service. She has never hesitated to give unstintingly of her time and energy to the work of the committee regardless of whether that work was of vital urgency or of almost routine drudgery. The gentlewoman from California is, and has

been, a mainstay on the committee. While we understand the reasons which led to her decision, her going will leave a vacancy that will test the legislative skill and try the mettle to the utmost of whoever tries to succeed her.

There was an organizational meeting in San Francisco at the home of Edward Macauley. Fred Farr of Monterey was there, and Anna Emmons from Salinas, Fred Henry of Bakersfield and Ivo Blank of Fresno. Out of it came the decision that Ruth Lybeck would run my campaign in Southern California and Harold Tipton would be the Northern California chief.

Jimmy Roosevelt declared himself the candidate for governor. There had been a high-level meeting of Democrats on September 14 to attempt to unify the party, now badly split in California between Democrats who remained committed to the principles of the New Deal and Democrats like Downey who had drifted into conservativism that was indistinguishable from Republican platforms.

The back-room strategists considered several options. One was that Downey would get a federal judgeship and leave room for Jimmy Roosevelt to run for the Senate in his place. Roosevelt wasn't popular with all Democrats. President Truman was keeping an eye on the situation and was rumored to favor Downey remaining as senator. Downey apparently didn't like any of the judgeships that were available then and decided to run again. That left Jimmy with no room to maneuver except in the gubernatorial race.

Most of California's major newspapers had opposed my candidacy in the past and I assumed they would be against me now, but I depended on the Los Angeles *Daily News*, my only bigcirculation champion, to be on my side. Manchester Boddy, who ran it, was a personal friend. I received a phone call from Leslie Claypool, head of the political desk on the *News*. He said he was coming to Washington and he was anxious to see me. We arranged to have breakfast, the only space I could find in my schedule.

Over eggs and coffee he said, "You know we think a great deal of you, Helen. We admire what you're doing in Congress. But you're wrong on one issue, the right of the state to control the tidelands. You haven't studied all the factors involved. All I'm asking you to do is take these books I've brought. They've got all the information you need to understand why those leases don't belong in the federal jurisdiction."

Les gave me several handsome-looking books that the oil companies had prepared to present their point of view. The books were propaganda, of course, with the statistics carefully selected to present a compelling argument for states' rights. To understand the issue properly, what mattered was what was left out of the books. There was nothing, for instance, to indicate that an ecological problem was even involved.

Another approach was made by John B. Elliott, an important and wealthy Democrat who supported Roosevelt in 1932. Elliott was an oilman and had wanted to be Roosevelt's Secretary of the Interior. Roosevelt wouldn't give him the appointment, which went to Harold Ickes, because in that portfolio Elliott would have been a cat in a canary cage.

From then on, Elliott worked against Roosevelt with the zeal of the spurned. Roosevelt was amused. Every time I sat next to him at dinner in the White House he would inquire, "How is Black Jack Elliott, Helen?" and I would describe Elliott's latest scheme.

Elliott was a likable, affable man and I couldn't help running into him at various social and political functions. He opposed me when I first ran for Congress because he didn't want to see a woman elected when there were perfectly good men candidates available. As time went on, his opinion of me didn't improve. He fought me in every election.

One day he called. "Helen," he said, "if you can't beat 'em, you join 'em. I give up. I guess you're the smartest person in the California delegation and I want to be your friend. I want to be *with* you. And to show you that I mean it, I want to give a dinner for you. Will you come?"

I told him I would be happy to. He said he planned to invite newspaper publishers, a gesture I appreciated because I didn't know many of the press moguls in the state. Elliott asked me to arrive a little early and when I did he escorted me into his study.

"Helen, there isn't anything you want politically that you can't have. *Anything.* But there's one issue that would prevent me from being wholeheartedly in your corner. That's the tidelands issue. You're dead wrong on it. Now, I'm not asking you to change your vote. I'm only asking you to study the problem."

And he handed me the same set of books I had been given before.

I managed not to laugh. I thanked him and we went in to dinner. After the meal I was asked to speak. I considered carefully and then decided I would never have a better opportunity to tell the leading publishers of California why they were wrong to support the Standard Oil position on control of oil leases in the tidelands. I was aware that Jack Elliott would be furious with me but it was a chance to put forward the argument in favor of federal controls, so I spent ten minutes or so talking about the tidelands.

It was not what they wanted to hear, of course, and it ended my brief reconciliation with Jack Elliott. He became an implacable enemy and when he heard that I was challenging Sheridan Downey he put all his rage and resources into fighting me. Mrs. Mattison Boyd Jones, the woman who was still bitter over my election as national committeewoman, volunteered to help him. Some of the most vicious material used against me before the primary came from his office. Nixon later claimed that he didn't invent the "dirty tricks" in his campaign against me, that he only embellished what Democrats like Jack Elliott had begun. There is some truth in that.

David Halberstam, in *The Powers That Be*, reveals that it was a telephone call from Kyle Palmer to Richard Nixon late in 1949 that led to Nixon's decision to run for the Senate. Nixon was on record in favor of removing the 160-acre limitation in the Reclamation Act and state control of the tidelands leases, and in favor of other measures favored by the big resource companies. Though he was only a two-term member of the House of Representatives, Nixon had leaped to the front pages of newspapers everywhere with his active participation in the House Un-American Activities Committee, where he was a key figure in the Alger Hiss-Whittaker Chambers confrontation. All of this made him a very attractive candidate in an era that was dominated by fear of communists.

Nixon told Kyle he was willing to run for the Senate and Kyle, according to Halberstam, made one telephone call to the Republican party's chief fund raiser, Asa Call. He sold Call on Nixon's worth to the party and the likelihood that he could defeat an ailing Senator Downey. "That's all it took," writes Halberstam. "Two men."

My feeling is that Nixon intended to run against Downey in 1950 anyway and had been preparing himself diligently throughout his four years in Congress. Kyle's telephone call and backing by Asa Call just made it easier.

Richard Nixon's vehicle for quick public notice was communist-bashing—and his timing, "his lucky star," as he called it, was impeccable. In 1949 the Soviet tested an atomic bomb and plunged Americans into panic. People were ready to believe that thousands upon thousands of communist spies had infiltrated Washington and were working to destroy democracy. The climate of fear was exacerbated that same year when communists under Mao Tse-tung drove the Nationalist Government off mainland China and took control of the world's most populous nation.

California, always more sensitive to events in Asia than other parts of the country are, was very uneasy. In such an environment of apprehension, a junior congressman who single-mindedly went after spies, traitors and other subversives could quickly be seen as a savior.

Nixon announced that the elections of 1950 allowed Americans "the choice between freedom and state socialism." He saw little distinction between Fair Deal programs for the disadvantaged, which he called "squandermania," and creeping communism.

"Call it planned economy, the Fair Deal, or social welfare," he said, "but it is still the same old socialist baloney any way you slice it."

Nixon wasn't anxious to oppose Sheridan Downey, whose political ideology was very similar to his own. He was rooting for me to win the primary because he would be able to use the same smear tactics that had worked so well to defeat Jerry Voorhis.

The designer of the Nixon-Voorhis campaign strategy was Murray Chotiner. Chotiner brought the same brilliant cunning to

Richard Nixon's senatorial campaign in 1950. Earl Mazo, in his book on Nixon, quotes Chotiner as saying:

"Quite frankly, we wanted her to be the Democratic nominee on the basis that it would be easier to defeat her than a conservative Democrat. So nothing was ever said pertaining to Helen Gahagan Douglas in the primary."

I was scarcely aware that Richard Nixon was holding back. In the months before the primary, I was too busy defending myself from Democrats. I suppose it is true that I said at the time, "I have utter scorn for such pipsqueaks as Nixon and [Senator Joseph] McCarthy." I was aware that Nixon traveled extensively in California, giving speeches with great effect in every whistlestop. His main issue, of course, was that he was needed in the Senate to fight the spread of communism.

Sheridan Downey was urged to respond to my many speeches about protecting the Reclamation Act. In November he challenged me to a debate on the Central Valley Project and the 160-acre limitation. I was delighted to accept and we put forth our different views on California radio stations. It is my understanding that Downey conducted a poll of listeners and discovered to his dismay that they were in favor of my position two to one. At that point rumors began to circulate that Downey was retiring from the race. He wavered for weeks. President Truman and others begged him to remain.

Drew Pearson, political columnist, revealed that Downey, whom he described as "a so-called Democrat," had retained Robert Franklin, a Republican, as his campaign manager and would raise his campaign funds chiefly from Republicans and the big farmers. Bill Malone held a luncheon in Fairmont and raised a huge sum for Downey.

In my campaign for the nomination I described the importance of the Central Valley Project and criticized Downey severely for opposing the Reclamation Act, charging him with ties to oil interests and the Associated Farmers. On March 29, 1950, Downey announced he was withdrawing from the campaign and gave as his reason ill health. He said he was not up to "waging a personal and militant campaign against the vicious and unethical propaganda" of his opponent.

The oil companies then needed another candidate to run against me. To my dismay, the one they put forward was my friend Manchester Boddy of the Los Angeles *Daily News*. It was years before I learned that oil interests held two million dollars of unpaid loans to the *News*. The Hearst organization was also involved in the pressure because Hearst was keeping the *News* afloat with $250,000 options to purchase, which it paid annually for five or six years. When they told Boddy to jump, he jumped.

The connection became clearer some time later when Sheridan Downey retired as the oil companies' lobbyist in Washington. He was replaced by Manchester Boddy.

Boddy was a good choice to run against me because the *News* had always supported me vigorously. His defection puzzled even my most ardent supporters, as it was meant to do. It was a crippling blow for me because his paper reached the southern part of the state where my support had been solid.

Lined up behind Boddy were all the moneyed interests who wanted to see me defeated, such as farmers with huge holdings, the oil people, lumbermen, and private power corporations. I had come out strongly in favor of public ownership of power on the basis that nonrenewable resources should be managed wisely, and rivers should not be exploited capriciously by individuals interested in short-range profit.

Ed Lybeck was concerned about money. My criticism of Downey and his backers had injured feelings within the Democratic party. These people turned to Boddy as the instrument for their revenge.

Downey's campaign had set the tone of portraying me as a maverick Democrat who didn't support Truman. He made a great deal of my vote against the Greek-Turkish aid bill when it was first introduced but said nothing about my reasons for opposing it or the fact that I voted for aid to Greece and Turkey when a second bill was introduced. He suggested that my stands in Congress against that bill and funds for HUAC were welcomed by the Soviet.

I suspected that John B. Elliott played a major role in drawing up that strategy. By the time Manchester Boddy's campaign was rolling, both the tone and the accusations were rawer. As a background accompaniment, Californians could hear President Truman's warnings about the communist menace and the danger of being soft on Soviet sympathizers within the country. In February a physicist, Klaus Fuchs, confessed that he had given secrets to the communists. Editorials demanded that the administration do something to stop the subversives.

In the Senate, Sheridan Downey missed no opportunity to attack me and support Boddy. As Earl Mazo later wrote, Democrats in the weeks that followed "painted Mrs. Douglas in every insulting shade of red. Few of them bothered to acknowledge, even obliquely, that she was actually a vigorous foe of the Communist party and had fought Henry Wallace's Progressive party in a congressional district where that took considerable courage."

In his speech to launch his campaign and set the mood Boddy said, "There is indisputable evidence of a statewide conspiracy on the part of this small subversive clique of red-hots to capture, through stealth and cunning, the nerve centers of our Democratic party.

"Good California Democrats know the score," he continued. "[They] have taken up the banner to preserve the American way of life and protect the true liberalism and honest progressivism which has made the Democratic party great."

Boddy was a political novice whose platform was a fuzzy, ill-defined plea for Americans to avoid another Depression and to stay out of wars. Voters couldn't make anything of it but when he talked about Helen Gahagan Douglas and the "red-hots" in the same breath, they paid attention.

The labor movement remained staunchly loyal and so did most Democratic women. Many of them were people I had recruited into political activism myself during the years when I was national committeewoman. However, there were exceptions. The vice-president of the California Democratic Women's League, for instance, urged Democrats to vote against me because I showed my sympathies for the country's enemies when I voted against funds for HUAC. The Business and Professional Women's Clubs of Los Angeles were also opposed to me. I had canceled an arrangement to address a banquet meeting because I was needed for an important vote in Congress, which infuriated the members.

They gave my substitute, Jimmy Roosevelt, a rough time when he
tried to defend me.

I was commuting from Washington to California to campaign.
The magnitude of the distances I had to cover within the state
made it imperative that I abandon the traditional method of
transportation, automobiles, so I hired a helicopter to whisk me
from town to town. Boddy began to declare everywhere that my
attendance in Congress was deplorable, that I had the worst attendance of any of the California delegation. The figures he gave
were all taken from the period when I began to campaign.

In fact my attendance record was excellent, as Minority Leader
John W. McCormack attested. McCormack told Tom Ford that
I was "one of the ablest, one of the most sincere, and one of the
most courageous legislators that I have ever had the honor to
serve with in any legislative body."

Boddy's campaign was handsomely subscribed. Backers were
spending thousands on a paper with a circulation of a million and
on pamphlets distributed by the hundreds of thousands. The
thrust of the message always was to portray me as a disloyal
American and traitorous Democrat.

I kept plugging the issues I thought the electorate should care
about, such as protection of the Reclamation Act, federal control
of oil-drilling leases in the tidelands, cheap public power, slum
clearance, rent control, housing for middle-income people, extended social security, and stimulating the economy to provide
jobs.

I described a proposal I hoped to introduce in the Senate if
elected, in which HUAC would be scrapped and replaced with a
bipartisan committee of responsible citizens, chaired perhaps by
Eleanor Roosevelt and ex-President Herbert Hoover, which would
investigate accusations of subversion in a forum which would respect the civil rights of suspects.

Sheridan Downey made a statewide radio broadcast in which
he said that I "gave comfort to the Soviet tyranny by voting
against aid to Greece and Turkey," and "opposed an appropria-
tion to enable Congress to uncover treasonable activities." He
added that I "joined Representative Vito Marcantonio, an admitted friend of the Communist party."

Accepting congratulations
on winning congressional
election, November 1944.
*(Western History Collections,
University of Oklahoma)*

U.S. delegation to the
United Nations,
October 1946. Left to right,
Representative Charles A. Eaton
(Republican— NJ),
Charles Fahy of the State
Department, Eleanor
Roosevelt, Representative
Sol Bloom (Democrat— NY),
Senator Warren R. Austin
(Republican— VT),
Adlai Stevenson,
Representative Helen Gahagan
Douglas (Democrat— CA).
*(Western History Collections,
University of Oklahoma)*

Left, fighting for low-income housing at a committee hearing, 1945. *(Western History Collections, University of Oklahoma)* Right, "Market Basket" speech in Congress in defense of maintaining price control, 1947. *(Western History Collections, University of Oklahoma)*

At home in California with Melvyn and children, Mary Helen and Peter, 1950. *(Graphic Associates)*

Campaigning against Nixon in 1950 from a trailer. *(Western History Collections, University of Oklahoma)*

With Helen Hayes, 1968. *(Weissberger)*

With Gloria Steinem and Patricia Carbine, publisher of *Ms.* magazine, following cover story, October 1973. *(Impact Photos)*

Receiving an honorary degree from Barnard College in 1979. *(The Barnard Reporter)*

Marcantonio, an Independent from New York who sat in the House as a member of the American Labor party, was believed to be a communist. The suggestion was that we voted alike because I was also a communist.

"We know that every Democrat will be called a communist," I said in despair in a campaign speech in May. Newspapers referred to me as "decidedly pink," or "pink shading to deep red." On April 28 Boddy's paper, the *Daily News*, called me "the pink lady," a tag that stuck.

Richard and Pat Nixon toured the state in a station wagon equipped with a record player and a loudspeaker. Nixon was keeping his Republican affiliation in the background as much as he could in the hope of Democratic support. If he could win both primaries, he would be spared the need for an election. Murray Chotiner, his campaign manager who was introducing a personality-based, media-blitz campaign of the sort which has since become commonplace, sent out one piece of literature which was titled, *As One Democrat to Another*.

Another circular asked IS HELEN DOUGLAS A DEMOCRAT? THE RECORD SAYS NO! and went on to say, "How will a real Democrat vote in this election?" The correct answer was to support Richard Nixon, "the man who puts country above party."

Ingrid Winther Scobie, a California journalist who researched the 1950 campaign, reports that some Democrats were offended. Others, however, began to establish groups calling themselves "Democrats for Nixon."

I was too preoccupied by keeping up with my responsibilities in Congress and trying to cram in hasty campaigning in California to appreciate what was going on. My campaign workers were exposed to it daily but I really wasn't. I did notice, however, a change of atmosphere as time went on. Something unhealthy was developing, a mood of pure hatred.

The results of the primary gave me a comfortable lead of 730,000 votes over Boddy's 400,000. Richard Nixon got 300,000 *Democratic* votes. Counting totals from the cross-filing, he had one million votes, narrowly edging my 900,000.

As Ed Lybeck put it, what my campaign now needed was some

luck. We got it—all bad. On June 25, 1950, the Democratic People's Republic of Korea, as the North Korean communist government called itself, invaded South Korea and almost swept its anti-communist regime off the peninsula.

For a shocking while it appeared possible that the Soviet and
China would support North Korea and the United States would
help defend South Korea. We would have a Third World War,
this time with atomic weapons on both sides. That calamity was
averted when the United Nations agreed to send in an army
made up of units from fifteen member countries. On July 1,
American troops landed in South Korea under the blue flag of the
United Nations and *lost* every one of their first engagements.

Americans reeled in horror. It appeared that communists were
advancing upon us from all sides. An industry mushroomed to
supply people who were building fallout shelters in their back-
yards and stocking them with emergency food and medical
supplies.

The panic was most acute in California, which saw itself closest
to the outbreak of hostilities on the far side of the Pacific. The
University of California dismissed 157 employees who refused to
sign an oath of loyalty to the United States. The Veterans of Foreign Wars demanded the dismissal of all those responsible for
putting "radicals and homosexuals into government departments." The FBI spoke of 12,000 dangerous communists loose in
America, half of them citizens. The Attorney General, J. Howard
McGrath, went further: he said the FBI knew of 500,000 communists trying to undermine the nation.

Suddenly a lot of people had statistics on the extent of subversion. J. Edgar Hoover spoke of a "potential fifth column" of
540,000 who were "using every trick they can to hide their illegal
activities." Hoover said there were exactly 6,977 communists working underground in California alone, where the movie industry
was said to be riddled with traitors.

The Los Angeles *Times* ran a daily list of American casualties
in Korea as the United Nations continued to lose every engagement. President Truman announced that he was asking Congress
for a $4-billion appropriation to send military supplies to non-

communist countries. There were stories of Russian and Chinese troops massed on the Korean border ready to enter the war.

The country swung hard toward conservatism. When people are nervous, they are ready to believe in muscle without asking too many questions. In Florida a respected New Deal senator, Claude Pepper, was defeated in the primaries by a hard-line right-wing congressman, George Smathers, whose campaign strategy centered on calling his opponent "Red Pepper." Senator Frank Graham of North Carolina lost to someone who accused him of taking the country down the road to socialism.

All over the country aspiring senators and congressmen rewrote campaign literature to show themselves as ardent anti-communists. In California the candidate for state attorney general, Edmund G. (Pat) Brown, displayed his credentials as a Red-basher and said he supported spending $25,000 on a program to find California's subversives. Jimmy Roosevelt, running hard for governor, said the amount wasn't big enough.

I was a day late reporting for Congress after the primary. Following roll call I went directly to the Speaker's platform to pay my respects to Sam Rayburn. He congratulated me on my victory and cautioned me not to make any mistakes in the campaign against Nixon.

Glancing at Richard Nixon, who was seated to the left of his dais, Rayburn said, "His is the most devious face of all those who have served in Congress in all the years I've been here."

The bill before us was called the McCarran-Wood bill but essentially it was the old Mundt-Nixon bill with a few minor revisions. The Mundt-Nixon bill to outlaw communism had passed in the Republican-dominated House of Representatives in 1948 but was killed in the Senate. President Harry Truman declared that he agreed with those who believed, as I did, that it violated a basic freedom guaranteed in the American Constitution. If the McCarran-Wood bill passed the House and Senate, Truman announced, he would veto it. He said:

"Unwise or excessive security measures can strike at the freedom and dignity of the individual which are the very foundation of our society—and the defense of which is the whole purpose of our security measures. . . .

"We already have tested legal defenses against treason, espionage, sabotage and other acts looking toward the overthrow of our government by force or violence . . . We must, therefore, be on our guard against extremists who urge us to adopt police state measures . . .

"Legislation is now pending before the Congress which is so broad and vague in its terms as to endanger the freedoms of speech, press and assembly protected by the First Amendment."

The debate was heated as liberals protested the opportunism and panic that had seized the Hill. After a stormy session, the Senate passed the bill. In the House of Representatives there was a tense silence as the call came for us to register the "yeas" and "nays" one by one.

When the clerk was halfway through the names beginning with A, Chet Holifield, my closest friend in the California delegation, left his seat and came over to see me. He squeezed into the row behind me and stood at the back of my chair. Richard Nixon was sitting in almost a direct line across from us on the Republican side of the House, laughing and talking with Les Arends who was standing behind him.

"Helen," Chet whispered urgently, "don't vote against this bill."

Surprised, I looked up at him and asked, "You're voting against it, aren't you?"

"Yes, but I'm not running for the Senate against Richard Nixon. You won't be able to get around the state fast enough to explain why you voted against the bill after he gets through telling voters that you did it because you're soft on Reds. He'll beat your brains in."

The clerk started calling names beginning with C.

One by one, California congressmen squirmed through the narrow space behind our seats and pleaded with me. "Don't vote 'no' on this bill, Helen," each said. "It'll cost you."

I stopped answering them.

"Why jeopardize your campaign? This bill is going to pass overwhelmingly. Your vote won't matter. Anyway, Truman will veto it."

I remained silent. One by one they gave way to my stiff back and left me.

The clerk began on the *D*'s.

I knew they were right. Nixon would use my vote against me in the same terrible way that he had destroyed Jerry Voorhis. It would give him ammunition to accuse me of being a communist.

But election strategy wasn't a compelling reason to vote against conscience on a bill that struck at the heart of the First Amendment of the Bill of Rights. What Nixon did was his responsibility. How I voted on the McCarran-Wood bill was my responsibility.

"Douglas of California."

"No."

When all present had answered the roll call and the votes were counted, the clerk announced the result. Only twenty-five of us had voted against the McCarran-Wood bill. It would go to the President for veto.

I went to the small dining room reserved for members of the House and approached the round corner in the table at which John McCormack presided. The men rose politely to their feet to greet me. One said, "How does it feel to be a dead statesman, Helen, instead of a live politician?"

I said, and meant it, "Just fine."

When President Truman vetoed the bill I made a speech in Congress about it. I said:

> Those who have used the Korean crisis to enlarge the wave of fear and panic that they might force through legislation to fetter the mind and spirit of America are sapping the well-springs of our strength. . . .
>
> The McCarran–Wood bill which the President has vetoed would not deal accurately with the dangers of communist action. Instead, it would undermine those American freedoms which make our fight against communism essential. . . .
>
> It would be tragic indeed if we were to undercut the freedom of our own people.

I explained why I had voted against the McCarran-Wood bill in order to have my reasons in the Congressional Record. I declared that the bill:

would be entirely ineffective to prevent communist espionage and
sabotage, while undermining fundamental liberties guaranteed
under the Constitution. I have voted for every measure which I
felt was genuinely aimed at making America strong against communist attack from within and without our borders.

In 1947 I had voted against Truman's loyalty bill because I was
unable to persuade Congress that it should be accompanied by
civil rights safeguards. It was back before us in July 1950 in the
same terrible form. It permitted the summary and arbitrary dismissal of federal workers without any provision for appeal or review. People would be fired with "discharged for loyalty reasons"
on their record, almost a guarantee in 1950 that they would be
permanently unemployed and socially ostracized.

An amendment was framed to put proper safeguards in the bill,
allowing dismissed or suspended federal employees the right of
appeal to the Civil Service Commission. I voted for that amendment but it lost in the belligerent House by a vote of 193 to 144.
Then we voted on the bill, which passed by 327 to 14. I was one
of the fourteen.

Happily the Senate voted in the amendment.

That summer the courts handed down important decisions
about the right of Congress to establish committees such as
HUAC, which went farther in investigating and grilling citizens
than any had before. Judge Learned Hand ruled that Congress is
entitled to legislate and require affidavits and therefore, inferen-
tially, can investigate as it pleases when ascertaining the loyalty of
Americans.

The first contempt of Congress citation after Judge Hand's decision and one similar to his came before the House on August
10. In view of the clarification of the jurisdiction supplied by the
courts, I voted for the citation. I supported it also because the
person concerned not only had refused to answer the question of
whether he was a communist but had also pleaded the Fifth
Amendment in refusing to reply to one hundred other questions,
most of them innocuous.

In the wake of the court ruling I voted for contempt citations
against more than fifty people. I didn't do so arbitrarily but always consulted with lawyers and others who were informed about

the particulars of each case. Some contempt citations I supported, some I did not.

In the end I became a sort of court of appeal in the House, since I insisted on knowing all the facts and was not prepared to rubber-stamp each citation. It was a dangerous situation for people hauled before HUAC with all the hysteria that was rising that summer. The atmosphere of fear was contagious. There were some congressmen who were afraid they wouldn't be considered 100 percent Americans unless they voted for terrible legislation like the McCarran-Wood bill.

I regretted that people who were committed to communism didn't feel they could say so. In a country devoted to freedom of speech, they should have been able to feel comfortable about declaring their beliefs and we should have been ready to respect them for it. Many who refused to answer questions were not communists at all, of course, but people who were silent because of principle.

Many Hollywood stars were in that category. They didn't know who was a communist and who wasn't, and they weren't going to be placed in a position where their speculation would hurt innocent people. So they took the Fifth. In those days, unfortunately, "taking the Fifth" was considered an admission of guilt.

But I did uphold contempt citations for people who wouldn't give even their name to HUAC. They were silly.

In August I voted for President Truman's loyalty program. I spoke in favor of it on the same day it came to the House because it contained proper safeguards for people accused of disloyalty to appeal. I declared:

> I support the recommendations which the President now makes as necessary to tighten certain security laws. But I will continue to oppose, as I have always opposed, those measures which, as the President says, "strike at the very heart of our free society" and which "would undermine freedom in the name of security."
>
> I have always fought totalitarianism in all its forms: communism, fascism, and Naziism. I have also fought, and I join with the President in fighting, against those extremists who now urge us to adopt police state measures. Those who advocate such mea-

sures cannot have the love of liberty which they profess. Otherwise they would not ask us, in the name of freedom, to adopt
measures which would end freedom. . . . Laws forbidding dissent
do not prevent subversive activities—they merely drive them into
more secret and dangerous channels. Police states are not secure;
their history is marked by successive purges, and growing concentration camps, as their governments strike out blindly in fear of
violent revolt. Once a government is committed to the principle
of silencing the voice of opposition, it has only one way to go,
and this is down the path of increasingly repressive measures,
until it becomes a source of terror to all its citizens and creates a
country where everyone lives in fear.

I felt demeaned by having to state that I was a loyal Democrat
and a loyal American, but the times seem to require that I do so.

Seasoned political analysts who studied the voting trend in the
primaries, and the results in California particularly, came to the
conclusion that I could not win, barring a miracle. Nixon had
polled more votes than I did *before* the outbreak of war in Korea,
despite the fact that registered Democrats outnumbered Republicans three million to two million.

If Ed Lybeck or anyone else in my campaign office agreed with
that prediction of doom, I didn't know it. For myself, I was optimistic after the primary. I believed the worst was over. The Democratic turnout had been light for the primaries and would certainly improve. Nixon also was gambling on those Democrats not
yet counted; he thought they could be persuaded to vote for him.
His staff was cautioning supporters to avoid blanket attacks on
Democrats.

Harry Truman intervened to ask Sheridan Downey to endorse
me and heal the wounds the party had suffered during the vicious
primary race. Though such a courtesy is customary and expected,
Downey refused. Like many other conservative Democrats, he
wanted Richard Nixon to win.

George Creel, who had been one of the first to urge me to run
for national committeewoman in California, couldn't forgive me
for challenging Downey. He threw himself into organizing
"Democrats for Nixon" groups, which were springing up every-

where in the state. Many other leading Democrats, I was discovering, either worked against me actively as Creel and Jack Elliott did or else stayed neutral until it was over. Bill Malone was quoted as saying, "I truly do support Helen Douglas and I want her to be elected," but he didn't help me one bit.

It hurt that many friends, Democrats who had worked with me in my years as national committeewoman, fought hard against me in the election. It was the reclamation issue that turned them around, I think. Like most people in the state who lived in the cities, they hadn't taken time to study it very well. As they saw it, they were California patriots and I was a carpetbagger.

Campaign contributions were skimpy. At one point there were stories in the newspapers that I was in such financial difficulty that I was ready to throw in the towel, but that was an exaggeration.

George Creel said bitter things against me. He spoke of my "perverted point of view" and then linked me to organizations I had addressed in 1945 and 1946 which now were regarded as communist fronts.

Murray Chotiner, Nixon's friend and chief strategist, was a clever Beverly Hills lawyer for whom winning a campaign justified whatever means were required. Later he was implicated in spying for Nixon on George McGovern in the presidential campaign of 1972. Chotiner's technique was one of sustained attack on the opponent. Stay away from the strengths, he advised, and go for the weak side. My prestige in the House and my stands on civil rights and social welfare legislation were my strengths. My weakness, as Nixon and Chotiner saw it, was that I had opposed HUAC, the Mundt-Nixon bill and the McCarran-Wood bill, stands which could be twisted to show that I was a communist.

"The autumn of 1950 was made for mean electioneering," Earl Mazo observed.

A story was planted with George Rothwell Brown, Hearst columnist, ten days before the campaign officially opened. He wrote that Helen Gahagan Douglas "has generally been found voting in the House of Representatives with Vito Marcantonio."

"If Vito Marcantonio had not existed in the late 1940's and early 1950's," Frank Mankiewicz said in *Perfectly Clear: Nixon from Whittier to Watergate,* "Richard Nixon (or, more properly, Murray Chotiner) would have had to invent him."

Frank added, "The 'found voting' is a nice touch; obviously it is more sinister to be 'found voting' than merely to have voted."

Bernard Brennan, manager of Nixon's campaign in Southern California, stepped up the attack on August 30, saying that I was "soft on communism" and referring to me as "the pink lady." He described Marcantonio and me as "heroes" of the communist movement. Brennan then charged that Marcantonio and I had voted alike 353 times. He put it, "On 353 times, the actress-candidate voted exactly the same as Vito Marcantonio, the notorious communist party-line Congressman from New York." He added, "The import of the votes is more significant than the numbers."

I don't know why I didn't go on the air at once and straighten out the charges that I voted with Vito Marcantonio. My only excuse is that I was always off-balance, working so hard and fast to cover the state, going back and forth to Washington all the time, that I simply didn't think of it. We had limited funds and a limited number of people working on the campaign so we often didn't have the energy and resources to step back and see the whole picture.

I should have said, "There isn't any Vito Marcantonio program. This is a lie. This is a deliberate lie." That would have been simple enough, though my friend Frank Mankiewicz tells me that it wasn't an easy matter to explain rather complex patterns of congressional voting.

Some years later, in 1956, I worked out a statement which I gave to the Scripps-Howard papers in response to persistent requests. Eleanor Roosevelt, for one, had been imploring me to set the record straight but every time I tried I found myself taking forever to describe how we voted and why. Finally I figured out a way to put it succinctly and it turned out that it wasn't so difficult after all.

Vito Marcantonio was a loner in the House of Representatives. Since he represented no party when he voted on a bill, he had the choice of voting with the Democrats or voting with the Republicans. He did both. Since the Republicans tended to be isolationist, which suited Marcantonio's politics, he voted with them on foreign bills such as the Marshall Plan and NATO, which they opposed. On domestic legislation such as public housing, rent control, civil rights and social security, he was more likely to vote with us.

Consequently he voted as I did a total of 353 times, as Brennan said, or 354 times, as Nixon counted it. Nixon didn't mention, of course, that he and Marcantonio voted alike 113 times. The disparity reflected the ratio between the greater number of bills on domestic issues than on foreign affairs.

I don't know to this day whether Marcantonio *was* a communist. He certainly was very, very left. He certainly seemed to be following very much the Communist party approach on foreign policy, but beyond that I don't know.

Late in the campaign when I grew desperate to counteract the effect of Nixon's repetition of "354 times," I started to include in my speeches and literature the fact that Nixon and Marcantonio also voted together. My intention was not to paint Nixon as a fellow traveler, which patently would have been absurd, but to explain rather ineptly how Marcantonio switched his vote around. It wasn't helpful to me and it didn't relieve the confusion. As Earl Mazo wrote, "When compared with the surgeons of the Nixon camp, Mrs. Douglas's operators performed like apprentice butchers."

Nixon launched his campaign on September 18 with a statewide radio address. His voice was calm and reassuring. He said, "There will be no name-calling, no smears, no misrepresentations in this campaign . . . [but] to the extent that Mrs. Douglas does not reveal, or conceals her record, I feel that I have an obligation to expose that record to the voters of California."

With that, we were off. Nixon never let up on the theme that I had voted with Vito Marcantonio 354 times. People could draw their own conclusions from that.

"Irrational fear of communism is being used in many quarters to blind us to our real problems," I protested.

When Nixon declared that I had tried to defeat the McCarran-Wood bill, which would help the United States rid itself of communist traitors, I could only reply, "With pride I was one of those twenty-five who stood fast against this bill."

Chotiner's strategy of keeping on the offensive made me feel I was standing in the path of tanks. That effect was exactly what he intended. His instructions to Nixon workers were to refer to me as "a supporter of the socialist program running on the Democratic ticket." In 1955 he was asked to conduct a seminar to teach aspiring Republicans how to win elections. He said then, "You keep hammering and hammering on weak points until your opponent can no longer exist. . . ."

Chotiner also told the seminar, "I believe in all sincerity that if you do not deflate the opposition candidate before your own campaign gets started, the odds are you are doomed to defeat."

In light of that statement, I can see the logic of the peculiar event that occurred a day or two before the primaries. I was at the University of Southern California, where I had strong student support, addressing an open-air rally on the sidewalk outside the Doheny Library on the campus.

A hay wagon came along the street and sitting on top of it were a number of young men in top hats, cutaway dinner jackets and underpants. They held siphons of water with which they soaked and scattered people who were listening to me.

The president of the university sent me a letter of apology and the students who invited me were mortified, but the damage was done. The young men succeeded in breaking up the meeting.

I still get letters from people who were youngsters in 1950 and saw something or heard something unpleasant that was done to me. Around the time that Richard Nixon was involved in the Watergate scandals, I heard from a number who said such incidents had stuck in their minds all those years.

One came from James McAree, professor of history at Pennsylvania State University, who told me he was present at the water-bombing. He wrote in his letter that "it is rare that historians are witnesses to events, however minor, that illustrate the work which occupies them personally" and supplied an explanation for that bizarre attack.

Professor McAree said that on the day of my rally there was an initiation into a secret society known as the Skull and Dagger. This society sought as members men who had distinguished themselves on campus and men who had been active in another campus society, the Trojan Horse. The hay wagon was part of that initiation.

"As the wagon drew abreast of where you were standing," Professor McAree wrote, "the boys reached into the hay and brought out the siphon bottles. They proceeded then to squirt you with soda water and shower hay upon you." They were directed from the edge of the crowd, Professor McAree thought, by two graduates. One was Joe Holt, who later became a member of Nixon's Senate staff, and the other was Patrick Hillings, the Republican candidate in the Twelfth District where Nixon's congressional seat was vacant.

Nixon was accused of being behind the incident but he dismissed it as a college prank. Jesse Unruh, who had arranged for me to speak that day, steadfastly maintained that the Skull and Dagger Society was part of the Nixon machine at the University of Southern California. Interestingly, Watergate turned up many who figured in that hay ride either as members of the Skull and Dagger or of the Trojan Horse or both—among them Donald Segretti, Gordon C. Strachan, Dwight Chapin and Herbert W. Kalmbach.

To protect myself from the onslaught of Nixon's slurs about my alleged communist leanings, I referred in the campaign to my voting record in the House and the Foreign Affairs Committee, where many of the bills I supported were anti-communist. Chotiner sent out a notice to all Nixon campaign chairmen: "Helen Douglas is trying to portray a new role as a foe of communism. DO NOT LET HER GET AWAY WITH IT! It is a phony act."

That's when his chairman in Southern California, Bernard Brennan, picked a sentence out of my 1946 speech in Congress about my democratic beliefs, in which I said, "Communism is no real threat to the institutions of this country." That quote was to appear in Nixon campaign literature until voting day. Since 17,000 Americans were casualties of the war against communism in Korea by that time, it had a devastating effect on my credibility. The next parts of the speech were never cited. I went on to say, "I don't think we value democracy highly enough," and "The best way to keep communism out of our country is to keep democracy in it," and "Communism was born out of hunger, slavery, illiteracy, superstition, degradation. Communism has no place in our society."

Two communist papers, *People's World* in California and New York's *Daily Worker*, printed editorials in support of my candidacy. Richard Nixon's staff pounced on them to add to the "evidence" that I was a communist.

Occasionally Nixon and I appeared on the same platform. The second time it happened was in San Francisco before the Commonwealth Club. He spoke first. He had a telegram in his hand and he held it up, saying it was an endorsement from Eleanor Roosevelt.

My face showed so much shock and dismay that the audience roared with laughter. That was the purpose of the trick, of course, to throw me off balance. It was supposed to be a joke but he caught me with my sense of humor down. I could only think that it must be true, that no one would lie publicly about something that could so easily be denied. If I had thought faster I would have asked, *which* Eleanor Roosevelt sent the telegram—because it certainly wasn't Mrs. Franklin Delano Roosevelt.

I telephoned her immediately after the meeting and received her assurances that she had sent no message to Richard Nixon.

Nixon was an impressive public speaker. He had the appearance of a worried, decent man courageously doing his best for his country. He would say at the opening, "I have been advised not to talk about communism," as if it were foolhardy to speak out, "but I am going to tell the people of California the truth." The "truth" always was that Helen Douglas tried to stop Americans who dared to fight communism.

"If she had her way," he said early in the campaign, "the communist conspiracy would never have been exposed, and Alger Hiss would still be influencing the foreign policy of the United States."

As Frank Mankiewicz pointed out, I had nothing to do with the Hiss case, and Alger Hiss, far from "influencing the foreign policy of the United States," had left the government before Nixon heard of him.

Later Nixon, looking perplexed and concerned, asked an audience, "Why has she followed the communist line so many times?" He added that if I had my way there would be no draft (I had voted against peacetime compulsory service), Greece and Turkey would have "gone communist," and the House Un-American Activities Committee wouldn't exist.

Dick Miller, captain of the debating team at the University of California in Berkeley, went to hear Nixon and came away awed. He wrote me that Nixon was "one of the cleverest speakers I have ever heard."

With the opening of the campaign Nixon issued the "Pink Sheet," the single most damaging piece of literature used against me. It was headed DOUGLAS-MARCANTONIO VOTING RECORD and subheaded VOTES AGAINST COMMITTEE ON UN-AMERICAN ACTIVITIES and VOTES AGAINST LOYALTY AND SECURITY LEGISLATION and COMMUNIST-LINE FOREIGN POLICY VOTES.

Nixon "has voted *exactly opposite* to the Douglas-Marcantonio AXIS!," proclaimed the Pink Sheet. The phrase "354 times!" was used liberally in a document that bristled with dates and legal language. It concluded, WOULD CALIFORNIA SEND MARCANTONIO TO THE UNITED STATES SENATE?

Murray Chotiner always maintained that the color was an accident. He said he wanted something other than white but the printer had only two choices, brown or pink. He picked the pink and insisted that he didn't realize until later how it fit with the charge of "pink lady."

The first printing was for 50,000 but the Pink Sheet was such a success that a few days later Chotiner ordered another 500,000.

Nixon used the Pink Sheet everywhere he went and referred to it in every platform and radio speech. The repetition, as Ernest Brashear said in *The New Republic*, "had a fearful impact . . . anti-communist sentiment was at a hysterical peak. Nixon, a powerful and convincing speaker . . . made the most of this Moscow-created opportunity."

I sent a telegram to close friends: I HAVE RUN INTO A FRIGHTENING CRISIS. I NEED YOUR HELP, YOUR ADVICE, YOUR SUPPORT. WILL YOU COME TO DINNER AT MY HOUSE TUESDAY SEPTEMBER 26 7PM SO THAT WE CAN TALK OVER THIS TERRIBLE SITUATION AND HOPEFULLY FIND A SOLUTION.

The "terrible situation" to which I referred was not only the

Pink Sheet, which was being waved at me wherever I spoke, but the massive defection of leading Democrats. George Creel, declaring he couldn't support me "because of her record in Congress," had gathered statewide support for "Democrats for Nixon" and enlisted a good many of the most stalwart Democrats in California to help defeat me.

I remember that I came away from that dinner with friends fully determined to wage my own campaign and ignore the tactics of my opponent. I wasn't going to descend to that level. My stand was never to recognize Nixon's tactics, not even to talk about them. I always believed that campaigns should be a time when voters had an opportunity to be educated about the issues and I stuck to that premise grimly. I talked about what reclamation had meant to California and why the 160-acre limitation mattered, and I talked about tidelands oil leases.

As I look back almost thirty years, I know we were affected by Nixon's tactics but at the time I thought I was rising above them. Perhaps our approach should have been different. Perhaps I shouldn't have been so above-it-all, sticking to my record all the time with Gahagan stubbornness. I don't mean I should have played his game—winning isn't everything—but that I should have defended myself better.

Still, every time I heard myself explaining that I really was a good, loyal citizen, I felt ashamed and debased.

New accusations came at me daily from one part of the state or another. If I paid attention to them all I would never have had time to talk about anything else, and I was determined to talk about the issues. We did retaliate a bit toward the end, but not much when you consider what kind of a campaign it was.

Nixon's hecklers were at every meeting asking why I supported "communist bills." I would give an explanation why that bill was good for the United States, and how important our liberties are, and that the bill wasn't communist, and which distinguished congressmen also had voted for it, but before I could finish another heckler planted in the crowd would bring up another "communist bill." I kept struggling to buttress myself on one side, only to find that the attack was coming from another.

With a great deal of help from Evelyn Chavoor, who with

Juanita Terry moved from Washington to work on my campaign, we put together the "Blue Book," which was titled, "HELEN GAHAGAN DOUGLAS versus RICHARD NIXON; *Here Is The Full Record Of Their Votes In Congress*—How They Stood On Agriculture, Civil Rights, Defense, Foreign Policy, Housing, Labor, Monopoly & Anti-Trust, Power & Resources, Rent Control, Social Security, Taxes, Veterans Affairs."

The blue cover declared, "This is the *authoritative* record of *Helen Gahagan Douglas* and her opponent—from the *official Congressional Record*."

Inside were seventy foolscap-length pages showing how Richard Nixon and I voted on a wide range of bills, giving excerpts of my speeches, a summary of the legislation, and comments on it by Democrats and Republicans who shared my view of it. The Blue Book was expensive to produce, laborious for anyone but a dedicated liberal to read, and quite unsuccessful in matching the flair and focus of the ubiquitous Pink Sheet.

Evelyn and Juanita and I would work until one or two in the morning preparing my speeches for the next day, searching through documents to get the facts right, and then we would struggle out of bed at five to make connections to a remote part of the state where I was expected for breakfast. I was trying to cover the Central Valley area, among others, because I wanted to reach the conservatives who were against me. I believed that if they knew the whole story, if they had the facts, they would change their minds.

I always took the Blue Book with me, since it was the basis of my campaign, but it was evident that voters weren't interested in details of legislation. People would point to something in a newspaper, a report of a Nixon speech, and ask me to explain it. When I did, I felt they closed their ears to rational comment. The fabricated stories came at me like a mudslide; I couldn't keep up with it.

In union meetings or church basements, everywhere, people would drop a word or two about "the pink lady." The "Did you know . . ." kind of thing. Word-of-mouth vilification.

Richard Nixon never said openly that I was a communist. He didn't have to—his people took care of that. The state was saturated with Nixon people paid to work wherever they could find a crowd. They were posted on street corners, for instance, where pedestrians waited for the light to change. They would pass out campaign literature and start a discussion about Helen Gahagan Douglas being a communist.

If someone showed interest, they would give examples taken from the Pink Sheet. One day Mickey Simone, a friend I'd known for years, was walking in a congested area of Los Angeles and was stopped by a Nixon worker who told her that I was a communist and the country wouldn't be safe unless I was defeated.

At that time, Communist China had entered the Korean War. In California in the autumn of 1950 it was quite possible to believe that a communist invasion was imminent.

If the person approached seemed resistant, the Nixon staffer would be more cautious in the accusations; that person would get only hints and innuendos. Special-interest groups received a different approach. It was explained to them that whatever it was they wanted—easy oil leases, cheap migrant labor, better schools —they would have a better chance with Nixon because I was opposed to anything that was good for Americans.

They managed to generate a lot of hatred that way. I really think it was the ugliest part of the campaign, that atmosphere of hate. It made people say and do things they normally wouldn't.

It had nothing to do with the issues because the issues weren't being discussed. It was a whispering campaign of, "This woman mustn't go to Congress. What will happen to us if she does? We must stop her."

That was the basis of the campaign. And it worked. I'm told I had a chance even after the Korean War started but that when the Chinese communists started fighting Americans, I was dead. I know that's true. There was the United States fighting communism and I was the person who said we should limit the power of the military and try to disarm the world and get along with Russia.

Korea was the critical element in Nixon's victory. I think that with it, he didn't need his smear tactics; he would have won anyway without character assassination and misrepresentation of my record. I had been all over the country talking about the United Nations and what it could do to avert war—and here we were at war in Korea under a United Nations flag. I talked about world cooperation—and men of many nations were killing one another in Korea. I had warned about the arms race—and now we were rushing guns to Korea. I said we had to live together—and men were dying together.

My opposition to the Greek-Turkish aid bill could be seen as my wanting communists to get ahead of America, in the light of the fighting in Korea.

The feeling was: she's for the United Nations and the United Nations hasn't worked! We're at war again. *She's wrong!*

California voters were manipulated in that election in a way that Judge Learned Hand predicted many years earlier when he warned of the danger the mass media pose for democracy. People can be stampeded, especially when they are fearful as they were in California that year, by a clever and cynical campaign waged in the media.

I could answer the charges on a platform but I couldn't be everywhere to counteract the rest of it. Our campaign was like a calm center, with all that hysteria going on around us while we plugged away with daily speaking schedules, unable to touch it. Even though I used a helicopter, something new in campaigning, I couldn't get to enough places in such a large state to keep ahead of what was being done to my reputation.

The first day I was to fly in the chopper, which normally was used for crop-dusting, the pilot picked me up at one of the San Francisco Bay piers. I was alarmed that there was no cabin. One was strapped into a seat that was completely open to the sky. Lifting off, straight up, was nerve-racking to say the least. To make it worse, the pilot decided to test me by making such a tight turn that we were almost upside down. I clenched my teeth and made not a sound of complaint; I was afraid he would refuse to take me to my destination.

For each speaking engagement, the people there had to obtain permission for us to land in some designated place, which was almost never conventional. One time it was a railway station in

Northern California. When the pilot saw the tiny platform where he was supposed to set me down, he was outraged.

"Those people *can't* want you to land there!" he shouted above the noise of the engine. "They'll kill you!"

I consulted my itinerary, which clearly instructed me to land at the railway platform. I told the pilot to go ahead. He tipped the helicopter to give me a better view of the target. It was indeed tiny, about four feet wide by seven feet long, and raised four feet above the ground.

"We'll be all right," I told him with a confidence I didn't feel. "Besides, I can see the welcoming committee. Let's show them we aren't afraid."

He gave me a sharp look, banked the chopper carefully, and after much maneuvering gently set it down exactly on the top of that plinth. When the engine was shut off I noticed that the people waiting for me were white-faced. They had expected us to land in the nearby field.

Another time I was scheduled to speak at ten and noon in Apple Valley and then fly to the San Joaquin Valley for some afternoon rallies. Between the two valleys there is a mountain range that has to be crossed with a favorable wind. We thought we were in good time to catch it, but we weren't. The helicopter rose in the air and stopped, unable to make headway.

The pilot found a gap in the mountain eventually, took us through it, and landed.

"Now what?" I asked.

"We're out of gas," he explained.

He walked a mile and a half to a place where he could get gas. It made us about an hour and a half late arriving at our destination, Visalia, where I was to address migrant farm workers.

As I climbed out of the chopper I saw that some people were kneeling in prayer. Those who came toward me were strangely subdued. They led me to an empty orange crate which was to be my dais and silently stood around me. I began by apologizing for the delay. A man interrupted.

"It doesn't matter," he said. "You're safe, Mrs. Douglas. We feared something had happened to you."

I talked only a short time, knowing how weary they must be,

and told them about the Reclamation Act and the importance of preserving it because it affected the lives of all rural people and, ultimately, city dwellers as well.

When I finished a man approached with tears in his eyes.

"They haven't made you afraid," he said; "they haven't made you afraid."

I was too moved to reply.

On our first flight the pilot warned me that he was a Republican. On our last flight, he told me that he'd changed his mind. After listening to me, he was a Democrat.

The crowds I was addressing *looked* all right but I was aware of the defections—Democrats, Catholics, union people from the building trades.

Nixon's strategy to win Democrats obliged him to be careful not to advance his Republicanism too forcefully. In fact, as he had before, he represented himself as a Democrat. One campaign pamphlet titled MEET RICHARD NIXON opened with, "In Congress Nixon has joined with the majority of Democrats . . . who have put country above partisanship." He said that I had "gone against the majority in her own party and joined with the small left-wing clique led by the communist party-liner Vito Marcantonio."

Another document asked, HOW DEMOCRATIC IS HELEN DOUGLAS? IS THIS A DEMOCRATIC VOTING RECORD?

What was I supposed to be? I thought interestedly. A Republican?

I failed to take his attacks seriously enough. The communist thing was so ludicrous, so preposterous. I wasn't nearly shocked enough when I saw the Pink Sheet. I just thought it was ridiculous, absolutely absurd. I remembered that when I voted against the McCarran-Wood bill I happened to catch Nixon's eye. He was grinning broadly. I knew then that he would twist the issue so that my vote against the abuse of civil rights in the bill would be presented as a vote for communism, but I thought that few people would pay much attention to such an outrageous accusation.

In my Fourteenth District, of course, Nixon got nowhere. I kept my district well informed about my stands and why I voted as I did. Nixon could not misrepresent me in the Fourteenth.

Catholics, however, alarmed by the atheism of communism as much as by its political implications, were easier to influence. I think many well-meaning Catholics were taken in by the Pink Sheet. The church in general felt that anything that advanced communism was a danger to Catholicism. Since seventy-five percent of the Catholics in California were registered Democrats, this was a group well worth Nixon's while.

Whether by coincidence or design, Nixon received powerful help from Archbishop J. Francis A. McIntyre of Los Angeles, who sent a letter to all his parish priests ordering that for four successive Sundays in October their sermons should deal with the dangers of communism, with special mention of the number of communists who had infiltrated high positions in government.

The priests were instructed not to name anyone at the altar but all were given a list of the candidates the archbishop wanted to see defeated in November. Many priests got around the first admonition but observed the intent by telling their congregations that "the woman" running for high public office should not be elected. There was but one woman running for high public office, me.

Outside the churches—not all, but many of them—Nixon's campaign workers were posted to distribute the Pink Sheet and other scurrilous literature to the departing flocks.

Many Catholics with long memories had not forgiven me for denouncing Francisco Franco, fascist dictator of Spain. They saw the civil war in Spain only in terms of the faith. If you were for the church, you supported Franco. If you were anti-Catholic, you supported the other side. While I was in Congress I often encountered priests lobbying to get the United States to recognize Franco's Spain. Mostly they approached Catholic congressmen. They never came to me because I was, in their terms, anti-Catholic.

Frank Chambers, chairman of my Northern California campaign, was a Catholic. With some other Catholics who were upset by what was happening, he went to see the bishop in San Francisco. The delegation told the bishop that I had a fine record in Congress and that I wasn't anti-Catholic.

The bishop replied that the Catholic Church didn't participate in politics. "I know Mrs. Douglas's record," he said. "There is nothing objectionable in her record, nothing whatsoever. But the church never mixes in politics."

The delegates might have mentioned that Archbishop McIntyre in Los Angeles was very much mixing in an election, but I didn't ask. I didn't know whether churches in the northern part of the state behaved differently, but certainly in the south the Catholic establishment tried its best to defeat me.

Zita Doneghan Remley, a Catholic, was one of my campaign workers. She wanted to volunteer her services but I insisted on paying her and she ran my headquarters with tireless dedication. She put together a pamphlet, *Catholics for Douglas,* which was signed by some well-known Catholics. Archbishop McIntyre reprimanded her for it but she defied him. I had a very strong Catholic committee. Other Catholics dropped in to the headquarters to say they were outraged by what was happening.

Richard Rogan, a lawyer who was one of the "Catholics for Douglas" committee, wrote a letter of protest to a church official in which he said, "California is not France, and Archbishop McIntyre is not Richelieu."

I suppose that at the very least this opposition created problems for my campaign fund raisers. Paul Ziffren raised money in the south and Ellie Heller in the north. Her husband refused to help me, but she did. The Macauleys, Jean and her husband, were also active. Jean was honorary chairman of the campaign in the north and Sue Lilienthal was vice-chairman. Sue and Ernest Lilienthal raised a good deal of money. In the south a number of actors and directors donated generously and helped round up funds.

What was most touching was that we received donations of coins—nickels and dimes—from poor people.

The film colony was divided about my campaign. HUAC's investigations of alleged communists in the movie industry had torn the community apart. Several people, Ronald Reagan among them, worked hard for me but many campaigned furiously against me. Zasu Pitts, who was livid on the subject of communism, made a particularly vicious speech about me.

I was in the campaign headquarters one day when my daughter

324 A Full Life

Mary Helen called. She was twelve then. She was crying. "Mummy, mummy," she sobbed, "what are they saying about you on the radio? They are saying terrible things about you." I was shattered. I consoled her as best I could.

Melvyn was on the road, touring in a play, *Two Blind Mice*. He was out of California for the entire campaign. I learned later that several times there were threats of picket lines outside the theater where he was appearing. Protesters wanted to warn people to avoid the communist inside. We talked on the telephone as often as we could and he sent a radio speech supporting me strongly, but there wasn't much he could do.

My record was known in the eastern part of the country. It would have been difficult for Nixon to misrepresent me there. That year *Liberty* magazine said of me, "You can count on your fingers the congressmen better versed in world affairs and social economics." Vice-President Alben Barkley was one of the major figures in the Democratic party who came from Washington to speak on my behalf. So did Attorney General J. Howard McGrath, Secretary of Labor Maurice Tobin, Secretary of Agriculture Charles F. Brannan, Secretary of the Interior Oscar L. Chapman, and Truman's presidential assistant W. Averell Harriman.

Juanita Terry remembers that she typed the speech Averell gave, working at his hotel on a special typewriter that printed huge letters that were easy to read on large cardboard cards. He was gracious to her, she told me, and sent her a warm thank-you note afterward.

When Attorney General McGrath praised my voting against HUAC, explaining that I was demonstrating my faith in democratic principles and civil rights in so doing, Nixon took time from attacking me to deliver an unpleasant speech impugning McGrath's loyalty.

Some Democrats in Alameda, led by Frank S. Richards, announced they were voting for Nixon.

The building trades, which were heavily Catholic, were reported to be solidly against me. The CIO and AFL, however, endorsed me. A newspaper criticism noted that Nixon was using "home talent," while I was bringing in "the Foreign Legion of Harry Truman."

Not all eastern Democrats were for me. I have a third-hand story by way of John Cowles of *Look* magazine who served with Judge Charles Wyzanski and John F. Kennedy on the Harvard Board of Overseers. In 1956, according to my informant, Kennedy told Cowles that he had made a campaign contribution to Nixon in 1950. Judge Wyzanski learned of it from Cowles and asked Kennedy to confirm it.

"Yes, I did donate to Nixon," Kennedy said. "It was the biggest damfool mistake I ever made."

Eleanor Roosevelt came to California to campaign for me and her son James, running against the popular incumbent governor, Earl Warren. She was worried for us both. For our part, each of us was keeping a careful distance from the other. I didn't want to draw him into the line of fire aimed at me. Jimmy, I think, shared my concern up until the end of the campaign, when polls showed that his support was even weaker than mine.

Warren was something of a lone wolf politically. One of the secrets of his success as a Republican in a state where Democrats had a majority was that he rarely endorsed other Republicans. He hadn't helped Nixon against Voorhis and he didn't come out for Senator William Knowland until the last few days of his campaign.

The Nixon campaign organization became obsessed by the goal of making Earl Warren support Nixon. He steadfastly resisted all the pressure they brought to bear, so they decided on a circuitous plan. They would force me to declare myself for Jimmy Roosevelt, which they expected would annoy Warren into supporting Nixon.

Accordingly, Joe Holt, head of the Young Republicans and later a congressman, attended every rally, every press conference, every speaking engagement I had. He asked but one question: *Who do you support for governor?*

The question was pretty silly on the face of it. Jimmy and I were both Democrats, I was known to be a friend of his family, and we had appeared on platforms together. Still, I hesitated to risk hurting him so I answered evasively by pointing out that I was a Democrat and I was running on the Democratic ticket.

Joe Holt kept it up and kept it up. With only a few days left in the campaign, I broke down and answered. Witnesses later wrote that I had tears in my eyes but I don't remember feeling that way. I said, "I hope and pray he will be the next governor, and he will if the Democrats vote the Democratic ticket."

Murray Chotiner telephoned some reporters friendly to Nixon and they told Earl Warren what I'd said. Warren made no comment until the next day, when he issued a statement: "I have no intention of being coy about this situation. As always, I have kept my campaign independent from other campaigns. The newspaper report from San Diego that Mrs. Douglas says she hopes and prays Mr. Roosevelt will be the next governor does not change my position. In view of her statement, however, I might ask her how she expects I will vote when I mark my ballot for the United States Senate next Tuesday."

Warren couldn't have been more vague but Chotiner seized on the statement anyway. He put out a press release saying, "Every voter in California who reads his statement will realize that Earl Warren intends to mark his ballot for Dick Nixon on election day."

There are people who are convinced that on election day in 1950 Earl Warren voted for Helen Gahagan Douglas.

I didn't know everything that was being done. I didn't know about the anti-Semitism directed against Melvyn, for instance. My campaign people did but they didn't tell me. Anti-Semites such as Gerald L. K. Smith and Wesley Swift moved through the state asking impressionable people who would listen to "help Richard Nixon get rid of the Jew-communists."

There was a telephone campaign as well. People would pick up the phone and a voice at the other end would say, "Did you know that Helen Gahagan Douglas is married to a man whose real name is Hesselberg?"

George Creel grew meaner as the campaign unfolded. He started describing my alleged connections to the Soviet Union and my "pro-communist" stands in the House of Representatives. At the same time Nixon brought in Senator Joseph McCarthy, national hero of the Red hunt, to speak on his behalf. McCarthy expressed his grave doubts about my loyalty.

Columnist Drew Pearson, passing through the state, wrote a sympathetic column about the keelhauling I was getting. He said that powerful forces "have combined in a skillful throat-cutting campaign." He described the tenor of the Pink Sheet and spent several paragraphs refuting its allegations. Later, when he again wrote a column supporting me, he predicted that he would be canceled by Republican newspapers in California if I lost.

The Los Angeles *Times*, the biggest newspaper in the state, was relentless in its attacks on me. Editors called Nixon "gutsy and courageous" for going after communists in high office. David Halberstam says:

"It was all red-baiting. Pink lady. If anything, the editorial voice of the *Times* was even harsher than that of Nixon. Mrs. Douglas's voice was never heard. She was never covered; she was only attacked, that was all that was permitted.

"Any conservative Democrat who backed Nixon made page one. If a Marine fighting in Korea sent back a five-dollar campaign contribution to Nixon—to keep America the way it had been when he left—it was fully reported. Any women's volunteer group was given great news space ('*This* is the group that did such a fine job in the primary and they want to repeat it and keep Helen Gahagan Douglas out of the Senate next November 7').

"There was no way, other than buying ads, that Mrs. Douglas could even get her schedules into print. It was a wonderful free ride for Nixon; he could speak to civic clubs and by raising eyebrows even imply that there was something sexual going on between Mrs. Douglas and Harry Truman (there was not, of course), but it was never reported.

"There was no attempt by any newspaper to assign a reporter to a candidate and have the reporter record the charges of that candidate; thus the candidates were unusually free to say what they wanted without any real accountability."

John Dodds, an editor at William Morrow publishers, was one of those who heard Nixon on one of the occasions when he said, "Helen Gahagan Douglas is pink right down to her underwear."

The *Times* published an appeal for volunteers to work in the

Nixon campaign to "keep left-wing Helen Gahagan Douglas out of the Senate."

The major newspapers in the East, the New York *Times* and the Washington *Post*, frequently carried stories about the shockingly abusive campaign Nixon was conducting against me and praised my record, but they carried little influence with California voters. As an example of the tone of California press coverage of the election, there was the cartoon in the San Francisco *Examiner* which showed Nixon on guard with a net labeled "Communist Control" against a horde of rats identified as "Appeaser" and "Professional Pacifist Propagandist," and so on.

A few years ago the Department of Communication and Journalism at Stanford University did an analysis of the content of political coverage during the Nixon-Douglas campaign, monitoring twelve representative newspapers from September 1 to November 7, 1950. The sampling represented about 45 percent of daily and Sunday circulation of California papers.

The results surprised me. The students found that almost 70 percent of unfavorable statements referred to me and about 30 percent of unfavorable statements were about Nixon. It was my impression at the time that only a few small papers had anything good to say about me. It was one of these, the *Independent Review*, which coined the name "Tricky Dick" Nixon.

Less than a week before voting day F. Joseph Donohue, former United States Attorney General, came to speak on my behalf. Since he had prosecuted Harry Bridges, his credentials as a communist-fighter were impeccable. He came at his own expense and told an audience at Sacramento the charges that I was a communist sympathizer were utterly false. The next day I held a rally at Union Square in San Francisco and was introduced by Congressman John F. Shelley, who for the first time on a platform referred to my opponent as "Tricky Dick."

At my campaign headquarters our morale was not improved by desperate financial problems. California was a garden of Richard Nixon billboards, reported to have cost his backers about $25,000 a month for seven months. He appeared to have unlimited funds for pamphlets, workers, Pink Sheets, radio broadcasts and bunting for his bandstands. By the end of October, with voting day a week away, I had taken in $42,757.

A good part of the money came from union people. The California Labor League for Political Education donated $4,260; $2,000 was from the ILGWU Political Education Fund, and $2,000 came from the Restaurant and Bartenders Union.

Harold Ickes wrote an appeal for donations to my campaign in *The New Republic*. He referred to me as "outstanding not only for her intelligence but for her courage—if she were a man I would say 'guts.' If even half our Senators and Representatives had Mrs. Douglas's courage and deep concern for the people, we would have the most outstanding parliament in the world."

In his plea for funds, Ickes said, "Unfortunately it has always been true in this country that those candidates who honestly believe in the people and would unselfishly serve them very often have to run impoverished campaigns. Show me candidates such as . . . Nixon, whose treasuries are bulging from the contributions of the rich and of selfish interests, and I will show you candidates who deserve to be defeated."

Some people felt that being a woman would have hurt me in that Senate race even if all other factors had been normal. There was grudging acceptance in California that a woman could serve in the House of Representatives but it was something else if she aspired to the Senate. I had little real evidence of that. Outstanding men such as Laurence Hewes, who had headed the Farm Security Camps, and Frank Graham, president of the University of North Carolina, worked hard for me.

Support of that caliber was unusual for a woman running for Senate. Still, I never felt in Congress or while campaigning that I was treated differently because of my sex. It seemed to me there was always a sincere, direct discussion of the issues. Even Richard Nixon did not say that I was a lightweight because of my sex.

Perhaps I received that kind of treatment because I expected it. I was used to strong, opinionated men because of my father and brothers and I was accustomed to arguing with them without feeling threatened. Thanks to them I learned to be at ease whether men agreed with me or disagreed with me.

If you're comfortable about what you're doing, there doesn't

seem to be much impediment between you and other people.
You haven't created a psychological problem for yourself that
can become a barrier. I had nothing to solve in being a congressman. It never occurred to me that because I was a woman I
was less qualified than some man. It just never crossed my mind.

If people are prepared when they talk, and know what they are
talking about, they are listened to seriously. If they don't know
what they are talking about, whether male or female, they aren't
listened to.

Mary McLeod Bethune was one of the prominent women who
spoke on my behalf. She said in a speech during the campaign,
"There has never been such a time when the voice of strong
women were more needed in building this great world-wide humane program than today . . . Helen Gahagan Douglas is the
voice of American democracy. . . . She has not failed the minority groups of America. We cannot fail her now."

On the other hand, clubwomen all over California received a
special mailing urging them to vote for Nixon and make sure that
a communist-supporter didn't go to the Senate.

The Los Angeles *Times* ran an editorial saying that California
was "the only state where communism becomes the main issue."
I was described as a "glamorous actress who, though not a communist, voted the Communist Party line in Congress innumer-
able times." The editorial declared that I was "the darling of the
Hollywood parlor pinks and Reds."

Though it made us miserable to do so, Melvyn and I issued
statements to attest to our loyalty. Melvyn's read, in part:

> I am informed that certain devious persons are attempting to
> defeat [Helen] by taking advantage of my absence from the state
> to spread malicious rumors to the effect that I am, or have been,
> a communist or fellow-traveller. . . .
>
> Whoever makes such a statement is an unmitigated liar and
> whoever believes it is either painfully inept or woefully misin-
> formed. . . .

He then listed his activities: working for the election of Culbert Olson; resigning from the Motion Picture Democratic Committee when it refused to condemn Russia's invasion of Finland;

member of the California State Board of Public Welfare; campaigner for Franklin Delano Roosevelt in 1940; on the record as opposing the Russo-German nonaggression pact; a member of the Fight for Freedom committee which urged passage of Lend-Lease programs; volunteering his services in Washington two days after Pearl Harbor; enlisting in the army as a private early in 1943; joining the Americans for Democratic Action in 1946; a supporter of President Truman and a critic of Henry Wallace and the Progressives. He concluded:

> As the husband of Helen Gahagan Douglas and as an individual citizen, I endorse my wife's candidacy whole-heartedly and I trust that the voters of California will not be deluded by a group of delinquents whose campaign tactics consist of dirty words and stink bombs.

I also listed my credentials in painful detail. I pointed out that I worked in the cause of migrant farmers but I had opposed certain proposals from the union because I believed them to be communist-dominated. Along with Congressman Chet Holifield, I had refused to file on the third-party ticket in 1948, though 30,000 voters had signed a petition to put the third party on the ticket and I had won my election in 1946 by a margin of only 10,000 votes. I declared:

> I am opposed to the Committee on Un-American Activities because I believe in the separation of powers in government. I do not believe we can make a committee of Congress into a court and maintain justice. I do not believe in trial by headline.
>
> Congress is subject to all kinds of political pressures. Congress is the legislative branch of our government. We have our judicial branch of the government and every man is entitled to his day in court and a fair trial.

Elmer Davis, radio commentator who enjoyed a large following, made a broadcast the week before voting day in which he protested that "the real issues have been beclouded by a dust storm raised not only by Mr. Nixon's supporters but by Mr. Nixon himself—the familiar phony cry of communism."

Davis had received the Pink Sheet in the mail and was scandal-

ized. He pointed out, "Senator Taft has voted the same as Marcantonio . . . but that doesn't make Mr. Taft a communist. . . .

"When campaigns are fought that way I don't know whether it
is much use to suggest that the citizens look at the facts. . . .

"George Creel . . . seems to think that communists and liberals are the same thing. . . . This is silly, of course; but it is
what a lot of people are trying to tell the voters."

Harry Truman declared in a press conference on November 3
that I was a true and loyal member of the Democratic party. Accusations that I wasn't a good Democrat, he said, were untrue.
People in the eastern part of the country who weren't aware of
the bloodbath of the California campaign thought it was a curious statement for one Democrat to have to make about another.

The anonymous telephone calls to tell voters that I was a communist began midway in the campaign but reached a peak in the
final few days. They were the same as those used to destroy Jerry
Voorhis. People picked up their phones and a person with a pleasant, concerned voice would say, "Did you know that Helen
Gahagan Douglas is a communist?" and hang up.

An MGM producer who received such a call was so angry that
he later paid for some investigation of the magnitude of the operation. He told me that he believed the total was half a million
calls. Certainly, it was a remarkably thorough blitz of the state.

The calls must have been a factor in the unpleasant incidents
which occurred a few times in the past days of the campaign,
when the station wagon in which I traveled was pelted with
stones. What was printed against me was only a small part of
what was done. Nixon and Chotiner had woven a spider's web of
sticky lies, a deadly whispering campaign that was impossible to
fight.

As a sample, there was an incident one of my workers
witnessed where Nixon greeted a woman holding a baby and said
to her, "If you vote for Douglas we will still be at war in Asia
when he's old enough to fight." To appreciate how devastating
such a remark could be, you have to remember that Americans
were dying in a war in Korea against communists.

Toward the end of the campaign, I knew I would lose. There
was nothing tangible, no poll reliable enough to trust, but failure

was in the air. When I traveled in the northern part of the state, my campaign team insisted on sending guards along to protect me. The mood of the crowd had become dangerously ugly.

"I accuse my opponent . . . of trying to steal this election by drugging the voters with political poison concocted of misrepresentation and false charges," I told audiences. It had a brave sound, but I knew that it was hopeless. Ed Lybeck and other seasoned politicians also were aware that Nixon would win but they worked doggedly anyway. Making between ten and fifteen speeches a day, I was almost too tired sometimes to drag myself out of the car and up the steps to the podium, but I was determined not to quit.

On the day before the election, cities were showered with leaflets offering prizes of silver tableware to people who answered "Vote for Nixon" when called by Nixon's headquarters staff. They followed through, too, and placed a blizzard of calls all over the state. Delighted recipients told their friends until it seemed that everyone was saying "Vote for Nixon" instead of "Hello." It may have won some votes, but I deplore that kind of tactic. It patronizes voters and shows contempt for the democratic process.

My major concern was not whether I would lose, because I knew that I would, or by how much, because I was quite certain that Nixon's victory would be smashing. I was worried about how I would feel the morning after the election. I didn't want Richard Nixon to have the final victory of destroying me along with my political career.

I had been in politics a total of ten years, four of them working within the party in the state and six of them in the U. S. Congress. On several occasions I was present when candidates lost; often I saw them over a long period after their defeat. In almost every case, they seemed to take what had happened to them on a personal level. It was as though their intrinsic worth as human beings had been held up to the light, examined carefully and impartially, and rejected. Their pride was hurt but they covered by saying that their only regret was for the country because they were needed in government.

I believe it is wrong for a losing candidate to have that perspective. In our system it isn't the case that only one person, or even two or three in a given district are uniquely qualified to serve in Congress. There are always a number of fine people in both parties who can do a fine job of representing a district. We are a varied people and a variety of views in Congress is a healthy thing.

Just because one person has done an adequate job in Congress doesn't mean that a different person can't follow and also perform adequately. The country isn't lost irrevocably even when a superior congressman is unseated. That is a totalitarian view; it is against our whole system. With all its faults and imperfections, our system is the best that has yet evolved. Its strength is that the absence of a fine congressman or the presence of a poor one doesn't disturb the roots a bit.

I was depressed therefore to see how some politicians react to defeat. They allow themselves to be destroyed by their belief that they have been mutilated and rejected, which makes them bitter and angry. In some cases, they are consumed afterward by hatred of the person who won the election. When you meet them, even years later, they talk about the campaign as though the events leading to their demise had occurred a week ago. They carry their opponent with them still.

I didn't want Nixon's defeat of me to take anything more away from me than my place in Congress.

My first campaign hadn't been a picnic, but this had been shocking. The worst moment, a sight I couldn't shake, was when children picked up rocks and threw them at my car, at me. I knew that in order to survive I would have to accept the rocks and the Nixon campaign, shrug them off and move on. I wondered if I would be able to do it.

In the final few days it was on my mind a good deal. I thought, "All right, Helen, you've seen other defeated candidates go to pieces. What's going to happen to you?" I didn't brood about it. There was so much to do, for one thing, what with planeloads of alarmed Democrats coming from Washington to help me with last-minute defenses of my character. But I did think about it several times as the campaign was ending.

When I woke up the next morning I felt free, uninjured, whole. Nixon had his victory but I had mine. There wasn't any part of me that was twisted. I wasn't a soul in torment who would brood about Richard Nixon for years to come. He hadn't touched me. I didn't carry Richard Nixon with me, thank God.

I had lunch not long ago in San Francisco with Millie Logan, who worked on the 1950 campaign. We were reminiscing and she looked at me seriously.

"You know, Helen, you're the only one who got through unscathed."

I know that India Edwards, vice-chairman of the Democratic National Committee, felt that Nixon did destroy me politically. Afterward people wondered why I wasn't given some appointment such as in the Department of the Interior or the United Nations. India replied that I couldn't have been appointed dogcatcher.

Drew Pearson wrote that Oscar Chapman talked to Harry Truman early in 1952 about appointing me Assistant Secretary of the Interior. Truman's reply was, "We may be taking on too many fights at this time. Let me think about it."

But Millie was right. I wasn't destroyed as a person. I woke up the morning of the election positively lighthearted.

Nixon defeated me by a margin of 680,947 votes, the biggest victory of any Senate election that year. While he was going from one victory celebration to another, playing "Happy Days Are Here Again" on the piano, my campaign headquarters was a desolate scene. Most of the people who worked in the office hadn't accepted the possibility that I would lose. When the returns showed Nixon's landslide, they suffered a brutal shock.

Their pain was the most distressing aspect of that night. I sat at my desk and took phone call after phone call from friends who were shattered by what had happened. A wealthy vintner in the Bakersfield-Fresno area was one of the callers. He was almost weeping. He said, "Don't concede, don't concede." I was startled. The man hadn't been one of my supporters. I learned later that he needed a large loan and pressure had been brought to bear. If he had come out in favor of me, he wouldn't have gotten the loan. So when he saw me losing, he was full of remorse.

A newspaper picture the day after the election shows me in my office. Juanita Terry looks stricken. She told me it felt like the end of the world. Another woman is crying openly. And I am smiling. The caption read, as I remember it, *Helen Gahagan Douglas Consoles Her Staff*.

In the next few days I went all over the state thanking people who had helped me. It was clear to me that they felt worse than I did. I was so pleased that I had escaped the terrible burden of hating Richard Nixon that I was almost elated.

Before Watergate and its revelations of Nixon's character, I was among those who didn't believe it was possible for him to be a great President. Even if he had succeeded in the White House, it would not have offset the kind of campaign he waged in 1950, the campaign he waged against Jerry Voorhis in 1946, the one against Adlai Stevenson for the presidency, what he said about Dean Acheson, about Harry Truman.

Richard Nixon had developed certain habits that became his technique for winning. The habits were consistent whenever he was under stress. I believe that people do revert to patterns of behavior that are basic to them whenever they are in trouble. Nixon established his basic pattern when he defeated Jerry Voorhis by destroying his opponent's reputation rather than fighting on the issues.

That same pattern emerged when Nixon was preparing for his second presidential campaign. It resulted in people close to him sending burglars into the Democratic party headquarters in the Watergate Hotel. It was the reason the FBI was used in the way it was. Under stress, Nixon reverted to what had served him in the past, which was to wage a dirty campaign. When frightened, people do revert that way.

I had a habit too. My habit, instilled in me by my father, was the habit of analyzing what was the best course of action. That habit, to tell the truth, was quite enough to occupy my forces fully. I sat down and figured out what was right, and then I did it. After that, I never worried about what was going to happen to me.

That's why I woke up free on the morning after the election. I harbored no burden of resentment. I felt no need to go around explaining that I really wasn't a communist and that I wasn't plotting the overthrow of my country. I didn't do that. I had done the best job I could in the Congress. I was proud of my record. I knew I was respected in Washington by my colleagues, even some who didn't agree with me, and by people who know what is going on in Congress.

I made the race for reasons that were proper, to save the 160-acre limit in the Reclamation Act, and I think it helped. Sheridan Downey resigned from the Senate immediately after my defeat to make way for Richard Nixon to be a senior senator. Downey then took a job with the oil companies as their lobbyist on the Hill, but with him out of the Senate there was less heat on the reclamation program for a long time. Attacks almost ceased, in fact, and when they did happen there were others in Congress who leaped to its defense.

John Rankin, my antagonist from Mississippi, was one of those who fought brilliantly against erosion of the Reclamation Act. We disagreed on almost every other subject but we stood together on that one.

One indication of the disappointment I must have felt, but scarcely acknowledged, was that I didn't want to talk about the campaign. I steered my friends off the doleful postmortems and refused totally to disinter the events of the campaign in the media. Far from feeling a compulsion to talk about Nixon and what he did, I avoided the subject. It was unpleasant. I wanted to forget it.

Juanita Terry went to work for Hubert Humphrey and stayed with him for six years, taking care of the problems his constituents raised. Then she became Jimmy Roosevelt's administrative assistant for six years, functioning as the indispensable person for him in the same way as Evelyn Chavoor had for me.

Evie remained in Washington and carved for herself a remarkable career that included working for Abe Fortas for a time and then Senator Blair Moody of Michigan. When Moody was defeated in 1952, Evie went to work in the Democratic National Committee as assistant to the director of the Research Division.

Because her family needed her from time to time, she was in California to help Richard Graves when he ran for governor and then, back in Washington, was the first woman to be named assistant to the Democratic National Chairman, who was then Paul

338 A FULL LIFEA FULL LIFE

Butler. Following that, my brother Walter persuaded Evie to be office manager for the Gahagan Dredging Corporation, which was engaged in some exciting work in Venezuela, dredging some 150 million cubic yards of muck out of the Orinoco River for U. S. Steel. Thanks to Walter, who was turning the moribund family business into a huge international success, the eighth-largest river in the world was opened to navigation, connecting rich iron ore deposits to the sea.

As for me, I observed my fiftieth birthday two weeks after my defeat with my mind already made up that I would go back to the stage or, better still, retrain my voice so that I could sing again. Meanwhile, I had to deal with my campaign debts.

I was touched that a few people, three or four, sent money after the campaign when they heard that my donations, $156,172, didn't cover all expenses. Evie Chavoor paid off the most pressing creditors, which left me with a relatively small amount owing, some $16,000.

When Melvyn and I put our house in the Outpost up for sale, rumor had it that I was forced to do it to pay my campaign debts. That wasn't true. We made that decision because Melvyn was living much of the time in New York to be near the theater. It was a nuisance to keep finding suitable tenants for it, and the house was too expensive to maintain empty. So we decided to put it on the market.

Eventually I paid off my debts, every cent, from the money I got from giving lectures. I come from a family of talkers, so it was an easy matter for me to go on the lecture circuit and give speeches with such titles as "Dollars Will Not Win the Cold War."

Some people turned out because they expected I would use the occasion to talk about Richard Nixon. Reporters dogged me asking questions about that 1950 campaign. To everyone I said politely and firmly that the subject was closed. I had come to discuss an issue and that was all I was prepared to talk about.

I took great pride in settling my campaign debts myself. Melvyn helped by paying the income tax on my earnings so the whole amount from the lectures could go on the campaign bills. He was amused at my insistence on discharging my debts myself. He said it would be simpler for him to just take care of it, but I couldn't allow that.

Richard Nixon declared donations of $62,899, less than half of mine. I could only laugh. Using the cost of his billboards, which is considered a reliable gauge of campaign expenses, estimates of his outlay are about $1.75 million. This seems realistic in view of the amount I know Jimmy Roosevelt spent, $1.5 million.

One of Nixon's donations was $52,000. Drew Pearson mentioned in his *Diaries* that Nixon reportedly had $52,000 from Union Oil in California in 1950. Pearson had a carbon copy of a letter to that effect.

Pearson also commented on a conspiracy launched by H. L. Hunt, the oil tycoon, by which enormous donations from oil companies were pumped into Nixon's coffers in 1950 and again in 1952 when Nixon succeeded in his campaign to be named running mate to Dwight D. Eisenhower. Pearson's informant, Lawrence Westbrook, heard the story while helping Sam Rayburn campaign in Texas. Westbrook said that Eisenhower never knew that oil interests were funding Nixon.

Two years after defeating me, Richard Nixon, at thirty-nine, was Vice-President of the United States.

My brother Walter Gahagan met a man at a fancy resort in Florida one time who appeared to have something on his mind. Walter let him steer the conversation around to the California campaign of 1950. The man seemed to know a lot about it. After a pause he said, very contritely, "We hated to do it to such a nice woman but we wanted Richard Nixon in the Senate. We spent three hundred and fifty thousand dollars on the people who did the whispering campaign."

As I moved about the state in the aftermath of the election, my campaign workers told me the horror stories they had been concealing. It was sickening stuff. Over the years I heard more of those stories in bits and pieces. A lot of Catholics couldn't forgive the sermons in the churches and the Nixon people posted outside with the Pink Sheets. Harold Tipton, my Northern California campaign manager, studied the election returns and came to the conclusion that "Catholics put Nixon in the Senate."

He said, "The campaigning of the Catholic church, especially in the building trades unions in the north, was very important."

Some of my workers committed themselves passionately to politics as a result of what they saw in 1950. They were to help Adlai Stevenson run against Eisenhower and Nixon, and I saw them again when I campaigned for John F. Kennedy. They and their children are still helping liberal Democrats.

One such is Phillip Burton, who in 1974 was chairman of the Democratic caucus in the House of Representatives. He said his decision to run for political office was made during the 1950 campaign. "I took a private oath after Helen was defeated by Nixon's despicable campaign that I was going to work to see the day that man would be retired from public life," he said.

Iphigene Sulzberger, daughter of Adolph Ochs who bought the New York *Times* in 1896, had somewhat the same reaction. In an interview in *New York* magazine in January 1977, she told writer Lally Weymouth, "I always thought that he [Nixon] was an evil man. My conscience is clear from the beginning; from the time he ran against Helen Gahagan Douglas, I never had any use for him."

I read in David Halberstam's book *The Powers That Be* that Nixon owed $5,000 when the campaign ended. Asa Call's wife said it would be her pleasure to write a check for the entire amount, and she did.

When people criticized Nixon for the smear tactics he used against me, he defended himself with a number of justifications. One was that he couldn't avoid making communism an issue because Manchester Boddy's campaign already had accused me of every red affiliation, short of actually saying that I was a communist. Or he said that he was famous for his involvement in the Alger Hiss case and so was expected to continue to guard America against communists.

Nixon denied that his office made the phone calls about me being a communist. He even claimed for a time that such calls never happened. Faced with irrefutable proof that they did, he declared that my supporters had placed the calls in order to create an issue!

In 1957, when Richard Nixon was still Vice-President, he received a number of distinguished British journalists and publishers. Richard Stout, respected writer for *The New Republic*, was there and asked Nixon how he could have run such a dreadful campaign against Helen Gahagan Douglas. According to those present, Nixon, who was born in 1913 and so was thirty-seven in 1950, looked shamefaced and sorry and said, "I want you to understand I was a very young man."

Nixon's simple objective in that 1950 campaign was to take Democratic votes away from me. He decided the way to accomplish that was to destroy confidence in my integrity. As he saw the election, it was a question of mathematics. No scruples stood in his way to correct the imbalance of Republicans and Democrats in the state.

There's not much to say about the 1950 campaign except that a man ran for Senate who wanted to get there, and didn't care how.

Speaking Out

After the defeat I went back to Washington to finish my term in the House of Representatives. I found it a special wrench to be meeting for the last time on the Foreign Affairs Committee. Three others were also there for the last time. Mike Mansfield and Jack Javits also had run for the Senate in 1950 and Abe Ribicoff made himself a candidate for governor in Connecticut.

When I was presented with an engraved parchment resolution about my value to the committee, signed by all the members, Republican and Democrat, I was deeply moved. I discovered, however, that each of us departing the committee had received one.

I do treasure Adolph Sabath's remarks delivered on the floor of the House on December 6, 1950, after Nixon's victory:

> The California delegation will show the absence of three exceptionally fine members, among them Mrs. Helen Gahagan Douglas.
>
> I have been in the House for forty-four years and have served with many efficient ladies. History will record in years to come that the membership of this, the Eighty-first Congress, excelled the membership of all previous Congresses.
>
> Mrs. Douglas, in my opinion, has been one of its foremost members, industrious, courageous, unafraid, able and efficient. I know we will miss her charming presence and helpfulness.

The assumption was that I would lick my wounds awhile and run again. Democrats in Nevada came to see me about running for Congress in that state. I considered another offer from a district in Northern California where people were anxious to have me. A third offer came from the Northwest.

Sometimes I was tempted but I turned them all down. I decided that my children and my husband had suffered enough. As

I told Alis de Sola, I suspected that my marriage could not have survived another term in Congress.

People speculated that our marriage was in trouble because in those days it was highly unusual for a couple to be separated for long periods, except during a war. I think we were just ahead of our time. Nowadays many people work out a relationship that accommodates two careers and results in extended periods of separation. That kind of arrangement isn't uncommon now, but thirty years ago people found it strange. Gossip had it that we were no longer a marriage except in name.

That was untrue. In fact, the reality was exactly the opposite. If we hadn't cared so much we would never have dared put such a strain on our marriage. When you truly love someone, you're bound to that person whether you are with him or not. No one has to talk about it, or explain, or wonder. It simply happens.

I see separateness in two ways. There is the fundamental separateness of all active people who pursue individual paths in order to achieve growth and satisfaction. And there is the separateness which is liberation and independence. Minorities struggle for that kind of separateness and so do women; and so do adolescents. No one can give you that but yourself. No one.

When you love deeply, you give up a part of that achievement naturally because you become aware of the other person. Your decisions are less free because they take the other into consideration. Consciously and unconsciously, you calculate what course of action is best for you as a couple rather than for just you as an individual. If you value your marriage highly, and I did, the decisions you make aren't painful in the least. They feel right. Far from being a loss to give up a career in politics, it was satisfying.

Who would want to be like a lost star out there in the sky? Wherever I went, however preoccupied I was, I always felt part of a network of lives intensely tied to mine: Melvyn, Peter and Mary Helen, Lilli, my mother, my brothers, my nieces and nephews. It changed nothing that I didn't see them for a few weeks or even months.

The situation with the children was different. Peter and Mary Helen had been without me for a long time and were showing unmistakable signs of the stress such absences place on children. They were good about it and never complained but I was brought up in a household where mother was always home, and it made me uneasy that they were growing up in a household where mother was almost never there.

I once was asked how I saw the contrary pulls of working and mothering by *Parents* magazine, which published my replies to a number of questions in July 1972. I said then that a working mother can often enrich the lives of her children because she looks at the world from a broader perspective. She can enlarge their outlook as well.

When she isn't able to be at home, there is no doubt in my mind that the best substitute for her presence is a good, professionally staffed day-care center. Young women can continue their careers and raise a family at the same time, as I did, but it is not easy.

Some careers demand a great deal of time and so do babies and little children. In my case, social life outside the home was cut to a bare minimum so that all free time could be devoted to the children. Happily, Melvyn and I were able to afford excellent people to care for them while we were away.

For a career woman, marriage and a family can surely be a continuing, developing and sustaining experience—not only for her, but for her husband and children as well. When a marriage works, nothing on earth can take its place.

I was still turning over my decision to leave politics while I disposed of my house in Washington, packed the files in my office and finished my term in the House of Representatives. That done, I returned to California. Melvyn was still on the road and the children were at Chadwick School, coming home only on weekends. I rented the big house for what was to be the last time and moved into an agreeable furnished apartment in a building frequented by actors.

I found myself drawn to New York. I started to read plays, looking for something suitable, and happily threw myself into working on retraining my voice. When we discovered that the house in the Outpost would need expensive repairs, I took it as

an omen. Since Melvyn had no intention of ever again tying himself to Hollywood films, he readily agreed that we should sell it
and settle in the East. What leaped to mind immediately was
Vermont. We could winterize Cliff Mull, I thought, and make it
our year-round base.

When I talked to my brother Walter about selling the house
in California, he was amazed when I told him blissfully, "I will
have the house in Vermont." It sounded so good aloud that I
said it again.

We could have stayed in California—in Carmel perhaps, which
Melvyn loved—and some friends suggested we try Connecticut. I
never had anything else in mind but returning to Vermont. I
spent hours in raptures of planning how I would renovate and restore Cliff Mull. I had lived in three major centers of America—
New York, Washington and California—and I found charming,
even handsome houses in all three. I was attached to none of
them; Vermont was pulling at me.

I felt the way I did in my childhood when I couldn't wait for
the summer to begin and the family to move to Vermont. I used
to nag, Can't we go early? Do we have to stay until the end of
school? What difference does a few more days in school make?
Why can't we go early? When we neared Cliff Mull I'd always
beg to get out of the car down below the road and run the rest of
the way. When I came to the driveway I would hug every tree
and talk to each one, saying "I'm so glad we're here," and "How
was the winter?" And I was sixteen years old.

Melvyn was very sweet and understanding about my obsession
with Vermont. We started by living in the lower house where the
chauffeur's quarters had been while the big house, shuttered for
years and falling apart, was being repaired. Little by little, we did
the renovations. One of the things I wanted was to put windows
all the way around the living room so I could see the marvelous
light of Vermont from every perspective. Melvyn groaned. He
said we would freeze every spring and fall with so much glass
around us.

"Certainly not," I retorted. "We'll have Thermopanes. Why
would anyone want to be closed up in a house without being able
to see outside?"

In the third summer of our return East, we moved into Cliff Mull and my joy was complete.

When people ask me, "Where do you live?" I answer, "Vermont." They look confused because their understanding is that we live in New York. "Oh, that." I explain, "We do have an apartment on Riverside Drive but we don't live in New York in the sense of *living*." At which some look even more confused.

Happily, Melvyn turned into a Vermonter too; Vermont slowly took him over. He also watches the light change and the lovely colors of the mountains and lake. He was always interested in birds but he became more absorbed in trying to spot the rare ones. The autumn when my illness required me to be in New York for treatment, Melvyn remained behind in Vermont for a while. He told me that he hated to leave. He could have said nothing that would have given me greater pleasure. I thought to myself, "Aha, you'll soon be trapped." Perhaps someday we will stay there year-round—and freeze, as he predicted.

My brother Walter and his wife also love Vermont. The whole generation of our children and their two children are attached to Cliff Mull and the houses that surround it. Lilli's children also are ardent Vermonters but she never shared my passion for Cliff Mull. She loved the ocean and relaxed only when she was beside the sea. We were very different in that respect. I get bored with the sea; even the storms aren't as thrilling as our Vermont storms.

We had a hurricane in Vermont in 1977 that caught Mary Helen and me in our car as we were returning from shopping. The road to the house is curved and steep between giant trees. The scene was wild, with branches whipping through the air and trees crashing to the ground around us. Melvyn was in the house, motioning frantically for us to stay in the car. He thinks of me as a frail person who might well have been blown off the face of the hill by the winds.

To his horror, he saw an enormous tree begin to topple straight down onto us. We were unaware of it and kept driving on as it crashed inches behind our small car. Melvyn's expression told us that something drastic had happened so we obeyed his signals to sit still until the worst was over.

When we surveyed the shambles a few minutes later we found

that some forty trees were down all over the place, so we couldn't get the car out. Because wires were also down, the electric pump for our artesian well wasn't working and the house was without power and telephones. The tree that missed us so narrowly was stretched across our road and the road to my nephew's place as well.

Mary and I trudged around, marveling at the force nature had unleashed. Melvyn, still shaken, remained inside. I think he thought my enthusiasm for the storm's power was somewhat misplaced, but my spirits could not be dampened. A Vermont storm does take you into its middle. The experience is fearful but you have the exultation of being one with nature. You feel how fragile you are, how fragile the world is. I feel at home in a storm and Vermont storms are pure heaven.

Melvyn Douglas:

Helen didn't like to talk about her insides. She was not an introspective person—or if she was, if she looked inside herself, she did it very, very privately. She didn't talk to anyone, including me, about her feelings. I can count on the fingers of one hand the times when we've talked and Helen dug into herself. I would not even say that she did that to any great extent in terms that people today do so much of. She rather disliked that. It was distasteful to her.

The only emotional outburst that I remember happened after her first operation for cancer, a mastectomy, which delayed our getting to Vermont. We'd made some more renovations on the house and she was tremendously enthusiastic about them. Because she couldn't actively supervise the work, other people went out of their way—her niece Joan, her nephew Herbert Walker, and others—to make it as lovely as possible.

She couldn't wait to get up to Vermont and fretted for the month or six weeks of her recuperation and treatment. We got out of the car and had to walk around to reach the side of the house where the new part was. When she came face to face with it she just stood there. Tears welled out of her eyes and poured down her cheeks. She was happy beyond words. It obviously was a joyous experience for her and I think maybe she had felt that she mightn't see it.

But she didn't say these things.

As our family settled in New York and Vermont I found a play that I wanted to do. It was *First Lady,* by Katharine Dayton and George S. Kaufman, which the New York City Theatre Company produced. We opened in Washington on May 23, 1952, in the New Gayety Theatre with me in the title role and a cast that included Edna Best and Peggy Ann Garner. The reviews were fine and we brought the show into New York a week later.

I went around to see Madame Cehanovska, who was nearing her nineties but still listened to former pupils and gave stern advice on voice improvement. I was working on a repertoire of songs for the concert stage. A record company approached me to put some of the songs on records but I don't believe they were released. I did have the pleasure of reading Emily Dickinson's poems on the Caedmon *Great American Poetry* series.

That summer I campaigned for Adlai Stevenson against the Republican candidate for the presidency, Dwight D. Eisenhower, and his running mate, Richard Nixon. Though I found that interest in the 1950 campaign in California was remarkably alive wherever I went, I avoided any mention of it. I talked about the issues. It was the same choice I made in 1950; I know only one way to campaign.

Adlai Stevenson was defeated by the Eisenhower-Nixon ticket. With heavy heart I wrote him a note. "You were magnificent in the recent campaign," I told him. "You never hit a false note. You have won the confidence, the admiration and the affection of millions of people. I hope for the sake of our country that you will lead the Democratic party for the next four years and that you will be the Democratic candidate in 1956. . . ."

With the Republicans in power in Washington, the fanatics of the House Un-American Activities Committee, now headed by Senator Joseph McCarthy, grew in influence and terror. They were reaching out to destroy all those good people prominently associated with Franklin Roosevelt's New Deal. Charles Hogan was being accused of communism. Agents asked the superintendent of his building, his grocer, his friends, "Did you ever hear Charles Hogan say that he was in favor of admission of Red China to the United Nations?"

And of course they had, because Hogo believed that it was folly to try to pretend that one of the world's largest countries didn't exist. I prepared a sworn testimonial that Charles Hogan was not a communist, much as it outraged me that such a defense was required. In it I declared that I had known Hogo and his wife Betty Ballantine for many years, including the period when he was connected with the San Francisco School for Social Studies, which I said developed "educational techniques somewhat like a New England Town Meeting, open discussion and exchange of viewpoints in direct antithesis to Communist party activities and ideals."

I declared, "If Mr. Hogan at any time advocated a position which indicated an adherence to the Communist party line in any degree, I would have been instantly aware of it. To the contrary, I say without hesitation that he was and still is a consistent liberal who has always been aware of the dangers of communism and of the purposes behind communist advocacy of certain policies."

The loyalty of Catherine Bauer Wurster was also questioned. I had appointed her assistant chairman of the Northern California Democratic Committee in 1940 and said in an affidavit concerning her, "She is a brilliant woman of independent mind and her attitudes are completely inconsistent with membership in the Communist party or adherence to the Communist party line."

My great friend Alexander Meiklejohn was also attacked. I drew up another sworn statement in which I said, "He is so much of a purist in the matter of civil liberties that his entire life is devoted to the proposition that we should not go back an iota from the great democratic achievements which have already been obtained. His great independence of mind and his consistent refusal to accept any dogmas, regardless of the proponent of that dogma, makes it inconceivable to me for him to be a member of the Communist Party."

Most Americans, it seemed, readily accepted the line that the country was in peril from subversives. Conservatives in office could exploit those fears to discredit those in or out of public office who believed in such "pinko" causes as Equal Employment Opportunity, Medicare and housing for the poor. The most sensationalized hearings before HUAC concerned the "Hollywood Ten," the leftist screenwriters who stood accused of plotting against their country. Among those almost destroyed in the purges at the studios were John Garfield and Edward Dmytryk, the director.

The public panicked because Americans had the delusion that we alone had the secret of the atom bomb and that we could guard it if we were zealous about rooting out traitors. The weakness of that position was that once the bomb was dropped on Hiroshima it was no longer a secret, but this was never understood. In trying to make something new, half the undertaking lies in discovering whether it can be done. Once it has been established that it can, duplication is inevitable.

The process by which the bomb was produced was part of scientific research that had been going on in many parts of the world for years. In fact, we weren't the first. Albert Einstein warned President Roosevelt that the Germans were working on such a bomb before we started. Roosevelt's reaction was to pull together a crack team of scientists, give them unlimited funds and order them to build the bomb for America ahead of the Germans. At that point secrecy was vital to prevent Germany from hurrying its own scientists, but after Hiroshima secrecy was irrelevant.

Unfortunately the Cold War distorted this truth. Americans grew to be so neurotic on the subject of secrecy that they did a number of foolish things which eventually led to McCarthyism.

I'm sorry that the Baruch plan proposing international control of atomic energy didn't succeed. The Russians weren't frightened because we had the bomb—they were sophisticated enough to know that it was only a matter of time before they would have it also. The fear of spies that destroyed so many reputations and careers was created by politicians to gain office. That kind of fear can spread quickly because it is so simple to grasp. Americans bought the silliness that we should protect secrets, that we *could* protect secrets.

In 1945, before the world started to line up with Russia on one side and the United States on the other, there was a space where sanity might have prevailed. Before every nation started on the disastrous course of the arms race, we might have gained a tight, effective ban on the worst weapons.

I support those organizations such as World Federalism, the International League for Peace and Freedom, the SANE Nuclear Policy Committee and others who say that we have to work for total disarmament under international controls and a World Court, with *power*, or we are going to end up in the last terrible holocaust.

In such an environment of shared authority, McCarthyism could not have existed. In the early 1950s, however, it dominated our lives. Melvyn and I watched in agony as our friends suffered. I determined that if I were attacked I would fight back. When Zasu Pitts made some vile statements during the 1950 campaign about my loyalty, I was dissuaded from suing her by J. Ray Files, a prominent Los Angeles lawyer and Democrat. Reluctantly I accepted his advice that the area of one's patriotism is too nebulous to bring before the courts. You can't prove you're an American by waving Old Glory.

Early in 1953 the Los Angeles *Times* printed a headline: RED DISCUSSIONS DECLARED HELD EACH WEEK AT HELEN GAHAGAN DOUGLAS' HOME. The story concerned a libel action laid by Assemblyman Vernon Kilpatrick against Beverly Hills police chief G. H. Anderson. A woman witness at the trial stated that nine or ten years earlier Kilpatrick had invited her to my house, where a group of people discussed methods of bringing about the economic collapse of America.

Kilpatrick was a fine assemblyman who worked hard all his life for less advantaged people, for which he was pilloried as a communist. The defense against his libel action was to smear me as well.

I drafted a letter which I proposed to send to the *Times*. It began: "Many of my friends in California have gotten in touch with me to express their indignation at the testimony of a woman whose name I have never heard before and about whom I know nothing. . . . According to your paper this woman testified that some nine or ten years ago Mr. Kilpatrick allegedly invited her to an open house meeting at my home and allegedly told her that this meeting was of people who planned or hoped to bring about the economic collapse of our country.

"No group ever met at my home at open house or any other time, for any such purpose. To say that I have anything to do with such ideas is untrue, fantastic, and utter nonsense. . . .

"I have never been a communist and I'm prepared to swear to it . . ."

Before sending the letter I consulted people I trusted. One of them was Lillian Ford, wife of the former California congressman. Lillian replied promptly. "Everything you say is true and your comments are valid," she wrote. "The comments of that Mrs. Haines at the Kilpatrick trial are a disgrace. But Florence Reynolds and others agree that it is extremely unwise for you to answer at this time.

"As sure as you make the statement 'I have never been a communist and I'm prepared to swear to it,' trouble will follow. You'll be called before HUAC and once you're sworn they'll produce crackpots who'll claim to have attended communist meetings where you advocated communism. Then you'll be prosecuted for perjury.

"We all think that this is a trap. I know it seems cowardly to keep quiet under such outrage, but you mustn't invite and lay yourself open to prosecution."

I could see her point. Americans no longer were protected by our constitutional guarantees of freedom of opinion and freedom of speech and freedom of assembly. Those had vanished under McCarthyism. The tyrants who had seized control of the House still had public support for the atrocities they were committing against decent Americans.

Lillian Ford urged me to wait out the madness. It would pass, she counseled. Meanwhile I would have to be wary and watchful. Certain congressmen would like nothing better than to drag me before HUAC and hire witnesses to testify against me, falsely and effectively.

"The fever will pass," she repeated, "as all hysterically induced movements do."

What she recommended was exactly the opposite of what I wanted to do. I longed to confront the lies and slanders against me. But I could see the wisdom of what she said. The United States was indeed in an unnatural period when justice seemed to be suspended.

My lawyer felt the same way when I asked about suing for libel. He told me such an action would drag on for months and months. "It'll take so much out of you," he warned. "You don't realize what this will cost you. You were able to rise above the campaign of 1950. This could be the last experience that you'll have to rise above."

So I dropped my plans to protest. I sat still. But I didn't stop trying to protect my friends from similar slanders and attacks. When I heard that Myer Cohen was being hauled before a loyalty board, I sent a sworn statement on his behalf. I said that he was a teacher in the San Francisco School of Social Studies when I met him and displayed "an abhorrence of communism and other forms of totalitarianism.

"These are people," I wrote (Myer's wife was also accused of being a communist), "whose lives have been devoted to making people think for themselves so that they may be better citizens— just the opposite of the communist approach."

I had begun the first of what was to become an enriching part of my life, study tours of evolving nations where I could discover firsthand what was happening and what was needed. The American Christian Palestine Committee sponsored a visit to Egypt, Cyprus and the new state of Israel. Cyprus became part of the tour because it was impossible then to travel directly from Egypt to Israel.

I was astounded by the change in Israel in the nineteen years since Melvyn and I had made our romantic trip around the world. Where there had been barren hills there now were terraces and forests. I marveled at the resourcefulness, ingenuity and courage it had taken to assimilate 300,000 homeless, destitute European Jews in only two and a half years. Israel had saved more Jewish lives than the rest of the world's countries put together.

We visited the holy places, spent two days at the Sea of Galilee, toured a hospital with Hadassah women, visited a school and the beautiful Weizmann Institute of Science, named for the man whose wartime discovery of a formula for cordite overcame

England's shortage of high explosives and contributed significantly to the Allied victory.

Afterward I returned to the lecture circuit to talk in glowing terms about what Israel was doing. The brochures produced by the people who arranged my speaking engagements listed accolades that had come my way. The editors of the Book of Knowledge named me "one of the twelve smartest women in the world," and *Pageant* magazine polled 272 women journalists who picked me as one of the twenty women who exerted the greatest influence on American life.

My brother Walter took Lilli and me into the flourishing Gahagan Dredging Corporation. I was named secretary and spent a good deal of time in the New York office. One of my projects was to work on a history of the eighty-eight-year-old family company and another was to advise Walter on political and economic developments in the far-flung countries where he was considering operations.

Later, when Walter returned to the United States, Lilli took complete charge of the Venezuela office. Besides dredging a 180-mile waterway in the Oronoco River, Gagahan Dredging also engineered for the Venezuelan government on Lake Maracaibo, opening up the lake to oil tankers. Lilli, a business whiz, proved to be an invaluable asset.

Melvyn and I prepared a two-hander for the stage, a series of dramatizations chosen from some of our favorite writers, Chekhov, George Sand, Oscar Wilde, Stephen Vincent Benét, H. G. Wells, Alis de Sola, O. Henry, Shakespeare and, of course, Emily Dickinson.

Just before we were to begin a tour with it, Melvyn received a call. Paul Muni had developed cancer that required the removal of an eye, as a result of which he had to drop out of the play *Inherit the Wind*. The part was offered to Melvyn. It was the first major dramatic role that had come his way since he left Broadway for films, so the opportunity was too important to miss. Basil Rathbone replaced him in what we called *One Plus One* and we toured it cheerfully through Norfolk, Sioux Falls, Buffalo, Brooklyn, Johnstown, Nashville, Savanna, Auburn, Chicago, Oklahoma and other places for several months.

With that under my belt, I put together a concert I called "A Recital of Songs and Poems." The poems included several from Emily Dickinson: *I'm Nobody, If You Were Coming in the Fall, I Felt a Funeral in My Brain, Tie the Strings to my Life,* and *My Lord,* and some of Gertrude Stein and Marianne Moore. The songs were from Schumann, Joseph Marx, Richard Strauss, and Léo Delibes, and some haunting folk songs from the Hebrides.

To my great sorrow, Madame Sophia Cehanovska was not there to hear me. She died at the grand age of ninety-one just before I started the tour with Basil Rathbone. George and I sorrowfully conveyed her body to the crematorium where we took part in a simple farewell service.

My "Recital" opened in Carnegie Hall on September 27, 1956. The critics were kind but I could see that it was not possible for me, at fifty-six, to have a first-rate voice. The *Herald Tribune* review scrupulously reported on the contents of the program and added:

> The basic quality of her soprano is sturdy and hale and her powers of projection are enormous.

The New York *Times* commented:

> The singing was interspersed with poetry readings . . . employing her large, deep-sounding voice like the accomplished actress she is. These low-pitched sounds also extended to her singing. Although she calls herself a soprano, Mrs. Douglas has a voice definitely extending into the mezzo register. It is obviously a well-trained, cultivated voice, and Mrs. Douglas uses it in a musical manner.

A major music critic wrote that I had become "technically insecure." He said "vocal chords, like muscles, turn flabby for lack of use; and once they have given up their resilience they are woefully hard to retread. . . . Thus, for all her infinite charm, elegance and grace, her recital was musically of only passing interest."

Melvyn Douglas:
I think there were times when she deeply missed singing. It had meant so much to her, more than anything else on the stage. But she never spoke of it.

A few times after that I presented the "Recital." Once, for instance, I did it at the MacDowell Colony in Peterborough. But I knew my singing career definitely was over. It was being replaced by speaking engagements in colleges, which I hugely enjoyed. And, of course, I campaigned for Adlai Stevenson again in 1956.

Adlai wrote me a charming note to thank me. "My dear Helen," he said, "I have had so many glowing reports of your efforts on my behalf here in California that I feel I must send you this very special note of thanks. . . . That you have troubled yourself so much for me touches me deeply—and I am grateful indeed. . . ."

A few years earlier, in 1952, Richard Nixon had survived a nasty scandal about campaign contributions. He made a speech in which he admitted that he had received a dog named Checkers which his daughters loved, and he hoped that he would not have to give his children's pet back. Fern Marja of the New York *Post* sought me out to ask my reaction. I replied, in one of the few occasions when I allowed myself to refer to the 1950 campaign:

"What happened to me is not important in itself. It has significance only in terms of the decision confronting the country today [the presidential election]. In that sense the 1950 campaign is not dead. My impression of Dick Nixon is that of an opponent who was smart and adaptable, who dodged the real issues and who campaigned on character assassination. . . ."

When I was asked if I didn't think Richard Nixon was clever enough to change, I responded:

"I'd say that isn't a possibility, since there is nothing in his record to indicate he has strong convictions about anything except success. There is also nothing to indicate that Richard Nixon is capable of taking the right stand if the right stand is unpopular. That is the most interesting factor in the 1950 campaign and that, I repeat, is why that campaign is still alive today."

In that campaign Nixon once again employed his strategy of smearing his opponent. He said dreadful things about Adlai. He called him "The Appeaser," as if conciliatory efforts were treason, and declared that Adlai "got a Ph.D. from Dean Acheson's College of Cowardly Containment."

Adlai went down to defeat for a second time to Dwight Eisen-

hower and Richard Nixon. The Democratic party began to look
for a new candidate for the 1960 race.

My mother was then ninety. The only time she showed her age
was when she had to move from the apartment at Park and Fifty-
fourth where she had lived for twenty-five years. The building was
sold and she had no choice, but she hated giving up what had become so familiar. We found another apartment for her on the
East River at 50 Sutton Place. My brother Walter, newly back
from Caracas where he had supervised the Gahagan dredging,
took an apartment a few floors up and Lillian, divorced a second
time, lived with Walter and his wife, Gay.

They gave a dinner party in the autumn of 1956. A few close
friends and some of the family were there, including Mother.
Around eleven, as they were sipping coffee in the living room,
Mother said, "I think I'll go downstairs."

"Don't be a poor sport," Walter chided her affectionately.
"Don't leave us."

"I really think I will go, Walter," Mother said firmly. She said
her good-byes and Walter escorted her to her apartment.

The next day, a Saturday, Walter, Gay, Lillian and some
friends went to Princeton for a football game. That night Mother
had a heart attack and was taken to Lenox Hill Hospital. Because
the hospital was crowded and the staff overworked, Lilli and I
nursed her, taking turns staying overnight in a ward, the only
space available.

Mother then suffered a series of small strokes, making it obvious that she would not recover. We decided to bring her home.
We placed her in her big bed and arranged for nurses to care for
her around the clock. She lived four weeks more.

My brother William came from Summerville, South Carolina,
so we were all with her at the end. I never left her side, day or
night. Lilli and Walter were both too busy with business to stay
through the day but they turned up in the evenings to keep vigil.

Mother was in a coma but would come to every now and then,
smile at me and say something, her eyes fluttering, and then drift
away again. As she was dying I sang a lovely Hebridean song that
was written for someone dying; she loved music so. She smiled,

opened her eyes briefly, saw us all standing around her bed, and then died.

I hate leaving a person who has died. I have to stay close for a time afterward. William, Walter and Lilli rose to go, saying "Come on, Helen," but I told them I was staying the night. "I won't see Mother again," I explained.

It was so peaceful. There was nothing sad about it because she was ninety-one and had lived a beautiful life. And she died surrounded by people who loved her. In a mood of tender sweetness, we divided up the bits of furniture that meant something to us. I took her rocker.

Melvyn was playing in Washington in 1958 and I was with him. I wondered what Lyndon Johnson planned to do about the 1960 election and hoped that he would be a candidate. He was then majority leader in the Senate and very busy. When I contacted him the only space he had available on his schedule was a seven-thirty A.M. breakfast.

The Johnsons sent a car for me and I rehearsed my arguments in favor of his trying for the nomination. I believed him to be the best-qualified candidate the Democrats could offer the country but I knew he wasn't popular with liberals in the party because of his support for many of Eisenhower's proposals, particularly the strengthening of the military.

Few Americans were in favor of pushing for international disarmament. The White House wasn't educating the American people to the folly of the arms race and time was running out. I thought Lyndon might just turn the tide if he really understood that *peace* is the issue of our time. The job was big enough even for him.

At breakfast the conversation was all about the bacon and the eggs and the toast and other chitchat, but there was no mention of politics. On the drive back to Washington with Lyndon, I was desperate to find an opportunity to bring up the subject of the presidency and the arms race.

No sooner had we entered the car and closed the doors than Lyndon picked up the telephone and called his office. He issued some instructions about what he wanted his staff to do, put down the receiver, and immediately called an aide, and then a Senator, and then various other people. We were almost at our destination before I could break in.

"Lyndon," I asked hurriedly, "are you thinking about offering yourself as a possible candidate for the presidency?"

I couldn't read his expression. I went on, spilling out my concern about the arms race and my conviction that disarmament was our only hope for attaining peace.

Lyndon looked at me and looked away. "I was born in the wrong place at the wrong time," he said.

"Not if you recognize that the human race needs *peace* to survive!" I protested.

His reaction was nothing. He got out of the car. "Peace!" I called after him. He waved good-bye and was gone.

I didn't feel his lack of response was due to being too tired or too preoccupied. He simply wasn't interested. I was very discouraged.

About eight months later, India Edwards called me and said that she had just talked to Lyndon. He had decided he would try for the nomination as the party's candidate for the presidency in 1960. "I've agreed to head a women's group to support him," India told me. "Lyndon would like you to work with me."

"I can't do it," I told her.

"You can't do it! Why not?"

"Because I have never lied to the voters," I explained. "Whatever my value has been in politics, it has been that I have only said what I know to be true. Sometimes I was mistaken, but what I said was what I believed at the time to be true. And I don't know where Lyndon stands on the arms race. I don't know where he stands on the issue of our time.

"Please tell him I cannot support him, I will not. I think he is eminently qualified, better than anyone we have, but I don't know how he stands on this issue. And everything else is wrong if this issue isn't right."

So I didn't work for him and Lyndon didn't get the nomination. John F. Kennedy won it and Lyndon was his running mate. I campaigned for Kennedy and Lyndon in the northeastern states. The national committee provided most of my schedule, though some of the speaking engagements came from a state committee or even a candidate's committee. I would be contacted directly and I would accept unless there was a conflicting commitment. I was talking day and night, which gives people the impression that you probably can crowd in one more speech, or two. Or three.

I didn't know Kennedy personally but I felt comfortable talking about Lyndon. I could be helpful, especially in the eastern states where people were concerned that Lyndon's support of liberal causes was weak. Minority groups would ask, "What about his votes?" and I would answer, "I don't care about his votes. When the pressure is on, it's the kind of man you're electing that matters. And I'm telling you that this man does not have prejudice."

With my record of support for minorities, I could be believed when I said that Lyndon was a decent man. I don't know that Lyndon ever knew that I campaigned hard for him in that election. I never heard from him about it.

Despite the fact that John F. Kennedy's opponent for the presidency was Richard Nixon, I did not allow myself to make bitter comments. I stuck to the positives in the Democratic platform and restricted myself to such mild criticism of Richard Nixon as "his record falls short of the mark."

I was speaking one evening at a Ford Hall Forum in Jordan Hall of the New England Conservatory of Music in Boston. The affair was a rally arranged by Kennedy supporters. I had just finished my talk and was answering questions from the floor when I heard a sound like light bulbs exploding around me. Someone was pelting me with eggs.

Justice Reuben Lurie gallantly put himself between me and the assailant while ushers frantically tried to find the egg-thrower. I remained calm and when the person was collared and escorted from the hall I called for more questions and went on. When it was over, people stood and applauded and cheered for five minutes, which was very gratifying.

A few weeks later John Fitzgerald Kennedy was President of the United States and Lyndon Baines Johnson was the Vice-President. I wired congratulations.

I was fresh from another trip to Israel when I started to campaign. This journey was unplanned. Melvyn and I made the decision to go very suddenly when we read that Syrian soldiers had killed a shepherd in the region of a kibbutz, Ha-Gosherim. Our daughter, Mary Helen, was working at that kibbutz.

A few months earlier Mary, saying nothing to either of us, had visited the Israeli Consulate in New York with a view to volunteering to work at a kibbutz. She happened to encounter Chaim Ber, who was in the United States on business for the Congress of the Kibbutzim, and they were charmed by each other. Chaim arranged for her to be posted to his family's kibbutz, Ha-Gosherim, and within weeks our nineteen-year-old had sailed for Israel.

Though Mary assured us that she was a full two miles from the Syrian border and that the kibbutz had an adequate underground shelter in case fighting broke out, we were not comforted. Melvyn and I decided to see for ourselves that Mary was safe.

A rapturous Mary Helen, toasted by the Mideastern sun, met us in Jerusalem looking buoyantly healthy. Chaim Ber and his wife Sarka kindly made arrangements for us to stay in a rest home reserved for visitors and grandly showed us around. During our few days there we were able to appreciate how much pluck and hard work and talent it takes to create gardens in what had been desert.

After five fascinating days we went to Jerusalem to stay with Miles and Gita Sherover, friends of my sister Lilli, and from there to a hotel by the sea not far from Tel Aviv, where we had the magical experience of visiting Haifa at midnight and seeing it lying still under the moonlight. The strong shapes of the ancient port buildings, washed and sharpened by the moon, were intoxicating. We returned to our hotel in reverent stillness.

Before leaving Israel I wanted to experience the legendary heat of the Gulf where Solomon had mined copper. Melvyn wisely declined to accompany me. I flew to Elat on the Gulf of Aqaba with a member of the Israeli foreign service as my escort. As we emerged from the plane at midmorning, I was agreeably surprised to find that the temperature was only pleasantly warm.

We explored Elat and I marveled that the Israelis who built it and lived there had constructed an ingenious cooling system for their homes. Burlap strips were hung from the eaves and kept wet by water piped from the Gulf to the roofs. When the desert wind was burning hot, people turned on the water and the wet burlap lowered the temperature in the houses to a bearable level.

By eleven in the morning, as we toured the copper mine, the temperature was soaring. An American tourist, recognizing me, said angrily to my escort, "Are you trying to kill Mrs. Douglas by exposing her to the noon heat?" I protested that it was my idea; he looked incredulous.

The inside of the car that carried us to a hotel for lunch was like a furnace. I endured it by concentrating on a heavenly image, that of running icy cold water over my wrists. I hurried to the ladies' room as soon as we arrived and turned on the tap. The water came out—boiling hot. I was so disappointed that I felt faint.

Melvyn met me at the hotel and put me to bed. I had a slight fever, my skin was lobster red, and I was bloated from head to foot. It was twenty-four hours before my reaction to heat subsided and I was normal again. But I wouldn't have missed that side trip. It gave me some understanding of what Israelis coming from northern climates had endured in learning to work and live in Elat. I'd gone to feel the heat. Well, I'd felt it.

I returned to New York to find that the spirit of McCarthy and Nixon lived on. The John Birch Society in a paper *From Counterattack* put out some slanderous material charging that I was a supporter of organizations which it claimed were communist-dominated. The list included the League of Shoppers, Consumers Union, an African famine relief committee, SANE Nuclear Policy, an American-Soviet cultural exchange, and many others.

There were some I had never heard of. I wrote to Evie Chavoor asking her help in identifying them. She couldn't trace most of the groups mentioned. The Hollywood Democratic Committee on the list was the one from which Melvyn resigned in 1939 when it rejected his motion to protest Russia's invasion of Finland. The American-Soviet Friendship organization was one I had addressed in 1945 when Russia was an ally. Disgusted, I gave up trying to sort out the tangle of invention and distortion.

Eleanor Roosevelt died in 1962. We had been in touch on a regular basis for more than twenty years. A reunion especially dear to us all occurred every year on Lorena Hickok's birthday. It had been Mrs. Roosevelt's practice when she was the First Lady to give a birthday luncheon for Hick. When she left the White House, she continued the birthday parties, first in the apartment off Washington Square in New York which she had rented just before her husband died, and later in a house she bought on the Upper East Side.

It was always the same small group: Judge Marion Harron, Nannine Joseph (Mrs. Roosevelt's literary agent), the actress Jean Dixon (one of Hick's closest friends), Congresswoman Mary Norton, and me. After Mrs. Roosevelt's death, I gave Hick's next birthday party in my apartment.

It was the last. That year Hick's health deteriorated so much that she was unable to leave her small home in Hyde Park. Because of diabetes, she was losing her eyesight rapidly. She was working on a book about Walter Reuther. To help her with it, Jean Dixon and I sent her a tape recorder.

Jean Dixon had been a pupil of Sarah Bernhardt. She played on Broadway in many productions, one with Helen Hayes and another with Melvyn, which is when I met her. Jean met Hick in Minneapolis when she was on tour, introduced by a hairdresser they shared. When Jean became ill, Hick went with her to the theater every night and almost literally boosted her onstage. Later Jean and Hick had a falling out, to Mrs. Roosevelt's great distress. It was the birthday parties that brought them back together.

As an example of Hick's warmth and strength in her friendships, there is the time I called to cancel a visit I had planned. "Hick," I told her, "I'm really sorry, but I can't make it."

She was instantly alert. "What's the matter?" she asked sharply.

"Well," I told her reluctantly. "I woke this morning vomiting blood—"

"Who's with you?" she interrupted.

I admitted that I was alone. She exploded.

"You never have any sense. You have no sense about yourself, none! I don't know how you go on living. Honest to God, Helen,

you have *no sense*. Will you please put down this phone and call
your son. Tell Peter to come over at once. When he gets there,
have him call me so I'll know that he's in charge."

I decided she was right. In order not to alarm Peter unduly, I
called Nan Stevens for help. Nan Stevens is a resourceful, funny
and kind woman who had done secretarial work for Melvyn when
he was in New York. After we left California and moved into a
Park Avenue apartment she became my secretary and then, like
Evie Chavoor, a person who seemed to be able to do anything.
Her management of the details of my complex affairs smoothed
my day.

"Nan," I said, "don't get upset, but I'm vomiting blood."

Nan said calmly, "I'll be right over." She arrived minutes later,
as I finished talking to Peter. Peter made the arrangements for
me to be taken to Lenox Hill Hospital. The problem was related to an ulcer and was quickly diagnosed and brought under
control. I phoned Hick to tell her about it and found her still
fuming that I hadn't reacted more promptly.

Whenever I visited Hick I found young people clustered
around her. She fascinated them, as she had Peter and Mary
Helen, with her stories of the politicians and events she had
known. In return they helped any way they could: buying gro
cer-
ies, reading her manuscript pages to her so she could make revisions, typing transcripts of her tapes as needed.

On one of my last visits, I was shocked to see that Hick had
lost the use of her legs. She could no longer rely on a cane or
walker to move about but was forced to use a wheelchair. Gamely
she continued to take care of herself, even preparing her own
meals. When I left I carried away a picture of a woman of rare
courage and intelligence who had justly earned the respect and
affection of so many.

Hick died two months after her seventy-fifth birthday, on May
1, 1968. About ten years later I heard from a writer, Doris Faber,
who said she was putting together a book based on letters ex-
changed by Hick and Mrs. Roosevelt. Hick had placed them in a
branch of the National Archives, the Franklin Delano Roosevelt
Library in Hyde Park, with instructions that they were to be
made available ten years after her death.

I agreed to talk to Doris Faber about Hick and Mrs. R. and we had an agreeable interview. Later I learned that the early letters between the two women, those written in the period before I met them, were openly affectionate and rumor had it that they could be interpreted as evidence of a lesbian relationship.

Sick with anger and indignation, I called the writer to protest. I followed our telephone conversation with a letter. "Had I known the intent of your book about Mrs. Roosevelt, I would not have consented to an interview," I wrote. "I have asked you not to use my name in connection with it. You have agreed not to do so.

"I was a close friend of Mrs. Roosevelt as well as of Lorena Hickok. You are making a grievous error in your interpretations of some of Hick's letters. I find this most regrettable."

I discarded one draft of the letter in which I said, "I know Mrs. Roosevelt was not a homosexual." The suggestion seemed to me too outrageous to be dignified with a denial. When the book appeared I was relieved to be informed by Mary and Nan, who read it, that nothing from my interview with Doris Faber was included nor was there any innuendo to discredit Mrs. Roosevelt.

Not long after Mrs. Roosevelt died, I received a call from a publishing house, Hill and Wang. Aaron J. Ezickson had assembled some remarkable photographs of Eleanor Roosevelt and Hill and Wang wanted me to write a brief text to accompany them in a book that would be titled, *The Eleanor Roosevelt We Remember*. They showed me the cover photograph, one by Philippe Halsman that I had never seen before. It has since become familiar and is, I think, the best ever taken of her; it is really beautiful.

The deadline, I was told, was four weeks away.

"How can I do it?" I asked. "It's impossible."

Simple, they said. They wanted a chronological record of my friendship with Mrs. Roosevelt. I had only to string together some stories.

"There are people who knew her better than I did," I protested. "We had a warm, loving friendship but I'm not in any way prepared to write a book that pretends to be her biography."

"No, no," I was told. "We don't want that. We just want *your* story."

I said I would let them know. I wanted to check with people close to Mrs. Roosevelt to ask if they approved of my doing such a book. I called Nannine Joseph, who had been Mrs. Roosevelt's friend for many, many years as well as being her literary agent. Nannine said, "Yes, Helen, I definitely think you should write it."

The difficulty for me was not to embroider. I didn't want in any way to build more into my first meeting with Mrs. Roosevelt than was there but I didn't know where else to begin the book. I thought about it for days, going over those early times in my mind. Then in bed at night with the lights out, I would review each occasion and try to recall the impressions I'd had then. Without turning on the light, I would scrawl on a pad by my bed. In the morning I had pages of almost illegible notes, enough to get me started the next morning, dictating to Nan Stevens.

The book grew scene by scene, like putting together a script. Four weeks later it was finished. I asked two people to read the final draft. One was Hick and the other Marie Rodell, my literary agent who handled the contract with Hill and Wang. Marie was also Rachel Carson's agent and a close friend.

Three of the pictures in the book had to do with times when Mrs. R. and I were together. One was taken when she toured the migrants' camps in 1939 and shows her in a crowd with Laurence Hewes, Melvyn and me. Another was taken in Washington in 1959 when she attended a conference of the National Advisory Committee on Farm Labor. In the picture with her are Secretary of Labor James Mitchell, Frank Graham, me, John M. Seabrook and A. Philip Randolph. The other shows me in 1946 when I was an alternate delegate to the United Nations. Eleanor Roosevelt is photographed talking to me and Senator Warren Austin, head of the delegation.

The book is dedicated "To the thousands who knew and loved Eleanor Roosevelt and the millions who never knew her but loved her."

I heard from Lyndon Johnson, now Vice-President of the United States. He told me that he decided to run with John F. Kennedy against Richard Nixon because of what Nixon had done to me in 1950. I don't think that was true but Lyndon liked to think that was his reason.

Nixon hadn't changed at all since the 1950 campaign against me. In 1962, running for governor of California, Nixon charged that his opponent, Governor Edmund G. Brown, "is not capable of dealing with the communist threat within our borders." Nixon declared that Brown's record "shows not a single item of anti-subversive legislation in four years." Nixon promised to make California "a model effectively dealing with an alien system—communism."

This time the old magic of raising the bogey of the Red Menace didn't work; Nixon lost.

Lyndon came to New York to address a luncheon and I went to hear him. I shared a table with my brother Walter and Helen Fuller, who was a close friend of John Kennedy's. Halfway through the speech I could tell by the quick look in Lyndon's eye that he had spotted us. When he finished, one of his aides tapped me on the shoulder and said, "The Vice-President would like you to go back to his hotel with him."

I explained that I was with some other people and couldn't. The aide went away and returned to say that Lyndon invited us all.

When we arrived in his suite I found Lyndon in a miserable and sour mood. Both times that I saw him while he was Vice-President he was utterly depressed. He wasn't running things and it didn't suit his nature at all. He complained that the aides hadn't yet arrived. He went on at some length about the indignity Lady Bird suffered, coming from Washington with her dress for the evening's reception over her arm. You're not disturbed by details like that if you aren't unhappy, and if you're not also a man given over obsessively to details and the way things are run.

The second time I saw Lyndon while he was Vice-President, he and Lady Bird had invited me to stay at their home when the three of us were to attend a formal dinner in the new building of the State Department. The Johnsons were hosts that night. We chatted as we waited for cars to take us to the affair, and again Lyndon was morose and testy. Then we drove to the dinner and the moment he entered the room he was charm itself—buoyant, outgoing, loving. His good spirits lasted until we were back in the car headed for home. He slumped in his seat and that veil of despondency settled on him again. I took a light tone and jibed him about something that had happened in Congress. He didn't reply. Perhaps I had been indiscreet since the chauffeur could hear me, but I think Lyndon was just too unhappy for conversation.

In his inaugural speech, John F. Kennedy announced a unique program aimed at helping Latin-American countries. He vowed that the United States would join hands with nineteen neighbors to the south, 200 million people crushed by poverty, to promote a better life.

I saw the Alliance for Progress, as Kennedy called it, as a profoundly important change in American foreign policy, as radical in our time as the Monroe Doctrine had been. The scheme originated with Juscelino Kubitschek, former president of Brazil, in 1959. The next year Congress authorized a Fund for Progress to assist inter-American partnership. A sum of $500 million was appropriated to launch it.

Kennedy fleshed out the details of the plan in 1961 and the next year the charter for the Alliance for Progress was signed at Punta del Este in Uruguay.

The Alliance has been compared to the Marshall Plan but it isn't the same. Western Europe recovered rapidly after the war with brief, intensive economic help from the United States, but Europeans had technical expertise in abundance. The goal of prosperity and economic self-sufficiency will take much longer in Latin America because there is no reservoir of know-how. Some of the countries are inhabited by primitive people who are at a very elementary stage of development. In many ways, Latin America is a century behind the highly industrialized nations of the world.

In his Good Neighbor Policy of the 1930s, Franklin Roosevelt recognized that truth and started to formulate policies that would build bridges to Latin America. After World War II began, that beginning collapsed under the pressure to respond to events in Europe.

In 1946, when I was at the United Nations, I was approached many times by South American delegates who described the desperate poverty of their countries. They said they were in as great need of aid from the United States as any nation in Europe. I agreed, but at the time the United States couldn't undertake aid programs to both Europe and Latin America. Their pleas went unanswered until John Kennedy came along.

North Americans in the main believe the travel posters about Latin America. They see the beautiful beaches of Rio de Janeiro, the colorful shawls on beaming peasant women, the glorious architecture in Lima and Santiago. In the early sixties I made two study tours to South America to see for myself. On another occasion I went to Panama with my brother Walter at the request of the government, which had just been refused a loan from the United States to improve conditions in the black neighborhoods. Walter and I agreed that crowded, unsanitary conditions there could lead to race riots. On my return I wrote a strong letter to Adolf Berle, who had influence in the State Department, and warned him that the situation in Panama was explosive unless the United States granted the loan.

The two study tours confirmed the impression that Panama had given me: Latin America was on the verge of violent upheaval. The first trip was a brief one to Venezuela and Uruguay in June 1960, undertaken in part on business for Gahagan Dredging. Walter wanted my opinion of the political stability of those countries. I advised him that the countries were deeply troubled.

"There is much to do," I reported to him. "It can't be done fast enough, even if you had the sympathy of the elite and privileged . . . and you don't."

I came home by way of Puerto Rico, where I was a guest of my old friend Muñoz Marín, the governor. I gave Walter a favorable report on the political situation and subsequently our family company commenced dredging operations there.

The second study tour began on June 1, 1962, and ended more than two months later. In the nine weeks I visited twelve countries: Mexico, Venezuela, Panama, Puerto Rico, Guatemala, Costa Rica, Colombia, Peru, Bolivia, Chile, Argentina and Brazil. Most of my trip was arranged by Robert W. Hudgens in the Department of Agriculture through his position in the Rockefeller Foundation, which was funding many programs in South America.

My purpose was to see the work of the Alliance for Progress

and to visit Peace Corps, CARE and YMCA projects to examine the impact North Americans were having on South America. I traveled along a network of knowledgeable people—ambassadors, missionaries, teachers, scientists and young idealists—and insisted on going to remote villages deep in the jungle and into the dreadful slums that gird Latin America's glorious cities.

Everywhere I went I found great contradictions because of the lopsidedness between the economic and social development. According to the U. S. Agency for International Development at the time of the Kennedy initiatives, the United States was to provide external aid while Latin-American countries revised their economic base in order to increase exports. The Alliance charter pledged capital and technical assistance which was expected to improve exports and thereby relieve poverty.

Latin-American countries at that time depended on exports of basic commodities in order to survive. When the world price for coffee, sugar and tin fell in the fifties, they had difficulty paying for the manufactured imports they needed from the United States. The imbalance depleted their meager resources and increased their foreign debt.

The U.S. solution appeared logical on the surface, but the expectations were wrong. My one overriding impression of Latin America was that the social change the United States anticipated in a ten-year period was going to take much, much longer, and that eruptions probably would take place in almost every South American country because people would think the Alliance for Progress wasn't working. People were so miserable that they weren't going to be able to wait for gradual improvement; they would attack their governments.

During the study tour I was to see the same conditions repeated everywhere. Blacks brought to South America as slaves and South American natives exploited by Spaniards and Portuguese as serfs had been kept for centuries in a deplorable state of poverty and neglect. The elite of European descent has amassed enormous wealth over the years, establishing with the church a monopoly over the land and other natural resources. It spends almost nothing on relieving the misery of the poor.

I found that many roads were unpaved, so in seasons of heavy rain they were almost impassable and in the dry season the dust was suffocating. I discovered what "underdeveloped" means: there were few schools and fewer teachers, and in some rural areas teachers had not gone beyond the fourth grade. There weren't enough books or facilities to print books.

Illiteracy is widespread. In Argentina it runs between 25 and 50 percent; 16 percent in Uruguay, 18 percent in Costa Rica, 22 percent in Cuba (before Castro), 38 percent in Panama, 37 percent in Chile, 48 percent in Colombia, 56 percent in Brazil and Peru, 80 percent in Guatemala, and as high as 84 percent in Bolivia. By United States estimates, there are 50 million illiterate, unskilled adults in Latin America.

Most housing was a hut with a dirt floor and no water, no power, no sewers. There weren't enough hospitals and the few available to the poor were short of doctors, nurses and equipment.

Though the land is suitable for agriculture, most Latin-American countries import food, which contributes to the national debt. People cannot live on a diet of sugarcane and coffee beans, the principal crops. Rural people often go hungry and many drift toward cities where they look for work in vain. They cluster in slums around the perimeters of cities in communities lacking schools, electricity, sewers, clean water and medical services.

The cities of South America are exceedingly beautiful, with lovely parks and graceful buildings, music halls, fine hotels, good restaurants, superior private schools, broad boulevards and luxurious homes. All this loveliness exists within a festering ring of destitution and despair.

For fifteen to twenty million children there are no schools. The Alliance in 1962 was planning to build 17,000 classrooms but this was scarcely more than a drop in the ocean.

The middle-level leadership group so vital for modern society is small throughout Latin America and in some countries doesn't exist. There is a vast shortage of men and women with secondary- and vocational-school training, the basis of a middle class that makes a society go. This is the critical lack in Latin America, and it can be corrected only by education—which takes time, years and years of time.

North Americans must understand this and not be impatient

when progress is slow. Progress will depend on the leadership of the middle class, something we in North America never lacked.

Anisio S. Teixeira, the foremost educator in Brazil, gave a paper on education in Santiago, Chile, in March 1962, in which he traced the fate of Latin-American countries after Columbus. The transplantation of Europeans to Latin America after the fifteenth century was conducted under the guise of bringing the approved form of Christianity to the heathens, but in truth the real motive was plunder.

"The life of the recently discovered continent was therefore characterized from the very outset by this basic contradiction," Dr. Teixeira said. "Jesuits and *bandeirantes*, faith and conquest. Thus from birth we were caught between real and ostensible aims."

That master-slave division of society he described is one of the basic causes of underdevelopment in the southern half of this hemisphere. The master-slave psychology is in large part responsible for the illiteracy and ignorance today of millions of people and for the nonpractical, nonutilitarian education that was imposed on children of the elite in schools run by the Jesuits. The curricula designed for French and Spanish aristocracy were imposed on a raw continent that needed skilled youth. The schools didn't grow from the culture of the countries in which they existed and they didn't produce leaders who could relate to the needs of their communities.

Latin America is just beginning to realize that the former system of education will not do. There must be education for all, free from social classification. Secondary schools must be developed as part of the public educational system. Each student must be given what he or she needs and what is best suited to that student's abilities.

This was one of the objectives of the Alliance for Progress. The Alliance goals encountered opposition from landowning aristocrats who were determined to protect their status quo by any means. They were also opposed by communists who believe that only violent revolution can bring about desired change.

The prerevolutionary pressures in Central and South America that I witnessed were not communist or communist-inspired.

Communists take advantage of such pressures wherever possible and manipulate them to their own ends, but communists are not the cause of the trouble. If there were no such system as communism in the world, the southern half of this hemisphere would still be in ferment.

Political explosions are not new to Latin America. Its past has been peppered with civil war since Simón Bolívar and the War of Independence. In one country after another, power has changed hands but the living conditions of the people—Indian, mestizo, negro, mulatto, the indigent foreign immigrant—have remained, with few exceptions, very much the same.

The fact-finding tour during which I came to appreciate all this began inauspiciously in Tampa, Florida, where I suffered a recurrence of an eye problem.

I wrote to Melvyn and Mary Helen a few days later while flying from Miami to Guatemala:

> Oh yes, the day before in Tampa, as a last precaution I saw an eye specialist. My left eye *again* had been giving me trouble. Red, swollen. What a drama. Same kind of lump in lid as I had had in New York. Grit or growth in gland. Dr. Fortes operated. I had little to say about it. What an office! First of all, it was a clinic. The doctor was operating on one person after another. It reminded me of a cafeteria. There is maybe segregation in Florida but there wasn't in his office. A miserable Negro man—about to be operated on—was told to get off the table. A fresh piece of paper was put on, after which I was ordered on same.
>
> Then the terrible business began. Three nurses running around; the doctor giving orders; patients sitting around looking on—all performed in the most casual, relaxed manner to the accompaniment of orders, social conversation and instructions to all.
>
> It might have been a field hospital, wartime, under fire, for there was a tense nervousness and haste underlying the work in the clinic.
>
> A sense of too many patients, not enough time.
>
> . . . I was a mess when I left.
>
> Went home to Gay's [Walter's wife], led by the hand—could not see at all. Went to bed with an ice bucket beside me. The left side of my face, eye and cheek, blood red. Next morning I

rose at six A.M. Packed with Gay's help—and looked as if I should be in the hospital instead of departing for South America. . . .

As I write I am holding ice to my face. This, just to remind you I am still red and swollen although slightly better than yesterday. I feel a thousand times stronger and wide awake. I look forward to Guatemala. . . .

One of the reasons I was eager to visit Guatemala was to find the people who made a scarf I had bought at the airport there three years previously. The scarf had become my favorite possession. It made friends for me—strangers stop to comment on it and everyone wants to touch it, to feel it. It has an extraordinary power to make people feel warm and glad just to look at it.

A few days after my arrival I was driving with some CARE people in the mountains when I suddenly saw a woman hurrying down a path. I cried out, "My scarf!" She wore a scarf identical to mine. I learned that every Indian in northern Guatemala has one and they prize them as much as I do mine. The scarf is used to carry children, wrap parcels, provide warmth, spread on the ground for sitting. The scarf became a bond between us; we all loved that bright, beautiful scarf.

Jim and Ellen Loeb, who invited me to stay with them in the American Embassy in Lima, Peru, insisted that I have an escort for part of my journey to Bolivia because, they said, the route was dangerous. My traveling companion was a very blond, pale young man, Nicky McCausland, a member of the U. S. Consulate staff in the northern part of Peru.

We traveled the 350 miles from Lima to Cuzco, where we learned that the train to Puno on Lake Titicaca, where I was to take the boat to Bolivia, was not running. There was a strike. I proposed that we hire a taxi.

"Good for you!" Nicky said. "I don't think that's been done before. We'll buy white wine, sandwich food, hire a taxi, and start tomorrow at dawn."

The trip to Puno took all day and we arrived covered with the high (over 12,000 feet) *altiplano* dust. Nicky left me there with instructions to the taxi driver to stop in a certain town the next day so that I could have breakfast. The driver spoke no English and I possess only a few words of Spanish, but we managed.

Since the boat was not available, we drove around the lake. The trip lasted four and a half days. At the border crossing, the Bolivian inspectors relieved me of all my Peruvian papers and refused to allow the taxi to enter the country. The taxi driver unloaded my luggage and piled it in the customs office. I looked around. Nicky's telegram to our embassy in La Paz apparently had not reached its destination. There was no one to meet me. There was also no telephone or telegraph office in the town.

The taxi man prepared to leave. I begged him not to desert me but he didn't seem to understand. In my desperation, I remembered the lyrics of an aria in *Cavalleria Rusticana* where the heroine pleads with her lover not to go. They were in Italian but they would have to do. "*Non me abondo nato!*" I cried to the cab driver. "*Non me abondo nato!*" He didn't get the words but he understood the idea. He made a gesture of helplessness with his hands—and drove away.

I discovered that there was one automobile in the village. It belonged to a doctor in La Paz who was visiting his family. I sat on a bench where I could keep the vehicle, a small truck, in view. I wasn't nervous but I had to go to the bathroom. Where? I didn't dare move. I hung on grimly until, to my joy, I saw the doctor approaching his car. He was followed by four children, three men and three women. My heart sank. There would be no room.

The kind Bolivians cheerfully made space for me. A third of the way to La Paz we met the embassy car making its third attempt to find me. I rode the rest of the way in roominess, though still aching to find a bathroom.

In Brazil I went up the Araguaia River to visit a tribe in the Amazon Valley. We traveled the final part of the way in pitch blackness. When the motorboat touched the shore, I could see nothing. We groped our way to the village where I witnessed a very moving initiation rite for a young girl, which reminded me strongly of the tenderness my Grandmother Hannah had shown me when I reached womanhood.

On my return I lectured across the United States on three

topics. One was the problems that Latin Americans faced and my concern that the Alliance for Progress did not have realistic goals. Another speech, entitled "Little Man? Big Machine! Small World? Big Question!," dealt with what was happening to the individual in the twentieth century. The third speech was about the arms race. In it I usually quoted John F. Kennedy's good comment, "Mankind will put an end to war or war will put an end to mankind."

I found appreciative audiences everywhere. Someone wrote after a talk at Southern Methodist University in Dallas that I had "related well to students," which was what I hoped to accomplish. Phoenix College said that I was "most generous" in giving of my time and "we were particularly happy that she was able to meet and talk with small groups during the day."

At the University of the Pacific, Stockton, California, they commented, "She gave so much of herself that I am sure her visit here will be long remembered." Patrick Beville, of the Veterans Administration in Huntington, West Virginia, wrote, "Huntington is better for Mrs. Douglas's visit here. . . . This republic needs citizens who are able and willing to do the work she is doing." At Goucher College in Baltimore the reaction was, "We are grateful to her for sharing her insights with us and for her lucid presentation of new ideas."

In a way, I was campaigning. I was bringing the issues to voters. When people approached me after the address, they often would start with, "There's something I want to ask you about, Mrs. Douglas." At first I would brace myself, expecting a question about Richard Nixon and the 1950 campaign, but always the question was about the issues. My opinion of the American electorate rose and rose; people *do* want to know what's happening in America and the world and they are capable of coming to good decisions when they have the right information.

On November 22, 1963, John F. Kennedy was shot and killed in Dallas. In Texas in those first tragic hours, Lyndon Johnson showed his mettle. He was magnificent in that hour of tragedy, fully in command. His steady hand prevented panic. He restored confidence in order, which helped ease the pain the country was feeling. He was thoughtful, solicitous, courteous.

And Lady Bird Johnson is no less deserving of appreciation and praise for her response to the personal tragedy of the Kennedys and the national confusion and despair.

In the next two years we heard praise on every hand for Lyndon. People kept saying, "He is going to be a great President." He was a master at working cooperatively with Congress. He put through social improvements and legal changes that were long overdue, much of it legislation that President Kennedy had proposed without success. Everything seemed to work well for the new President.

In domestic concerns and matters his fine mind, his fairness, his instinctive decency, his personal experience and knowledge of the United States served him well. He could balance and weigh the reports of those who were experts in the various fields and disciplines. In the matter of foreign relations, it was a different matter.

I don't remember his discussing foreign policy very often as did those who were preoccupied with international issues and the serious threat of the new weapons. Did his work on the Military Affairs Committee condition his thinking? Is that why he put his faith in the military and what led him to make the civil war in Vietnam an American war? Or was it respect for power? Did he become intoxicated with the power of the United States?

All the failures of the postwar period, twenty-five years of them, hatched on LBJ's doorstep when he became President. Neither his education nor his habits served his fine mind when the pressure was turned on. He did not relate to the Vietnamese in the personal way he did to Americans. He could not; he didn't have the background. The result was that he who had manipulated Congress with such dexterity was himself manipulated.

I think the relationship that develops between congressmen and the House committees on which they serve is worthy of study. Lyndon Johnson's orientation in the House was the military. He must have been drawn to it for strong reasons, as I was drawn to the Foreign Affairs Committee for my reasons. In the crisis of Vietnam he depended on the group he knew most intimately, where he knew the power was unlimited, rather than on his own strength.

I believe it was faith in the military that led him to intervene in the Vietnam civil war. It was against everything he did and believed in at home. I often in my mind imagine a scene that he might have had with the military, one that comes out of what I know of his character. He was vain about his ability to get things done, scornful of those who couldn't do the job. He was impatient with the United Nations, which he described as "all those people talking up there, and what are they getting done?"—or some such comment.

When he became President he wanted to be the greatest President who ever sat in the White House. And he certainly worked at it. And so here was our involvement in Southeast Asia. Two Presidents before him had sent some assistance to South Vietnam. I would think he probably called his friends in the military and said, "What's going on here? You've got the experts. Why don't we finish this thing up! Those poor little miserable people running around with no shoes on their feet. You've got everything. You come in here year after year looking for so much money. Why don't you finish it up?"

I can imagine their replying, "Well, Mr. President, we haven't been given any authority. We can't do anything."

"Well, all right, you've got the authority," Lyndon would say, as I construct it. "How long is it going to take you?"

Some simplistic approach such as that may have been the beginning. In the end he was suffocated by the mantle he himself wove. This was a loss not only for Lyndon Johnson, but for his country.

Senator Fulbright suggested that Lyndon exerted "an arrogant use of power." He wanted to do something two Presidents had failed to do. He wanted to close out the situation in Southeast Asia, clean it up, get it out of the way. That pushed aside the proper concern, the proper study to know what was happening, what the real conditions were, to come to know the Vietnamese people.

I think Lyndon's paternalism showed there. He knew what was best for the Vietnamese, what was needed, what was good. He never seemed to doubt the capacity of the United States to deliver. After the military cleaned up—finished their job—he planned to make everything right. In the darkest days of his administration he was sending the experts to Vietnam. He ordered the blueprints drawn for grandiose plans for reconstruction and development once the war was won. He had land projects, reclamation projects. He was going to raise the living standards of all those people in Asia, that's what he really wanted to do.

A word about the presidency. The daily pressures on the President of the United States are intense and exhausting; there is no escape from them. A President is in constant danger of being manipulated by events unless he is solidly grounded. In order to hew his own course, a President must have a design and a conviction strong enough to stand against the forces that would push him off it.

I believe that Lyndon Johnson insisted on his policy for Southeast Asia because he believed that he was hewing to his course. I think he was trapped in Vietnam because of his ignorance of what was happening around the world. A few trips to a foreign country don't give you experience enough for foreign policy, and bringing home a camel driver doesn't help.

He wasn't well read; he wasn't conversant. This hadn't been his field. He was certainly not one to examine the motives of United States foreign policy too critically. He suffered from the national malaise—the belief that Americans are the good people, that everything we do is prompted by the best and highest motives. I don't think we can take for granted that we're always good.

As the tragedy of Vietnam grew in size, as the supporters of his Asian policy turned against him, as the country became more and more divided, as there was less and less of the money that had once seemed unlimited for the building of the Great Society, Lyndon Johnson became more and more isolated from the people he loved. He sacrificed a second term in office, with all that it might have meant to him and for the country.

Historians, no doubt, and psychologists will try to understand why this man with his fine brain and his instinctive decency could not face the facts in Vietnam, could not admit that he had been wrong.

Not long after Lyndon Johnson became President I was one of the guests of honor at a banquet given by the Washington

women's press corps. The Johnsons also were guests of honor.
When they came in, they passed my table. Lyndon's face lit up
and he said, "Oh how lovely. Come right after this thing is over
and spend the night with us in the White House."

I accepted against my better judgment, since I had to catch an
early plane the next morning for the Northwest. I went straight
to bed and the Johnsons came in later, so I didn't see them that
night. The next morning Lyndon talked to me on the telephone
—he wasn't going to be able to join us for breakfast.

He was in a good mood, telling me proudly that he was cleaning up the military, getting rid of old bases.

"Oh Lyndon," I said. "When you really begin to cut the meat,
all right. But that naval base in Brooklyn, for heaven's sake,
hasn't been operating for years. That's not the real thing at all."

Then he switched the subject to mention the two women he
had appointed to high office. I got the impression that his eye was
on the effect he was making on the media rather than seriously
considering the worth of women in public life.

He was flying to New York that morning and wanted me to go
with him so we could talk more but I explained I couldn't. I had
to be in Oregon to deliver a lecture that night.

I went down and had breakfast with Lady Bird. We discussed
general subjects relating to the White House and the presidency.
I listed what I thought were Lyndon's opportunities, what was
needed in the world, the contribution he could make. I remember
her saying something odd, "If he just gets through . . ."

"There's no possibility of 'just getting through'!" I exclaimed.
"Events won't allow Lyndon to do that. The world is moving at
such a pace that no one can just 'get through' the presidency. It's
no longer possible."

I understood Lady Bird's concern for her husband. Lady Bird
was greatly admired in Washington. The press preferred her to
Jackie Onassis. I don't think Lyndon Johnson was easy to live
with or work for at all, so she didn't have an easy life. But she
gave no indication that it wasn't easy. Her whole life was devoted
to her family and to helping any way that she could.

I once heard Lady Bird speak in New York at a gathering of
Democratic women. Before she rose to speak I would say that

more than half were prejudiced against her. One woman at my table muttered to me, "I just can't bear to hear that Southern accent."

"Well," I retorted, "I think the Southern accent will sound very sweet when you hear it because I'm sure you'll like what she has to say."

The audience was utterly captivated by Lady Bird that day. I made a point of reporting that back to the White House. She had a grace and naturalness that were irresistible.

In January 1964 Lyndon Johnson appointed me his emissary to Liberia on the occasion of President William V. S. Tubman's fifth inauguration. It was also the one-hundredth anniversary of the establishing of diplomatic relations between that country, founded as a refuge for freed slaves, and the United States.

The gift from America was a portfolio of papers that had passed between President Abraham Lincoln and Liberia. It was chosen by President John F. Kennedy and was accompanied by a letter from him which is believed to be the last official document he signed before his assassination.

In delivering it, our American delegation asked for a special audience with President Tubman. He granted it just before the celebrations began and I presented him with a letter which I said our new President, a Southerner, wanted him to have. The message in it was that Lyndon was concerned about Africa and civil rights. And Tubman cried. During his inaugural address, Tubman referred to Lyndon's letter and how much it meant to him.

On my return to New York I repacked breathlessly and spent a month vacationing in Cuernavaca with Melvyn. Then I had some speaking engagements in Allentown, Pennsylvania, and Corvallis, Oregon, to talk about South America. After that, in April, I left for Moscow, one of the delegation of the Women's International League for Peace and Freedom.

I first came in contact with the ILPF, which was founded in 1915 by Jane Addams, when I chaired a subcommittee of the congressional Foreign Affairs Committee through hearings on the United Nations. Women came to it from all over the country to testify in support of the United Nations and peace efforts. Some of the most knowledgeable of them were members of the ILPF. After I left Congress, I joined.

The International League for Peace and Freedom has chapters all over the world, wherever people are free to criticize their governments. For that reason, there are none in communist countries.

Eleanor Roosevelt, Mrs. Eugene Meyer of the Washington *Post* and the singer Marian Anderson sponsored a conference in 1961 at Bryn Mawr which was attended by a delegation of women from the Soviet Union. The Soviet group made a poor showing. The members were not well informed and they didn't discuss the issues as freely as American women did. That must have rankled in the Kremlin because it was two years before arrangements could be completed for a reciprocal visit.

As we discovered upon our arrival in Moscow, this time the top women in the Soviet Union were involved. They were enormously gifted, charming scientists, professors and government people who were easily the match for the women of our delegation, even though we had some outstanding people.

After our sessions in Moscow, we were allowed a brief tour. In Leningrad we were greeted by the mayor, a woman. By the time we reached Leningrad, however, I was in agony from the pain in my back. I think it came from carrying around a thick briefcase stuffed with papers—I was suspicious enough of Soviet snoopers not to want to leave it unguarded in my room. The resulting discomfort, however, was almost unbearable.

I was taken to a hospital in Leningrad where all the doctors were women. They worked diligently on me but nothing seemed to help. I carried on anyway and enjoyed the imperial palaces of Leningrad, which properly is called the Venice of the North. Then we went to Tashkent and Samarkand, which made us appreciate how huge and varied the Soviet is. The people there are Oriental and I noted that the Moscow women accompanying us showed them great respect, which I thought very revealing.

Nikita Khrushchev was in power in the Kremlin at that time and the Soviet Union was a more relaxed place for foreigners to visit but still I had the feeling sometimes that I was suffocating

and longed to be on my way home. There was no evidence whatsoever of any duress while we were there but I found their so-
called modern farms were really quite primitive and there was the
prevailing hand of the state on everything.

I picked up in casual conversation how much control there was
over the lives of the people, even to such matters as deciding
where they would have their vacations. I learned that most Soviet
citizens seemed to have friendly feelings toward the United States
but they were in dread of China.

I knew that Lyndon Johnson had made some proposals for disarmament that the Russians had rejected but I felt that the
United States should persist in view of the steadily improving
relations between our two countries. I believed that a breakthrough might be possible in 1964 and that the Chinese might
come along at that point too. It was early enough in the arms
escalation for such things to seem possible.

Just before we left, a young Russian woman came to me. She
knew that I was a friend of Lyndon Johnson's and had access to
the White House. I don't think she would have said what she did
to just anyone in the delegation.

The essence of the message she gave me, which I had the impression came directly from Khrushchev's wife, was that the Soviet leader wanted a gesture from the White House to enable
him to make the kinds of concessions in disarmament that both
countries could live with. The military was pressing him to do
otherwise and what he needed to resist them was an olive branch
from Washington.

There was no question in my mind but that the message was
authentic. Later I sent a letter to Lyndon Johnson through certain channels I could trust. It said, in part:

> Dear Lyndon, dear, dear Lyndon: . . . Nikita Khrushchev is an
> old man and he wants to help the cause of peace in his final ac-
> tive years . . . he needs reassurance that you are sincere in saying
> that peace is your prime concern . . . he is fearful of putting his
> head in a noose . . . such assurance could be a letter from you
> delivered by someone he trusts . . . there are those who oppose
> efforts to reach disarmament agreements, but if Khrushchev is
> convinced, many things are possible. . . .

The U. N. Disarmament Commission got hold of the letter and sent word that it was the best report to come from anyone that year on what was happening in the Soviet. People there were very excited at the news that Khrushchev possibly was seeking a route to better relations with the United States.

We had a second chance then, I believe, and we lost it. I did not hear from Lyndon Johnson about my letter and there was no attempt to approach Khrushchev in the manner that was suggested. Lyndon, a restless, vain, insecure man, was not inclined to get ahead of the crowd. He operated on the safer basis of consensus politics. When the pressure was on, he tended to become conservative and cautious.

I remember thinking after John Kennedy was killed that one thing was sure, we had heard the last frank response to a question from the press. Lyndon Johnson was constitutionally unable to open himself to the press as Kennedy did. Perhaps that can be seen as one of the factors that contributed to his downfall.

On my way home from the Soviet Union by way of London I went to a great woman chiropractor about my back. She put me under anesthetic and cracked my spine. It was so badly out of line from carrying the heavy weight of my papers that she didn't want to straighten it with me conscious. After that I went to bed and slept for two days and was fine. I had to remind myself that I could expect such problems; I was almost sixty-five.

Lyndon Johnson was the Democrats' nominee for the presidency in 1964. As he launched his campaign he said, "We should not send American boys to fight in Asia to do the job Asian boys ought to do." I had been troubled by America's increasing involvement in Southeast Asia and was relieved to hear his statement.

Of course I believed him. I campaigned hard for him in that election on the basis of my faith in his word. Did he deliberately lie to the voters, or did he believe what he said? I do not know. It is possible that no one knows except Lyndon, not even Lady Bird. It is possible that Lyndon himself didn't know the truth.

Senator Albert Gore once described a conversation he had with Lyndon soon after the election. His account of it is part of the Congressional Record. Gore related that he went to the

White House and learned that Lyndon was planning to send
American soldiers to Vietnam in contradiction to his election
promises.

Lyndon reviewed the situation for Gore as he saw it. Eisenhower had sent advisers, Kennedy sent advisers, technicians and
aides; it wasn't enough. He, President Johnson, either had to
withdraw all advisers, technicians and aides or else send in combat troops.

Lyndon said to Gore, "I'm not going to be the first President
to run."

I encountered Lyndon only once during the campaign. I went
to hear him give a speech in big old Madison Square Garden.
The audience was very warm and Lyndon went on interminably.
He never wanted that speech to end. He kept putting out his
hands as though he would embrace the audience. When he left,
people wanted to touch him. It was a very loving time, every bit
of it.

One has to have that picture of him to realize what it meant in
the last year of his term when he couldn't appear in public. He
didn't dare face the public. He had to give his speeches at army
bases, navy bases. His unhappiness over that must have been very
great.

The Johnsons invited me many times to visit them in the
White House but unfortunately I was never able to accept.
Either I was in Europe or I was lecturing somewhere on every
date suggested.

After the troops went to Vietnam I began to associate myself
with protests against the war. I didn't try to contact Lyndon. I
felt, after his silence following my letter about Khrushchev, that
it was no use. He couldn't listen. It would be just one more
harassment.

Toward the end of his last term in office, when my position on
Vietnam was well known, I was among a large number invited to
a reception at the White House. I went down the receiving line
and shook Lyndon's hand. He looked at me with a glassy stare,
no recognition in his face, and said nothing. I moved on in shock.

Afterward I joined Lady Bird and Tex Goldschmidt in another
room away from the crowd and we talked of old times. When she

left, Tex turned to me in consternation. He had witnessed the President's snub.

"It isn't possible that the President didn't recognize you!" Tex cried.

I shook my head in despair. Of course he recognized me. It was just that he had nothing to say. That struck me as sad—not for me at all, but because it indicated his misery and what he was undergoing. And what the country was undergoing, and what we all suffered.

Soon afterward I was part of one of the most moving protest meetings of that period. I was the emcee for an evening of poetry readings, called "Poets for Peace," in the Town Hall of New York University. Present were six Pulitzer Prize winners, Stanley Kunitz, Robert Lowell, W. D. Snodgrass, Mark Van Doren, Richard Wilbur and Arthur Miller. Among those who spoke that evening were Daniel Berrigan, Paul Goodman, Julian Bond, Anaïs Nin and a Buddhist monk and poet from Vietnam, Thich Nhat Hanh. The proceeds of the evening went to civilian relief in Vietnam.

That year I was also a member of the National Committee for a SANE Nuclear Policy. At a Board meeting on April 27, 1967, which was also attended by Dr. Benjamin Spock, Norman Thomas, Jane Buchenholz and Norman Cousins, we approved the famous advertisement that showed Benjamin Spock and began, "DR. SPOCK IS WORRIED . . . And if you've read my books on raising children, you know I don't worry easily. But our nation's involvement in Vietnam causes me the gravest concern—particularly now that U.S. bombs are falling again on North Vietnam. . . ."

The Gahagan family was celebrating a notable achievement. Walter had received a plaque from the American Society of Civil Engineers for "the outstanding achievement of 1966," which was the work the Gahagan Dredging Corporation did on the launch complex at the Kennedy Space Center. Our company literally put the earth under the moon shot; our dredges provided the fill for the pads, access channels and the Vertical Assembly Building. Walter also had a personal commendation from NASA and the Chief of Army Engineers for that work.

Lilli came from Caracas to New York with terror in her eyes. She went into the hospital and we learned that she had cancer which had invaded her liver.

Nan Stevens offered to take care of Lilli's tiny Yorkshire terrier Bombi while the tests were being made. Afterward Nan said to me, "Is Lilli all right?"

I found it difficult to speak of it. I started to give some evasive answer but Nan's direct look stopped me.

"She has cancer," I said. "She isn't all right at all."

Lilli went to Virginia and the family took turns, a week at a time, staying with her. Toward the end, I didn't leave her.

Melvyn Douglas:

Lilli's death was the hardest for Helen to bear of all the deaths of people she loved. The sisters were very close. Helen went to stay with Lilli at the stage where she was helpless. She used to carry her to the bathroom, that sort of thing. She went through the horrors of seeing her beloved sister in great pain, of watching her die.

Helen handled grief stoically. Not for one moment did she beg for support. She accepted support, liked support, responded to it, but she didn't ask for it. When she learned four years after Lilli's death that she herself had cancer, she accepted the news in much the same way, keeping her feelings completely to herself.

Lilli died in March 1968, and after that I refused all speaking tours for a year or two. I would accept individual requests to speak if I felt the occasion demanded it, but I preferred to have a quieter life. I was appalled by the violence in Chicago when the Democrats chose Hubert Humphrey as their presidential candidate. Because Humphrey did not repudiate the war in Vietnam, I did not campaign for him.

Humphrey's opponent was Richard Nixon. A Virginia journalist, Jean Polk, asked me to comment on Nixon and his 1950 tactics against me because he was using the same techniques to impugn Humphrey's loyalty.

"A campaign of vilification does not clarify basic issues," I told her, "though it may hot up the contest between candidates. If candidates for public office are allowed by the voters to avoid the issues, democratic processes are undermined. The voter gives his support without being told what candidates will be voting for or against in his name. The voter has been led down the primrose path. He has not used his voice to guide policy."

When Jean Polk asked what I was doing at the time, I made no mention of the fact that my beloved sister had died a few weeks earlier. I replied, "My current activities are an extension of my work over the last thirty years. . . . I continue to support the work of the United Nations. I have opposed the Vietnam adventure from the beginning. I deplore and oppose the arms race.

"I believe a disarmed world under international control is the only guarantee that man will have of a future in which to mature.

"As long as there continues to be such universal ignorance of the inescapable laws of this new age we have entered—the nuclear age—the disarmed world is unachievable. Therefore I travel to better know people, to acquaint myself with conditions under which people live at home and abroad so that I can think and act reasonably in our time."

In truth, I was doing little traveling or speaking. My back problems had returned and I was in excruciating pain much of the time. When I could, I helped collect my papers for the University of Oklahoma at Norman.

After much work by Evie Chavoor, Nan Stevens and many others we assembled enough material to fill 217 boxes with memorabilia, correspondence, printed and manuscript material relating to my theatrical, legislative, diplomatic and political careers and my participation in national and international organizations concerned with global questions.

We located several hundred photographs of me, posed and candid, and I sent along some of the honors I had received, such as the George Washington Carver Award of 1947, the Scroll of Honor from the National Council of Negro Women in 1946, and the papers signed by President Truman in September 1946 appointing me as alternate representative of the United States to the United Nations.

Jack D. Haley, assistant curator of Oklahoma University's Western History Collection, spent several days with me, sorting and cataloguing the collection. Haley told me that it had "great research value."

The Helen Gahagan Douglas Collection is available under supervision to scholars, historians and people who are interested in the theater and music. I understand that Box 207 and Box 208 excite the most attention. The first contains my campaign material from the 1950 election when I was defeated by Richard Nixon and the second includes the Pink Sheet as well as some of the speeches endorsing me at that time.

Richard Nixon became President of the United States in 1968. I had letters from people who remembered that 1950 campaign and were alarmed. One such came from Wilfred Myll, an Episcopal clergyman in Louisville, Kentucky. I replied to him in much the same way I answered the others. I wrote on January 24, 1969:

> As I watched Richard Nixon take the oath of office as President of the United States, my reactions were quite normal, completely objective.
>
> I judge President Nixon as I do any political figure. I have my doubts about this administration and they are very grave ones. But I must add that no partisan supporter of Richard Nixon will be more satisfied than I if Richard Nixon proves to be a good and wise President.
>
> The country can afford no less. The world can afford no less.

In 1968 Walter liquidated the Gahagan Dredging Corporation and made a generous distribution of the profits to the remaining members of the family. He felt it was time for him to retire and there was no Gahagan to take over. He and Gay moved to a beachside penthouse in Fort Lauderdale, Florida, where they spend their winters in good works. He and Gay were honored as "the couple of the year" in March 1979, in recognition of their philanthropic activities. I know that Walter, who was president of the Boys' Athletic League of New York from 1970 to 1974, made a donation in six figures to that organization.

In the summers Walter and Gay live at Gay-Walden in Vermont, which continues to pull our scattered families together from all over the world.

Nixon's election produced a flurry of interest in me. I had requests from Radcliffe College and Boston University, among others, for my papers, which were already in Oklahoma. Regularly I sat down with scholars to contribute to oral histories such as those of Lyndon Johnson and Eleanor Roosevelt. I had a note from Amelia R. Fry, known to friends as Chita, director of the Earl Warren History Project, University of California at Berkeley. She wanted my recollections of Earl Warren, and subsequently launched an oral history of my life. We became warm friends: Chita Fry spent months and months, over many years, working with me on the Helen Gahagan Douglas oral history that is now stored in the Bancroft Library. Our agreement is that it will not be released until this book is published.

I also devoted considerable time to correcting tapes for a series of books being prepared by the University of Pittsburgh covering my years on the Foreign Affairs Committee.

A reporter asked if I had any regrets about being out of politics. "No." I grinned. "Why should I? I never left the stage, you know."

It gave me great pleasure to be on the board of directors of Creative Arts Rehabilitation in New York, which provides remarkably effective therapy through the medium of music, art, dance, drama or poetry to help the emotional repair and growth of adults and children. Headed by the actress Celeste Holm, it really pioneered that kind of community-based approach to mental illness.

I also served a three-year term, beginning in 1970, on the advisory council of the Columbia School of Social Work, and remained active in SANE and in the Women's International League for Peace and Freedom. When I gave speeches at colleges, where students were having confrontations with faculty and police over the Vietnamese war and other issues, I argued as strongly as I could for an approach to problems based on reason rather than fury.

After I spoke at Alma College in Michigan, a student there told a reporter from the Alma *Record-Leader,* "I've been moving toward the left and I convinced myself that violence could be

justified. After talking with Mrs. Douglas, I'm beginning to think
I'm wrong."

As a visible woman, I was one of those approached for my
views on the women's movement which was beginning to stir. On
January 5, 1971, I told Enid Nemy of the New York *Times*:

> Women's movements are not sufficiently preoccupied with the
> peace issue. I don't know what it would take to arouse women.
> Why don't they take this issue and make it theirs? None of the
> other things we all want will happen until we get this
> straight. . . .
>
> I've certainly always been for women's liberation. There are in-
> disputable goals of equal opportunity and pay but I think there
> are peripheral undertakings that are frivolous.
>
> I don't think women will get anywhere by just demanding.
> One way to get attention is to work at grass roots level until we
> have sufficient strength so we must be consulted. . . .

I observed that my Grandmother Hannah hadn't marched in
the streets demanding the right to run for office on the school
board. She just rounded up supporters and ran. As I see it, that's
the way to succeed. Don't complain that you can't do it—just do
it.

In the spring of 1972 I discovered a lump in my breast. I went
into the hospital to have it, and my breast, removed.

Melvyn Douglas:

> I was completely undone. I was terribly afraid of the effect that
> it was going to have on Helen psychologically. Once in her youth
> she was called "ten of the twelve most beautiful women in the
> world." I think this meant a great deal to Helen. Helen was
> aware that people found her beautiful and she relished it, enjoyed
> it.
>
> I can remember in the first year of our marriage when we were
> driving across the mountains in California. Something fell on the
> floor of the car and I leaned down to pick it up and almost went
> off the road. I had to jam on the brakes and Helen was thrown
> forward and hit her head on the windshield. The impact broke
> open her forehead.
>
> I never had such guilt feelings in my life. I felt I had disfigured

the ten most beautiful women in the world. We rushed her to a great plastic surgeon but the worry went on for two years that it wouldn't heal properly. I know Helen was worried about it. Her face was part of her career at that time.

After the children were born, Helen became extremely full-breasted. Without consulting me, without saying anything about it, she made arrangements to have plastic surgery to reduce the size of her bust. I was horrified. However, she went through with it.

To this day, despite what the doctors have told me, I'm not sure that it didn't have something to do with her developing cancer in her breast.

While she was being operated on to remove the cancer, I had the same dread as when her face was hurt. I thought that when Helen awoke from the anesthetic and found that she had lost part of her body, it would destroy her.

Mary Helen and I went out to eat while the operation was going on and I couldn't help sobbing. I couldn't bear to think how Helen would feel when she realized that part of herself was gone. I thought it would be impossible to bear.

No such thing happened. She had none of the pep talks that women get after a mastectomy because she didn't need them. She went through it like a skylark. She showed no psychological effect at all. She had no inhibition about exposing herself, about asking for advice. She was amazing. She even showed off her scar. All the fears and torments I'd gone through were unwarranted. Helen made up her mind that the operation was necessary to save her life, and that was that.

Nan Stevens:

Helen was seventy-two when the cancer started. For a woman of that age, she was incredible. Her back was absolutely straight and she walked so vigorously that I always seemed to be ten steps behind her. She once said that her father had walked like that.

When she found out that her breast would be removed, she went up to Vermont by herself. She delayed going into the hospital and said there was something up there that she had to take care of. I think she went really to prepare herself for what was coming. When the surgery was over, she went back to Vermont as soon as she could. Vermont was where she pulled herself together.

That summer of 1972 I found myself too sore from the mastectomy to do many public appearances but I had an interview with
Parents magazine in which I explained why I was so drawn to
speaking to college students. I said:

> I have always welcomed the opportunity to talk with young
> people . . . [to] describe how this government of the people op-
> erates. If they are to work for changes within the system, there
> must be a clear understanding of the system. As far as I can, I
> make sure they do. I explain the relationship between the execu-
> tive, the Congress and the court, trace the steps that must be
> taken before a proposal becomes law, explain why this govern-
> ment of the people needs the continuing watchful support of the
> people to work *for the people*, why an uninformed vote in the
> Congress or in the voting booth can be harmful to the general
> welfare, remind them that eternal vigilance is the price of lib-
> erty. . . .
> Today the average new voter is better informed than fifty-two
> years ago. This voter, man or woman, will get off to a better start
> —can have a more important position in the political life of the
> nation. I am betting on the new voters. I think there will be
> changes.

I was impatient with some of the manifestations of the
women's movement. Asked for my reaction to a New York *Times*
story about the efforts of some militant women to be served in an
all-male bar, I told the interviewer from *Parents:*

> I cannot see that this has anything to do with liberation. . . .
> What we want to get at is the root of woman's problem—in-
> feriority. At the beginning of this century a few women tena-
> ciously worked, struggled, endured ridicule—even imprisonment
> —to obtain the vote. They believed we must share political power
> if we were to gain independence. They won the first round.
> The question now, it seems to me, is how to activate the inac-
> tive woman, the woman who is brought up to believe that mar-
> riage is "all of it"—and finds that it isn't. Life for her can be
> boring, an empty shell, devitalizing, if nothing occurs to shock
> her out of her state of somnambulism. . . .
> I wish Women's Liberation would interest itself in the early
> childhood of female children. The female has to be trained from

childhood to develop interests and abilities, to be aware of her capacities. Capacity differs. But training, to be successful, must be geared to developing the potential. A woman must be given the resources necessary to build an inner life so she can respect herself.

I was asked about the Black Power movement, which had become a political force. I said:

> I have never thought the prime issue for blacks was mixing and living with whites. Once their acceptance in our society is wholehearted and relaxed, their preference for association with whites or blacks will seem quite natural. The blacks want to be judged and accepted as every other citizen should be in a democratic society, on the basis of character and ability. They need and rightly demand the same opportunity to develop and then to function in society on the same equal basis of ability as white people. They do not ask, have never asked, for a free ride.

My advice to citizens who want to be better informed about the issues and want to be part of responsible organizations concerned with problems of the day was first of all to obtain and read the Congressional Record. I have a copy delivered daily to my home. Next, study the voting record of your congressman.

> The entire record of a congressman can be obtained for nominal cost from the Congressional Quarterly, 1735 K Street NW, Washington, D.C. 20006.
>
> This service sends to subscribers weekly reports on the words and works of the President, the Congress, the Court, and the Cabinet. If one has the time, a daily study of the Congressional Record of the House and Senate is enlightening. One can request that it be sent to them by some member of their delegation in Congress or, if that is not possible, order a Congressional Record from the Public Printing Office, Washington, D.C. and pay the Office for it.
>
> Such citizen committees as Another Mother for Peace, or Common Cause, or SANE, or Public Citizen Inc. (Ralph Nader's organization), the International League for Peace and Freedom, ADA, can be an introduction to meaningful organized political action.

I had become a board member of The Population Institute, along with such worthy people as Arthur Ashe, Isaac Asimov, Joan Baez, Simone de Beauvoir, John Cowles, Sr., Margaret Truman Daniel, John Kenneth Galbraith, Clare Boothe Luce and Mary Tyler Moore. The focus was on explaining the why of family planning rather than the how. We produced radio spots which didn't put out the message that people should have fewer children but rather spoke of upgrading the quality of life in the family and the community.

By autumn I was stronger and I spent ten weeks stumping for George McGovern, who was running against Richard Nixon for the presidency. I didn't think I'd have the strength for it, but I did.

Nixon couldn't get far accusing McGovern of being a communist, so he had other tactics. He tried to diminish his opponent by describing him as a man who doesn't understand what's going on, who changes his mind, whose staff work is poor. He was still not discussing the issues.

"It's not just me who got smeared by Nixon in an election," I told Democratic rallies, "it's everybody from Voorhis to Adlai Stevenson and now to George McGovern."

The issues, as I saw them in that campaign, were the failure of Nixon to end the war in Vietnam, the scandals associated with his administration, the rise in inflation and the record deficit.

McGovern's campaign got off to a rocky start because he began by defending himself against Nixon's attacks on his character. I thought this was a tactical error. It was more fruitful, I thought, to stick to the issues. Everywhere I went around northern New York State I spoke of the war in Vietnam and asked a question that intrigued me: Why didn't Nixon reveal the source of his campaign funds?

In California in 1950 the money came from oil interests. I wondered who was supplying it this time.

In Springfield for a round of coffee parties, I held a press conference in which I raised the matter of the strange incident in the Watergate apartments where five men with close ties to the Republican Committee to Reelect the President were arrested in the Democratic party's national headquarters. It was clear that they were spying on behalf of Richard Nixon and it seemed essential for the country to know whether the President had condoned or authorized the crime.

Mostly, however, I spoke of the tragedy of the war in Vietnam. I was backing McGovern, I said, for his stand on social issues and that war—"the most divisive experience" in recent history in the United States.

"It is even worse for the nation than the Civil War was," I said, "because it has led to cynicism that is very dangerous for America. There is a prevailing lack of trust in government."

Nixon brought out new accusations against McGovern, saying that George was in favor of unilateral disarmament. That wasn't true and Richard Nixon knew it wasn't true. George McGovern deplored the war, recognized it as a frightful error and understood what it was doing to us as a people. He proposed to take the fat out of the military and put it in schools and drug and crime control.

My speaking itinerary in New Hampshire and Vermont in October required up to five appearances a day, starting with a morning coffee party, and included radio and television and newspaper interviews in between. Someone asked if I didn't find it a taxing schedule so soon after a radical mastectomy. I replied:

"I am so anguished at what is being done in my name in Vietnam that I couldn't be still if I had to get up from my deathbed."

The mystery of what was behind the burglaries in the Watergate continued to interest me. Nixon was making statements denying any involvement. I said, "What has been done to us is the greatest snow job in history."

On November 1, I did a performance of readings in the Westport Country Playhouse that netted $5,000 for McGovern's campaign fund. A few days later, Americans went to the polls and reelected Richard Nixon as President of the United States.

During the next year I stepped up efforts to make Americans aware of the horror of the accelerating arms race. I was in close contact with my dear friend Philip Noel-Baker, a British Quaker and pacifist who in 1959 received the Nobel Peace Prize. His book *The Arms Race: A Program for World Disarmament*, published in 1958, is still one of the finest sources of information for those who wish to appreciate the folly of the military buildup all over the world.

I give two samples of letters to me from Philip Noel-Baker to illustrate the nature and content of our exchanges. One was written from the airport as he was departing New York for London. It is dated "Saturday, 2.5.59" and reads:

> Dear Helen, I can't leave without a line. I must tell you how I have loved seeing you and thank you for being so good to me.
>
> I sent back a lot of stuff today, all of highest value. Humphrey's speech is very promising; we must get him lined up on our UNA programme! I'm sure that's the big hope.
>
> I sent the two papers to the Editor of the New York *Post*.
>
> Plane just leaving; see you in Greece (I hope). My love and gratitude again. As always, Philip N.B.

The other comes from his London address in South Eaton Place and is dated November 20, 1969. He writes:

> Dear Helen:
>
> Thank you very much for several letters. First I must thank you for your help over the National Rifle Association. Edward Kennedy's letter and the book *No Right to Bear Arms* give me exactly what I need to know.
>
> Second, I must thank you for sending me the transcript of the picture made by N.E.T. which you tell me is to be shown over here by the B.B.C. I hope I am not too late to see the picture on the B.B.C. My sporting friends (ICSPE, UNESCO), gave me a marvellous colour television set for my eightieth birthday so, if I can get it on the B.B.C., I shall see it in the best conditions. I shall, in any case, try to get the film shown at the House of Commons for our Labour Party Foreign Affairs Group and others.
>
> All gratitude again, and love. Yours ever, Philip N.B.
>
> P.S. When are you coming over? The years go by.

Though I could see that I was having no impact on the arms race, I could not let the subject alone. In one of the hundreds of speeches I made on the subject, I said:

> The continued expenditure for exotic new weapons when we already have more weapons than we need, and when there is such a need for schools and hospitals, and our cities are deteriorating, is reprehensible. The White House says there is not enough

money for day care centers or for adequate help for children and the elderly but there is never a suggestion that we have to cut back on any expense for the military.

In the spring of 1973 I had good news. A report from the cancer specialists I was consulting said my blood count was normal. It appeared that the radical mastectomy had cleared away all the malignancy.

As the conspiracy behind the Watergate burglary began to unfold and Richard Nixon clearly was implicated, I threw myself into the movement to impeach the President. That summer a number of reporters remembered that I was one of Richard Nixon's earliest victims. One who came to visit me in Vermont was Lee Israel of *Ms.* magazine. The story appeared in the October 1973 issue, which bore my picture on the cover.

She reviewed the events of the 1950 election in California and dwelled at some length on my childhood and years on the stage. Lee Israel pondered my refusal to defend myself adequately against Nixon. The article ended:

> Driving home from Vermont, I tried to grapple with the Helen Douglas dilemma, not hers to be sure, but mine, ours. Is the road to hell really paved with small compromises, as my college ethics teacher had insisted? Do chinks inevitably become yawning gaps? Or is the human animal equipped with an on/off switch, or at least a variety of gears? Must we settle so frequently in politics for evil because the good are not willing or able to shoot a little dirty pool?
>
> I can imagine that my Jesuitical ethics prof would have responded: "Yes, but you see Helen Gahagan Douglas would not be Helen Gahagan Douglas if . . ."
>
> "Yes, professor, but neither would she be Richard Nixon."

For months afterward, *Ms.* magazine received inquiries from people who wanted to know how to contact me. The editors reported breathlessly, "The response is incredible." I found myself besieged by an avalanche of letters and requests for interviews and speeches.

When I spoke in Boston in November 1973, seven hundred New England Democratic women showed up. The Boston Sunday *Globe* remarked that I was in danger of becoming a cult figure. I refused to see what was happening in that light. I said,

"You do what you must do and that's all. Each of us has a responsibility to follow our beliefs."

In truth I welcomed the sudden attention because it gave me fresh opportunities to talk about the arms race. I found I was drawing huge audiences. When I was announced as the emcee of a fund-raising banquet sponsored by the National Committee of the Democratic party in Washington, thirteen hundred attended. My friend William O. Douglas of the Supreme Court introduced me and described the time in 1947 when the Hollywood Ten were cited for contempt of Congress for refusing to answer such questions put to them by HUAC as, "Do you believe in communism?" He went on to say:

> Nine out of ten (as I recall) did not plead the Fifth Amendment but the First Amendment, which says "Congress shall make no law . . . abridging the freedom of speech." That freedom in our Western world has covered beliefs. "Do you believe in God?" "Do you believe in the unearned increment of Henry George?" "Do you believe in peace?" All questions of belief are taboo. They are none of the government's business. For failure to disclose their "belief" nine of the ten were convicted. They brought the case to our court where the *certiorari* was denied. But Hugo Black and I voted to grant.
>
> But the important fact concerns Helen. On November 24, 1947, she voted against the contempt citation of the Hollywood Ten. Hollywood, following the example of Charles Dickens, sometimes produced films whose minor theme was exploitation by the free enterprise system. This was the kind of theme that sent the Hollywood Ten to prison.
>
> The vote in the House was 260 ayes and 16 nays. Helen Douglas said, "I refuse to accept the insidious doctrine that any reflection on established wrongs that may be found in American movies, the American radio, or in the American press are communist-inspired.
>
> "When I took the oath of office I swore to uphold the Constitution and the Bill of Rights. Any infringement upon freedom of speech is a violation of the First Amendment. I consider it my clear duty to oppose the Committee on Un-American Activities."
>
> I have the honor to present a First Amendment friend who has truly lived in the tradition of Thomas Jefferson—Helen Gahagan Douglas.

People stood and cheered, while I struggled for composure.

The next day I spoke at the regular luncheon of the Woman's National Democratic Club, which normally draws an audience of fifty. More than five hundred wanted tickets, so the organizers accommodated most of them by having tables removed and rows of chairs substituted. The women dined on an austere meal of cheese sandwiches which they balanced on paper plates on their laps.

The story in the Washington *Post* about the event was headlined: ANGER WITHOUT MALICE. I was not enjoying Richard Nixon's disgrace as the scandal of Watergate continued to unfold and I refused to make capital of his downfall. Reporters all over the country wanted my reaction to Watergate and expected me to talk about the 1950 campaign; I preferred not to do so.

It was a matter of taste. My opponent for a seat in the Senate was now President of the United States. In no way did I want to give the impression that I would take the unhappy Watergate affair as my opportunity to get back at Richard Nixon. It wasn't the time to say, "And by the way, look at what he did to me."

I would much rather, for the good of the country, that Richard Nixon were the President he thought he was. I couldn't take pleasure from the distress of our country.

I was told of a bumper sticker: DON'T BLAME ME. I VOTED FOR HELEN GAHAGAN DOUGLAS. I could laugh about that, but there was nothing in the abasement of the White House that I could enjoy.

Nan Stevens:

It was true. People rather expected that she would be gloating over Richard Nixon finally being found out, but she was only sad. She thought it was terrible for the country and for America's reputation abroad. I know that makes her sound almost too good to be true, but she *was* good. I'm not saying Helen didn't have feet of clay, because she did. But you had to look awfully hard to find her tiny clay feet.

In January 1974 I was the final speaker at a rally sponsored by the Citizens' Lobby for the Impeachment Process. It was coordinated by outraged citizens in Queens, Nassau and Suffolk counties and coincided with the investigation into Watergate that was being conducted by the Select Committee on Presidential Campaign Activities of the Senate.

Two months later I was in Los Angeles to address a Democratic Women's Forum. It was held in the Beverly Hills Hotel but I was told that the sponsors could have booked the Hollywood Bowl for it.

To my delight, the event turned into something of a reunion. Among those who attended was Jerry Voorhis. He too was being asked a lot about Nixon; we compared notes.

Laurence and Patsy Hewes wrote me:

> No one who has lived as a liberal for the last four decades could witness the Nixon downfall without thinking of you and the principles for which you have stood.

Many of the letters I received were in the same vein. Russell W. Ballard, former director of Hull House in Chicago and a liberal who suffered under McCarthyism, said:

> I write in appreciation and in sorrow that this man was responsible that your official political service to the nation was curtailed.

I told the Knight News Service reporter who asked about Nixon, "One feels sorry—for the family and for him at this moment. You can't help but feel sorry . . ."

I hoped that impeachment would go through because I thought it was better for the country to clear the air. I thought the Judiciary Committee should submit the charges against Nixon to Congress so that our elected representatives could determine whether impeachment proceedings should begin.

Instead Nixon abruptly left the White House and turned the office of President over to Gerald R. Ford, who promptly repaid the favor by pardoning Nixon. It was, I thought, a grievous miscarriage of justice but I was as relieved as anyone else in the country that the long agony was ended.

I was one of the sponsors of a seminar at the United Nations conducted by the Women of the World United for Peace. My hope that the women's movement would concern itself with the arms race was beginning to be realized. Among those who also sponsored that seminar were Bella Abzug, Joan Baez, Angela Davis, Simone de Beauvoir, Ruby Dee, Betty Friedan, Eleanor McGovern and Susan Sontag.

Soon afterward I signed a telegram from the National Abortion Rights Action League to Birch Bayh strongly protesting amendments that were being introduced to limit Medicaid payments for abortion, thus denying low-income women that same choice that middle-class women had.

That autumn I chaired a dinner in Washington for Democratic Senators up for reelection: James B. Allen of Alabama, Frank Church of Idaho, Adlai Stevenson III of Illinois, Russell B. Long and others.

I was enthusiastic about the Women's Campaign Fund that had been launched to help worthy women candidates and I signed some letters appealing for donations. I helped put a board of directors together for Women's Lobby Inc., which launched the *Women's Lobby Quarterly* to provide an analysis of legislation affecting women and reveal how individual congressmen spoke and voted on these issues.

I signed a fund-raising letter that went to 12,000 potential donors in the first mailing and 35,000 more in the second. In it I explained that the Women's Lobby was working on Capitol Hill to inform congressmen of women's problems and what was needed in legislation. There are 105 million women in the United States. Six million school children have working mothers and many of these are the head of the family. The country needs quality day care, full pension benefits for women equal to those of men, tax reform, and evenhanded credit.

I was also interested in the Gray Panthers movement. When I addressed members in Washington in March 1974, I told them about Dorothy McCall of Oregon who at eighty-five declared she was ready to succeed her son as Governor of the state, since Tom McCall was ineligible to succeed himself.

I quoted Dorothy McCall's spunky comment that she wasn't ready to be put out to pasture. She added, "I urge everyone from fifty-nine to ninety-five to get involved in productive living. If any

boy can grow up to be President, surely a grandmother like me
can aspire to be governor."

At seventy-three myself, I heartily concurred. The following
spring I was at Marlboro College in Vermont to address the com-
mencement. I spoke, of course, about the arms race:

> We have the capability of destroying life on this planet. As I
> see it, nothing will come right if we do not stop the arms race.
> Nations still talk of peace and the need to control nuclear weap-
> ons but the arms race that began in the fifties between the Soviet
> Union and the United States goes on at an accelerated pace—
> and the nations around the world that can ill afford to do so have
> been buying non-nuclear weapons at an accelerated rate.
>
> Albert Einstein had this to say about the arms race of the
> fifties: "The unleashed power of the atom has changed every-
> thing save our modes of thinking, and we thus drift toward un-
> paralleled catastrophes. . . ." The United States and the Soviet
> Union together have already stockpiled nuclear weapons with the
> force of ten tons of TNT for every man, woman and child on
> earth. But apparently that's not enough. . . . In this bicentennial
> year, we must reeducate ourselves to the American dream. Ideas
> are powerful in the evolution of the human family. We will not
> strengthen democracy by the power of our weapons but by the
> example we set here at home of a vital democracy.
>
> Graduation is not the end of learning. Learning goes on daily
> or one stagnates. As you go through life you will have to make, at
> times, decisive decisions, under strain, which will affect your fu-
> ture and your character. . . .
>
> Success, more often than not, depends on the fulfillment of
> one's maximum potential, rather than on competition with one
> another. If one is trustworthy, if one's word is one's bond, he or
> she will have stature. It is so with a nation.
>
> Character isn't inherited. One builds it daily by the way one
> thinks and acts, thought by thought, action by action. If one lets
> fear or hate or anger take possession of the mind, they become
> self-forged chains. The challenge to us all is to stay alive in life,
> to remain open, receiving, responding to nature, friends, pas-
> sersby; to learn the art of love, of giving one's self, and asking
> nothing in return.

Though most of my speeches dealt with the arms race, there
were some of a lighter nature. In October 1975 I was in Cleve-

land to give an address to mark the sixtieth anniversary of the Play House. Wearing a loose jacket to conceal a back brace that supported two broken ribs, I spoke of the power of living theater. I said:

> Everything one does that is verbal helps to make the mind function. When we attend living theater we make an effort to get there. We set an evening aside for a special entertainment, rather than having it come into our homes via a television set. We purchase tickets. Then, there is an impact between the actor and the listener. The more knowledgeable the audience is about itself, and about the world, the better the actor.

My cancer had returned. It began with weakness in my legs and was diagnosed at Sloan-Kettering Memorial Hospital as cancer of the bone marrow. Surgery was impossible but a course of heavy chemotherapy was indicated. I was warned that it would result in the loss of my hair.

Melvyn Douglas:

When I heard about what would happen to her hair, I again thought it would be a terribly difficult experience for her. Long before her hair began to come out, I went to considerable trouble to find the best wig man in New York. He came to the apartment and saw Helen, cutting some samples of her hair to take away with him. Then he made one of the most beautiful wigs that I think ever was made.

Helen was utterly delighted with it. She acted as though she couldn't wait to wear it. When her hair loss began, she put on the wig with obvious pleasure.

Then there was a second delight because when the chemotherapy ended her hair came back, and it came back charmingly.

Nan Stevens:

She wasn't in the least self-conscious about her bald head. She wore the wig only when she had to go out. She never wore it around the house.

So that when I saw her for the first time after she had been in Vermont all summer, I was surprised that she received me with the wig on. I made some comment about it.

"It isn't a wig," she told me impatiently. "My hair has grown back."

It was true. It grew back snow-white and luxurious.

When Mary Helen heard that my illness had been diagnosed as bone cancer, she immediately sent me Adelle Davis's books about healthful anti-stress diet. I began to follow the suggestions at once and I have not stopped. My cancer is still with me but, after almost six years, so am I; emphatically.

Lately I have added to the natural vitamin approach a new vitamin that has been developed recently. I'm studying every article and book that I can find to aid me. I cherish a quote of Dr. Charles Mayo: "No case of cancer is hopeless."

In the fall of 1976 I was doing well on modified chemotherapy when a new pain developed in the right side of my back. Together with the constant ache in my right leg, it gave me great discomfort. With Mary Helen's help I devised a schedule by which I ate six small meals a day rather than three larger ones and took quantities of brewer's yeast and vitamin E. Ginseng tea, I discovered, helped me cope with the nausea that followed chemotherapy.

I also took laetrile, a controversial treatment for cancer that the American Medical Association had not approved. It was still being debated hotly but I saw no reason why I should not try it.

That spring I was interviewed by Ruthe Stein of the San Francisco *Chronicle*, who wanted to know what I thought of the Democrats who were campaigning hard for the presidential nomination. I said, "I'm listening to Carter. I'm not as frightened of him as some people are. I like Church very much, and I like Udall. . . ."

I added earnestly, "We need excellence. The problems are so different today. We need new ideas and new approaches."

In November 1976 the United States elected James Earl Carter as our new President. Some of my activities during his campaign had been directed by what the Democratic party called its Senior Citizens Desk, which hoped that the concerns of the elderly would receive adequate attention under the new administration. A few days after the victory I received a letter from Jimmy

Carter. Writing from Plains, Georgia, on November 10, 1976, he said:

> Our Chairman, Bob Strauss, has told me of your prompt and generous response to our Demo-Gram and even though belatedly I want to tell you how much I appreciate the additional contribution you made to help assure the victory we won. It is because you cared enough to help when help was needed that our Party succeeded and will go on now to restore a government that will be worthy of the trust and aspirations of the American people.
>
> Thank you again for the sacrifices you have made and for what you have done to help make this a better country.
>
> Sincerely, Jimmy Carter.

Two days later I had a letter from Cooki Lutkefedder, national coordinator of the Committee for 51.3 Percent, which was the women's branch of the campaign. She wrote:

> We have just won a victory that did not come easily, one that might not have been possible without your time and energy. The Committee for 51.3% was created because Jimmy Carter cares and 51.3% has been extremely important in this election.
>
> The work you did on behalf of the 51.3% Committee and Jimmy Carter—and for women throughout the country—helped form the nationwide resource network that was instrumental in achieving our tremendous impact during the campaign. You are part of that network. Now that the election is over and the transition period is in progress, it is extremely important that you keep in touch with us. We've come a long way together and we will continue to need your help and support in order to fulfill our role in the Carter administration.
>
> As women become an integral part of the new administration, we will need your counsel—your suggestions and ideas can be of great help.
>
> Thank you for all your efforts—they have certainly paid off. I look forward to hearing from you soon.

I was still hoping that women would take more interest in disarmament. In 1977 I signed an appeal that was addressed to women everywhere in the world to address themselves to arms escalation. It read:

The escalating arms race wastes a billion dollars a day. A billion dollars a day could wipe out poverty and hunger. That amount of money could bring day care, health care, decent housing, jobs, clean water, and safe energy to all. By denying these human needs, the arms race itself kills and maims. Children and women are its first victims. . . .

Let all women stand together to demand disarmament now.

In March 1977 there was a reunion in Washington of New Dealers. I attended the event in the ballroom of the Mayflower Hotel and mingled with dear friends and comrades of my vintage. "We were so young then," I said to a New York *Times* reporter. "We had such hope."

Thomas (the Cork) Corcoran was there, the lawyer who helped draft the New Deal legislation. He said, "We never thought we'd be alive this long—we've cheated heaven."

President Carter couldn't attend but sent a message. Hubert Humphrey, thin, frail, near death from cancer, was there. So were India Edwards, Claude Pepper, I. F. Stone and eight hundred others. The party marked the forty-fourth anniversary of Franklin Roosevelt's first inauguration, and the presence of FDR and Eleanor was felt by all of us. Rexford Tugwell, who had been Under Secretary of Agriculture in the Roosevelt administration, was the speaker.

Benjamin Cohen, a Roosevelt Brain Truster, said it for all of us in the *Times:* "We were the lucky ones. For us it was a time when to be alive was joy and to be young was very heaven."

I managed to keep in touch with the National Advisory Committee on Farm Labor, of which I was still a member. Farm workers, "the slaves we rent," were still in a miserable condition in 1977. It was estimated that year that forty-two states depended on millions of migrants for cheap, disposable labor. According to Department of Agriculture figures, the average income for a migrant worker in America is $2,714 a season. Many have no other employment.

In the spring of 1978 there was an International Peace Ball at the United Nations. I wasn't well enough to attend it but I was a member of the National Committee Planetary Citizens who pulled it off. Other sponsors were Norman Cousins, Marshall

McLuhan, Isaac Asimov, Marcel Marceau, Robert Hutchins, Buckminster Fuller, John Updike and Victor Reuther.

President Carter was supposed to attend but canceled at the last minute. I sent him a telegram:

DEAR JIMMY CARTER: THIS WEEK HAS BEEN A BITTER DISAP-
POINTMENT FOR THOSE OF US WHO EXPECTED YOU WOULD AT-
TEND THE UNITED NATIONS DISARMAMENT CONFERENCE. HELEN
GAHAGAN DOUGLAS.

Though I found traveling too exhausting, I was able to keep active by mail. The 1978 Women's Campaign Fund received my support. It was directed at the inequity of a Congress composed of 515 men and only twenty women. Nationally women hold less than 7 percent of all elective offices. I wrote in a fund-raising letter, "After 200 years of debate about equality, public office remains the fortress of inequality. 51.3% of the population is not represented in our government."

I also appeared on the letterhead of the World Peace Tax Fund, which launched a write-in campaign aimed at Washington telling the government and the IRS that Americans don't want most of their tax dollars to go to the military.

The Women's International League for Peace and Freedom issued a protest, which I endorsed heartily, against the stockpile of leaking nerve gas bombs stored at Rocky Mountain Arsenal in Denver, Colorado, at the Tooele Depot in Utah, and other places. We wanted Congress to pass a resolution that would clean up those sites.

And I worked on this book. The first half, the part covering my life until I reached Congress, was in manuscript but the remainder dealing with the 1950 campaign and my life since was still in pieces. I sorted through letters, speeches, clippings, playbills, photographs, broadsheets, posters and reports, a process that not infrequently sidetracked me completely.

I mused about the deplorable tendency in modern political rhetoric to throw around charges that one country or another is an "imperialist." I don't think that word can be applied to nations. There is imperialism certainly in industry when it seeks to influence the changes of government in foreign countries, but the rest is nonsense.

In the industrial age the world became interdependent because industry had to be supported. Raw materials came from this country, manufacturing happened in that country, and sales were made everywhere. We are now at the point of development where we won't survive unless we find new styles of cooperation to replace the old, which were based to a large extent on profits.

Nationalism in the old sense doesn't exist anymore in a world that can be destroyed in a few hours. Imperialism becomes a sloppy term. We need to define interference more precisely. The Soviet Union tries to exert influence; *we* try to exert influence. What we both must strive to do is stop trying to achieve short-term gains. We must work cooperatively for goals related to the survival of *all*.

Nothing can be controlled by one country today; *nothing*.

I still think as I did when Harry Truman was President, that United States aid should be channeled through the United Nations. This is especially true when the aid is intended for a country where we might be accused of self-interest in keeping a despotic government in power. We could avoid criticism and the help would appear evenhanded.

I don't think the United Nations is an empty symbol, as I told *Parents* magazine years ago. It is man's best hope for world disarmament. It needs only the sustaining faith and support of peoples. It needs the support of governments. Only the most able ministers should be sent to the United Nations to negotiate.

The United States is not guiltless in weakening the United Nations. The first flagrant disregard of the Charter was by the United States in 1948 when we took matters into our own hands in Greece and Turkey. We have since bypassed it whenever it suited us, at the cost of grievous moral, psychological and physical injury.

Instead of giving sincere leadership to the building of peace, we have fallen back on the old arguments, the old formulas. Step by step, we have led the way in turning the world into an armed camp.

The United States and the U.S.S.R. have opted for a balance of terror—a balance that never balances—as each strains for a higher margin of overkill. Each year the resarch and development of even more monstrous weapons is carried on.

Preoccupation with military affairs has left little time to devote to the correction of conditions that threaten to undermine society. No wonder violence and crime are widespread. We live today in a military state. It is conditioning us to accept as a matter of course our role as the world's policeman. Are we not the good people?

We accept with less and less shock our domination of others, the use of the big stick. My Lai was a mirror in which we could catch a glimpse of ourselves and, since nothing stands still— neither organic nor inorganic bodies—what we may become if we don't change course.

There is still time for sane people to set things right. But time is running out.

Nan Stevens:

Helen went downhill physically but she never lost the brilliance of her mind. Depending on the drug she was using, she sometimes would seem wiped out physically, but there was no change in her powers of observation or her capacity to react to what she felt was unjust.

She was in the hospital just before Christmas in 1979 and she put enormous effort into getting gifts for the staff. And she did something that year for children in the neighborhood. Like the times of those parties in the Farm Security Camps of California, she thought Christmas was for children.

Dr. William Cahan, her physician:

She is a prime example of a person so hooked on living she won't let a little thing like cancer deter her—from writing her autobiography, enjoying her family, doing things like making that speech about federal assistance for cancer research.

When she comes to Memorial Hospital for treatment they worship her, from the top to the lowliest employee. They all want to talk to her.

And when she was in the most profound despair in one of her

worst times, she noticed that the man sweeping the halls had
holes in his shoes. She was furious with the hospital for not providing better for him.

Nan Stevens:

My God, she created a lot of good. And she was so thoughtful.

I was with Melvyn and Mary in the apartment a few days before Thanksgiving. Helen called from the hospital and asked to
talk to me. "Nan," she said, "would you like to come here and
have Thanksgiving lunch with me?" "I'd adore it," I said. We
dined alone, just Helen and me.

I went often to see her in the hospital. We would sit and talk
or I'd push her wheelchair through the lovely indoor garden they
have at Memorial Hospital. She was hoping to finish her book before she died but it was difficult. Her handwriting got very bad.
Still, she kept trying.

Melvyn Douglas:

When she was approaching her seventy-ninth birthday, which
was to be her last, she was determined to have a big party to cele-
brate it. She loved parties. She was very nervously anxious to have
a wonderful party, and she did. The next spring, April 5, 1980,
she went through the same strenuous efforts to have a marvelous
party for our forty-ninth wedding anniversary, which was also my
seventy-ninth birthday. She wore herself out getting those parties
accomplished.

I'm sure it was because she had a sense that she might not be
here for another one. But that wasn't said.

Nan Stevens:

She got very thin. While she was still at home she'd be dressed
every day. Her hair was always combed and Mary Helen would
help her into her chair. She'd work for hours on the book or correspondence.

One day Melvyn asked me to type something for him while he
was being interviewed in the living room. The typewriter was in
Helen's room and she was in bed resting. I asked if it would disturb her if I typed. She said it wouldn't. While I worked, she
dropped off to sleep.

In a while Melvyn came into the room. He stood beside the

bed looking at her. Gently, tenderly, he bent over and kissed her on the forehead. The gesture was so loving, so protective, so intimate, that I turned my head.

Nan Stevens:

In March that year Melvyn was very ill with pneumonia. He wasn't a well man anyway because he had severe arthritis and was also a diabetic. He recovered slowly and despite being very weak went off somewhere, Canada I think, to make a film.

When he returned in June we went immediately to Memorial to see Helen. I remember the day, Thursday June 26, 1980. Helen was so weak she could do nothing but lift a hand in greeting. Then she closed her eyes wearily without speaking.

Melvyn Douglas:

Mary Helen was in New York with me but Peter was in Vermont with his wife and children. No one expected that Helen would die so quickly. The next day the hospital called that she was sinking and I should hurry if I wanted to see her. Mary and I rushed to Sloan-Kettering and found Helen in a coma. Nan Stevens arrived a few minutes later. Mary Helen leaned over to arrange the cushion under her mother's head. Helen opened her eyes and said with her old independence:

"Leave me alone. *I'm all right.*"

That was the last distinct thing she said.

Nan Stevens:

Melvyn, Mary and I stayed with Helen all that day. It grew dark. At 3:35 A.M. June 28, 1980, I saw Helen take her last breath.

In the taxi leaving the hospital Melvyn wept. He said he had always thought he would go first.

When I got home I started to make the necessary calls—the New York *Times*, radio and television stations, and so on. It took hours. I repeated over and over, "Helen Gahagan Douglas died this morning." It hurt every time to say it. But somehow I had the feeling that Helen was there. I could hear her saying, "I know you can handle it, Nan." She was always great at giving people encouragement.

Melvyn Douglas:

Even now, when something happens that impresses me or pleases me or excites me, I think, "I have to go home right now and tell Helen about it."

Los Angeles *Times* editorial July 1, 1980:

Helen Gahagan Douglas, who died Saturday in New York at 79, was a gracious person of many talents. She distinguished herself as an actress and on the operatic stage before entering political life in California in 1940. Her testimony before a state committee on the problems of migrant workers attracted wide attention, and soon afterward she was elected as Democratic national committeewoman from California.

Elected to Congress in 1944 from the 14th District of Los Angeles, she was immediately named to the House Foreign Affairs Committee, an appointment that carried with it explicit recognition of her superior abilities. She was an effective member of Congress for three terms, but will be best remembered for her political courage.

Her service in Congress coincided with the Cold War, and although she had no sympathy with communism, she refused to be stampeded into voting for measures that she was convinced would undermine democracy. She was, for example, one of only 17 representatives who voted against contempt citations for the Hollywood Ten, writers and producers who declined to answer questions before the House Un-American Affairs Committee.

In 1950 she ran for the U.S. Senate, and her record made her vulnerable to attack by her opponent, Richard M. Nixon, whose campaign was a model of its kind—innuendo piled on innuendo. Helen Gahagan Douglas responded to defeat with characteristic courage, and went on for many years to live a full, productive and principled life.

The Philadelphia *Inquirer* editorial July 1, 1980:

It was characteristic of Helen Gahagan Douglas that as she hastened to finish a manuscript of her autobiography while suffering terminal cancer, she refused to take drugs to ease her pain. "I want to keep my mind as clear as I can as long as I can," she told an interviewer last year. "I never wrote a book before, but I used to write my own speeches."

Mrs. Douglas, 79, died Saturday in New York with the final chapter of her manuscript unfinished. Even so, when her autobiography is published it is certain to be worth reading, for as a gifted actress, sensitive politician and indomitable, caring person, Mrs. Douglas was an inspiration to all who were fortunate enough to come in contact with her.

Considering the depth of her courage and all that she accomplished, it is somewhat ironic that she probably will be remembered most for having lost to Richard M. Nixon in a classic liberal vs. conservative race for the U.S. Senate in California in 1950. Mrs. Douglas had represented a Los Angeles district in the House of Representatives when she opposed Mr. Nixon, then a two-term congressman from a nearby district in Southern California. It was a bitterly fought race which revealed Mr. Nixon's dark side for the first time and would never be forgotten by those who participated in it.

After her defeat, Mrs. Douglas remained involved in politics but never again ran for public office. She returned to the theater and with her husband, actor Melvyn Douglas, was active in liberal and humanitarian causes. If she had any bitterness over the vicious tactics that were used against her in the Senate race, she never revealed it, but it was not until after the Watergate scandal drove Mr. Nixon from the White House that she felt fully vindicated. Long before 1974, the Douglases had made their home in Vermont and that fall, as Mrs. Douglas campaigned in shopping centers for Patrick J. Leahy, the Democratic candidate for The state's U.S. Senate seat, time and again people approached her and said, "I just want to tell you, Mrs. Douglas, I'm sorry. We didn't know."

Cancer wasted Mrs. Douglas's body but it could not weaken her spirit. She leaves us the example of her talented, gracious life and the words she often uttered when refusing to criticize Nixon for the excesses of his 1950 campaign. "One must always look to the future," she would say, "not the past."

Letter from Jerry Voorhis in the Claremont *Courier* July 15, 1980:

Dear Editor: The death of Helen Gahagan Douglas marked the end of a truly noble life. Even while she suffered from what she knew was a terminal illness she was actively administering to the needs of others more afflicted than she.

She was a humanitarian in the best, most truly religious sense of that often misused word. All her life she sought to relieve the want and suffering of those who seemed to need her help most. In the days of the Dust Bowl and the coming of the so-called "Arkies" and "Okies" to California she visited their labor camps and worked to improve the conditions there.

She was an ardent crusader for women's rights but always in the context which working women understood.

She was a talented actress and opera singer. A star in a number of motion pictures. With her husband, Melvyn Douglas, one of the best of movie greats, she gave to politics in California devoted and constructive services. The Douglases were frequent guests at the Roosevelt White House, their counsel and their help deeply valued by both F.D.R. and his remarkable wife Eleanor. Helen Douglas served three terms in the House of Representatives. She probably sacrificed what could have been a seat in the U.S. Senate when she refused to vote to hold in contempt ten Hollywood actors who had refused to testify before the House Un-American Affairs Committee. For it was that vote more than anything else that was used by Richard Nixon in defeating Helen Douglas for the U.S. Senate in 1950. It was supposed to be evidence that she was "soft on communism"—as false an accusation as was ever made in American politics.

Helen Gahagan Douglas will not be forgotten. She will live on through the years as symbol of the Gallant American Lady.

Alan Cranston of California, speaking in the Senate August 5, 1980:

On June 28, 1980, a great American died, already a legend in our times: Helen Gahagan Douglas. To those of us who had the privilege of knowing her personally, her death is a great loss. We mourn her, not only for her fellow Californians but all Americans who love and respect the values she stood for. And she stood for them staunchly through good and bad times in our history, ever firm in her commitment to liberty of thought and action, to truth and to justice.

I believe Helen Gahagan Douglas was one of the grandest, most eloquent, deepest-thinking people we have had in American politics. She stands among the best of our 20th-century leaders, rivaling even Eleanor Roosevelt in stature, compassion, and simple greatness. For those of us who loved her—and there are so many

—mere words cannot do justice to the spirit and soul of this woman. But the Sacramento *Bee*, in a July 2 editorial, pays tribute to Helen Gahagan Douglas in a way which I know will evoke many memories in the hearts of her admirers. I would like to share this tribute with my colleagues here in the Senate.

The editorial follows:

HELEN GAHAGAN DOUGLAS

"One of the several faces of courage is just being true to oneself in one's own place and in one's own time. Such was the courage of Helen Gahagan Douglas, the actress-turned-Congresswoman whose political career ended in a bitter clash with Richard M. Nixon in 1950. Douglas, actress, singer, wife of actor Melvyn Douglas, political activist, served in the U.S. House of Representatives from California along with Nixon for two terms, 1946–1950. She was the Democratic nominee for the Senate in 1950 and was defeated by Nixon in a campaign that made history for its vicious smear tactics.

"It was the time of Korea and McCarthyism and, despite the charges that she was a communist sympathizer, Douglas refused to run a campaign based on innuendo and smear. Instead, she emphasized preservation of the 160-acre limit on water from federal reclamation projects and federal control of California's vast tidelands oil resources. She stuck to the issues despite the personal attacks.

"In the best of all possible Americas, Helen Gahagan Douglas might have become an influential and respected U.S. Senator. When she died Saturday of cancer in a New York hospital, this country lost a gifted person, a principled advocate of women's rights, civil liberties and world disarmament whose contributions to society were eclipsed by the Cold War controversy and the agonies created by the smash-and-grab politics of the 1950's. She strove for freedom, justice and equality that never go out of style, and, in her personal relationships, extended a warmth and respect that are no less the mark of a person who cares about others."

Senator Howard M. Metzenbaum of Ohio, in the U. S. Senate June 30, 1980:

On Saturday, June 28, America lost a rare and wonderful person when Helen Gahagan Douglas died at the age of 79. Helen Gahagan Douglas was a brilliant artistic talent—a Broadway star at the age of 22, a classical singer who performed in the world's great opera houses and a contemporary in the film industry of legendary actresses like Greta Garbo and Marlene Dietrich. But she was more than a brilliant artistic talent, more than an outstanding Member of Congress. Helen Gahagan Douglas was a brilliant human being who stood up bravely all her life for what she knew to be right and decent.

After seeing at first hand the terrible human cost of the Great Depression, she began her life-long commitment to building a fairer and juster society in America. In the late 1930's, after witnessing at first hand the vicious Nazi regime in Germany, she canceled her contract to sing in that country and devoted herself to organizing aid for the growing flood of Jewish and other anti-Nazi refugees who were desperately fleeing from the malignancy called "National Socialism."

In the 1940's, she served three distinguished terms in the House of Representatives, only to lose a Senate bid in 1950 after a campaign that is still notorious for the tactics of smear and innuendo employed by her opponent. Those tactics, which included casting doubt upon her loyalty to the country and that of her husband—himself a volunteer in both world wars—brought prematurely to an end her career in public office. But let us remember now that her career was marked by the kind of compassion, by the sense of decency and by a large and generous vision of America that to me constitutes patriotism in its highest form.

Mr. President, Helen Gahagan Douglas was a brave and beautiful human being. I honor her memory and I extend on behalf of the Metzenbaum family our deepest sympathy and most profound condolences to Melvyn Douglas, her husband of more than 50 years, and to her family.

Mr. President, I ask that an article on Mrs. Douglas by Edith Evans Asbury that appeared in the June 29, 1980, edition of the New York *Times* be printed in the Record.

The article follows:

"Helen Gahagan Douglas, the actress and former United States Representative whose defeat in 1950 for a Senate seat from California launched Richard M. Nixon into international prominence, died early yesterday at Memorial Sloan-Kettering Cancer Center. She was 79 years old and had lived in Riverside Drive in Manhattan. . . .

"Mrs. Douglas's life was marked by sudden, unpredictable

changes, usually the result of her own firm choice, always followed through with courage. . . .

"One of Mrs. Douglas's final public pleas was an appeal to Congress for Federal funds for cancer research. On June 19, 1979, she spoke to a Congressional hearing in Washington by telephone from the bedroom of her Riverside Drive apartment, a frail but determined figure braced by pillows and cushions.

"Dr. William Cahan, a cancer specialist and her physician, was in the room as she spoke. At a bridge table against the wall, piled high with files, clippings and books, a young actor doing research for her was typing notes for the autobiography she was determined to finish.

"Mrs. Douglas was persuaded to write the autobiography by a literary agent who had suggested that it would be a good way to take her mind off her illness.

"'Later I discovered that she had cancer and she died,' Mrs. Douglas said of the agent during an interview in the summer of 1979. 'It's as if I have a commitment to her to finish the book before I pass on.

"'When they wanted to give me drugs to ease the pain I wouldn't let them,' she said. 'I want to keep my mind as clear as I can for as long as I can. I never wrote a book before, but I used to write my own speeches.'

"Besides her husband and daughter, Mrs. Douglas is survived by a son, Peter, a step-son, Gregory Hesselberg; a brother, Walter H. Gahagan, and several grandchildren. The family said there would be no funeral and contributions in lieu of flowers should be made to the Memorial Sloan-Kettering Cancer Center. A memorial service was to be held later at an as yet undetermined time and place in New York or Vermont."

A MEMORIAL SERVICE FOR
HELEN GAHAGAN DOUGLAS

ALL SOULS UNITARIAN CHURCH
1157 LEXINGTON AVENUE
NEW YORK

Tuesday, December 2, 1980   4:30 P.M.

Arthur Goldschmidt at the Memorial Service:

We all remember the first time we saw the Grand Canyon, Niagara, or other great wonders of nature. Similarly, people always seem to remember their first meeting with Helen Gahagan Douglas.

In my own case, it was in the early forties in California before she first ran for Congress. Ours was not a casual meeting; she had been told of my work on public power and my interest in ensuring that the anti-speculation and benefit-sharing provisions of the reclamation laws would not be set aside to suit vested interests in the great Central Valley of California. As a consequence of this introduction, I found myself subjected to an intense cross-examination by Helen—grilling might not be too strong a word—in her drive to understand the controversial issues. She wanted to know what, why and how—and accepted no vague generalities. Her questions were not naïve; she knew a lot about landlessness and unemployment; she had worked for the migrant Okies and Arkies and had concerned herself with unemployed youth in California.

I came away from that meeting enchanted and with a sense of wonder at Helen's display of energy—at the physical, emotional and mental drive of this beautiful and glamorous person. And to this day I have not lost that enchantment and sense of wonder. Nor was I ever spared similar examinations on issues of interest to Helen in the years since. In this experience, I am only one of many; mine was a narrow band in the broad spectrum of Helen's interests. In her work she mastered many fields in addition to land, water and resource policy; she gained expertise in inflation and price control, migration, welfare and social security, housing, foreign aid, atomic energy, disarmament and the overridingly important field of civil rights, including especially the "loyalty" issue that chilled so many otherwise warm people in the Cold War climate of her later years in Congress.

This is not a random sampling or capricious listing; on each of these areas Helen had a profound and lasting influence. Her mastery of them involved her in discussions with lawyers, academics, labor leaders, newspaper people, diplomats and others as well as government officials. In addition to my boss and other Cabinet members and Justices of the Supreme Court, I can recall offhand people like Ben Cohen, Wilson Wyatt, the Keyserlings, Bill Walton, Averell Harriman, Paul Sifton, Alan Barton, Jim Newman, the Reuther brothers, and many others who were subjected to her intense search for answers and became her unquestioned admirers and friends. . . .

Why did people like us respond so readily to Helen? Her charm, her warmth, her beauty, her glamor might well have been enough. But there was always something more: her commitment, her energy and her courage made us sure that she would get things done. Helen brought to her work in the House of Representatives, as to all else she did, an elegance of style, a brilliance of performance, and a commitment so passionate that it has rarely, if ever, been equaled. It was thrilling and deeply satisfying to play even a small part in her battles. . . .

Abe Fortas at the Memorial Service:

We are told that perfection is beyond human attainment, and I suppose that's so; but Helen Gahagan Douglas came as close to perfection as the divine order permits. She was remarkably endowed: beautiful in face and form; elegant in carriage and movement; her eyes and her voice were magnificent instruments of communication; her mind was hard-edged; her heart was tender.

These marvelous gifts she put to great use: her intelligence was direct, clear and relentless; her energy was boundless; her compassion and sensitivity were inexhaustible; and her courage—her willingness knowingly to expose herself to injury for a cause in which she believed—was as firm as steel.

It is, after all, the fundamental human obligation to use to the utmost the talents with which we have been endowed. Helen Gahagan Douglas's accounting, in summation of her life, is remarkable: artist in the theater and on the operatic stage; citizen; benefactor of people; warrior; loving and beloved friend, wife and mother . . . her life was well and truly lived.

It is illuminating of this remarkable woman's character that she did not take the easy and obvious road; she might have chosen to respond to conscience's call merely by being *helpful* in the great social struggle, while continuing her career as an artist. Most of us seek the easier course; we seek to respond to the cry of distress by a gift of time or money or convenient participation. Helen gave it her life.

She was not a compromiser; she was not a dilettante; she gave herself entirely; her dedication was complete. And when she responded to the observed anguish of her time, in marvelous partnership with Melvyn, it was a total commitment—a commitment of all her vast energy, talent and courage . . . of her life.

In the paranoia of 1950, there was no chance that Helen could survive an attack of the intensity which was launched against her largely on the basis of her civil rights record. I shall not dwell upon the ingenuity and diabolic fury of the attack, or the distortion and misrepresentations which characterized it. Nor will I suggest that we seek to comfort ourselves by describing the retribution that was ultimately visited upon Helen's assailant, Mr. Nixon. Helen would not approve of this.

Even as the sordid events of Watergate were unfolded and it became common parlance to point to the evil aspects of Mr. Nixon's record, Helen remained silent and aloof—a gentlewoman, a person of impeccable taste and essential kindness in vindication as she had been in battle and in defeat. . . .

I should like to conclude with a personal recollection. I remember my last meeting with Helen. In December 1977 she was asked to participate in a public reading of the Constitution as part of the celebration of the inquiry honoring Justice William O. Douglas. She agreed, although she was nearing the end of her life.

On the night of December 10, she rose before a large audience in a New York theater. Breathtakingly beautiful, radiant despite her terminal illness, she read the magnificent words of the Fifth Amendment to our Constitution. The ovation that followed was for her—a tribute for a lifetime dedication which she once expressed as follows:

I have stood firm for the rights and privileges of American citizens under the Constitution. I will not be stampeded by hysteria, nor will I waver for political expediency. My record and my conscience are clear. We who love our country cannot let this heritage of freedom be whittled away.

INDEX